SECOND EDITION

HEALTH & PSYCHOSOCIAL
Rehabilitation

JODY L. WEIGEL • EMILY S. LOGAN

KIRKWOOD COMMUNITY COLLEGE

Kendall Hunt

publishing company

Kendall Hunt
publishing company

www.kendallhunt.com
Send all inquiries to:
4050 Westmark Drive
Dubuque, IA 52004-1840

Printed in the United States of America

DEDICATION

A special thanks to my wife, Jill, and my three beautiful daughters, Morgan, Rachel, and Olivia for all of their support.

—Jody Weigel

Thank you to Josh, Annika, Brendan, and Vivienne for giving me the courage to follow my dreams.

—Emily Logan

CONTENTS

Dedication   iii

Preface   ix

Key Abbreviations   xi

About the Authors   xiii

CHAPTER 1: Psychosocial Rehabilitation and Ethical Practice   1

Psychosocial Rehabilitation   2

Did You Know?   3

Case Study   4

Ethical Principles   4

Laws   5

154C.1 Definitions   6

CHAPTER 2: Physical Health and Safety   25

Health Disparities   26

Personal Protective Equipment (PPE) Reduces Exposure to Bloodborne Pathogens   30

CHAPTER 3: Neurodevelopmental Disorders   39

What Is Disability and Who Is Affected by Disability?   40

Understanding Characteristics of People with Disabilities   43

Developmental Disabilities   43

Learning Issues   45

Traumatic Brain Injury (TBI'S)   45

Suggestions—TBI   46

Pervasive Developmental Disorders (PDD)   47

Asperger's Syndrome or Disorder   47

Austism   47

Suggestions—Autism   48

Understanding Specific Disabilities   53

Developmental Disabilities   58

Case Study   59

Internet Sites: At-Risk and Developmental Disabilities   59

Internet Research Questions: At-Risk and Developmental Disabilities   60

Journal Discussion Questions: At-Risk and Developmental Disabilities   61

CHAPTER 4: Mental Health   63

Case Study   64

Quick Facts on Mental Illness   64

Depression   64

Dual Diagnosis   76

HIV Prevention News   96

HIV Assessment News   99

HIV Treatment News   103

Psychiatric/Psychological/Psychosocial/Spiritual Care   103

About Suicide   113

References   115

CHAPTER 5: Substance Use, Abuse, and Co-occurring Disorders   119

Case Study   120

Substance Abuse   120

Alcohol   126

Overview   126

Alcohol Abuse   127

Women and Alcohol   128

Illegal Drugs of Abuse   147

Iowa 2007 Nasadad State Snapshot on Methamphetamine   152

Legal Drugs of Abuse   154

Discussion Questions   157

Overview of Co-occurring Disorders   160

Co-occurring Marijuana Use and Mental Illness   161

Posttraumatic Stress Disorder (PTSD) and Substance Abuse   161

Integrated Approach for Treatment of Mental Illness and Substance Abuse   165

Harm-Reduction Model of Prevention   167

Synthetic Drugs in Iowa Update   174

CHAPTER 6: Child and Dependent Adult Abuse   181

Case Study   182

Child Abuse, Dependent Adult Abuse, and Elder Abuse   182

Child Abuse: A Guide for Mandatory Reporters   185

CHAPTER 7: At-Risk Populations   311

Case Study   312

Addressing Racial Disproportionality in Child Welfare   315

The Child and Family Services Reviews   317

Alzheimer's Disease   320

Major Depressive Episode and Treatment for Depression among Veterans Aged 21 to 39   327

SAMHSA News Release   332

Homelessness among Veterans   334

Sharayna: A Young Woman Who Experienced Homelessness and How She Turned Her Life Around   336

How Many People Experience Homelessness?   337

HIV/AIDS and Homelessness   342

APPENDIX   345

Citations Using APA, 6th Edition, 2010   345

INDEX   353

PREFACE

The purpose of this textbook is to provide students with a resource to take with them on their future journeys. It is expected that most students that read this text are headed toward careers that involve direct contact with people. While the desire to "help" people can be very strong, unfortunately, emerging practitioners can become easily frustrated when starting their human services journey. Our thoughts were to be as realistic and straightforward with our documents and information, so as to let students know that the disillusionment of all people wanting to be healthy can be addressed. The content of this textbook includes introductory information about disabilities, mental health, substance abuse, abuse and neglect, and what rehabilitation means for people facing these challenges. While it is not a complete discussion of any topic, it is the hope of the authors that it is a strong base upon which deeper understandings can be built.

While it has been a challenge to put the text together, it has also been a wonderful learning experience. We are humbled by the opportunity and could not do so without the support, guidance, and direction of many people. Specifically, we thank our families, colleagues, and Kirkwood Community College for supporting us in this endeavor.

KEY ABBREVIATIONS

AACP = American Academy of Child and Adolescent Psychiatry
CDC = Centers for Disease Control
CMHS = Center for Mental Health Services
CFHC = Collaborative Family Healthcare Coalition
CSAT = Center for Substance Abuse Treatment
DEA = Drug Enforcement Administration
DHS = Iowa Department of Human Services
DHHS = United States Department of Health and Human Services
NACOA = National Association for Children of Alcoholics
NAMI = National Alliance on Mental Illness
NASW = National Association of Social Workers
NIDA = National Institute on Drug Abuse
NIMH = National Institute of Mental Health
OJJDP = Office of Juvenile Justice and Delinquency Prevention
SAMHSA = Substance Abuse and Mental Health Services Administration
SGRMH = Surgeon General's Report on Mental Health
USCB = United States Census Bureau
USCCFY = United States Select Committee on Children, Families, and Youth

ABOUT THE AUTHORS

Jody L. Weigel is Associate Professor and Program Coordinator for the Human Services and Certified Alcohol and Drug Educational track at Kirkwood Community College in Cedar Rapids, Iowa. He holds a Master of Social Work degree from the University of Iowa and a Bachelor's degree from the University of Northern Iowa. Mr. Weigel serves on several local community and state level boards. His background is primarily in child welfare (foster family care/adoptions), domestic violence and family systems (including adult services). Mr. Weigel has work experience in state public welfare and Iowa public school systems and is licensed in the state of Iowa.

Emily S. Logan, MSW, LISW, is an Instructor in the Human Services Program and Certified Alcohol and Drug Educational track at Kirkwood Community College in Cedar Rapids, Iowa. She holds a Master of Social Work degree from Grand Valley State University and a Bachelor's degree from Central College. Ms. Logan's professional background includes work in substance abuse counseling, infant adoption, intercountry adoption, and special needs adoption. She served as the Iowa coordinator for the Infant Adoption Awareness Training Initiative.

CHAPTER 1

PSYCHOSOCIAL REHABILITATION
AND ETHICAL PRACTICE

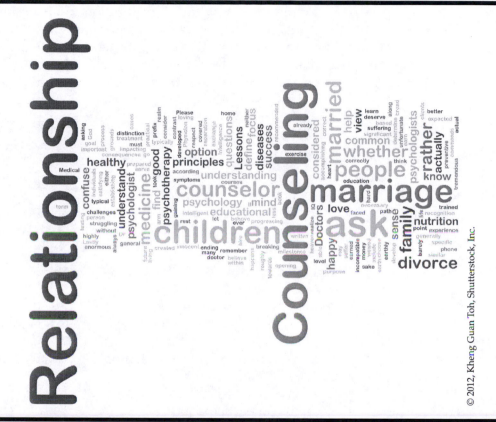

© 2012, Kheng Guan Toh, Shutterstock, Inc.

Chapter Objectives

- Define and discuss the goals of psychosocial rehabilitation.
- Review ethical principles that guide human service work.

NOTES

The term psychosocial rehabilitation is one that covers several areas and can be confusing for entry level practitioners, as well as individuals that have been working in the human services arena for a period of time. We will be working with a definition that was developed by Susan Simon, *Kirkwood Community College, 1985*.

PSYCHOSOCIAL REHABILITATION

- Facilitating an individual's restoration to an optimal level of independent functioning in the community;
- Encourages persons to participate actively with others to attain mental health and social competence goals;
- Emphasizes wholeness and wellness of the individual;
- Utilizes a comprehensive approach that includes vocational, residential, social, recreational, educational, and personal adjustment services.

Also according to the definition, we need to be aware of the principles that come along with psychosocial rehabilitation. These principles may or may not apply to individuals that you are working with, but it is of utmost importance that as a professional, you allow for the principles to be known to the individuals with whom we are working with. Some of the principles of psychosocial rehabilitation are:

- Equipping people with skills: social, vocational, educational, interpersonal, etc.
- People have the right and responsibility for self-determination
- Services should be provided in as normalized environment as possible
- Emphasis on social, rather than medical, model of care
- Early intervention
- Environmental approach
- No limits on participation
- Work-centered process
- Emphasis on the client's/consumer's strengths, rather than on pathologies
- Emphasis on the "here and now" rather than on problems in the past.

We need to be focused on the fact that people are motivated by a need for mastery and competence in areas which allow them to feel more independent and self-confident. We need to make sure that we believe that new behaviors can be learned, and that people are capable of adapting their behavior to meet their basic needs.

By allowing the above, we are hopefully dealing with the assumptions of psychosocial rehabilitation as outlined in the above bullet points.

DID YOU KNOW?

In 1999, the Surgeon General's Report on Mental Health reported that more than 54 million Americans have a mental disorder in any given year, although, fewer than 8 million seek treatment. Of the 54 million reported, depression and anxiety disorders are the two most commonly illness that the individuals were diagnosed as, with approximately 19 million individuals ending up with one of these labels.

Adult Caucasians who have either depression or anxiety disorders are more likely to receive treatment than adult African Americans with the same disorder even though the disorders occur in both groups at the same rate, taking into account socioeconomic factors.

Also according to the SMRMH report, at least 10 to 20% of widows and widowers develop clinically significant depression within one year of their spouse's death, and that among adults aged 55 and older, 11.4% meet the criteria for having an anxiety disorder.

We continue to see numbers escalate in this area, with fewer and fewer resources being available to the individuals. What we need to explore is the differences with gender; age, ethnicity, socioeconomic status, sexual orientation, and abuse issues just to name a few.

Some of the questions that we need to focus on and dissect are:

1. Why are more and more teenagers dealing with depression?
2. Why do our youth believe that regular alcohol and drug usage is not dangerous? We are they experimenting and using at a younger and younger age?
3. Why are children with parents addicted to alcohol and/or drugs more likely to develop substance abuse and mental health problems than other children?
4. Are genetic factors a role in why females more likely to develop depression than their male counterparts?
5. Is suicide one of the leading causes of death among youth ages 15 to 24? What about our aging population? Are they more likely than any other group to commit suicide? If so, why?
6. Misdiagnosis??? Why does this happen? What are some of the factors that contribute to this? Are there cultural barriers? What else creates the "inadequate treatment and identification of issues"?

Taking into consideration some of the above questions and the limited information that you have regarding mental health, addictions, socioeconomic status, cultural barriers, etc, what are the major concerns? What seems to be the most urgent? What should be done about it? What can you do about it?

CASE STUDY

Tiffany is a Caucasian nineteen-year-old female. She grew up in a small Midwestern city.

Tiffany resided with her mother after her parents separated when she was eight years old. Tiffany described her early childhood as "tough," recalling frequent arguments and physical altercations between her parents. Her father, Pete, owned a bar and was often under the influence of alcohol. Tiffany described drinking alcohol as "a part of our life," adding that her dad is still a "drinker." Tiffany reported she liked living with her mother, Phyllis, but added that she dealt with long-term back problems from an earlier injury that often left Phyllis homebound and unable to work.

When Tiffany's mother decided to move to Texas after meeting a man through an Internet dating site, Tiffany decided to stay in her hometown, moving in with her father. Tiffany was fourteen years old and a freshman at the local community high school. Having spent little time with her father over the previous six years, Tiffany found Pete to be either working at his bar or spending time with his friends. Tiffany disliked her dad's girlfriend, who was eighteen years younger than him and closer in age to Tiffany. Tiffany missed her mother and found it difficult to understand her mother's decision to move so far away. While they texted and called each other frequently, Tiffany often felt lonely and isolated.

Tiffany has presented to a local shelter requesting housing, appearing exhausted, disheveled, and wearing stained clothing. She has what appears to be bruising on her face and blood-crusted cuticles.

ETHICAL PRINCIPLES*

National Association of Social Workers (NASW) Ethical Principles

The National Association of Social Workers (NASW) states that social work's core values are service, social justice, dignity and worth of the person, importance of human relationships, integrity, and competence. Ethical principles are based in these values. Social workers should practice ethically and uphold these principles and ideals.

When considering the value of *service*, the related ethical principle is that social workers' primary goal is to assist people in need as well as address problems of society. Social workers are expected to prioritize

*This information was adapted from the National Association of Social Workers, 2010, www.socialworkers.org.

service over self-interest. Social problems are addressed with social work knowledge, values, and skills. Volunteering professional skills is encouraged (pro bono service).

Regarding the social work value of *social justice,* social workers' ethical principle is to challenge injustice. Not only will social workers pursue social change on behalf of vulnerable and oppressed populations, but also promote awareness and sensitivity in the community. These populations include, but are not limited to, people in poverty, unemployed persons, and minority groups. Social workers strive to give all persons access to information, resources, and services. In so doing, individuals will have the power to make their own decisions, experience opportunity and meaningful participation in society.

The value of *dignity and worth of the person* is related to the ethical principle that social workers will respect people, no matter what. Social workers are mindful of diversity and treat each person as a unique individual. Clients' self-determination is promoted. Social workers are aware that there is a dual responsibility to clients and to society. Therefore, when conflicts between interests arise, social workers will seek to resolve them in a manner consistent with the ethics of the profession.

Regarding the *importance of human relationships,* social workers recognize that relationships are a change-agent. Social workers engage and collaborate with clients through the helping process. Social workers strive to enhance relationships between people to restore and maintain the health and well-being of individuals, families, social groups, organizations, and communities.

The value of *integrity* means that social workers are trustworthy. Social work practice must be consistent with the profession's mission, values, and ethics. Ethics will also be promoted in the workplaces of social workers.

Finally, the value of *competence* promotes social work practice only in areas of competence. Furthermore, continuing education, practice, and research should enhance professional proficiency. The knowledge base of the profession will be enhanced by research and practice.

LAWS

Laws are contained in the Iowa Code. They are enacted by the Iowa Legislature and provide statutory authority to the professional licensure boards.

154C.1 DEFINITIONS

As used in this chapter unless the context otherwise requires:

1. *"Board"* means the board of social work established in chapter 147.
2. *"Licensee"* means a person licensed to practice social work.
3. *"Practice of social work"* means the professional activity of licensees which is directed at enhancing or restoring people's capacity for social functioning, whether impaired by environmental, emotional, or physical factors, with particular attention to the person-in-situation configuration. The social work profession represents a body of knowledge requiring progressively more sophisticated analytic and intervention skills, and includes the application of psychosocial theory methods to individuals, couples, families, groups, and communities. The practice of social work does not include the making of a medical diagnosis, or the treatment of conditions or disorders of biological etiology except treatment of conditions or disorders which involve psychosocial aspects and conditions. The practice of social work for each of the categories of social work licensure includes the following:
   a. Bachelor social workers provide psychosocial assessment and intervention through direct contact with clients or referral of clients to other qualified resources for assistance, including but not limited to performance of social histories, problem identification, establishment of goals and monitoring of progress, interviewing techniques, counseling, social work administration, supervision, evaluation, interdisciplinary consultation and collaboration, and research of service delivery including development and implementation of organizational policies and procedures in program management.
   b. Master social workers are qualified to perform the practice of bachelor social workers and provide psychosocial assessment, diagnosis, and treatment, including but not limited to performance of psychosocial histories, problem identification and evaluation of symptoms and behavior, assessment of psychosocial and behavioral strengths and weaknesses, effects of the environment on behavior, psychosocial therapy with individuals, couples, families, and groups, establishment of treatment goals and monitoring progress, differential treatment planning, and interdisciplinary consultation and collaboration.
   c. Independent social workers are qualified to perform the practice of master social workers as a private practice.
4. *"Private practice"* means social work practice conducted only by an independent social worker who is either self-employed or a member of a partnership or of a group practice providing

diagnosis and treatment of mental and emotional disorders or conditions.

5. *"Supervision"* means the direction of social work practice in face-to-face sessions.

ADMINISTRATIVE RULES

The professional licensure boards adopt rules to interpret and implement the Iowa Code. Administrative rules have the force and effect of law.

The following rules apply to your specific licensure board. Press the chapter you are interested in and you will be linked directly to the rule.

CHAPTER 282: PRACTICE OF SOCIAL WORKERS

645—282.1(154C) Definitions.

"Client" means the individual, couple, family, or group to whom a licensee provides direct social work services.

"Clinical services" means services provided by an LMSW or LISW which involve the professional application of social work theory and methods in diagnosing, assessing, treating, and preventing psychosocial disabilities or impairments, including emotional and mental disorders.

"Counseling" means a method used by licensees to assist clients in learning how to solve problems and make decisions about personal, health, social, educational, vocational, financial, and other interpersonal concerns.

"Psychosocial therapy" means a specialized, formal interaction between an LMSW or LISW and a client in which a therapeutic relationship is established and maintained to assist the client in overcoming or abating specific emotional, mental, or social problems and achieving specified goals for well-being.

Psychosocial therapy is a form of psychotherapy which emphasizes the interface between the client and the client's environment. Therapy is a planned, structured program based on a diagnosis and is directed to accomplish measurable goals and objectives specified in the client's individual treatment plan.

645—282.2(154C) Rules of conduct.

282.2(1) *Informed consent.*

a. A licensee shall provide services to clients only in the context of a professional relationship based, when appropriate, on valid written informed consent. A licensee shall use clear and understandable language to inform clients of the proposed services, purpose of the services, risks related to the services, limits to services because of the requirements of a third-party

NOTES

payer, relevant costs, reasonable alternatives, a client's right to refuse or withdraw consent, and the time frame covered by the consent.

b. If a client is not literate or has difficulty understanding the primary language used in the practice setting, a licensee shall attempt to ensure the client's comprehension. This may include providing the client with a detailed verbal explanation or arranging for a qualified interpreter or translator whenever possible.

c. If a client lacks the capacity to provide informed consent, a licensee shall protect the client's interests by seeking permission from an appropriate third party and shall inform the client consistent with the client's level of understanding. In such instances, a licensee shall seek to ensure that the third party acts in a manner consistent with the client's wishes and interests. A licensee shall take reasonable steps to enhance the client's ability to give informed consent.

d. If a client is receiving services involuntarily, a licensee shall provide information about the nature and extent of services and about the extent of the client's right to refuse services.

e. The provision of social work services to an individual in this state through any electronic means, including the Internet, telephone, or the Iowa Communications Network or any fiberoptic media, regardless of the location of the licensee, shall constitute the practice of social work in the state of Iowa and shall be subject to regulation in accordance with Iowa Code chapters 147 and 154C and the administrative rules of the board. A licensee who provides services via electronic media shall inform recipients of the limitations and risks associated with such services.

f. A licensee shall obtain a client's informed consent before audiotaping or videotaping the client or permitting a third party to observe services provided to the client.

282.2(2) *Competence*.

a. A licensee shall provide services and represent oneself as competent only within the boundaries of the licensee's education, training, license, certification, consultation received, supervised experience, or other relevant professional experience.

b. A licensee shall provide services in substantive areas or use intervention techniques or approaches that are new only after engaging in appropriate study, training, consultation, and supervision from people who are competent in those areas, interventions, or techniques.

c. When generally recognized standards do not exist with respect to an emerging area of practice, a licensee shall exercise careful judgment and take responsible steps, including appropriate education, research, training, consultation and supervision, to ensure competence and to protect clients from harm.

282.2(3) *Supervision.*

a. A licensee shall exercise appropriate supervision over persons who practice under the supervision of the licensee.

b. A licensee who provides supervision or consultation shall have the necessary knowledge and skill to supervise or consult appropriately and shall do so only within the licensee's areas of knowledge and competence.

c. A licensee who provides supervision or consultation is responsible for setting clear, appropriate, and culturally sensitive boundaries.

d. A licensee shall not engage in any dual or multiple relationships with supervisees if there is a risk of exploitation of or potential harm to the supervisee.

e. A licensee shall not engage in sexual activities or sexual contact with a supervisee, student, trainee, or other colleague over whom the licensee exercises professional or supervisory authority.

f. A licensee shall not employ, assign, or supervise an individual in the performance of services that require a license if the individual has not received a license to perform the services or if the individual has a suspended, revoked, lapsed, or inactive license.

g. A licensee shall not practice without receiving supervision, as needed, given the licensee's level of practice, experience, and need.

282.2(4) *Privacy and confidentiality.*

a. A licensee shall not disclose or be compelled to disclose client information unless required by law, except under the following limited circumstances:

(1) If the information reveals the contemplation or commission of a crime. This includes situations in which the licensee determines that disclosure is necessary to prevent serious, foreseeable, and imminent harm to the client or another specific identifiable person.

(2) If the client waives the privilege by bringing criminal, civil, or administrative charges or action against a licensee.

(3) With the written informed consent of the client that explains to whom the client information will be disclosed or released and the purpose and time frame for the release of information. If the client is deceased or unable to provide informed consent, a licensee shall obtain written consent from the client's personal representative, another person authorized to sue, or the beneficiary of an insurance policy on the client's life, health, or physical condition.

NOTES

(4) To testify in a court or administrative hearing concerning matters pertaining to the welfare of children.

(5) To seek collaboration or consultation with professional colleagues or administrative superiors on behalf of the client.

(6) Pursuant to a validly issued subpoena or court order.

In the event of a disclosure of information under any of the circumstances stated above, the licensee shall disclose the least amount of confidential information necessary and shall reveal only that information that is directly relevant to the purpose for which the disclosure is made.

b. Before the disclosure is made, a licensee shall inform a client, to the extent possible, about the disclosure of confidential information and the potential consequences of the disclosure. This requirement applies whether a licensee discloses confidential information on the basis of client consent or other legal basis.

c. A licensee shall discuss with clients and other interested parties the nature of confidentiality and limitations of a client's right to confidentiality. A licensee shall review with clients the circumstances under which confidential information may be requested and when disclosure of confidential information may be legally required. This discussion should occur as soon as possible in the professional relationship and as needed throughout the course of the relationship.

d. When a licensee provides counseling or psychosocial therapy services to families, couples, or groups, the licensee shall seek agreement among the parties involved concerning each individual's right to confidentiality and obligation to preserve the confidentiality of information shared by others. A licensee shall inform participants in family, couples, or group counseling or psychosocial therapy that the licensee cannot guarantee that all participants will honor such agreements.

e. A licensee shall inform clients involved in family, couples, marital, or group counseling or psychosocial therapy of the licensee's, the licensee's employer's, and agency's policy concerning the licensee's disclosure of confidential information among the parties involved in the counseling or therapy.

f. A licensee shall not disclose confidential information to third-party payers unless a client has authorized such disclosure. A licensee shall inform the client of the nature of the client information to be disclosed or released to the third-party payer.

g. A licensee shall not discuss confidential information in any setting unless privacy can be ensured. A licensee shall not discuss confidential information in public or semipublic areas such as hallways, waiting rooms, elevators, and restaurants.

h. A licensee shall protect the confidentiality of clients during legal proceedings to the extent permitted by law.

i. A licensee shall protect the confidentiality of clients when the licensee is responding to requests from members of the media.

j. A licensee shall protect the confidentiality of clients' written and electronic records and other sensitive information. A licensee shall take reasonable steps to ensure that client records are stored in a secure location and that client records are not available to others who are not authorized to have access.

k. A licensee shall take precautions to ensure and maintain the confidentiality of information transmitted to other parties through the use of computers, electronic mail, facsimile machines, telephones, telephone answering machines, and other electronic or computer technology.

l. A licensee shall transfer or dispose of client records in a manner that protects client confidentiality and is consistent with federal and state statutes, rules and regulations and the guidelines of the licensee's employer or agency, if applicable.

m. A licensee shall take reasonable precautions to protect client confidentiality in the event of the licensee's termination of practice, incapacitation, or death.

n. A licensee shall not disclose identifying information when discussing a client for teaching or training purposes or in public presentations unless the client has consented to disclosure of confidential information.

o. A licensee shall not disclose identifying information when discussing a client with consultants unless the client has consented to disclosure of confidential information or there is a compelling need for such disclosure.

p. Consistent with the preceding standards, a licensee shall protect the confidentiality of deceased clients.

282.2(5) *Record keeping.*

a. A licensee shall maintain sufficient, timely, and accurate documentation in client records. A licensee's records shall reflect the services provided, facilitate the delivery of services, and ensure continuity of services in the future.

b. A licensee who provides clinical services in any employment setting, including private practice, shall maintain timely records that include subjective and objective data, assessment or diagnosis, a treatment plan, and any revisions to the assessment, diagnosis, or plan made during the course of treatment.

c. A licensee who provides clinical services shall store records in accordance with state and federal statutes, rules, and regulations governing record retention and with the guidelines of

NOTES

the licensee's employer or agency, if applicable. If no other legal provisions govern record retention, a licensee shall store all client records for a minimum of seven years following the termination of services to ensure reasonable future access.

282.2(6) *Access to records.* A licensee who provides clinical services shall:

a. Provide the client with reasonable access to records concerning the client. A licensee who is concerned that a client's access to the client's records could cause serious misunderstanding or harm to the client shall provide assistance in interpreting the records and consultation with the client regarding the records. A licensee may limit a client's access to the client's records, or portions of the records, only in exceptional circumstances when there is compelling evidence that such access would cause serious harm to the client. Both the client's request and the rationale for withholding some or all of a record should be documented in the client's records.

b. Take steps to protect the confidentiality of other individuals identified or discussed in any records to which a client is provided access.

282.2(7) *Billing and fees.*

a. A licensee shall bill only for services which have been provided.

b. A licensee shall not accept goods or services from the client or a third party in exchange for the licensee's services.

c. A licensee shall not solicit a private fee or other remuneration for providing services to clients who are entitled to such available services through the licensee's employer or agency.

d. A licensee shall not accept, give, offer or solicit a fee, commission, rebate, fee split, or other form of consideration for the referral of a client.

e. A licensee shall not permit any person to share in the fees for professional services, other than a partner, employee, an associate in a professional firm, or a consultant to the licensee.

f. A licensee who provides clinical services shall, when appropriate:

  (1) Establish and maintain billing practices that accurately reflect the nature and extent of services provided.

  (2) Inform the client of the fee at the initial session or meeting with the client. A licensee shall provide a written payment arrangement to a client at the commencement of the professional relationship.

  (3) Ensure that the fees are fair, reasonable, and commensurate with the services performed.

282.2(8) *Dual relationships and conflicts of interest.*

a. "Dual relationship" means that a licensee develops or assumes a secondary role with a client, including but not limited to a social relationship or business association. For purposes of these rules, "dual relationship" does not include a sexual relationship. Standards governing sexual relationships are found in subrule 282.2(9).

  (1) Current clients. A licensee shall not engage in a dual relationship with a client.

  (2) Former clients. A licensee shall not engage in a dual relationship with a client within five years of the termination of the client relationship. A licensee shall not engage in a dual relationship with a former client, regardless of the length of time elapsed since termination of the client relationship, when there is a risk of exploitation or potential harm to a client or former client.

  (3) Unavoidable dual relationships with current and former clients. If a dual relationship with a current or former client is unavoidable, the licensee shall take steps to protect the client and shall be responsible for setting clear, appropriate, and culturally sensitive boundaries. The burden shall be on the licensee to show that the dual relationship was unavoidable. In determining whether a dual relationship was unavoidable, the board shall consider the size of the community, the nature of the relationship, and the risk of exploitation or harm to a client or former client.

b. Conflicts of interest.

  (1) A licensee shall avoid conflicts of interest that interfere with the exercise of professional discretion and impartial judgment.

  (2) A licensee shall not continue in a professional relationship with a client when the licensee has become emotionally involved with the client to the extent that objectivity is no longer possible in providing the required professional services.

  (3) A licensee shall inform the client when a real or potential conflict of interest arises and take reasonable steps to resolve the issue in a manner that makes the client's interests primary and protects the client's interests to the greatest extent possible. In some cases, protecting the client's interests may require termination of the professional relationship with proper referral of the client.

  (4) A licensee shall not take unfair advantage of any professional relationship or exploit others to further the licensee's personal, religious, political, or business interests.

NOTES

(5) A licensee who provides services to two or more people who have a relationship with each other shall clarify with all parties, when appropriate and in a manner consistent with the confidentiality standards of subrule 282.2(4), which individuals will be considered clients and the nature of the licensee's professional obligations to the various individuals who are receiving services. A licensee who anticipates a conflict of interest among the individuals receiving services or who anticipates having to perform in potentially conflicting roles shall clarify, when appropriate and in a manner consistent with the confidentiality standards at subrule 282.2(4), the licensee's role with the parties involved and take appropriate action to minimize any conflict of interest.

282.2(9) *Sexual relationships.*

a. Current clients. A licensee shall not engage in sexual activities or sexual contact with a client, regardless of whether such contact is consensual or nonconsensual.

b. Former clients. A licensee shall not engage in sexual activities or sexual contact with a former client within the five years following termination of the client relationship. A licensee shall not engage in sexual activities or sexual contact with a former client, regardless of the length of time elapsed since termination of the client relationship, if the client has a history of physical, emotional, or sexual abuse or if the client has ever been diagnosed with any form of psychosis or personality disorder or if the client is likely to remain in need of therapy due to the intensity or chronicity of a problem.

c. A licensee shall not engage in sexual activities or sexual contact with a client's or former client's spouse or significant other.

d. A licensee shall not engage in sexual activities or sexual contact with a client's or former client's relative within the second degree of consanguinity (client's parent, grandparent, child, grandchild, or sibling) when there is a risk of exploitation or potential harm to a client or former client.

e. A licensee shall not provide clinical services to an individual with whom the licensee has had prior sexual contact.

282.2(10) *Physical contact.* A licensee shall not engage in physical contact with a client when there is a possibility of psychological harm to the client as a result of the contact. A licensee who engages in appropriate physical contact with a client is responsible for setting clear, appropriate, and culturally and age-sensitive boundaries which govern such contact.

282.2(11) *Termination of services.*

a. A licensee shall terminate services to a client when such service is no longer required or no longer serves the client's needs or interests.

b. A licensee shall take reasonable steps to avoid abandoning clients who are still in need of services. A licensee shall assist in making appropriate arrangements for continuation of services when necessary.

c. A licensee shall not terminate services to pursue a social, financial, business, romantic, or sexual relationship with a client.

d. A licensee who anticipates the termination or interruption of services to a client shall notify the client promptly and seek the transfer, referral, or continuation of services in relation to the client's needs and preferences.

e. A licensee who is leaving an employment setting shall inform clients, to the extent possible given the nature of the termination of the employment relationship, of appropriate options for the continuation of services and of the benefits and risks of the options.

f. If the employer who terminates a licensee is also a licensee, the employer shall provide notice to clients or allow the licensee the opportunity to provide notice to clients to ensure appropriate case closure or continuation or transfer of services if continued treatment is necessary.

g. A licensee who provides clinical services shall comply with the following additional standards regarding termination of the client relationship:

  (1) Termination of a client relationship shall be documented in the client record. Absent written documentation of termination, the professional relationship shall be considered ongoing.

  (2) A licensee who practices in a fee-for-service setting may terminate services to a client who is not paying an overdue balance only if the financial contractual arrangements have been made clear to the client, if the client does not pose an imminent danger to self or others, and if the clinical and other consequences of the current nonpayment have been addressed and discussed with the client. Prior to terminating services under this subrule, a licensee shall make reasonable efforts to collect the unpaid fees and shall make appropriate referrals for the client.

282.2(12) *Misrepresentations, disclosure.* A licensee shall not:

a. Knowingly make a materially false statement, or fail to disclose a relevant material fact, in a letter of reference, application, referral, report or other document.

b. Knowingly allow another person to use the licensee's license or credentials.

c. Knowingly aid or abet a person who is misrepresenting the person's professional credentials or competencies.

d. Impersonate another person or misrepresent an organizational affiliation in one's professional practice.

e. Further the application or make a recommendation for professional licensure of another person who is known by the licensee to be unqualified in respect to character, education, experience, or other relevant attribute.

f. Fail to notify the appropriate licensing authority of any human services professional who is practicing or teaching in violation of the laws or rules governing that person's professional discipline.

g. Engage in professional activities, including advertising, that involve dishonesty, fraud, deceit, or misrepresentation.

h. Advertise services in a false or misleading manner or fail to indicate in the advertisement the name, the highest relevant degree and licensure status of the provider of services.

i. Fail to distinguish, or purposely mislead the reader or listener in public announcements, addresses, letters and reports as to whether the statements are made as a private individual or whether they are made on behalf of an employer or organization.

j. Engage in direct solicitation of potential clients for pecuniary gain in a manner or in circumstances which constitute overreacting, undue influence, misrepresentation or invasion of privacy.

k. Fail to inform each client of any financial interests that might accrue to the licensee for referral to any other person or organization or for the use of tests, books, or apparatus.

l. Fail to inform each client that the client may be entitled to the same services from a public agency, if the licensee is employed by that public agency and also offers services privately.

m. Make claims of professional superiority which cannot be substantiated by the licensee.

n. Guarantee that satisfaction or a cure will result from the performance of professional services.

o. Claim or use any secret or special method of treatment or techniques which the licensee refuses to divulge to professional colleagues.

p. Take credit for work not personally performed whether by giving inaccurate information or failing to give accurate information.

q. Offer social work services or use the designation of licensed bachelor social worker, licensed master social worker, or licensed independent social worker; or use the designations LBSW, LMSW, or LISW or any other designation indicating licensure status; or hold oneself out as practicing at a certain level of licensure unless the licensee is duly licensed as such.

r. Permit another person to use the licensee's license for any purpose.

s. Practice outside the scope of a license.

282.2(13) *Impairments.*

a. A licensee shall not:
   (1) Practice in a professional relationship while intoxicated or under the influence of alcohol or drugs not prescribed by a licensed physician.
   (2) Practice in a professional relationship while experiencing a mental or physical impairment that adversely affects the ability of the licensee to perform professional duties in a competent and safe manner.
   (3) Practice in a professional relationship if involuntarily committed for treatment of mental illness, drug addiction, or alcoholism.

b. A licensee who self-reports an impairment or suspected impairment to the board may be eligible for confidential monitoring by the impaired practitioner review committee. The licensee shall be provided the Impaired Practitioner Report form to initiate the process. Standards governing the impaired practitioner review committee may be found in 645—Chapter 16.

282.2(14) *Research.* If engaged in research, a licensee shall:

a. Consider carefully the possible consequences for human beings participating in the research.

b. Protect each participant from unwarranted physical and mental harm.

c. Ensure that the consent of the participant is voluntary and informed and that each participant executes a signed informed consent form which details the nature of the research and any known possible consequences.

d. Treat information obtained as confidential.

e. Not knowingly report distorted, erroneous, or misleading information.

NOTES

282.2(15) *Organization relationships and business practices.* A licensee shall not:

a. Solicit the clients of colleagues or assume professional responsibility for clients of another agency or colleague without appropriate communication with that agency or colleague.

b. Abandon an agency, organization, institution, or group practice without reasonable notice or under circumstances which seriously impair the delivery of professional care to clients.

c. Deliberately falsify client records.

d. Fail to submit required reports and documents in a timely fashion to the extent that the well-being of the client is adversely affected.

e. Delegate professional responsibilities to a person when the licensee knows, or has reason to know, that the person is not qualified by training, education, experience, or classification to perform the requested duties.

282.2(16) *Discrimination and sexual harassment.*

a. A licensee shall not practice, condone, or facilitate discrimination against a client, student, or supervisee on the basis of race, ethnicity, national origin, color, sex, sexual orientation, age, marital status, political belief, religion, mental or physical disability, diagnosis, or social or economic status.

b. A licensee shall not sexually harass a client, student, or supervisee. Sexual harassment includes sexual advances, sexual solicitation, requests for sexual favors, and other verbal or physical conduct of a sexual nature.

282.2(17) *General.* A licensee shall not:

a. Practice without receiving supervision as needed, given the licensee's level of practice, experience, and need.

b. Practice a professional discipline without an appropriate license or after expiration of the required license.

c. Physically or verbally abuse a client or colleague.

d. Obtain, possess, or attempt to obtain or possess a controlled substance without lawful authority; or sell, prescribe, give away, or administer controlled substances.

282.2(18) *Relationship between the board's rules of conduct and the National Association of Social Workers (NASW) Code of Ethics.* The NASW Code of Ethics is one resource for practitioners with respect to practice and ethical issues, and selected sections from the NASW Code of Ethics have been incorporated into the rules of conduct. A licensee's professional conduct is governed by the board's rules of conduct, and a licensee may be disciplined for violation of these rules. These rules are intended to implement Iowa Code chapters 21, 147, 154C, and

272C. [Filed 8/14/03, Notice 6/11/03—published 9/3/03, effective 10/8/03]

CHAPTER 283: DISCIPLINE FOR SOCIAL WORKERS

[Prior to 9/19/01, see 645—Chapter 280]
[Prior to 9/3/03, see 645—Chapter 282]
645—283.1(154B) Definitions.
"Board" means the board of social work.
"Discipline" means any sanction the board may impose upon licensees.
"Licensee" means a person licensed to practice social work.
[**ARC 8371B**, IAB 12/16/09, effective 1/20/10]
645—283.2(272C) Grounds for discipline. The board may impose any of the disciplinary sanctions provided in rule 645—283.3(272C) when the board determines that the licensee is guilty of any of the following acts or offenses:

283.2(1) Fraud in procuring a license. Fraud in procuring a license includes, but is not limited to:

   a. An intentional perversion of the truth in making application for a license to practice in this state;
   b. False representations of a material fact, whether by word or by conduct, by false or misleading allegations, or by concealment of that which should have been disclosed when making application for a license in this state; or
   c. Attempting to file or filing with the board or the department of public health any false or forged diploma or certificate or affidavit or identification or qualification in making an application for a license in this state.

283.2(2) Professional incompetency. Professional incompetency includes, but is not limited to:

   a. A substantial lack of knowledge or ability to discharge professional obligations within the scope of practice.
   b. A substantial deviation from the standards of learning or skill ordinarily possessed and applied by other social workers in the state of Iowa acting in the same or similar circumstances.
   c. A failure to exercise the degree of care which is ordinarily exercised by the average social worker acting in the same or similar circumstances.
   d. Failure to conform to the minimal standard of acceptable and prevailing practice of licensed social workers in this state.

283.2(3) Knowingly making misleading, deceptive, untrue or fraudulent representations in the practice of social work or engaging in unethical conduct or practice harmful or detrimental to the public. Proof of actual injury need not be established.

NOTES

283.2(4) Practice outside the scope of the profession.

283.2(5) Use of untruthful or improbable statements in advertisements. Use of untruthful or improbable statements in advertisements includes, but is not limited to, an action by a licensee in making information or intention known to the public which is false, deceptive, misleading or promoted through fraud or misrepresentation.

283.2(6) Habitual intoxication or addiction to the use of drugs.
  a. The inability of a licensee to practice with reasonable skill and safety by reason of the excessive use of alcohol on a continuing basis.
  b. The excessive use of drugs which may impair a licensee's ability to practice with reasonable skill or safety.

283.2(7) Obtaining, possessing, attempting to obtain or possess, or administering controlled substances without lawful authority.

283.2(8) Falsification of client records.

283.2(9) Acceptance of any fee by fraud or misrepresentation.

283.2(10) Negligence by the licensee in the practice of the profession. Negligence by the licensee in the practice of the profession includes a failure to exercise due care, including negligent delegation of duties or supervision of employees or other individuals, whether or not injury results; or any conduct, practice or conditions which impair the licensee's ability to safely and skillfully practice the profession.

283.2(11) Conviction of a felony related to the profession or occupation of the licensee or the conviction of any felony that would affect the licensee's ability to practice social work. A copy of the record of conviction or plea of guilty shall be conclusive evidence.

283.2(12) Violation of a regulation, rule, or law of this state, another state, or the United States, which relates to the practice of social work, including, but not limited to, the rules of conduct found in 645—282.2(154C).

283.2(13) Revocation, suspension, or other disciplinary action taken by a licensing authority of this state, another state, territory, or country; or failure by the licensee to report such action in writing within 30 days of the final action by such licensing authority. A stay by an appellate court shall not negate this requirement; however, if such disciplinary action is overturned or reversed by a court of last resort, the report shall be expunged from the records of the board.

283.2(14) Failure of a licensee or an applicant for licensure in this state to report any voluntary agreements restricting the individual's practice of social work in another state, district, territory or country.

283.2(15) Failure to notify the board of a criminal conviction within 30 days of the action, regardless of the jurisdiction where it occurred.

283.2(16) Failure to notify the board within 30 days after occurrence of any judgment or settlement of a malpractice claim or action.

283.2(17) Engaging in any conduct that subverts or attempts to subvert a board investigation.

283.2(18) Failure to respond within 30 days of receipt of communication from the board which was sent by registered or certified mail.

283.2(19) Failure to comply with a subpoena issued by the board or failure to cooperate with an investigation of the board.

283.2(20) Failure to comply with the terms of a board order or the terms of a settlement agreement or consent order.

283.2(21) Failure to pay costs assessed in any disciplinary action.

283.2(22) Submission of a false report of continuing education or failure to submit the biennial report of continuing education.

283.2(23) Failure to report another licensee to the board for any violations listed in these rules, pursuant to Iowa Code section 272C.9.

283.2(24) Knowingly aiding, assisting or advising a person to unlawfully practice social work.

283.2(25) Failure to report a change of name or address within 30 days after it occurs.

283.2(26) Representing oneself as a licensed social worker when one's license has been suspended or revoked, or when one's license is on inactive status.

283.2(27) Permitting another person to use the licensee's license for any purpose.

283.2(28) Permitting an unlicensed employee or person under the licensee's control to perform activities that require a license.

283.2(29) Unethical conduct. In accordance with Iowa Code section 147.55(3), behavior (i.e., acts, knowledge, and practices) which constitutes unethical conduct may include, but is not limited to, the following:

  a. Verbally or physically abusing a client or coworker.
  b. Improper sexual contact with or making suggestive, lewd, lascivious or improper remarks or advances to a client or coworker.
  c. Betrayal of a professional confidence.
  d. Engaging in a professional conflict of interest.
  e. Mental or physical inability reasonably related to and adversely affecting the licensee's ability to practice in a safe and competent manner.
  f. Being adjudged mentally incompetent by a court of competent jurisdiction.

283.2(30) Repeated failure to comply with standard precautions for preventing transmission of infectious diseases as issued by the Centers for Disease Control and Prevention of the United States Department of Health and Human Services.

283.2(31) Violation of the terms of an initial agreement with the impaired practitioner review committee or violation of the terms of an impaired practitioner recovery contract with the impaired practitioner review committee.

645—283.3(147,272C) Method of discipline. The board has the authority to impose the following disciplinary sanctions:

1. Revocation of license.
2. Suspension of license until further order of the board or for a specific period.
3. Prohibit permanently, until further order of the board, or for a specific period the licensee's engaging in specified procedures, methods, or acts.
4. Probation.
5. Require additional education or training.
6. Require a reexamination.
7. Order a physical or mental evaluation, or order alcohol and drug screening within a time specified by the board.
8. Impose civil penalties not to exceed $1000.
9. Issue a citation and warning.
10. Such other sanctions allowed by law as may be appropriate.

645—283.4(272C) Discretion of board. The following factors may be considered by the board in determining the nature and severity of the disciplinary sanction to be imposed:

1. The relative serious nature of the violation as it relates to ensuring a high standard of professional care for the citizens of this state;
2. The facts of the particular violation;
3. Any extenuating facts or other countervailing considerations;
4. The number of prior violations or complaints;
5. The seriousness of prior violations or complaints;
6. Whether remedial action has been taken; and
7. Such other factors as may reflect upon the competency, ethical standards, and professional conduct of the licensee.

645—283.5(154C) Order for mental, physical, or clinical competency examination or alcohol or drug screening. Rescinded IAB 3/10/10, effective 4/14/10.

These rules are intended to implement Iowa Code chapters 147, 154C and 272C.

[Filed 8/30/01, Notice 6/13/01—published 9/19/01, effective 10/24/01]

[Filed 8/14/03, Notice 6/11/03—published 9/3/03, effective 10/8/03]

[Filed 8/9/05, Notice 6/8/05—published 8/31/05, effective 10/5/05]

[Filed 11/15/05, Notice 8/31/05—published 12/7/05, effective 1/11/06]

[Filed 2/14/06, Notice 12/7/05—published 3/15/06, effective 4/19/06]

[Filed ARC 8371B (Notice ARC 8101B, IAB 9/9/09), IAB 12/16/09, effective 1/20/10]

[Filed ARC 8587B (Notice ARC 8368B, IAB 12/16/09), IAB 3/10/10, effective 4/14/10]

NOTES

CHAPTER 2

PHYSICAL HEALTH AND SAFETY

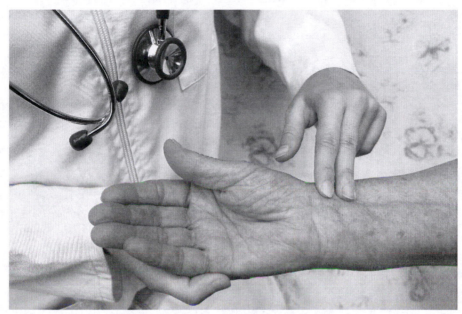

© 2012, LeventeGyori, Shutterstock, Inc.

Chapter Objectives

- Describe the impact of physical health on human service work.
- Describe meeting the needs of children and adults with physical or health care needs.
- Describe the impact of safety on human service work.

HEALTH DISPARITIES

YESTERDAY

- By 1980, average life expectancy in America had reached 74 years—25 years longer than at the beginning of the 20th century. However, African Americans, Hispanic Americans, American Indians, Asian Americans, and Native Hawaiians/Other Pacific Islanders, who represented 25% of the U.S. population, continued to experience significant health disparities, including shorter life expectancy and higher rates of diabetes, cancer, heart disease, stroke, substance abuse, infant mortality, and low birth weight.

- There was a growing awareness that racial and ethnic minority groups experienced poorer health compared to the overall population of the country. Scientists believed that the disparities were a result of a complex interaction between factors such as biology and the environment, as well as specific behaviors that could not be meaningfully addressed due to a shortage of racial and ethnic minority health professionals, discrimination, and inequities in income, education, and access to health care.

- In 1985, a Task Force on Black and Minority Health convened by the Secretary, DHHS, asked the NIH to determine why minorities were experiencing higher rates of diseases, disability, and death than the overall U.S. population and to work to eliminate such health disparities.

TODAY

- In 2010, Congress stressed its commitment to health equity by elevating the National Center on Minority Health and Health Disparities (NCMHD) to the National Institute on Minority Health and Health Disparities (NIMHD). NIMHD leads the planning, review, coordination, and evaluation of NIH's minority health and health disparities research activities. *The NIH Health Disparities Strategic Plan and Budget is the national blueprint for research to eliminate health disparities and for the educational and outreach efforts needed to translate research advances to health improvements.*

- Current NIH priorities include:
  - basic research focused on health disparities experienced by racial and ethnic minorities, the rural and urban poor, and other medically underserved populations;
  - population-specific community-based participatory research;

Fact sheet from National Institutes of Health. Updated October 2010.

- enhancing capacity to conduct health disparities research;
- recruiting and retaining racial and ethnic minorities and other underrepresented groups into the scientific research workforce;
- establishing health education programs for special populations; and
- promoting the inclusion of women, minorities, and other medically underserved groups in clinical trials

RESEARCH NIH is uncovering the causes of health disparities and determining how they can be eliminated.

- HIV/AIDS: The AIDS epidemic disproportionately affects racial and ethnic minorities. In 2007, African Americans comprised 13% of the U.S. population, but accounted for nearly half of persons living with HIV/AIDS. HIV/AIDS rates (cases per 100,000) were 77 among black/African Americans, 35 among Native Hawaiians/Other Pacific Islanders, 28 among Hispanics, 13 among American Indians/Alaska Natives, 9.2 among whites and 7.7 among Asian Americans.

  - The NIH-sponsored Center for AIDS Health Disparities Research (CAHDR) (http://www.mmc.edu/research/centers/chd/chdmission.html) at Meharry Medical College is investigating the biological basis for HIV/AIDS disparities among racial and ethnic minority groups. Recent CAHDR advances have explained the role of cholesterol in HIV entry and replication within a cell. The CAHDR has also identified a microbial agent, beta-cyclodexin (BCD), that can inactivate HIV and make cells resistant to infection by removing cholesterol from them. This discovery offers hope that compounds such as BCD can be used as microbicides to protect women against HIV infection.

- Cardiovascular Disease (CVD) and Stroke: Heart disease continues to be the leading cause of death in the U.S., and racial and ethnic minorities and individuals with low socio-economic status are strongly affected. Several large observational studies are examining the occurrence of CVD and its association with biological, demographic, social, environmental, and genetic determinants of risk in minority populations. They include the Strong Heart Study of American Indians (http://strongheart.ouhsc.edu/), the Jackson Heart Study of African Americans (http://jhs.jsums.edu/jhsinfo/), the Genetics of Coronary Artery Disease in Alaska Natives (https://gocadan.sfbrgenetics.org/) and the Hispanic Community Health Study of Americans of Mexican, Puerto Rican, Cuban, and Central American descent (http://www.cscc.unc.edu/hchs/). The Multi-Ethnic Study of Atherosclerosis (MESA) (http://www.mesanhlbi.org/) seeks to validate methods to detect CVD before it has produced clinical signs and symptoms in African Americans, Hispanic Americans, Asian Americans, and Americans of European heritage.

- **Cancer:** The National Cancer Institute offers a host of health disparities research and training programs, such as the Community Networks Program (http://crchd.cancer.gov/cnp/overview.html), the Comprehensive Partnerships to Reduce Cancer Health Disparities program(http://crchd.cancer.gov/research/miccp-overview.html), the Patient Navigation Research Program (http://crchd.cancer.gov/pnp/pnrp-index.html), and the Continuing Umbrella of Research Experiences (CURE) program (http://crchd.cancer.gov/diversity/cure-overview.html).

- **Addressing the Social Determinants of Health:** Recognizing that the biologic differences that cause health disparities are largely determined by a complex interplay of socio-economic, cultural, and environmental factors, NIMHD is spearheading NIH's research into the social determinants of health, and the application of faith-based approaches to understand health disparities. The NIH Centers for Population Health and Health Disparities conduct transdisciplinary research involving social, behavioral, biological, and genetic research to improve knowledge of the causes of health disparities and devise effective methods of preventing, diagnosing, and treating disease and promoting health.

- **Health Education:** Through Medline Plus and other outreach efforts, NIH educates the public about healthy lifestyles and many diseases and conditions including stroke, cancer, asthma, diabetes, drug addiction, mental illness, and cardiovascular, skin, musculoskeletal, and eye diseases. During *Stroke Awareness Month*, families across the Nation receive information about the symptoms of stroke and the need for prompt medical attention. The *Back-to-Sleep* campaign informs parents about the importance of placing infants on their back to sleep.

NIH's efforts to eliminate health disparities include the following key programs:

- Centers of Excellence—conduct research on health disparities in areas such as cancer, cardiovascular diseases, stroke, diabetes, nutrition, obesity, and maternal and infant health;

- Community-Based Participatory Research—enables partnerships among scientists and communities to conduct research and improve the health of communities;

- Loan Repayment Program—assists scientists to advance their careers in basic, clinical, and behavioral research focused on minority health or health disparities;
- Minority Health and Health Disparities International Research Training—supports young scientists conducting scientific research abroad;
- The Bridges to the Future Program—helps students in an associate's or master's degree program make the sometimes-difficult transition to the next level of training;
- Minority Biomedical Research Support, Building Research Infrastructure and Capacity, Research Centers in Minority Institutions, and Research Endowment—supports research and strengthens the biomedical research capability of the eligible institutions;
- Competitive Research (SCORE) Programs—supports the biomedical and behavioral research of faculty at institutions that serve minority populations ; and
- Clinical Trial Networks—enrolls a diverse population to ensure access and representation of the populations most affected by and vulnerable to the spread of HIV/AIDS (NIAID's HIV/AIDS Research Program) (http://www.niaid.nih.gov/topics/hivaids/Pages/Default.aspx).

TOMORROW

The Census Bureau predicts that racial and ethnic minority populations in the U.S. will grow to become half of the U.S. population in three decades. NIH has a research agenda in place to address the increasing health needs of racial and ethnic minorities, rural and urban poor, and other medically underserved populations in the midst of efforts to strengthen the healthcare system and improve access to care for millions of Americans. Eliminating health disparities is a priority for the NIH and involving diverse communities and partners will be critical in its effort directed at achieving health equity in America.

For more information, please contact the National Institute on Minority Health and Health Disparities (NIMHD):

- Website: www.nimhd.nih.gov
- Phone: (301) 402-1366
- E-mail: ncmhdinfo@mail.nih.gov

Personal Protective Equipment (PPE) Reduces Exposure to Bloodborne Pathogens

OSHA's Bloodborne Pathogens standard (29 CFR 1910.1030) requires employers to protect workers who are occupationally exposed to blood and other potentially infectious materials (OPIM), as defined in the standard. That is, the standard protects workers who can reasonably be anticipated to come into contact with blood or OPIM as a result of doing their job duties.

One way the employer can protect workers against exposure to bloodborne pathogens, such as hepatitis B virus (HBV), hepatitis C virus (HCV), and human immunodeficiency virus (HIV), the virus that causes AIDS, is by providing and ensuring they use personal protective equipment, or PPE. Wearing appropriate PPE can significantly reduce risk, since it acts as a barrier against exposure. Employers are required to provide, clean, repair, and replace this equipment as needed, and at no cost to workers.

Selecting Personal Protective Equipment

Personal protective equipment may include gloves, gowns, laboratory coats, face shields or masks, eye protection, pocket masks, and other protective gear. The PPE selected must be appropriate for the task. This means the level and type of protection must fit the expected exposure. For example, gloves may be the only PPE needed for a laboratory technician who is drawing blood. However, a pathologist conducting an autopsy would need much more protective clothing because of the different types of exposure (e.g., splashes, sprays) and the increased amount of blood and OPIM that are encountered. PPE must be readily accessible to workers and available in appropriate sizes.

If it can be reasonably expected that a worker could have hand contact with blood, OPIM, or contaminated surfaces or items, the employer must ensure that the worker wears gloves. Single-use gloves cannot be washed or decontaminated for reuse. Utility gloves may be decontaminated if their ability to provide an effective barrier is not compromised. They should be replaced when they show signs of cracking, peeling, tearing, puncturing, or deteriorating. Non-latex gloves, glove liners, powderless gloves or similar alternatives must be provided if workers are allergic to the gloves normally provided.

Gloves are required for all phlebotomies outside of volunteer blood donation centers. If an employer in a volunteer blood donation center judges that routine gloving for all phlebotomies is not

From OSHA Fact Sheet

necessary, then the employer is required to periodically re-evaluate this policy; make gloves available for workers who want to use them; and cannot discourage their use. In addition, employers must ensure that workers in volunteer blood donation centers use gloves (1) when they have cuts, scratches or other breaks in their skin, (2) while they are in training, or (3) when the worker believes that hand contamination might occur.

When splashes, sprays, splatters, or droplets of blood or OPIM pose a hazard to the eyes, nose or mouth, then masks in conjunction with eye protection (such as goggles or glasses with solid side shields) or chin-length face shields must be worn. Protection against exposure to the body is provided by protective clothing, such as gowns, aprons, lab coats, and similar garments. Surgical caps or hoods, and shoe covers or boots are needed when gross contamination is expected, such as during orthopedic surgery or autopsies.

In HIV and HBV research laboratories and production facilities, laboratory coats, gowns, smocks, uniforms, or other appropriate protective clothing must be used in work areas and animal rooms. Also, protective clothing must not be worn outside of the work area and must be decontaminated before being laundered.

EXCEPTION TO USE OF PERSONAL PROTECTIVE EQUIPMENT

A worker may choose, temporarily and briefly, **under rare and extraordinary circumstances**, to forego use of personal protective equipment. It must be the worker's professional judgment that using the personal protective equipment would prevent the delivery of health care or public safety services or would pose an increased hazard to the safety of the worker or coworker. When such a situation occurs, the employer is required to investigate and document the circumstances to determine if there is a way to avoid it from happening again in the future. Employers and workers should be aware that this is not a blanket exemption to the requirement to use PPE. OSHA expects that this will be an extremely rare occurrence.

DECONTAMINATING AND DISPOSING OF PERSONAL PROTECTIVE EQUIPMENT

Employers must ensure that workers remove personal protective equipment before leaving the work area. If a garment is penetrated by blood or OPIM, it must be removed immediately or as soon as feasible. Once PPE is removed, it must be placed in an appropriately designated area or container for storage, washing, decontamination, or disposal. In addition, employers must ensure that workers wash their hands immediately or as soon as feasible after removal of gloves or other personal protective equipment.

HOW TO TAKE VITAL SIGNS: RESPIRATION

Respiration refers to how rapidly you breathe. The ideal respiration is quiet, rhythmic and effortless. A rapid respiration rate is common after exercise, when a person has a fever, and when a person goes into shock. Respiratory diseases will also contribute to a rapid respiration rate. A rapid respiration rate will increase a person's pulse.

A slow respiration rate will result in a lowered pulse rate. Slow respiratory rates can be also caused by narcotic use, sedatives and sleeping.

RESPIRATION NORMS

Adults—12–20 respirations or breaths per minute.
Children are faster.

GUIDELINES FOR TAKING RESPIRATION

- Observe the rise and fall of the person's chest.
- Count the number of breaths.
- Note the regularity of the person's breaths and any periods of apnea.
- Note the quality of the breaths. Is it noisy or does it require effort?
- Record all information on the person's chart.

HOW TO TAKE VITAL SIGNS: PULSE

Pulse is the rate of blood flowing through the arteries. It is usually determined by placing the tips of the index and middle finger over the radial artery (base of the thumb). There are several points at which the pulse may be taken. These are the carotid, brachial, radial, femoral, apical, popliteal and dorsalis peds arteries.

PULSE NORMS

Adults—50–100 pulses per minute for adults (this may vary based on age and activity).
Children and babies have higher pulse rates.

GUIDELINES FOR TAKING A PULSE

1. Use the flat part of your fingers, not your thumb.
2. Place your index and middle fingers lightly on top of the artery to feel the pulse.
3. Do not compress the artery too much, or you will not be able to feel a pulse.

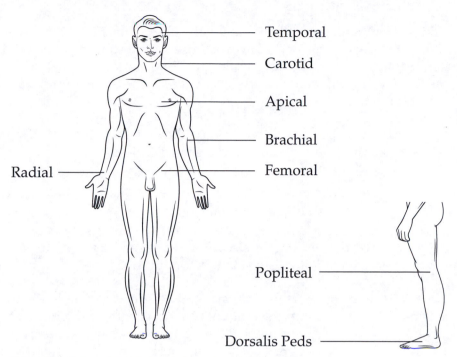

© Anna Rassadnikova, 2014. Used under license from Shutterstock, Inc.

4. Using a watch with a second hand, count the number of pulses. Make note of how regular the pulse is and any skipped beats. If you count the number of pulses for 10 seconds--multiply that number by 6, 15 seconds—multiply that number by 4, 30 seconds—multiply that number by 2.

HOW TO TAKE VITAL SIGNS: TEMPERATURE

A body's temperature is a good sign of overall health. Temperatures tend to rise a degree or two throughout the day and then lower at night. It is important to take vital signs at regular intervals or at the same time each day.

TEMPERATURE NORMS

- Centigrade = 37 degrees
- Fahrenheit = 98.6 degrees
- Rectal reading typically one degree above oral temperature reading.
- Axillary, (armpit) reading typically one degree lower than oral temperature reading.

GUIDELINES FOR TAKING TEMPERATURE ORALLY

Taking a temperature orally is usually the most convenient method as well as the least disruptive. However, this method should not be used with babies, people who have undergone oral surgery, have oral diseases, are confused, or are receiving oxygen. Procedure for traditional oral thermometers:

- Use the disposable sleeve or wipe the thermometer with disinfectant from bulb to tip and rinse in cold water.
- Shake down the thermometer to 97 degrees Fahrenheit or lower.
- Place the thermometer bulb under the tongue with lips closed for 3–5 minutes for an accurate reading.
- After removing the thermometer, record the person's temperature.
- Remove the disposable sleeve or wash the thermometer and again wipe it with disinfectant before putting it away.

Electronic thermometers that are made of plastic with a metal sensor are increasingly used because of concerns regarding the poisonous alcohol and mercury contents of the traditional glass thermometers.

In recent years there has been an increase in the use of **small ear thermometers** that measure temperature through the eardrum. A benefit, especially with children, is that the measurement can be taken quickly, often within one second.

HOW TO TAKE VITAL SIGNS: BLOOD PRESSURE

Blood pressure is the force of blood in artery walls. Blood pressure is taken with an instrument called a sphygmomanometer or blood pressure cuff. The first number is called the **systolic** number (when the heart is pumping). The second number is the **diastolic** number (when the heart relaxes). The diastolic number is the most important number.

BLOOD PRESSURE NORMS

Adults--Ranges from 100/70 to 150/90.
Children are lower than adults.
The average blood pressure is 120/80.

There is no real normal blood pressure, only a normal pressure for the individual: Elevations in blood pressure can produce headache, blurred vision, dizziness, pulsations in eyes, or may produce no symptoms.

High blood pressure is often a silent killer. An elevation in blood pressure is referred to as hypertension and a decrease in blood pressure is referred to as hypotension. People who are suffering from shock will often have severely decreased blood pressure.

GUIDELINES FOR TAKING BLOOD PRESSURE

1. Position the cuff over the brachial artery.
2. Inflate to 200, and slowly release.
3. Place the stethoscope over the artery. It will produce the sound of beats.
4. Take a reading at the sound of the first beat (first number is systolic).
5. Take a reading at muffle or the last audible beat (second number is diastolic).

STANDARD PRECAUTIONS

The Centers for Disease Control (CDC) recommend the following practices for the prevention of blood-borne pathogens. Training on these guidelines is mandated annually for all individuals who are identified as at-risk to occupational exposure for blood-borne pathogens.

HAND CARE

1. Wash hands with soap and water frequently.
2. If health science student, wash hands before and after all patient care. Wash hands immediately after exposure to blood and/or body fluids and after removing disposable gloves.
3. If working with heavy cleaning activities, each individual should have his/her own pair of utility gloves to wear during at-risk activities, and wash and disinfect gloves after each use.
4. Avoid chapped and cracked hands if possible. Use a water-based hand lotion frequently. Petroleum-based products and Vaseline break down latex.

Protective Barriers should be worn at all times when working with blood or blood products or body fluids or waste that may contain blood.

1. Protective eyewear should be worn whenever there is a risk of eye splash.
2. Gowns, boots, & masks should be worn when risk of contamination to clothes, feet, or face.

Individuals with open or draining lesions should not work directly with other people (health care students, food servers) while lesion is open or draining.

NOTES

Do Not Recap; shear, or break needles at any time.

Discard needles and sharp objects in protective containers immediately.

Sterilize or disinfect reusable equipment that is to be used for more than one person. Do Not share equipment between roommates or friends.

Place items that contain a lot of blood in a red biohazard plastic bag which you can get from Student Health Service or Housekeeping. Return red bag to Student Health Service so that bag can be incinerated.

Do Not pick up broken glass with bare hands. Wear utility gloves or sweep it up. Dispose of broken glass in container that does not allow others to be cut.

Resuscitation: Mouthpieces or resuscitator bags should be used whenever resuscitation is carried out.

STANDARD PRECAUTIONS

GLOVES	WASH	GOWN/APRON	MASK EYE PROTECTION

Before touching blood, body fluids, mucous membranes, non-intact skin or performing venipuncture CHANGE gloves after contact with each patient.	Wash hands immediately after gloves are removed. Wash hands and other skin surfaces immediately if contaminated with blood or other body fluids.	For procedures likely to generate splashes of blood or other body fluids.	Masks and protective eyewear or face shields for procedures likely to generate splashes of blood or other body fluids.
SHARPS	**DO NOT RECAP BY HAND**	**RESUSCITATION**	**WASTE/LINEN**

Dispose of needles with syringes and other sharp items in puncture-resistant container near point-of-use.	Do not recap needles or otherwise manipulate by hand before disposal.	Mouthpieces or resuscitator bags should be available to minimize need for emergency mouth to mouth resuscitation.	Waste and soiled linen should be handled in accordance with disposal policy and local law.

GLOVE REMOVAL

— With both hands gloved, peel one glove off from top to bottom and hold it in the gloved hand.
— With the exposed hand, peel the second glove from the inside, tucking the first glove inside the second.
— Dispose of the gloves promptly.
— Never touch the outside of the glove with bare skin.
— Every time you remove your gloves wash your hands with soap and water as soon as possible.

ADDITIONAL INFORMATION

For more information, go to OSHA's Bloodborne Pathogens and Needlestick Prevention Safety and Health Topics web page at: https://www.osha.gov/SLTC/bloodbornepathogens/index.html.

To file a complaint by phone, report an emergency, or get OSHA advice, assistance, or products, contact your nearest OSHA office under the "U.S. Department of Labor" listing in your phone book, or call us toll-free at (800) 321-OSHA (6742).

CHAPTER 3

NEURODEVELOPMENTAL DISORDERS

© 2012, kentoh, Shutterstock, Inc.

Chapter Objectives

- Describe the characteristics of developmental disabilities.
- Describe the meeting of needs for children and adults with disabilities.

WHAT IS DISABILITY AND WHO IS AFFECTED BY DISABILITY?

Disabilities have been defined in many ways. In general, disabilities are characteristics of the body, mind, or senses that, to a greater or lesser extent, affect a person's ability to engage independently in some or all aspects of day-to-day life.

- Different kinds of disabilities affect people in different ways. The same kind of disability can affect each person differently.
- Many Americans will experience disability first hand.
- While all disabilities are as different as the individuals who experience them, the challenges and opportunities for persons with disabilities often are similar.

DISABILITY IS NEITHER INABILITY NOR SICKNESS

- Most persons with disabilities are as healthy as people who don't have disabilities; however, persons with disabilities are at greater risk for illness.
- Most people with disabilities can and do work, play, learn, and enjoy full healthy lives in their communities.
- One of the key challenges for a person with a disability is to be seen by the public, to be portrayed in the media, treated by health care professionals, as an individual with abilities, and not just seen as a disability.

DISABILITY CAN BECOME A FACT OF LIFE FOR ANYONE AT ANY TIME

- Today, 54 million people in the United States are living in the community with a disability. That's one in every five people. According to the most recent census data, around 52 million of them reside in the community (US Census Bureau 2002). Additionally, about 2 million people live in nursing homes and other long-term care facilities.
- Some people are born with a disability; some people get sick or have an accident that results in a disability; and some people develop a disability as they age.
- The reality is that just about everyone—women, men and children of all ages, races and ethnicities—will experience a disability some time during his or her lifetime.
- As we age, the likelihood of having a disability of some kind increases. The likelihood of having a disability increased with age. For those 45 to 54 years old, 22.6 percent have some form of disability; for those 65 to 69 years old, the comparable estimate is 44.9 percent; and for the oldest age group, 80 years old and over, the prevalence of disability is estimated to be 73.6 percent.

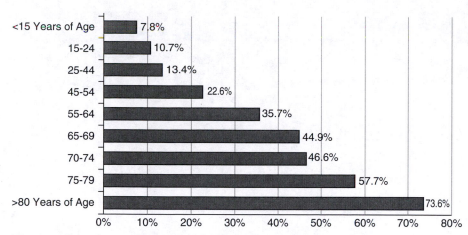

Figure 1: Prevalence of Disability by Age Group, 1997*

TABLE 1 POPULATION BY AGE AND DISABILITY		
Characteristic	**Total**	**Total %**
Population, Age 5 and over	**257,167,527**	**100.0**
With any disability	49,746,248	19.3
Population, Ages 5–15	**45,133,687**	**100.0**
With any disability	2,614,919	5.8
Sensory	442,894	1.0
Physical	455,461	1.0
Mental	2,078,502	4.6
Self-care	419,018	0.9
Population, Ages 16–64	**178,687,234**	**100.0**
With any disability	33,153,211	18.6
Sensory	4,123,902	2.3
Physical	11,140,365	6.2
Mental	6,764,439	3.8
Self-care	3,149,875	1.8
Difficulty going out	11,414,508	6.4
Employment disability	21,287,570	11.9
Population, Age 65 and Over	**33,346,626**	**100.0**
With any disability	13,978,118	41.9
Sensory	4,738,479	14.2
Physical	9,545,680	28.6
Mental	3,592,912	10.8
Self-care	3,183,840	9.5
Difficulty going out	8,795,517	20.4
Source: U.S. Census Bureau, Census 2000 Summary File 3 (adapted from Panko Reis et al 2004)		

WORKSHEET ON ABILITIES FILM

VIDEO: *WITHOUT PITY: A FILM ABOUT ABILITIES*

PERSONAL REFLECTIONS ABOUT INDIVIDUALS

Young Woman—Cerebral Palsy:

Man—Cerebral Palsy:

Remarkable Six Year Old—Without Arms/Legs:

Professor—Polio:

UNDERSTANDING CHARACTERISTICS OF PEOPLE WITH DISABILITIES

- They are individuals.
- They are more like their non-disabled peers than they are different.
- Characteristics of people with disabilities are different, even when they have the same disability.
- Knowledge of the abilities of individuals will be more valuable than general information about their disabilities.
- People with and without disabilities have the same rights to participate, to try, to succeed, and to fail.
- All people can learn.

DEVELOPMENTAL DISABILITIES

- Mental or physical impairment or both—manifested before age 22.
- Likely to continue indefinitely.
- Specialized plans and treatments—IEP or IHP.
- Three or more needs with:
  - Self care
  - Receptive and expressive languages
  - Learning difficulties
  - How to apply learning
  - Mobility
  - Self-direction (make decisions)
  - Capacity for independent living
  - Economic self-sufficiency

The DSM-5, published by the American Psychiatric Association in 2013, provides information about neurodevelopmental disorders, which are disorders that typically begin in early development. These disorders include:

- Intellectual disabilities (formerly called mental retardation)
- Communication disorders
- Autism spectrum disorders
- Attention Deficit Hyperactivity Disorder (ADHD)
- Neurodevelopmental motor disorders
- Learning disorders

Intellectual disability, also described as intellectual developmental disorder, begins during the developmental period. There are three

NOTES

main criteria that must be met for an individual to be diagnosed with an intellectual disability:

1. Intellectual functioning deficits, such as problems with planning, learning, reasoning, and problem-solving.
2. Problems in adaptive functioning, which includes failing to meet the sociocultural standards of social responsibility and personal independence.
3. The disorder begins during the developmental period.

Intellectual disabilities are specified in four severities which are similar to the former severities for the diagnosis for mental retardation:

1. Mild
2. Moderate
3. Severe
4. Profound

<u>Intelligence Quotient (I.Q.)</u>
      130—gifted/talented
      115 to 85—average I.Q.
      84 to 70—slow learners
      70 and below—mental retardation

<u>Levels of Mental Retardation:</u>
- **Mild—70 to 55 I.Q.**
  - The person doesn't look different
  - With support they can read at the 8th grade level (max.)

- Work and can count change accurately.
- Most graduate from high school.
- Many if not all have an active social life.
- **Moderate—54 to 40 I.Q.**
  - Difficulties living on their own and holding jobs. Usually live in a secure setting—usually a facility; has a work coach
  - Needs more support.
  - Difficulties with change.
  - More medical issues are involved.
- **Severe—39 to 25 I.Q.**
  - Physical needs are greater.
  - Chromosomal issues/genetics.
- **Profound—24 and lower I.Q.**
  - Can't speak.
  - Some signing can be learned.
  - Regular and constant care is required.
  - Can learn—their likes and dislikes.

LEARNING ISSUES

The individual diagnosed with mental retardation will learn more slowly than peers; will have difficulties with generalization (boys to men; girls to women); difficulty with cause and effect; poor memory; easily frustrated; difficulty with reading and with social interactions.

TRAUMATIC BRAIN INJURY (TBI'S)

May be an adult or a child—however, all are very complex and can even be described by some as a "mystery."

- Injury to the brain that results in loss of consciousness.
- Head injuries cause changes in or difficulties with:
  - **Physical abilities:** speaking, hearing, seeing, walking, writing, many motor difficulties
  - **Thinking and reasoning:** short/long term memory, concentrating, reading/writing, talking, listening and learning, don't know things day to day
  - **Social, behavioral, or emotional issues:** mood swings, denial, agitation, anxiety, depression, impulsive, different relationships to others, emotion are up and down.
  - **Smell:** complete loss of sometimes.

What we need to remember is to remain calm, be direct, explain things in detail to the individual.

NOTES

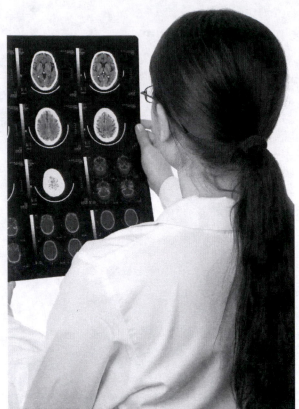

© 2012, Lusoimages, Shutterstock, Inc.

SUGGESTIONS—TBI

- Provide extra time for tasks.
- Directions should be given one at a time.
- Provide written directions and oral.
- Consistent routines.
- Establish a plan/follow it/routinize it.
- Reduce distractions.
- Simplify things.
- Provide opportunities to rest.
- Be flexible.
- Be patient.

"Executive Functioning"—located in the frontal lobes of the brain. Allows for the individual to move from one thing to another—transitioning—individuals with a TBI will have many issues in this area. Ultimately, it will cause lots of problems.

PERVASIVE DEVELOPMENTAL DISORDERS (PDD)

- Includes Autism and Asperger's Syndrome.
- Neurological Disorders—brain issues.
- Range of abilities.
- Common Characteristics:
  - Difficulty in social situations.
  - Communication skills.
  - Presence of stereotyped behaviors, interests, and activities.
  - Fascination with certain objects—train/airplane schedules.
  - Things are done repetitively.
  - Insensitivity to pain.
  - Spinning type motions are common.

ASPERGER'S SYNDROME OR DISORDER

- No delay in cognitive development or age appropriate help skills.
- No clinical delay in language.
- May have difficulty with subtleties (e.g., humor).
- Average intelligence.
- Impairment of social interactions.
- Repetitive stereotyped behaviors and interests.
- Later onset than Autism.

AUSTISM

- Developmental disability—onset before age 3.
- Impaired social development.
- Communication difficulties.
- Interference with learning.
- Sensory deficits.
- Inappropriate behaviors (self-stimulation, tantrums, isolation)
- Difficulty with change.
- Difficulty with generalization.
- Difficulty with abstract thinking.
- Hyperactivity often times accompanies Autism/Asperger's
- Follow own internal agenda.
- Usually a loner.
- Can lead to depression—at risk for depression to occur.
- Sensitive to texture, smells, feels, lots of sensory issues, noise sensitive too.

Examples of self-stimulation—rocking, waving, biting, pacing, head banging, rolling eyes—these could be self-harming or injurious.

SUGGESTIONS—AUTISM

- Provide direct instruction on alternative appropriate behaviors.
- Provide consistent routine.
- Provide numerous opportunities to practice.
- Great success with early intensive behavior modification programs.
- Usually are visual learners or tactile learners.

Lovaas—sensory—stimulation—reward—system of working with individuals diagnosed with Autism.

PECS—cards with pictures used to communicate with others for the non-verbal individual. Some of the cards are also three-dimensional.

More males are being diagnosed autistic or with Asperger's Syndrome than females.

VIDEO: *ASPERGER SYNDROME—LIVING OUTSIDE THE BELL CURVE*

1. Identify the symptoms of Asperger Syndrome described in the video.

2. Describe the effects of Asperger Syndrome on social development of individuals with the disorder.

3. Describe the effects on the family of individuals of individuals with the disorder.

4. Discuss the strategies for dealing with Asperger Syndrome.

5. As a staff member working with an individual with Asperger Syndrome, how can you use the information provided in the video?

VIDEO: *TRAUMATIC BRAIN INJURY*

1. Describe the effects of head injuries on learning and development.

2. Describe the symptoms or issues that family members and teachers recognized.

3. What are the short term and long term concerns of the family and school staff?

4. What accommodations are being made?

Case study discussion:

Beth, a child with a traumatic brain injury, is in eighth grade. You are part of the child study team that is focusing on Beth. She has difficulty concentrating and seems confused some of the time. She asks lots of questions and interrupts frequently.

Identify three goals that you would like to see implemented this year.

How should these goals be implemented?

Case study discussion:

You are working with an adult who sustained a head injury when he was 30 years old. He is now back at work, but is having some difficulties.

- Describe some typical issues that he may be having.

- How will you provide support for him in his work and in social situations?

VIDEO: *THE SPECTRUM OF AUTISM*

1.   Identify the symptoms of Autism described in the video.

2.   Describe the effects of Autism on social development of individuals with the disorder.

3.   Describe the effects on the family of individuals of individuals with the disorder.

4.   Discuss the strategies for dealing with Autism.

5.   As a staff member working with an individual with Autism, how can you use the information provided in the video?

UNDERSTANDING SPECIFIC DISABILITIES

INTELLECTUAL DISABILITIES

Individuals who have intellectual disabilities are defined by low scores on intelligence tests and limitations in adaptive behavior which refers to the way they meet ordinary social and personal demands. (Intellectual disabilities is divided into four levels of severity: mild, moderate, severe, and profound).

People with intellectual disabilities learn more slowly than their peers. They generally have the following difficulties which impact their learning:

- Poor memory.
- Difficulty learning new things.
- Inability to generalize—to take information learned in one setting and using it in another.
- Difficulty understanding cause and effect.
- Difficulty paying attention.

WORKING WITH PEOPLE WITH INTELLECTUAL DISABILITIES. **Individuals** can learn and retain information. We can help people with intellectual disabilities acquire skills.

- Use clear, specific language.
- Check for understanding.
- Use task analysis by dividing tasks into small parts. Teach each part sequentially.
- Teach by demonstration rather than just verbal instruction.
- Demonstrate appropriate social behavior.
- Provide specific feedback.
- Reinforce success frequently.

PHYSICAL AND NEUROLOGICAL DISABILITIES

The characteristics of individuals with physical and neurological disabilities vary based on the type and severity of their disabilities. There are many different physical and neurological disabilities; some of the more common types include:

Cerebral palsy—a physical and neurological impairment caused by damage to the nervous system before, during, or immediately after birth. Coordination, mobility, balance, and communication may be affected. Some individuals with cerebral palsy may also have intellectual disabilities.

NOTES

Epilepsy—an impairment characterized by temporary sudden brief changes in how the brain works which lead to loss of consciousness or seizures. An individual with epilepsy may experience a few moments of staring into space, or may display major convulsions. Most people with epilepsy take medications which partially or completely control the seizures.

Spina bifida—is a birth defect of the spinal cord that results in a permanent disability. Individuals typically experience motor impairment, muscle weakness, or paralysis. Some have difficulty with respiration, eating problems, infections and learning problems. In many cases, people with spina bifida also have hydrocephalus, fluid on the brain. Individuals benefit from assistive devices.

Muscular dystrophy—a progressive impairment that leads to deterioration of muscles connected to the skeleton. The impairment results in limiting movement and mobility. Individuals require assistive devices.

WORKING WITH PEOPLE WITH PHYSICAL AND NEUROLOGICAL DISABILITIES Teamwork is very important when working with people with physical and neurological disabilities. Often medical staff, physical and occupational therapists, parents and educators work together to help individuals be as independent as possible. Some lifting and transferring are often required.

LEARNING DISABILITIES

Individuals with learning disabilities are defined as those with significant problems in academic areas despite having average or above average intelligence. The disability is not caused by mental retardation or environmental factors.

Individuals with learning disabilities typically have difficulties in reading, or mathematics, or writing, or listening. They often have deficits in:

- Information processing
- Perception—may reverse numbers or letters
- Auditory or visual memory
- Attention
- Organization and time management
- Following directions
- Social skills

WORKING WITH PEOPLE WITH LEARNING DISABILITIES Individuals with learning disabilities need structured lessons that teach them not only information, but also the techniques for self management and independent learning.

- Combine visual and auditory information.
- Provide extra time
- Use task analysis
- Teach self management techniques
- Provide specific feedback

ATTENTION DEFICIT DISORDER—WITH AND WITHOUT HYPERACTIVITY

Individuals with attention deficit disorder have difficulty attending to tasks. Many pay attention to everything and have problems focusing. Individuals with attention deficit disorder may also have hyperactive tendencies and seem to move constantly. Some people who have attention deficit disorder are also learning disabled.

Individuals with attention deficit disorder are often given medication in combination with behavior modification and self management techniques.

WORKING WITH PEOPLE WITH ATTENTION DEFICIT DISORDER Provide a stable and consistent environment.

- Minimize distractions
- Provide a variety of activities
- Keep pace of activity rapid

BEHAVIOR OR EMOTIONAL DISABILITY

Individuals with behavior or emotional disabilities have extreme problems that affect their ability to perform at school, at work, and with social relationships. These individuals display significant behaviors over longer time and to higher intensity when compared to their peers.

These behaviors may include: aggression, violence, verbal threats, destruction of property, inappropriately seeking attention, tantrums, hyperactivity, compulsiveness, impulsiveness, irritability, or withdrawal.

WORKING WITH PEOPLE WITH BEHAVIOR OR EMOTIONAL DISABILITIES
Provide supportive and consistent interventions.
Listen carefully

- Provide social skill instruction
- Teach self management techniques
- Provide specific feedback.
- Reinforce success frequently

NOTES

© 2012, Lisa F. Young, Shutterstock, Inc.

Speech and language disorders

People with speech and language disorders have a variety of disabilities that affect the way individuals communicate. If the way a person communicates draws unwarranted attention to the individual, it may be considered a disability.

The speech disorders include articulation—production of sounds; stuttering—speech fluency; voice—speak too loudly, softly, or hoarsely. Language disorders include expressive and receptive language problems. Expressive language involves speaking clearly. Receptive language involves understanding spoken or written communication.

Working with people with speech and language disorders A
speech and language specialist or clinician often works individually and in small groups with people with speech and language disorders. The specialist recommends activities for speech and language interventions in natural environments such as classrooms, work sites, or family and community settings.

Visual impairment—includes blindness and low vision

Individuals with visual impairment have a variety of vision problems that range from blindness to visual limitations under some conditions. Their visual impairment affects their educational and vocational performance.

Individuals with visual impairments typically have average intelligence, but their impairments often lead to delays in cognitive, language and social development. Many need assistance with mobility and orientation. Some people with visual impairments read by using Braille. Assistive technology and adaptive devices such as computerized voice synthesizers and touch screens allow individuals with visual impairments to learn and become more independent.

WORKING WITH PEOPLE WITH VISUAL IMPAIRMENTS **Always ask if you can assist** people with visual disabilities. Do not assume that they need help. Keep the environment consistent. Ask the itinerant vision teacher or specialist for information on assistive and adaptive devices.

HEARING IMPAIRMENT—INCLUDES DEAF AND HARD OF HEARING

Individuals who are deaf cannot hear spoken language even with hearing aids. People who are defined as hard of hearing have losses which adversely affect their performance in school and work. Hearing impairments results in delays in language development.

Some individuals with hearing impairments communicate by using sign language. Others use speech reading, communication boards, or computers. Telecommunication devices change verbal messages into writing (TTY).

Technology has greatly improved adaptive devices for individuals with hearing impairments. These range from advanced hearing aids, assistive communication devices where a voice is transmitted directly to a receiver in the individuals' ear, and cochlea implants.

WORKING WITH INDIVIDUALS WITH HEARING IMPAIRMENTS **Speak clearly** without obstruction of your mouth and lips. Become familiar with the individual's favored method of communication, e.g. sign language or communication board. Ask the itinerant hearing teacher or specialist for information on assistive and adaptive devices.

AUTISM

People with autism have a condition that is characterized by severe disorders of communication and behavior which usually appears during the early developmental stages of childhood. These communication difficulties and behaviors interfere with the individual's learning, speech, developmental rate, response to the environment, and relations to others. Individuals may seem to be preoccupied with objects; they may display body rocking, head banging, unusual hand movements, or repeated speech.

NOTES

Many children with autism are receiving early intensive individualized behavior modification programs. The focus is often on developing alternative appropriate behaviors.

WORKING WITH PEOPLE WITH AUTISM **Provide highly structured environments with clear expectations and consequences for behavior. Activities should be regular and predictable.**

TRAUMATIC BRAIN INJURY

Individuals with traumatic brain injury experience trauma to the head that results in prolonged loss of consciousness or coma. The extent of their disabilities depends on the part of the brain that sustained injury and the severity of the damage.

The resulting disabilities can include intelligence, motor functioning, speech, language, memory, behavior and social adjustments.

WORKING WITH INDIVIDUALS WITH TRAUMATIC BRAIN INJURY **Working with the individual and the family is important.**

- Provide consistent interventions.
- Teach strategies for remembering.
- Present materials in small increments.
- Provide immediate feedback and reinforcement.
- Be prepared for emotional reactions.

DEVELOPMENTAL DISABILITIES

A developmental disability is defined as a severe and long lasting disability of a person which:

1. Is the result of a mental or physical impairment or both;
2. Is manifested before age 22;
3. Is likely to continue indefinitely;
4. Reflects the person's needs for specialized services and or treatment that are individually planned and coordinated;
5. Results in substantial functional limitations in three or more of the following areas of major life activity:

   a) <u>Self care:</u> daily activities enabling a person to meet basic life needs for food, hygiene, and appearance.

   b) <u>Receptive and expressive language:</u> communication involving verbal and non-verbal behavior enabling a person both to understand others and to express ideas and information to others.

   c) <u>Learning:</u> general cognitive competence and ability to acquire new behaviors, perceptions, and information; apply experiences to new situations.

d) <u>Mobility:</u> ability to use fine and gross motor skills; ability to move one's person form one place to another with or without mechanical aids.

e) <u>Self-direction:</u> management and taking control over one's social and personal life; ability to make decisions affecting and protecting one's self-interest.

f) <u>Capacity for independent living:</u> age-appropriate ability to live without extraordinary assistance.

g) <u>Economic self-sufficiency:</u> maintaining adequate employment and financial support.

CASE STUDY

Tiffany's son, Caleb, is nine months old. His pediatrician is concerned about Caleb's delayed development. Caleb is not babbling, does not respond to his own name, and makes little eye contact. Caleb does not bear weight on his legs and cannot sit up without support. He has just started to consistently roll over. Caleb weighs only 14 pounds and has difficulty eating baby foods.

Tiffany reported that she was diagnosed with ADHD "a long time ago." She added that she took Ritalin and that it seemed to help her in school. She added that she stopped taking the medicine around the time she moved in with her father.

INTERNET SITES: AT-RISK AND DEVELOPMENTAL DISABILITIES

National Dissemination Center for Children with Disabilities
www.nichcy.org

Brain Injury Association
www.biaia.org

Council for Exceptional Children
www.cec.sped.org

Iowa Vocational Rehabilitation
www.ivrs.iowa.gov

Learning Disabilities Association of Iowa
www.isa-ia.org

Grant Wood Area Education Agency
www.aea10.k12.ia.us

NOTES

Internet Research Questions: At-Risk and Developmental Disabilities

**Answer questions 1 and 2 and <u>either</u> 3 or 4

1. **<u>Advocacy Group:</u>** Go to the Brain Injury Association website www.biausa.org
   a. How does an advocacy group such as the Brain Injury Association educate the public and impact public policy?

2. **<u>Local Organization for information, programs and advocacy:</u>** Go to the Grant Wood Area Education Agency website www.aea10.k12.ia.us. Find Prog/Services and select Parent Educator Partnership.
   a. Read a recent issue of the PEP newsletter.
   b. Identify and review two articles in the newsletter that focus either on providing information or advocacy.
   c. Summarize the articles.
   d. Discuss how the information can be used by a staff member who works with a person or family with these issues?

3. **<u>Professional Organization:</u>** Go to the Council of Exceptional Children website www.cec.sped.org. Select either Current Special Education topics or Exceptionality/Topic Area.
   a. Select and identify a topic of interest to you.
   b. Summarize your findings.
   c. Discuss two current issues. (Not a definition) that is interesting or surprising to you. Explain why.
   d. Discuss how the information can be used by a staff member who works with a person with these issues.

4. **<u>National Information Center:</u>** Go to the National Dissemination Center for Children with Disabilities website www.nichcy.org. Go to A—Z topics.
   a. Select and identify a topic of interest to you. Examples: Asperger Syndrome, Learning Disabilities, etc.
   b. Summarize the information.
   c. Discuss two current issues. (Not a definition) that is interesting or surprising to you. Explain why.
   d. Discuss how the information can be used by a staff member who works with a person with these issues.

JOURNAL DISCUSSION QUESTIONS: AT-RISK AND DEVELOPMENTAL DISABILITIES

Students will respond to the following questions individually and record their responses in a "running journal" which will be turned in to be graded. Students will discuss their responses in small groups and share the responses with the larger class.

Be sure to use people first language.

1. Why is "at risk" a sensitive term? What is your definition of "at-risk"? Describe three strategies, interventions or programs that can be used to support those who you define as "at-risk". Why did you select these strategies?
2. How is an individual with a developmental disability the same and different than other individuals?
3. How can you maintain a balance between focusing on an individual's abilities and disabilities? Why is it important to do this?
4. Describe the similarities and differences of working with an individual with mental retardation, and one with traumatic brain injury.

CHAPTER 4

MENTAL HEALTH

© 2012, luxorphoto, Shutterstock, Inc.

Chapter Objectives

- Describe how mental health disorders are diagnosed.
- Identify the categories and classifications of Axis I psychiatric disorders.

NOTES

CASE STUDY

Tiffany reported she has felt depressed ever since she can remember. She added, "I've always watched other people look happy. I don't know how that feels." Tiffany reported she has considered suicide many times, even attempting suicide twice when she was sixteen, after she moved to her mother's home in Texas. Tiffany's arms, legs, and hips have scars from years of cutting. Tiffany reported that the cutting has helped her "calm down" when she was upset or angry. Tiffany has very short fingernails and cuticles due to frequent chewing and picking.

When asked if Tiffany is currently considering harming herself, she explained she cuts at least once per day and thinks of killing herself often. Tiffany denied having a specific plan.

Tiffany reported that the happiest she has ever felt was living with her best friend, Lena, until they "got into a big fight" two days ago.

QUICK FACTS ON MENTAL ILLNESS

DEPRESSION

Everyone feels blue now and then. It's part of life. But, if you no longer enjoy activities that you usually like, you may have a more serious problem. Being depressed, without letup, can change the way you think and feel. Doctors call this "clinical depression."

Being "down in the dumps" over a period of time is not a normal part of getting older. But, it is a common problem, and medical help may be needed. For most people, depression will get better with treatment. "Talk therapy," medicine, or other treatment methods can ease the pain of depression. You do not need to suffer.

There are many reasons why depression in older people is often missed or untreated. As a person ages, the signs of depression are much more varied than at younger ages. It can appear as increased tiredness, or it can be seen as grumpiness or irritability. Confusion or attention problems caused by depression can sometimes look like Alzheimer's disease or other brain disorders. Mood changes and signs of depression can be caused by medicines older people may take for arthritis, high blood pressure, or heart disease. The good news is that people who are depressed usually feel better with the right treatment.

From the National Institutes on Aging
http://www.nia.nih.gov/HealthInformation/Publications/depression.htm

WHAT CAUSES DEPRESSION?

There is no one cause of depression. For some people, a single event can bring on the illness. Depression often strikes people who felt fine but who suddenly find they are dealing with a death in the family or a serious illness. For some people, changes in the brain can affect mood and cause depression. Sometimes, those under a lot of stress, like caregivers, can feel depressed. Others become depressed for no clear reason.

People with serious illnesses, such as cancer, diabetes, heart disease, stroke, or Parkinson's disease, may become depressed. They may worry about how their illness will change their lives. They might be tired and not able to deal with things that make them sad. Treatment for depression can help them manage their depressive symptoms and improve their quality of life.

Genetics, too, can play a role. Studies show that depression may run in families. Children of depressed parents may be at a higher risk for depression. And, depression tends to be a disorder that occurs more than once. Many older people who have been depressed in the past will be at an increased risk.

WHAT TO LOOK FOR

How do you know when you need help? After all, as you age, you may have to face problems that could cause anyone to feel depressed. Perhaps you are dealing with the death of a loved one or friend. Maybe you are having a tough time getting used to retirement, and you feel lonely. Possibly, you have a chronic illness. Or, you might feel like you have lost control over your life.

After a period of feeling sad, older people usually adjust and regain their emotional balance. But, if you are suffering from clinical depression and don't get help, your depression might last for weeks, months, or even years. Here is a list of the most common signs of depression. If you have several of these and they last for more than 2 weeks, see a doctor.

- An "empty" feeling, ongoing sadness, and anxiety
- Tiredness, lack of energy
- Loss of interest or pleasure in everyday activities, including sex
- Sleep problems, including trouble getting to sleep, very early morning waking, and sleeping too much
- Eating more or less than usual
- Crying too often or too much
- Aches and pains that don't go away when treated
- A hard time focusing, remembering, or making decisions

- Feeling guilty, helpless, worthless, or hopeless
- Being irritable
- Thoughts of death or suicide or a suicide attempt

If you are a family member, friend, or healthcare provider of an older person, watch for clues. Sometimes depression can hide behind a smiling face. A depressed person who lives alone may appear to feel better when someone stops by to say hello. The symptoms may seem to go away. But, when someone is very depressed, the symptoms usually come back.

Don't ignore the warning signs. If left untreated, serious depression can lead to suicide. Listen carefully if someone of any age complains about being depressed or says people don't care. That person may really be asking for help.

GETTING HELP

The first step is to accept that you or your family member needs help. You may not be comfortable with the subject of mental illness. Or, you might feel that asking for help is a sign of weakness. You might be like many older people, their relatives, or friends who believe that a depressed person can quickly "snap out of it" or that some people are too old to be helped. They are wrong.

A healthcare provider can help you. Once you decide to get medical advice, start with your family doctor. Your doctor should check to see if your depression could be caused by a health problem (such as hypothyroidism or vitamin B12 deficiency) or a medicine you are taking. After a complete exam, your doctor may suggest you talk to a mental health worker, for example, a social worker, mental health counselor, psychologist, or psychiatrist. Doctors specially trained to treat depression in older people are called geriatric psychiatrists.

Don't avoid getting help because you may be afraid of how much treatments might cost. Often, only short-term psychotherapy (talk therapy) is needed. Treatment for depression is usually covered by private insurance and Medicare. Also, some community mental health centers may offer treatment based on a person's ability to Be aware that some family doctors may not understand about aging and depression. If your doctor is unable or unwilling to help, you may want to talk to another healthcare provider.

Are you the relative or friend of a depressed older person who won't go to a doctor for treatment? Try explaining how treatment may help the person feel better. In some cases, when a depressed person can't or won't go to the doctor's office, the doctor or mental health specialist can start by making a phone call. A phone call can't take the place of the personal contact needed for a complete medical checkup, but it might inspire the person to go for treatment.

Treating depression

Your doctor or mental health expert can often treat your depression successfully. Different therapies seem to work for different people. For instance, support groups can provide new coping skills or social support if you are dealing with a major life change. Several kinds of talk therapies are useful as well. One method might help you think in a more positive way. Always thinking about the sad things in your life or what you have lost might have led to your depression. Another method works to improve your relations with others so you will have more hope about your future.

Getting better takes time, but with support from others and with treatment, you will get a little better each day.

Antidepressant drugs (medicine to treat depression) can also help. These medications can improve your mood, sleep, appetite, and concentration. There are several types of antidepressants available. Some of these medicines can take up to 12 weeks before you feel like they are working. Your doctor may want you to continue medications for 6 months or more after your symptoms disappear.

Some antidepressants can cause unwanted side effects, although newer medicines have fewer side effects. Any antidepressant should be used with great care to avoid this problem. Remember:

- The doctor needs to know about all prescribed and over-the-counter medications, vitamins, or herbal supplements you are taking.
- The doctor should also be aware of any other physical problems you have.
- Be sure to take antidepressants in the proper dose and on the right schedule.

If you are still very depressed after trying different treatments, electroconvulsive therapy (ECT) may be an option. Don't be misled by the way some movies and books have portrayed ECT (also called electroshock therapy). ECT may be recommended if medicines or other therapies do not work for you. ECT is given as a series of treatments over a few weeks. Like other antidepressant therapies, follow-up treatment is often needed to help prevent a return of depression.

Help from family and friends

Family and friends can play an important role in treatment. You can help your relative or friend stay with the treatment plan. If needed, make appointments for the person or go along to the doctor, mental health expert, or support group.

NOTES

Be patient and understanding. Ask your relative or friend to go on outings with you or to go back to an activity that he or she once enjoyed. Encourage the person to be active and busy but not to take on too much at one time.

PREVENTING DEPRESSION

What can be done to lower the risk of depression? How can people cope? There are a few steps you can take. Try to prepare for major changes in life, such as retirement or moving from your home of many years. One way to do this is to try and keep friendships over the years. Friends can help ease loneliness if you lose a spouse. You can also develop a hobby. Hobbies may help keep your mind and body active. Stay in touch with family. Let them help you when you feel sad. If you are faced with a lot to do, try to break it up into smaller jobs that are easy to finish.

Regular exercise may also help prevent depression or lift your mood if you are somewhat depressed. Older people who are depressed can gain mental as well as physical benefits from mild forms of exercise like walking outdoors or in shopping malls. Gardening, dancing, and swimming are other good forms of exercise. Pick something you like to do. Begin with 10–15 minutes a day, and increase the time as you are able. Being physically fit and eating a balanced diet may help avoid illnesses that can bring on disability or depression.

Remember, with treatment, most people will begin to feel better soon. Expect your mood to improve slowly. Feeling better takes time. But, it can happen.

Children and teens who have a chronic illness, endure abuse or neglect, or experience other trauma have an increased risk of depression. National Institute on Mental Health (*NIMH*)

http://www.whatadifference.samhsa.gov/learn.asp?nav=nav01_3a&content=1_3_1_clinical

Major depressive disorder affects approximately 14.8 million American adults, or about 6.7 percent of the U.S. population age 18 and older in a given year. *NIMH*

http://www.whatadifference.samhsa.gov/learn.asp?nav=nav01_3b&content=1_3_2_dysthymia

As many as one in every 33 children and one in eight adolescents may have depression. *NMHA*

http://www.whatadifference.samhsa.gov/learn.asp?nav=nav01_3&content=1_3_depression

People with depressive illnesses do not all experience the same symptoms. The severity, frequency, and duration of symptoms vary depending on the individual and his or her particular illness.

SIGNS AND SYMPTOMS INCLUDE:

- Persistent sad, anxious, or "empty" feelings
- Feelings of hopelessness or pessimism
- Feelings of guilt, worthlessness, or helplessness
- Irritability, restlessness
- Loss of interest in activities or hobbies once pleasurable, including sex
- Fatigue and decreased energy
- Difficulty concentrating, remembering details, and making decisions
- Insomnia, early-morning wakefulness, or excessive sleeping
- Overeating, or appetite loss
- Thoughts of suicide, suicide attempts
- Aches or pains, headaches, cramps, or digestive problems that do not ease even with treatment.

http://www.nimh.nih.gov/health/publications/depression/what-are-the-signs-and-symptoms-of-depression.shtml

What illnesses often co-exist with depression?
Other illnesses may come on before depression, cause it, or be a consequence of it. But depression and other illnesses interact differently in different people. In any case, co-occurring illnesses need to be diagnosed and treated.

Anxiety disorders, such as post-traumatic stress disorder (PTSD), obsessive-compulsive disorder, panic disorder, social phobia, and generalized anxiety disorder, often accompany depression.[3,4] PTSD can occur after a person experiences a terrifying event or ordeal, such as a violent assault, a natural disaster, an accident, terrorism or military combat. People experiencing PTSD are especially prone to having co-existing depression.

In a National Institute of Mental Health (NIMH)-funded study, researchers found that more than 40 percent of people with PTSD also had depression 4 months after the traumatic event.[5]

Alcohol and other substance abuse or dependence may also co-exist with depression. Research shows that mood disorders and substance abuse commonly occur together.[6]

Depression also may occur with other serious medical illnesses such as heart disease, stroke, cancer, HIV/AIDS, diabetes, and Parkinson's disease. People who have depression along with another medical illness tend to have more severe symptoms of both depression and the medical illness, more difficulty adapting to their medical condition, and more medical costs than those who do not have co-existing depression.[7] Treating the depression can also help improve the outcome of treating the co-occurring illness.[8]

http://www.nimh.nih.gov/health/publications/depression/what-illnesses-often-co-exist-with-depression.shtml

BIPOLAR DISORDER

Bipolar disorder affects approximately 5.7 million American adults, or about 2.6 percent of the U.S. population age 18 and older in a given year. *NIMH*

http://www.whatadifference.samhsa.gov/learn.asp?nav=nav01_4&content=1_4_bipolar

What is bipolar disorder?

Bipolar disorder, also known as manic-depressive illness, is a brain disorder that causes unusual shifts in mood, energy, activity levels, and the ability to carry out day-to-day tasks. Symptoms of bipolar disorder are severe. They are different from the normal ups and downs that everyone goes through from time to time. Bipolar disorder symptoms can result in damaged relationships, poor job or school performance, and even suicide. But bipolar disorder can be treated, and people with this illness can lead full and productive lives.

Bipolar disorder often develops in a person's late teens or early adult years. At least half of all cases start before age 25.[1] Some people have their first symptoms during childhood, while others may develop symptoms late in life.

Bipolar disorder is not easy to spot when it starts. The symptoms may seem like separate problems, not recognized as parts of a larger problem. Some people suffer for years before they are properly diagnosed and treated. Like diabetes or heart disease, bipolar disorder is a long-term illness that must be carefully managed throughout a person's life.

http://www.nimh.nih.gov/health/publications/bipolar-disorder/what-is-bipolar-disorder.shtml

What are the symptoms of bipolar disorder?

People with bipolar disorder experience unusually intense emotional states that occur in distinct periods called "mood episodes." An overly joyful or overexcited state is called a manic episode, and an extremely sad or hopeless state is called a depressive episode. Sometimes, a mood episode includes symptoms of both mania and depression. This is called a mixed state. People with bipolar disorder also may be explosive and irritable during a mood episode.

Extreme changes in energy, activity, sleep, and behavior go along with these changes in mood. It is possible for someone with bipolar disorder to experience a long-lasting period of unstable moods rather than discrete episodes of depression or mania.

A person may be having an episode of bipolar disorder if he or she has a number of manic or depressive symptoms for most of the day, nearly every day, for at least one or two weeks. Sometimes symptoms are so severe that the person cannot function normally at work, school, or home.

Symptoms of bipolar disorder are described below.

NOTES

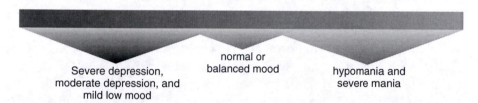

Severe depression, moderate depression, and mild low mood

normal or balanced mood

hypomania and severe mania

Symptoms of mania or a manic episode include:
Mood Changes
- A long period of feeling "high," or an overly happy or outgoing mood
- Extremely irritable mood, agitation, feeling "jumpy" or "wired."

Behavioral Changes
- Talking very fast, jumping from one idea to another, having racing thoughts
- Being easily distracted
- Increasing goal-directed activities, such as taking on new projects
- Being restless
- Sleeping little
- Having an unrealistic belief in one's abilities
- Behaving impulsively and taking part in a lot of pleasurable, high-risk behaviors, such as spending sprees, impulsive sex, and impulsive business investments

Symptoms of depression or a depressive episode include:
Mood Changes
- A long period of feeling worried or empty
- Loss of interest in activities once enjoyed, including sex.

Behavioral Changes
- Feeling tired or "slowed down"
- Having problems concentrating, remembering, and making decisions
- Being restless or irritable
- Changing eating, sleeping, or other habits
- Thinking of death or suicide, or attempting suicide.

NOTES

In addition to mania and depression, bipolar disorder can cause a range of moods, as shown on the scale.

One side of the scale includes severe depression, moderate depression, and mild low mood. Moderate depression may cause less extreme symptoms, and mild low mood is called dysthymia when it is chronic or long-term. In the middle of the scale is normal or balanced mood.

At the other end of the scale are hypomania and severe mania. Some people with bipolar disorder experience hypomania. During hypomanic episodes, a person may have increased energy and activity levels that are not as severe as typical mania, or he or she may have episodes that last less than a week and do not require emergency care. A person having a hypomanic episode may feel very good, be highly productive, and function well. This person may not feel that anything is wrong even as family and friends recognize the mood swings as possible bipolar disorder. Without proper treatment, however, people with hypomania may develop severe mania or depression.

During a mixed state, symptoms often include agitation, trouble sleeping, major changes in appetite, and suicidal thinking. People in a mixed state may feel very sad or hopeless while feeling extremely energized.

Sometimes, a person with severe episodes of mania or depression has psychotic symptoms too, such as hallucinations or delusions. The psychotic symptoms tend to reflect the person's extreme mood. For example, psychotic symptoms for a person having a manic episode may include believing he or she is famous, has a lot of money, or has special powers. In the same way, a person having a depressive episode may believe he or she is ruined and penniless, or has committed a crime. As a result, people with bipolar disorder who have psychotic symptoms are sometimes wrongly diagnosed as having schizophrenia, another severe mental illness that is linked with hallucinations and delusions.

People with bipolar disorder may also have behavioral problems. They may abuse alcohol or substances, have relationship problems, or perform poorly in school or at work. At first, it's not easy to recognize these problems as signs of a major mental illness.

http://www.nimh.nih.gov/health/publications/bipolar-disorder/what-are-the-symptoms-of-bipolar-disorder.shtml

ANXIETY DISORDERS

Anxiety is a normal reaction to stress. In general, it helps one cope. But when anxiety becomes an excessive, irrational dread of everyday situations, it has become a disabling disorder.

According to the CDC, the number of ambulatory care visits for anxiety: 6.2 million.

http://www.whatadifference.samhsa.gov/learn.asp?nav=nav01_2d&content=1_2_4_gad

TYPES OF ANXIETY DISORDERS ARE:

- Generalized Anxiety Disorder
- Obsessive-Compulsive Disorder (OCD)
- Panic Disorder
- Post-Traumatic Stress Disorder (PTSD)
- Social Phobia (or Social Anxiety Disorder)

GENERAL ANXIETY DISORDER (GAD)

People with general anxiety disorder deal with intense worry and tension nearly all the time. About 4 million Americans have GAD; twice as many women as men are diagnosed with it. The worry GAD causes brings about physical symptoms like fatigue, headaches, muscle tension and aches, trouble swallowing, trembling, twitching, irritability, sweating, and hot flashes. Mild GAD lets people function fairly well in everyday life, but more severe cases can overwhelm a person and cause serious difficulties. There's a variety of treatment and support options that can be effective including psychotherapy, medications, and support groups.

http://www.whatadifference.samhsa.gov/learn.asp?nav=nav01_2d&content=1_2_4_gad

OBSESSIVE COMPULSIVE DISORDER (OCD)

People with obsessive-compulsive disorder deal with persistent and unwelcome anxious thoughts (obsessions), which give rise to ritualistic practices (compulsions) that are intended to control the intruding thoughts. People may feel compelled to count objects or actions, check things repeatedly, or wash their hands over and over again. About 3.3 million Americans are living with OCD; men and women are equally affected. Severe cases can take up so much of a person's time and concentration that the actions of normal life are nearly impossible. There's a variety of treatment and support options that can be effective including psychotherapy, medications, and support groups as well as the acceptance and sensitive understanding of friends.

http://www.whatadifference.samhsa.gov/learn.asp?nav=nav01_2b&content=1_2_2_ocd

PANIC DISORDER

Imagine a sudden feeling of terror that sets your heart racing, your stomach churning, and your head spinning. Panic attacks occur without warning and can cause frightening physical symptoms that seem almost like a heart attack. About 2.4 million Americans suffer from panic disorder; twice as many women as men are directly affected. Left untreated, panic disorder can cause the person with it to avoid triggering situations or places, which can be extremely disruptive to his or her everyday life. In about a third of cases, it can even result in agoraphobia, a condition in which a person becomes isolated or housebound. Depression, drug abuse, and alcoholism often accompany panic disorder. It can be serious. Luckily, it's also highly treatable. There's a variety of treatment and support options that can be effective including psychotherapy, medications, and support groups as well as the acceptance and sensitive understanding of friends.

http://www.whatadifference.samhsa.gov/learn.asp?nav=nav01_2a&content=1_2_1_panic

POST-TRAUMATIC STRESS DISORDER (PTSD)

A terrifying experience—military combat, a car accident, sexual abuse, a natural disaster—can bring about a terrifying condition. PTSD affects about 5.2 million Americans, but more women than men are likely to develop it. A person with PTSD relives his or her trauma through nightmares or upsetting thoughts; this reliving can make him or her feel detached, numb, irritable, or aggressive. Ordinary events can trigger a flashback episode or cause a resurgence of the unpleasant thoughts. Some people recover soon after the troubling event, but others need more time—along with therapy and medication.

http://www.whatadifference.samhsa.gov/learn.asp?nav=nav01_2c&content=1_2_3_ptsd

SOCIAL ANXIETY DISORDER

People with this condition—about 5.3 million Americans—experience a debilitating fear of interacting with others or appearing in public. Some have problems with public speaking, some with eating in public, and some with just being around others. People with social anxiety disorder fear that other people are watching or judging them, and this can cause considerable difficulty in everyday life. It's hard to relate to others when you feel humiliated or embarrassed. Some of the physical symptoms include blushing, profuse sweating, trembling, nausea, and difficulty talking. There's a variety of treatment and support options that can be effective including psychotherapy, medications, and support groups.

http://www.whatadifference.samhsa.gov/learn.asp?nav=nav01_2e&content=1_2_5_sad

ATTENTION DEFICIT AND HYPERACTIVITY DISORDER (ADHD)

ADHD, one of the most common mental disorders in children and adolescents, also affects an estimated 4.1 percent of adults, ages 18 to 44, in a given year. *NIMH*

http://www.whatadifference.samhsa.gov/learn.asp?nav=nav01_2f&content=1_2_6_adhd

ADHD is a diagnosis applied to children (mostly) who consistently display behaviors like inattention, hyperactivity, and impulsivity. Two million American kids are diagnosed with ADHD; they have a hard time keeping their minds on a task and may get bored after just a few minutes. They can't sit still and may talk or dash about incessantly. Not every child—or adult—with these behaviors has ADHD; scientists have learned a lot about the condition over the past decade and are now able to recognize and treat it with medication and therapy. It's important to remember that people with ADHD aren't doing it on purpose—ADHD causes these behaviors, and the children aren't to blame.

ADHD usually becomes evident in preschool or early elementary years. The median age of onset of ADHD is seven years, although the disorder can persist into adolescence and occasionally into adulthood. *NIMH*

http://www.whatadifference.samhsa.gov/learn.asp?nav=nav01_2b&content=1_2_2_ocd

SCHIZOPHRENIA

Approximately 2.4 million American adults, or about 1.1 percent of the population age 18 and older in a given year, have schizophrenia. *NIMH*

http://www.whatadifference.samhsa.gov/learn.asp?nav=nav01_6&content=1_6_schizophrenia

Schizophrenia is a chronic, severe, and disabling brain disorder that has affected people throughout history. About 1 percent of Americans have this illness.[1]

People with the disorder may hear voices other people don't hear. They may believe other people are reading their minds, controlling their thoughts, or plotting to harm them. This can terrify people with the illness and make them withdrawn or extremely agitated.

People with schizophrenia may not make sense when they talk. They may sit for hours without moving or talking. Sometimes people with schizophrenia seem perfectly fine until they talk about what they are really thinking.

Families and society are affected by schizophrenia too. Many people with schizophrenia have difficulty holding a job or caring for themselves, so they rely on others for help.

Treatment helps relieve many symptoms of schizophrenia, but most people who have the disorder cope with symptoms throughout their lives. However, many people with schizophrenia can lead rewarding and meaningful lives in their communities. Researchers are developing more effective medications and using new research tools to understand the causes of schizophrenia. In the years to come, this work may help prevent and better treat the illness.

http://www.nimh.nih.gov/health/publications/schizophrenia/what-is-schizophrenia.shtml

DUAL DIAGNOSIS

DEFINITION

Dual **diagnosis** is a term that refers to patients who have both a mental health disorder and substance use disorder. It may be used interchangeably with **"co-occurring disorders"** or "co-morbidity." According to the U.S. Substance Abuse and Mental Health Services Administration (SAMHSA), an estimated 10 million people in the United States will have a combination of at least one mental health and one substance abuse disorder in any twelve-month period. Substance abuse is the most common and significant co-occurring disorder among adults with such severe mental illnesses as **schizophrenia** or **bipolar disorder**. It may also be observed in individuals with mental health diagnoses that include depression, anxiety, **post-traumatic stress disorder**, or eating disorders. The term "substance abuse" refers to substance use disorders that range along a continuum from abuse to dependence or **addiction**.

The term "dual diagnosis" is considered to be misleading by some professionals because most people with this diagnosis actually have many problems rather than just two discrete illnesses. Occasionally, the term is used to describe a person with developmental disabilities and/or a mental health disorder or substance abuse disorder. More commonly, dual diagnosis refers to those with severe mental illness and a drug or alcohol abuse disorder, and who receive therapy in the public treatment systems.

FACT SHEET   CENTER FOR MENTAL HEALTH SERVICES

EATING DISORDERS

What are eating disorders?

Most of us want to lose a few unwanted pounds at some point in our lives, and when we successfully shed them, we are satisfied. For some people, however, losing weight and keeping it off becomes an obsession that can cause permanent damage such as stunted growth, thinning or broken bones, infertility, damaged teeth and gums, kidney and heart failure, and even death (National Institute of Mental Health [NIMH], 2002; Mayo Clinic, 2002). Unlike those who diet occasionally, these people may have an eating disorder.

Research shows that more than 90 percent of those who have eating disorders are women between the ages of 12 and 25 (National Alliance for the Mentally Ill, 2003). However, increasing numbers of older women and men have these disorders. In addition, hundreds of thousands of boys are affected by these disorders (U.S. DHHS Office on Women's Health, 2000).

This fact sheet identifies the common signs, symptoms, and treatment for three of the most common eating disorders: anorexia nervosa, bulimia nervosa, and binge-eating disorder (NIMH, 2002). Various combinations of the signs and symptoms of these disorders also represent other eating disorders (National Eating Disorders Association, 2002). Regardless of the type, all eating disorders require professional help, and behavioral scientists continue to discover better ways to identify, understand, and treat them (NIMH, 2002).

Eating disorders often are long-term illnesses that may require long-term treatment. In addition, eating disorders frequently occur with other mental disorders such as depression, substance abuse, and anxiety disorders (NIMH, 2002). The earlier these disorders are diagnosed and treated, the better the chances are for full recovery.

If you believe you or a loved one has an eating disorder, seek help from a professional who is specifically trained to recognize and treat eating disorders. If you do not know of a therapist in your area, you can begin by contacting one of the resources listed at the end of this fact sheet.

What are the common signs of an eating disorder?

Anorexia nervosa

People who have anorexia develop unusual eating habits such as avoiding food and meals, picking out a few foods and eating them in small amounts, weighing their food, and counting the calories of everything they eat. Also, they may exercise excessively.

They often have an intense fear of gaining weight. Because they resist maintaining their body weight at what are considered normal levels for their height and age, they can literally starve themselves to death. Women of childbearing age often, or always, miss their menstrual periods (NIMH, 2002).

(continued)

A mental health therapist may determine that a person has anorexia if that person:

- Weighs at least 15 percent below what is considered normal for others of the same height and age.
- Misses at least three consecutive menstrual cycles (if a female of childbearing age).
- Has an intense fear of gaining weight.
- Refuses to maintain the minimal normal body weight.
- Believes he or she is overweight though in reality is dangerously thin (American Psychiatric Association [APA], 1994; NIMH, 2002).

Bulimia nervosa

People who have bulimia eat an excessive amount of food in a single episode and almost immediately make themselves vomit or use laxatives or diuretics (water pills) to get rid of the food in their bodies. This behavior often is referred to as the "binge/purge" cycle. Like people with anorexia, people with bulimia have an intense fear of gaining weight.

A mental health therapist may determine that a person has bulimia if that person:

- Has at least two binge/purge cycles a week, on average, for at least 3 months.
- Lacks control over his or her eating behavior.
- Seems obsessed with his or her body shape and weight (APA, 1994; NIMH, 2002).

Binge-eating disorder

People with this recently recognized disorder have frequent episodes of compulsive overeating, but unlike those with bulimia, they do not purge their bodies of food (NIMH, 2002). During these food binges, they often eat alone and very quickly, regardless of whether they feel hungry or full. They often feel shame or guilt over their actions. Unlike anorexia and bulimia, binge-eating disorder occurs almost as often in men as in women (National Eating Disorders Association, 2002.)

A mental health therapist may determine that a person has binge-eating disorder if that person:

- Has at least two binge-eating episodes a week, on average, for 6 months.
- Lacks control over his or her eating behavior (NIMH, 2002).

How do eating disorders affect the body?

Anorexia nervosa

Anorexia can slow the heart rate and lower blood pressure, increasing the chance of heart failure. Those who use drugs to stimulate vomiting, bowel movements, or urination are also at high risk for heart failure. Starvation can also lead to heart failure, as well as damage the brain.

Anorexia may also cause hair and nails to grow brittle. Skin may dry out, become yellow, and develop a covering of soft hair called *lanugo*. Mild anemia, swollen joints, reduced muscle mass, and light-headedness also commonly occur as a consequence of this eating disorder.

Severe cases of anorexia can lead to brittle bones that break easily as a result of calcium loss. In fact, people with anorexia are about twice as likely to have bone fractures as are those without an eating disorder. The risk of bone fractures remains high for as long as a decade following a diagnosis of anorexia.

Bulimia nervosa

In cases of bulimia, the acid in vomit can wear down the outer layer of the teeth, inflame and damage the esophagus (a tube in the throat through which food passes to the stomach), and enlarge the glands near the cheeks (giving the appearance of swollen cheeks). Damage to the stomach can also occur from frequent vomiting.

Irregular heartbeats, heart failure, and death can occur from chemical imbalances and the loss of important minerals such as potassium. Peptic ulcers, pancreatitis (inflammation of the pancreas, which is a large gland that aids digestion), and long-term constipation are also consequences of bulimia.

Binge-eating disorder

Binge-eating disorder can cause high blood pressure and high cholesterol levels. Other effects of binge-eating disorder include fatigue, joint pain, Type II diabetes, gallbladder disease, and heart disease.

What are some common treatments?

Anorexia nervosa

The first goal for the treatment of anorexia is to ensure the person's physical health, which involves restoring a healthy weight (NIMH, 2002). Reaching this goal may require hospitalization. Once a person's physical condition is stable, treatment usually involves individual psychotherapy and family therapy during which parents help their child learn to eat again and maintain healthy eating habits on his or her own. Behavioral therapy also has been effective for helping a person return to healthy eating habits. Supportive group therapy may follow, and self-help groups within communities may provide ongoing support.

For a person experiencing problems with anxiety and depression or spending large amounts of time performing elaborate food rituals, medication combined with psychotherapy has proven to be effective.

Bulimia nervosa

Unless malnutrition is severe, any substance abuse problems that may be present at the time the eating disorder is diagnosed are usually treated first. The next goal of treatment is to reduce or eliminate the person's binge eating and purging behavior (NIMH, 2002). Behavioral therapy has proven effective in achieving this goal. Psychotherapy has proven effective in helping to prevent the eating disorder from recurring and in addressing issues that led to the disorder. Studies have also found that Prozac, an antidepressant, may help people who do not respond to psychotherapy (APA, 2002). As with anorexia, family therapy is also recommended.

Binge-eating disorder

The goals and strategies for treating binge-eating disorder are similar to those for bulimia. Binge-eating disorder was recognized only recently as an eating disorder, and research is under way to study the effectiveness of different interventions (NIMH, 2002).

Eating disorders are serious mental and physical illnesses, but they are treatable. To learn more about eating disorders and specialists who treat these disorders, contact the resources listed below:

REFERRAL RESOURCES

National Association of Anorexia Nervosa and Associated Disorders
P.O. Box 7
Highland Park, IL 60035
Hotline: 1-847-831-3438
http://www.anad.org/services.htm

National Eating Disorders Association
Informational and Referral Program
603 Stewart Street, Suite 803
Seattle, WA 98101
1-800-931-2237
http://www.nationaleatingdisorders.org/p.asp?WebPage_ID=347

INFORMATION RESOURCES

healthfinder®
A Federal government web site developed by
the U.S. Department of Health and Human Services
P.O. Box 1133
Washington, DC 20013-1133
http://www.healthfinder.gov/scripts/SearchContext.asp?topic=267

¡Soy Unica! ¡Soy Latina!
A public education initiative sponsored by the
U.S. Department of Health and Human Services and
the U.S. Substance Abuse and Mental Health Services Administration
1-800-773-8546
http://www.soyunica.gov/mybody/bodyimage/default.htm

National Institute of Mental Health
Office of Communications and Public Liaison
6001 Executive Boulevard
Room 8184, MSC 9663
Bethesda, MD 20892-9663
301-443-4513
http://www.nimh.nih.gov/publicat/eatingdisorder.cfm

The National Women's Health Center
8550 Arlington Boulevard, Suite 300
Fairfax, VA 22031
1-800-994-WOMAN
http://www.4woman.gov/bodyimage/BodyImage.cfm?page=125
http://www.4woman.gov/BodyImage/Bodywise/bp/boys.pdf (boys and eating disorders)

KidsHealth
A web site project of The Nemours Foundation
http://www.kidshealth.org/kid/health_problems/learning_problem/eatdisorder.html

This is a list of suggested resources and is not intended to be comprehensive.

ANXIETY DISORDERS

Anxiety is an emotion that can signal just the right response to a situation. It can spur you on, for example, to add the finishing touches that elevate an essay, painting, or important work document from good to excellent. But if you have an anxiety disorder, exaggerated anxiety can stop you cold and disrupt your life. Like many other illnesses, anxiety disorders often have an underlying biological cause and frequently run in families. These disorders can be treated by several methods.

Anxiety disorders range from feelings of uneasiness most of the time to immobilizing bouts of terror. This fact sheet briefly describes generalized anxiety disorder, panic disorder, phobias, and post-traumatic stress disorder. It is intended only as a starting point for gaining an understanding of anxiety disorders. This fact sheet is not exhaustive, nor does it include the full range of symptoms and treatments. Keep in mind that new research can yield rapid and dramatic changes in our understanding of and approaches to mental disorders.

If you believe you or a loved one has an anxiety disorder, seek competent professional advice or other forms of support.

Generalized Anxiety Disorder

Most people experience anxiety—that knot in the stomach over a backlog of bills or just before a job interview—at some point in their lives. Such nervousness in anticipation of a real situation is normal. But if a person cannot shake unwarranted worries, or the feelings are jarring to the point of avoiding everyday activities, he or she most likely has an anxiety disorder.

Symptoms: Chronic, exaggerated worry, tension, and irritability that appear to have no cause or are more intense than the situation warrants. These psychological symptoms often are accompanied by physical signs such as restlessness, trouble falling or staying asleep, headaches, trembling, twitching, muscle tension, or sweating.

Formal Diagnosis: When someone spends at least 6 months worried excessively about everyday problems. However, incapacitating or troublesome symptoms warranting treatment may exist for shorter periods of time.

Treatment: Anxiety is among the most common, most treatable mental disorders. Effective treatments include cognitive behavioral therapy, relaxation techniques, and biofeedback to control muscle tension. Medication, most commonly antianxiety drugs, such as benzodiazepines and its derivatives, also may be required in some cases. Some commonly prescribed antianxiety medications are diazepam, alprazolam, and lorazepam. The nonbenzodiazepine antianxiety medication buspirone can be helpful for some individuals.

Panic Disorder

People with panic disorder experience white-knuckled, heart-pounding terror that strikes with the force of a lightning bolt—suddenly and without warning. Some people feel like they are being devoured by fear, going crazy, or that they are surely dying of a heart attack. And because they can not predict when a panic attack will seize them, many people live in persistent worry that another one could overcome them at any minute.

MOOD DISORDERS

More than one in four American adults will experience a mental disorder each year. In fact, mental illnesses are among the most common conditions affecting health today. Researchers believe most serious mental illnesses are caused by complex imbalances in the brain's chemical activity. They also believe environmental factors can play a part in triggering—or cushioning against—the onset of mental illness.

Like other diseases, mental illnesses can be treated. The good news is that most people who have mental illnesses, even serious ones, can lead productive lives with proper treatment. Mood disorders are one form of serious mental illness.

This fact sheet is intended only as a starting point for gaining an understanding about two of the most common mood disorders: depression and bipolar disorder, also known as manic-depressive illness. It is by no means exhaustive, nor does it include the full range of symptoms and treatments. Keep in mind that new research can yield rapid and dramatic changes in our understanding of, and approaches to, mental disorders.

If you believe you or a loved one has a mood disorder, seek competent professional advice.

Bipolar Disorder

Extreme mood swings punctuated by periods of generally even-keeled behavior characterize this disorder. For example, a person who has bipolar disorder may soar with happiness and feel capable of "taking on the world" for a while, only to be immobilized by crushing sadness and a sense of worthlessness some time later.

Bipolar disorder tends to run in families. This disorder typically begins in the mid-twenties and continues throughout life. Without treatment, people who have bipolar disorder often go through devastating life events such as marital breakups, job loss, substance abuse, and suicide.

Symptoms: Mania—expansive or irritable mood, inflated self-esteem, decreased need for sleep; increased energy; racing thoughts; feelings of invulnerability; poor judgment; heightened sex drive; and denial that anything is wrong. Depression—feelings of hopelessness, guilt, worthlessness, or melancholy; fatigue; loss of appetite for food or sex; sleep disturbances, thoughts of death or suicide; and suicide attempts.

Mania and depression may vary in both duration and degree of intensity.

Formal Diagnosis: Although scientific evidence indicates bipolar disorder is caused by chemical imbalances in the brain, no lab test exists to diagnose the disorder. In fact, this mental illness often goes unrecognized by the person who has it, relatives, friends, or even physicians.

If you suspect someone you know or love has bipolar disorder, you may actively have to help that person find appropriate treatment. It may also help to realize that this is a long-term illness: people who have it usually require treatment for the rest of their lives.

The first step of diagnosis is to receive a complete medical evaluation to rule out any other mental or physical disorders. Anyone who has this mental illness should be under the care of a psychiatrist skilled in the diagnosis and treatment of bipolar disorder.

Treatment: Eighty percent of people who have bipolar disorder can be treated effectively with medication and psychotherapy. Self-help groups can offer emotional support and assistance in recognizing signs of relapse to avert a full-blown episode of bipolar disorder. The most commonly prescribed medications to treat bipolar disorder are three mood stabilizers: lithium carbonate, carbamazepine, and valproate.

Depression

Everyone feels down in the dumps sometimes, especially when life's unavoidable pitfalls make just getting through the day a challenge. But when a person's feelings of sadness persist beyond a few weeks, he or she may have depression. In fact, one in four women and one in eight men can expect to develop depression at some time in their lives.

To a lesser extent than in bipolar disorder, depression appears to run in families. However, researchers do not know the exact mechanisms that trigger depression. Two neurotransmitters—natural substances that allow brain cells to communicate with one another—are implicated in depression: serotonin and norepinephrine.

Symptoms: Changes in appetite and sleeping patterns; feelings of worthlessness, hopelessness, and inappropriate guilt; loss of interest or pleasure in formerly important activities; fatigue; inability to concentrate; overwhelming sadness; disturbed thinking; physical symptoms such as headaches or stomachaches; and suicidal thoughts or behaviors.

Formal Diagnosis: Four or more of the previous symptoms have been present continually, or most of the time, for more than 2 weeks. The term *clinical depression* merely means the episode of depression is serious enough to require treatment. *Major depression* is marked by far more severe symptoms, such as literally being unable to drag oneself out of bed. Another form of depression, known as *seasonal affective disorder,* is associated with seasonal changes in the amount of available daylight.

Treatment: Some types of cognitive/behavioral therapy and interpersonal therapy may be as effective as medications for some people who have depression. In general, psychiatrists agree that people who have severe depression do better with medication or with a combination of medication and psychotherapy. Special bright light helps many people who have seasonal affective disorder.

Three major types of medication are used to treat depression: tricyclics; the newer selective serotonin re-uptake inhibitors (SSRIs), and monoamine oxidase inhibitors (MAO inhibitors).

The tricyclics and the SSRIs are most often prescribed for people whose depressions are characterized by fatigue; feelings of hopelessness, helplessness and excessive guilt; inability to feel pleasure; and loss of appetite with resulting weight loss.

SCHIZOPHRENIA

Contrary to the common misconception, schizophrenia does not mean "split or multiple personality." And, although people with schizophrenia often are portrayed as violent on television and in movies, that is seldom the case. In fact, people with schizophrenia are more likely to be victims of violence than perpetrators, and they tend to be shy and socially withdrawn.

Schizophrenia is one of the most disabling and puzzling mental disorders. Just as "cancer" refers to numerous related illnesses, many researchers now consider schizophrenia to be a group of mental disorders rather than a single illness. Generally, schizophrenia begins in late adolescence or early adulthood.

Research indicates a genetic link to the development of schizophrenia. A child who has one parent with schizophrenia, for example, has about a 10 percent chance of developing the illness, compared with a one percent chance if neither parent has schizophrenia. Current research implicates abnormalities in both the brain's structure and biochemical activities. Imbalances in the chemical messenger dopamine, for example, may underlie some cases of schizophrenia. Researchers also tend to agree that environmental influences—such as a viral infection, a highly stressful situation in adulthood, or a combination of these—may be involved in the onset of schizophrenia.

The good news is that more than 50 percent of those who have schizophrenia can work, live in the community or with their families, and enjoy friends if they receive continuous, appropriate treatment.

Symptoms: Psychotic, or "positive," symptoms include delusions (bizarre thoughts that have no basis in reality); hallucinations (hearing voices, seeing nonexistent things, and experiencing sensations, such as burning, that have no source); and disordered thinking (apparent from a person's fragmented, disconnected and sometimes nonsensical speech). Other "negative" symptoms include social withdrawal, extreme apathy, diminished motivation, and blunted emotional expression. Keep in mind that other psychotic disorders, such as those caused by drug use or exposure to toxins, can share many of these symptoms.

Formal Diagnosis: Active symptoms of the illness (such as a psychotic episode) for at least 2 weeks, with other symptoms lasting 6 months.

Treatment: People who have schizophrenia often require medication to control the most troubling symptoms. Antipsychotic medications help bring biochemical imbalances closer to normal. These medications—haloperidol and chlorpromazine, for example, and newer ones such as olanzapine, risperidone, and clozapine—significantly reduce the severity and intrusiveness of psychotic symptoms. The newer drugs may also be effective for symptoms such as social withdrawal, extreme apathy, and blunted emotional expression. More such drugs are being developed.

After these symptoms are controlled, psychotherapy and self-help groups can assist people who have schizophrenia learn to develop social skills, cope with stress, identify early warning signs of relapse, and prolong periods of remission. In addition, support groups and family therapy can give loved ones a better understanding of the illness and help them provide the compassion and support that play an important role in recovery.

Note: This fact sheet is intended only as a starting point for gaining an understanding about schizophrenia. It is by no means exhaustive, nor does it include the full range of symptoms and treatments. Keep in mind that new research can yield rapid and dramatic changes in our understanding of, and approaches to, mental disorders. This fact sheet should not be viewed as a replacement for seeking competent professional advice or other forms of support.

For more information, as well as referrals to specialists and self-help groups in your State, contact:

National Alliance for the Mentally Ill
200 North Glebe Road, Suite 1015
Arlington, VA 22203
Telephone: 800-950-6264
Fax: 703-524-9094
E-mail: membership@nami.org
www.nami.org

National Mental Health Association

1021 Prince St.
Alexandria, VA 22314
Telephone: 703-684-7722/800-969-6642
Fax: 703-684-5968
E-mail: aulm@nmha.org
www.nmha.org

Description

The prevalence of people with dual diagnoses became fully apparent to clinicians in the early 1980s. Initially, dual diagnoses were thought to be most likely in young adults with schizophrenia or bipolar disorder who also had extensive histories of drug or alcohol abuse. There was a widespread belief, often shared by family members of affected patients, that a young person's initiation into illegal drug use actually caused a subsequent mental illness. It is now more commonly thought that symptoms of the mental disorder generally appear first, and that the abuse of drugs or alcohol may represent the patient's attempt to self-medicate and alleviate the troublesome symptoms that accompany mental health disorders.

Today it is clear that the co-occurrence of mental illness and substance abuse is common: about 50% of individuals with severe mental illnesses are affected by substance abuse. A dual diagnosis is also associated with a host of negative outcomes that may include higher rates of relapse, **hospitalization**, incarceration, violence, **homelessness**, and exposure to such serious infections as HIV and hepatitis.

Despite almost twenty years of evidence regarding the prevalence and serious illnesses of people with dual diagnoses, the United States mental health and substance abuse systems continue to operate on parallel tracks, causing additional confusion to those with concurrent disorders. Refusal to combine services to provide better coordinated treatment has meant unnecessary suffering and expense for thousands of patients and their families.

For many people with dual diagnoses, the criminal justice system—juvenile as well as adult—becomes their *de facto* treatment system. Nearly two-thirds of incarcerated youth with substance abuse disorders have at least one other mental health disorder. The common association between **conduct disorder** or **attention-deficit/hyperactivity disorder** and substance abuse are two examples of combinations of serious and disabling disorders. A person in need of treatment for dual diagnoses who is in the current criminal justice system may not be evaluated or assessed, let alone provided with appropriate treatment.

Dual Diagnosis/Co-Occurring Disorders— Mental Health and Substance Abuse

Demographics

Children of alcohol or other drug-addicted parents are at increased risk for developing substance abuse and mental health problems. Disruptive behavior disorders coexist with adolescent substance abuse problems more often than not. Other special groups that may be affected include older adults with mood or anxiety disorders, especially those who are grieving numerous losses. They may drink or misuse or abuse prescription drugs to cope with their lowered quality of life. These factors can often complicate treatment of hypertension, diabetes, arthritis, and other health-related problems that affect the elderly as well.

Abuse of alcohol or other drugs may occur in persons with eating disorders in an effort to deal with guilt, shame, anxiety, or feelings of self-loathing as a result of bingeing and purging food. Many military veterans suffer from anxiety, depression or post-traumatic stress disorder and have histories of substance abuse. Services for veterans are woefully inadequate, adding to the chronic nature of dual diagnosis among them.

TREATMENT

One of the difficulties in treating patients with dual diagnoses is that most treatments for mental illness are usually developed for and validated by studies of patients with single diagnoses; therefore, many cases of co-morbidity may not be well treated by these approaches. Recent research on services provided to people with dual diagnoses, however, indicates that treatment can be successful, provided certain specific components are included in the treatment process. The critical elements identified as part of treatment programs with the most successful outcomes are:

- Staged interventions that begin with engaging the client; persuading him or her to become involved in recovery-focused activities; acquiring skills and support to control the illnesses; and then helping the patient with relapse prevention.
- Assertive outreach that may involve intensive **case management** and meetings in the person's home.
- Motivational interventions to help the client become committed to self-management of their illnesses.
- Counseling that includes cognitive and behavioral skills.
- Social network support and/or family interventions.
- An understanding of the long-term nature of recovery.
- Comprehensive scope to treatment that includes personal habits, stress management, friendship networks, housing, and many other aspects of a person's life.
- Cultural sensitivity and competence.

The success of 12-step programs in the treatment of substance abuse is well-established. Nevertheless, the level of confrontation sometimes found in a traditional 12-step group may feel overwhelming to people with mental illnesses. In addition, the use of psychotropic (mood- or behavior-altering) medications is controversial in some areas of the

NOTES

substance abuse recovery community. As a result, other models of consumer-led **support groups** specifically for people with concurrent disorders, such as Dual Recovery Anonymous and Double Trouble, are being developed.

WHY IS AN INTEGRATED APPROACH TO TREATING SEVERE MENTAL ILLNESSES AND SUBSTANCE ABUSE PROBLEMS SO IMPORTANT?

Despite much research that supports its success, integrated treatment is still not made widely available to consumers. Those who struggle both with serious mental illness and substance abuse face problems of enormous proportions. Mental health services tend not to be well prepared to deal with patients having both afflictions. Often only one of the two problems is identified. If both are recognized, the individual may bounce back and forth between services for mental illness and those for substance abuse, or they may be refused treatment by each of them. Fragmented and uncoordinated services create a service gap for persons with co-occurring disorders.

Providing appropriate, integrated services for these consumers will not only allow for their recovery and improved overall health, but can ameliorate the effects their disorders have on their family, friends and society at large. By helping these consumers stay in treatment, find housing and jobs, and develop better social skills and judgment, we can potentially begin to substantially diminish some of the most sinister and costly societal problems: crime, HIV/AIDS, domestic violence and more.

There is much evidence that integrated treatment can be effective. For example:

- Individuals with a substance abuse disorder are more likely to receive treatment if they have a co-occurring mental disorder.
- Research shows that when consumers with dual diagnosis successfully overcome alcohol abuse, their response to treatment improves remarkably.

With continued education on co-occurring disorders, hopefully, more treatments and better understanding are on the way.

WHAT DOES EFFECTIVE INTEGRATED TREATMENT ENTAIL?

Effective integrated treatment consists of the same health professionals, working in one setting, providing appropriate treatment for both mental health and substance abuse in a coordinated fashion.

The caregivers see to it that interventions are bundled together; the consumers, therefore, receive consistent treatment, with no division between mental health or substance abuse assistance. The approach, philosophy and recommendations are seamless, and the need to consult with separate teams and programs is eliminated.

Integrated treatment also requires the recognition that substance abuse counseling and traditional mental health counseling are different approaches that must be reconciled to treat co-occurring disorders. It is not enough merely to teach relationship skills to a person with bipolar disorder. They must also learn to explore how to avoid the relationships that are intertwined with their substance abuse.

Providers should recognize that denial is an inherent part of the problem. Patients often do not have insight as to the seriousness and scope of the problem. Abstinence may be a goal of the program but should not be a precondition for entering treatment. If dually diagnosed clients do not fit into local Alcoholics Anonymous (AA) and Narcotics Anonymous (NA) groups, special peer groups based on AA principles might be developed.

Clients with a dual diagnosis have to proceed at their own pace in treatment. An illness model of the problem should be used rather than a moralistic one. Providers need to convey understanding of how hard it is to end an addiction problem and give credit for any accomplishments. Attention should be given to social networks that can serve as important reinforcers. Clients should be given opportunities to socialize, have access to recreational activities, and develop peer relationships. Their families should be offered support and education, while learning not to react with guilt or blame but to learn to cope with two interacting illnesses.

WHAT ARE THE KEY FACTORS IN EFFECTIVE INTEGRATED TREATMENT?

There are a number of key factors in an integrated treatment program.

Treatment must be approached in **stages.** First, a *trust* is established between the consumer and the caregiver. This helps *motivate* the consumer to learn the skills for *actively controlling* their illnesses and focus on goals. This helps keep the consumer on track, *preventing relapse.* Treatment can begin at any one of these stages; the program is tailored to the individual.

Assertive outreach has been shown to engage and retain clients at a high rate, while those that fail to include outreach lose clients. Therefore, effective programs, through intensive case management, meeting at the consumer's residence, and other methods of developing a dependable relationship with the client, ensure that more consumers are consistently monitored and counseled.

NOTES

Effective treatment includes **motivational interventions**, which, through education, support and counseling, help empower deeply demoralized clients to recognize the importance of their goals and illness self-management.

Of course, counseling is a fundamental component of dual diagnosis services. **Counseling** helps develop positive coping patterns, as well as promotes cognitive and behavioral skills. Counseling can be in the form of individual, group, or family therapy or a combination of these.

A consumer's **social support** is critical. Their immediate environment has a direct impact on their choices and moods; therefore consumers need help strengthening positive relationships and jettisoning those that encourage negative behavior.

Effective integrated treatment programs **view recovery as a long-term, community-based process**, one that can take months or, more likely, years to undergo. Improvement is slow even with a consistent treatment program. However, such an approach prevents relapses and enhances a consumer's gains.

To be effective, a dual diagnosis program must be **comprehensive**, taking into account a number of life's aspects: stress management, social networks, jobs, housing and activities. These programs view substance abuse as intertwined with mental illness, not a separate issue, and therefore provide solutions to both illnesses together at the same time.

Finally, effective integrated treatment programs must contain elements of **cultural sensitivity and competence** to even lure consumers, much less retain them. Various groups such as African-Americans, homeless, women with children, Hispanics and others can benefit from services tailored to their particular racial and cultural needs.

MENTAL HEALTH INTERNET SITES

Center for Mental Health Services
http://www.mentalhealth.org/

National Institute of Mental Health
http://www.nimh.nih.gov/

The National Mental Health Association
http://www.nmha.org/

The National Alliance for the Mentally Ill
http://www.nami.org/

Mental Health: A Report of the Surgeon General
http://www.surgeongeneral.gov/library/mentalhealth/home.html

National Association for Rural Mental Health
http://narmh.org/

CASE ILLUSTRATIONS: CO-OCCURRING DISORDERS

Bethany is 45 years old. She has recently been discharged from a crisis housing facility and was referred to you to coordinate services for her. She suffers from severe depression and anxiety, bordering on panic, which seems to be enhanced while coping with a recently failed marriage, estrangement from her two daughters, and a related job loss. Bethany believes that the marriage failed because her husband thinks that she drinks daily – which she doesn't believe to be an issue. She has not received professional care beyond her use of antidepressant medications because her family/husband had always taken care of her. She isn't sure where she will go or what she will do to survive.

As her newly assigned case manager you need to determine with Bethany what she will need to be self-sufficient.

1. Identify/define what the issues/problems are that Bethany is currently dealing with.

2. What services/treatment would you recommend for Bethany?

3. How and where should these services be implemented for her?

Nate is a 25 year old, unemployed male with schizophrenia. Nate reportedly smokes marijuana on a "regular" basis to relieve stress. He lived with his mother, who held a full-time job, in a suburban neighborhood of a large Midwestern city. The parents are divorced, and his father lives a few hundred mile away. Nate was referred to the agency which you are employed after a hospital stay for an attempted suicide. Nate reports that he intentionally overdosed on prescription antipsychotic medications. Neither parent is willing to have Nate return to their home. What do you do?

1. Identify/define what the issues/problems are that Nate is currently dealing with.

2. What services/treatment would you recommend for Nate?

3. How and where should these services be implemented for him?

MENTAL HEALTH DISCUSSION QUESTIONS

Students will respond to the following questions individually and record their responses in a "running journal" which will be turned in for grading. Students will also be divided into small groups of three to four to discuss and then facilitate the responses shared in the small group discussion.

1. What values apply to practice in mental health?

2. Which professions make up the "traditional" mental health team? In what ways are these positions different? In what ways do they overlap?

3. Why are social workers skeptical about the use of classification systems like the *DSM-IV-TR*? Are there any advantages to using such a system to classify mental disorders?

4. Why is Dorthea Dix important in the history of mental health care?

5. What are the positive and negative implications of deinstitutionalizing for the mentally ill? For their families? For the community?

6. What are some of the interventions social workers/human service providers may use in their work with mentally ill clients?

MENTAL HEALTH CLASSROOM EXERCISES

Students will break into small groups of three or four to discuss these exercises. You must choose a scribe to record and report interesting points to the class after the group discussion. The group must also identify a spokesperson.

ACTIVITY #1:

Why do many hospitals that treat people with mental illness have policies requiring that social workers be part of their mental health team? What special expertise do social workers bring to a mental health team?

ACTIVITY #2:

How has the National Association of Social Workers been involved in influencing national social policy affecting people at risk of mental health problems?

ACTIVITY #3:

Do you think the primary purpose of case management is client service or cost containment? Explain your reasons.

ACTIVITY #4:

What are two major thrusts of recent national social policy reform efforts attempting to assist people with mental illness? How are these thrusts illustrated in former President Clinton's Mental Health Bill of Rights? The Mental Health Parity Act of 1996? What were some major problems with the 1996 law?

INTERNET RESEARCH EXERCISES

1. The National Institute of Mental Health offers information on bipolar disorder on its website (http://nimh.nih.gov/).
   a. What percentage of the U.S. adult population suffers from bipolar disorder?
   b. What are the symptoms of (1) depression and (2) mania?
   c. What evidence is given to support the thesis that bipolar disorder has some sort of genetic basis?

2. An evaluation of the effects of the Mental Health Parity Act of 1996 may be found on the Internet.
   a. Where did you find information about the act?
   b. What was the primary provision of the act?
   c. To what extent did employers drop or restrict mental health coverage as a result of the act?
   d. According to this evaluation, were the effects of the MHPA positive or negative? Explain.

3. In recent history, much happened in regards to the treatment of individuals with mental health issues.
   a. What can you find about mental health deinstitutionalization?
   b. Where did you find this information?
   c. In your opinion, why do people refuse treatment? Do you believe that this movement has been beneficial? Why or why not?

NOTES

HIV Prevention News

About adolescents and young adults

Brown et al. (2010) "used a structured computer interview to examine **the relationship between psychiatric disorders** (i.e., major depressive disorder [MDD], mania, hypomania, generalized anxiety disorder [GAD], posttraumatic stress disorder [PTSD], [conduct disorder] CD, [attention-deficit/hyperactivity disorder] ADHD, and oppositional defiant disorder [ODD]) **and sexual risk behaviors.** Adolescents meeting criteria were compared with adolescents who did not meet criteria but who were in mental health treatment" (p. 591). "The study was conducted in three sites: Providence (Rhode Island), Atlanta (Georgia), and Chicago (Illinois). Participants were recruited from 10 outpatient settings (hospital, community-based, and public) and five inpatient psychiatric units from 2004 to 2007" (p. 591) and included 840 adolescents "(56% female, 58% African American, mean age = 14.9 years) and their parents" (p. 590). The teens "completed computerized assessments of psychiatric symptoms[,] . . . reported on sexual risk behaviors (vaginal/anal sex, condom use at last sex) and completed urine screens for a sexually transmitted infection (STI)" (p. 590).

Brown and colleagues found that "compared with age- and race-adjusted national data . . ., this sample of youths in mental health treatment is no different in report of condom use, but they appear to be more likely to be sexually active (54% vs. 43%), to report four or more sexual partners (15% in the last 90 days vs. 14% lifetime), and to have a[n] STI (14% via urine screen vs. 6% lifetime history)" (p. 595). Moreover,

> adolescents meeting criteria for mania, externalizing disorders ([ODD], [CD], and [ADHD]), or comorbid for externalizing and internalizing disorders ([MDD], [GAD], and [PTSD]) were significantly more likely to report a lifetime history of vaginal or anal sex than those who did not meet criteria for any psychiatric disorder. . . . Adolescents meeting criteria for mania were significantly more likely to have 2 or more partners in the past 90 days . . . and to test positive for a[n] STI . . . relative to adolescents who did not meet criteria for a psychiatric disorder. (p. 590)

On the basis of these findings, the investigators stress that

> although adolescents in mental health treatment are at risk for HIV and other STIs, particular diagnoses convey additional risk. <u>Those with externalizing disorders, even with a co-occurring internalizing disorder, are more likely to be sexually active and thus should be carefully screened for intervention to reduce their</u>

A Quarterly Update from the Center for Mental Health Services (CMHS) of the Substance Abuse and Mental Health Services Administration (SAMHSA) Volume 12, Issue 1—Fall 2010

risk. <u>Adolescents with a history of mania are at increased risk because of more sexual partners and STIs</u>. <u>In addition to treatment of psychiatric symptoms, careful monitoring of behavior and contact with lower risk peers may be helpful</u>. Adolescents in treatment but without significant symptoms were the lowest risk group. It is possible that effective mental health treatment, without specific attention to sexual behavior risk, will reduce HIV/STI risk, but longitudinal studies are needed. For now, <u>youths with externalizing disorders and mania deserve careful attention, and all adolescents can benefit from strategies to increase safer sexual behaviors</u>. (p. 595)

Elkington, Bauermeister, and Zimmerman (2010) prospectively examined "the mediating or moderating **role of substance use on the relationship between psychological distress and sexual risk behaviors** . . . over the four high school years" (p. 514) among a sample of 850 urban, predominantly African American youth. The investigators found that

substance use was associated with psychological distress. Greater psychological distress was associated with increased sexual intercourse frequency, decreased condom use, and increased number of partners. Substance use fully mediated the relationship between psychological distress and intercourse frequency and condom use, and partially mediated the relationship between psychological distress and number of partners. [Elkington and colleagues] found no differences in mediation by sex or race/ethnicity and no evidence to support moderation of psychological distress and substance use on sexual risk. (p. 514)

Stated simply, these "findings suggest that psychological distress is associated with sexual risk because youth with greater psychological distress are also more likely to use substances" (p. 514). "Thus, psychological distress appears to be a more distal or indirect factor of sexual risk in [this] sample while substance use has a more proximal or direct effect. These results suggest that <u>efforts to address urban adolescents' psychological distress or improve their psychological well-being may have the benefit of both helping to reduce substance use and therefore sexual risk behavior</u>" (p. 523).

On this point, Elkington and colleagues lament the fact that

despite the strong association . . . [among] mental health problems, substance use and sexual risk behaviors, HIV/STI prevention programming for youth has typically not focused on mental health problems and substance use while also addressing sexual risk. Th[ese] . . . findings . . . suggest [that] <u>programs that address both psychological distress and substance use prevention may</u>

NOTES

be most effective for HIV/STI prevention as well. . . . Programs that identify triggers for engaging in both sex and substance use risk behaviors while also promoting mental health are necessary to address the comprehensive needs of youth at greater risk for HIV/STI infection. (p. 524)

ABOUT MEN WHO HAVE SEX WITH MEN

Wong, Kipke, Weiss, and McDavitt (2010) "examined the way recent experiences of a diverse set of stressors predict illicit drug use, alcohol misuse, and inconsistent condom use (i.e., unprotected anal intercourse) among an ethnically diverse cohort of [526] YMSM [young men who have sex with men]" (p. 463). The investigators found that "stress related to financial and health concerns . . . [was] associated with increased risk for substance use, while health concerns and partner-related stress were associated with sexual risk-taking. Additional analyses indicated drug use and alcohol misuse did not significantly mediate the impact that stressors have on sexual risk" (p. 463). These results

> highlight **the significant impact that stressful life events can have in the lives of YMSM** and . . . point to the importance of examining stressors related to both sexual identity and emerging adulthood as they have significant and distinct impact on HIV-risk behaviors. For example, when each risk behavior is examined separately, the experience of stress associated with financial difficulties consistently predicted both drug use and alcohol misuse. Level of sexual identity disclosure was only significantly associated with drug use. Stress related to one's own health concerns also predicted alcohol misuse. Partner-related stress and stress associated with concerns about ones' own health were significantly associated with sexual risk-taking.

> While previous research has linked alcohol use with risky sexual behaviors . . ., only illicit drug use significantly predicted inconsistent condom use in the current study. . . . However, drug use did not significantly mediate the effects of stress on unprotected anal intercourse. Despite this, drug use may be a significant mediator of other psychosocial processes not examined currently.

> Limitations associated with this study may affect the interpretation and generalizability of the findings. . . . Despite the limitations, findings . . . clearly show that emerging adulthood is an enormously stressful time in the lives of YMSM and that stressors from different life domains can have distinct impact on YMSM's risk-taking. The heterogeneity of these stressful experiences and their differential impact on risk behaviors suggest that

interventions may need to be targeted at specific sets of stressors if they seek to diminish YMSM's adoption of specific types of risk behaviors. (pp. 472–473)

In North Carolina, Hurt et al. (2010) "evaluated the hypothesized association between **primary** [or newly acquired] **HIV infection** (PHI) and having **older sexual partners** among [74 YMSM]" (p. 185). Of these 74 men,

20 had PHI (27%) [and 54 (73%) were uninfected]. Demographics (including age) were similar between groups; 39% were non-white and 74% identified as gay. The mean age of sex partners differed significantly: men with PHI had partners on average 6 years older than themselves, whereas uninfected men's partners were 4 months their junior. . . . After adjusting for race, sex while intoxicated, and having a serodiscordant/serostatus unknown partner, a participant had twice the odds of PHI if his sex partner was 5 years his senior. (p. 185)

According to Hurt and colleagues, these findings reinforce the importance of applying

an individualized approach to counseling when talking to young MSM about their sexual risk behavior. Provision of safe[r] sex messages should include both traditional [e.g., injecting drug use, unprotected intercourse] and nontraditional risk factors, directed at all age groups of sexually active individuals. Young men who have older sexual partners should be informed of the comparatively increased risk that such partnerships pose for HIV infection. In parallel, older MSM living with HIV and engaged in care should receive secondary prevention messages encouraging disclosure of their status to partners, maintenance of safer sex behavior, and [awareness] that [antiretroviral] treatment alone is not enough to prevent transmission. (p. 189)

HIV ASSESSMENT NEWS

PSYCHIATRIC ASSESSMENT

Serchuck et al. (2010) "evaluated the **prevalence of pain and psychiatric symptoms** in perinatally HIV-infected children" (p. 640) recruited from 29 sites in mainland U.S. and Puerto Rico. The study included 576 children –320 living with HIV and 256 "HIV-uninfected controls who were either perinatally HIV-exposed or living in a household with an HIV-infected person" (p. 641) –between the ages of 6 and 17 years, and their primary caregivers. The "most important finding," according to Serchuck and colleagues, "is a high prevalence of pain across all age groups, HIV-infected or not, with 37% of all subjects and 41% of HIV-infected children reporting pain during the two months prior to enrollment" (p. 644). Yet, "for all subjects, only 52% of caregivers recognized their child's pain and just 22% were aware that pain affected their child's daily activities" (p. 640). Moreover, "HIV-infected children who reported pain had higher symptom severity scores for anxiety and depression. Even after adjustment for age, gender, and HIV status, [Serchuck and colleagues] found that as the severity of generalized anxiety, major depression, or dysthymia symptoms increased, the odds of reported pain in . . . study subjects also increased, particularly among children with HIV infection" (p. 646). Additionally,

> an AIDS diagnosis was associated with increased [odds] of reported pain, yet contrary to expectations, disease severity . . . [was] not predictive of pain. Economic and family stressors appear to be less a factor in reported pain in HIV+ than HIV- uninfected children. The high proportion of reported pain amongst uninfected children underscores the importance of querying for these stressors in the primary care setting when providing services for children living in an HIV-affected household. Lastly, increasing severity of generalized anxiety, major depression, and dysthymia symptoms in HIV-infected children were associated with significantly increased odds of pain. Queries concerning pain and psychiatric symptomatology should be incorporated into the primary and specialty care of HIV+ children and adolescents: children HIV-uninfected despite prior exposure and those living in a household with an HIV+ individual. (p. 647)

"The discordance between patient and caregiver reports of pain and its impact on activities of daily living highlights that pain in children is under-recognized and therefore potentially under-treated" (p. 640).

Discordance was also evident in findings from Krug, Karus, Selwyn, and Raveis (2010), who **compared** "the **self-assessments of** 67 **late-stage HIV/AIDS patients** regarding their symptomatology, sense of self-worth, and several other aspects of their health-care situation, **to assessments** of that situation provided **by** their **informal caregivers**" (p. 23) among a convenience sample drawn from an urban health-care setting. Using a 10-item instrument, the investigators report that "substantial or moderate agreement . . . was found between patient and caregiver assessments with regard to only four items assessing physical or emotional states of the patient (pain, other symptoms, anxiety, and life worthwhile). Fair or slight agreement was found for the six remaining items, including those assessing the patient's sense of self-worth, family/friends' anxiety, interactions with family/friends, and practical matters" (p. 23). In fact, "a statistically significant difference was noted between the mean patient and mean caregiver ratings for one item—patient self-worth. On average, caregivers tended to rate patient self-worth lower than patients rated their own selfworth. In fact, 37% of caregivers stated that the patient had some or severe trouble with self-worth when the patient reported no trouble at all" (p. 30). Moreover,

> caregivers of HIV/AIDS patients . . . tended to assess the patient as being in poorer health and experiencing greater problems with physical symptoms than did the patient himself. For over a quarter of the sample, caregivers reported a problem with pain, the patient's sense of self-worth and/or the receipt of adequate, understandable information when the patient reported no such problem. In contrast, the finding that in those instances . . . [in which] the patient and caregiver agreed on the presence of a problem but not its severity, [it was] the patient [who] was more likely to describe the problem as `severe' suggests [that] reliance on proxy data might result in insufficient provision of care or services among those who need it most. (pp. 30–31)

> Krug and colleagues conclude that

> when circumstances allow, information on health-care outcomes is best obtained directly from the patient. . . . Although there was little evidence of systematic bias, patient and caregiver responses show substantial disagreement. Indeed, reliance on caregivers as proxy informants may contribute to both unmet need and delivery of unnecessary or unwanted care. . . . Conflicted dyads may especially benefit from an intervention designed to assist both patients and caregivers in com municating more effectively about healthcare issues, to help provide more accurate accounts of the patient's illness experience. (p. 31)

Neuropsychological assessment

A team of Swiss investigators (Simioni et al., 2010) set out "to deter-mine the prevalence of cognitive complaints and **HIV-associated neu-rocognitive disorders** (HANDs) **in** a cohort of aviremic HIV-positive patients" (i.e., **patients with undetectable viral loads**) and "to evalu-ate the relevance of the HIV dementia scale [(HDS)] to detect HANDs" (p. 1243). As a reminder to readers, "the new nosology for HANDs recognizes three conditions given hereafter by order of increasing severity: HIV-associated asymptomatic neurocognitive impairment (ANI), HIV-associated mild neurocognitive disorders (MNDs), and HIV-associated dementia (HIV-D)" (p. 1244).

In this study, 200 "HIV-infected patients with undetectable HIV-1 RNA concentrations in the plasma, no history of major opportunistic

NOTES

infection of the central nervous system [(CNS)] in the past 3 years, no current use of intravenous drugs, and no major depression answered a questionnaire designed to elicit cognitive complaints. Cognitive functions of 50 complaining and 50 noncomplaining HIV-positive patients were assessed" (p. 1243) with neuropsy-chological (NP) tests. Simioni and colleagues "found that 27% of HIV-positive patients with long-standing undetectable HIV-1 RNA concentration complained of neurocognitive disorders and 84% of them actually presented HANDs [ANI 24%, MND 52%, and HIV-D 8%]. Even in patients with no specific complaints, this percentage was 64% [ANI 60%, MND 4%, and HIV-D 0%]. . . . The message of [this] study is that the prevalence of HANDs remains elevated even in HIV-positive patients who are aviremic for a long time" (p. 1248). Importantly,

> to ensure that there was no other obvious cause than HIV itself to explain HANDs, [the investigators] tried to minimize confounding factors by not enrolling patients with major depression, active drug addiction, or opportunistic infection of the CNS. Some patients using methadone (8%) or having a remote history of cerebral toxoplasmosis (6%) were enrolled, but none of these factors was found to be associated with HANDs after correction for multiple comparisons. Patients with HCV [hepatitis C virus] coinfection (19%) were also accepted and were not found to have a higher prevalence of HANDs as compared with HCV-negative patients. . . .

Cognitive complaint was relatively predictive of the presence of HANDs (84% of patients) but not complaining certainly did not rule it out (64% of patients). However, whereas most complainers presented with MNDs or HIV-D, the vast majority of noncomplainers presenting with HANDs had ANI. Thus, in HIV-positive patients, contrary to HIV-negative patients . . ., cognitive complaints are predictive of actual impairment. Interestingly, a sensitivity analysis of the HDS revealed that a cutoff of 14 points or less was associated with a good sensitivity and a good predictive value to detect HANDs despite a somewhat decreased specificity, either in complainers or noncomplainers. . . . \Whereas the HDS alone is not sufficient to ascertain HANDs, [Simioni and colleagues] propose that HIV-positive patients with undetectable viremia and a[n] HDS score of 14 points or less should benefit from a thorough [NP] evaluation. . . .

Altogether, [these] results show that cognitive dysfunction is frequent in virologically optimally treated HIV-positive patients. These data point out the importance of an early diagnosis of HANDs and of a regular follow-up of HIV-positive patients, especially when they complain of cognitive disorders. (p. 1249)

HIV TREATMENT NEWS

MEDICAL CARE

Thompson et al. (2010), writing for the International AIDS Society—USA Panel, recently **updated** their "**guidelines for the use of anti-retroviral therapy in adults** with HIV infection" (p. 321) as follows:

> Patient readiness for treatment should be confirmed before initiation of antiretroviral treatment. Therapy is recommended for asymptomatic patients with a CD4 cell count $\leq 500/\mu L$, for all symptomatic patients, and those with specific conditions and comorbidities. Therapy should be considered for asymptomatic patients with CD4 cell count $> 500/\mu L$. Components of the initial and subsequent regimens must be individualized, particularly in the context of concurrent conditions. Patients receiving antiretroviral treatment should be monitored regularly; treatment failure should be detected and managed early, with the goal of therapy, even in heavily pre-treated patients, being HIV-1 RNA suppression below commercially available assay quantification limits. (p. 321)

The Panel's 2008 guidelines recommended initiating therapy for asymptomatic patients with a CD4 cell count $< 350/\mu L$, but

> increasing evidence that insidious damage occurs during "asymptomatic" HIV infection underscores the potential benefit of ART [antiretroviral therapy], even when the risk of traditional AIDS-defining diseases is relatively low. The prominence of non-AIDS events as a major cause of morbidity and mortality in those with ongoing HIV replication suggests that early ART initiation may further improve the quality and length of life for persons living with HIV. The strategic use of newer drugs can improve tolerability, as well as provide durable and potent viral suppression in initial and subsequent therapy. (p. 329)

PSYCHIATRIC/PSYCHOLOGICAL/ PSYCHOSOCIAL/ SPIRITUAL CARE

PSYCHOPHARMACOLOGY

Following up on a pilot study first reported in the <u>Spring 2005</u> issue of **mental health AIDS** (Rabkin, McElhiney, Rabkin, & Ferrando, 2004), Rabkin, McElhiney, Rabkin, and McGrath (2010) conducted "a 4-week randomized, placebo-controlled, double-blind trial" to assess "the efficacy and safety of **modafinil** [Provigil©; a wake-promoting agent]

NOTES

in the treatment of **fatigue** in patients with . . . HIV/AIDS[1] . . . and to assess [the] effect [of modafinil] on depressive symptoms" (p. 707). In total, 115 patients living with HIV who "had clinically significant fatigue (according to the Fatigue Severity Scale)" (p. 707) were randomized to the medication or to a placebo. "This was followed by an additional 8 weeks of open-label treatment for modafinil responders and 12 weeks for placebo nonresponders. . . . Visits were weekly for 4 weeks, then biweekly, with a follow-up visit at 6 months. Maximum trial dose of modafinil was 200 mg/d" (p. 707). Importantly, "markers of immunologic and virologic status were monitored for safety reasons because of the theoretical possibility of an inducer effect of modafinil on antiretrovirals (hastening their metabolism and thus reducing potency), since both drug classes share the same metabolic pathway" (p. 713). The investigators' analyses revealed that the

> fatigue response rate to modafinil was 73% and to placebo, 28%. Attrition was 9%. Modafinil did not have an effect on mood alone in the absence of improved energy. At week 4, CD4 cell counts did not change significantly; HIV RNA viral load showed a trend decline for patients taking modafinil but not for those taking placebo. At 6 months, [among the 97 patients who were reevaluated,] those still taking modafinil had more energy and fewer depressive symptoms than patients who were not taking modafinil, and only those still taking modafinil showed a significant decline from baseline in their HIV RNA viral load. (p. 707)

The investigators contextualize the effect on fatigue by noting that "modafinil was widely considered helpful and effective in enabling participants to carry out activities of daily living that previously had been restricted by fatigue. Examples include cleaning one's house, going outside more often, taking walks, socializing, and otherwise being less isolated and limited. However, initiation or resumption of more complex goals [such as taking classes or returning to work] was uncommon" (p. 714). Within these parameters, Rabkin and colleagues conclude that "modafinil appears to be effective and well tolerated in treating fatigue in HIV+patients. Consideration of its use is warranted considering the high prevalence of fatigue in the HIV community, its minimal side effects, and overall patient acceptance" (p. 707). As for achievement of more complex goals, "it seems likely that additional support and tailored interventions are needed to assist HIV+patients in achieving such goals[, as] . . . [m]odafinil alone did not bring about widespread behavior change of this nature" (p. 714).

[1]A recent review of predictors and treatment strategies for HIV-related fatigue (Jong et al., 2010) is highlighted in this issue's Resources **Tool Box**.

In a separate paper, McElhiney, Rabkin, van Gorp, and Rabkin (2010)

examined the efficacy of **modafinil** for HIV+ patients who sought treatment for fatigue in a placebo-controlled double-blind 4-week trial. A battery of standard [NP] tests was administered at study entry and Week 4, and change in performance was compared for 59 patients receiving modafinil versus 44 patients receiving placebo. A significant effect on fatigue was observed. In addition, **cognitive performance,** as measured by a global change score, improved more in the modafinil than in the placebo group although the effect was not specific to any cognitive domain. (p. 474)

Notably, "this overall effect for drug versus placebo on the global NP score may be of more than academic interest; [one study] . . . reported that this kind of global NP finding, even when slight, has been related to employment status in HIV+individuals" (p. 479). McElhiney and colleagues conclude that "findings show a positive effect of 4 weeks of modafinil treatment on overall cognitive function among HIV+adults with fatigue, in terms of both performance on NP tests and subjective perception of cognitive problems. Future research would usefully examine the effect of modafinil on patients with the primary presenting problem of cognitive impairment" (p. 479).

ADHERENCE TO TREATMENT

Hart et al. (2010) conducted a systematic review and meta-analysis to assess the impact of **directly observed therapy of highly active ART** (DOT-HAART) on adherence as well as virologic and immunologic response. Among the 17 peer-reviewed controlled studies published or presented through August 2009 and included in the analysis, "compared with control groups, DOT-HAART recipients were more likely to achieve an undetectable viral load . . ., a greater increase in CD4 cell count . . ., and HAART adherence of ≥ 95%" (p. 167). Importantly, when comparing randomized and nonrandomized studies,

the positive effect of DOT-HAART on virologic and immunologic outcomes among RCTs [randomized controlled trials] was attenuated and not statistically significant, whereas the association remained significant in nonrandomized studies. . . . Nonrandomized DOT-HAART experiences may have allowed greater flexibility in intervention design and modification and may have enrolled vulnerable populations in whom the intervention effect could be greatest.

. . . [Moreover, g]reater effect on virologic outcome was observed among substance-using and HAART-experienced

NOTES

cohorts. . . . Residence and methadone-based DOT-HAART interventions demonstrated greater treatment effect compared with clinic-based interventions, although the effect among methadone-based interventions was not statistically significant. Choosing a convenient site—such as a methadone clinic or the patient's residence—could enhance the effect of the intervention. Interventions delivered in patient homes, community-based vans, prisons, and methadone clinics may impose minimal additional burden on patients' routines. On the other hand, the time and expenses of daily travel to a site (e.g., HIV clinic, hospital) that is not part of a patient's daily routine may pose important barriers to DOT-HAART adherence. . . .

Not all DOT is the same. Enhanced DOT-HAART, defined as an intervention that provides additional material or behavioral adherence support not offered to the control group,[2] seemed to enhance treatment effect. . . .

Although there were few studies that assessed postintervention effect [i.e., beyond immediate outcomes], [the investigators] found that initial intervention effect may wane after completion of DOT support. . . . [E]xploring this time-limited effect may be . . . [particularly] important for DOT-HAART, if the mechanism of action is through improved adherence via direct supervision. If DOT-HAART is to have a sustained effect on postintervention outcomes, interventions must be designed to engender psychosocial and behavioral changes in patients through DOT encounters. . . . Efforts to sustain the benefits of DOT postintervention may . . . require closer attention to the transition from DOT to self-administration and to individualizing DOT through varied frequency, intensity, and duration of support. . . . If DOT-HAART effect is not durable, another option would be long-term or even life-long DOT-HAART for certain individuals or populations. . . . Creating and implementing durable HAART adherence interventions remains an enormous challenge. (p. 167)

[2]Hart and colleagues (2010) "defined 'enhanced DOT-HAART' as any intervention that included additional formal adherence support not offered to the control group (i.e., material or financial incentives/enablers) or a behavioral intervention or ancillary services aimed at improving adherence. Because certain services were often provided as necessary and ethical consequences of DOT, [the investigators] did not consider the following activities to constitute formal additional support: asking about side effects and adherence at DOT visits and reporting any problems to providers; prepackaging and delivering HAART via DOT visits; and referring patients to other social services unless additional staff (e.g., case manager, social worker) was integrated into the DOT team" (p. 169).

In short, according to Hart and colleagues,

> DOT-HAART seems to be effective among selected patient pop-
> ulations, such as those with a history of prior HAART experi-
> ence and/or substance use. Features of DOT-HAART which may
> increase treatment effect include nonclinic-based DOT and the
> provision of additional forms of adherence support. Because
> the impact of DOT-HAART on viro-logic response did not reach
> statistical significance when restricted to RCTs, the efficacy of
> DOT-HAART still remains in question. Areas for future research
> include assessment of long-term treatment effects and the refine-
> ment of DOT-HAART interventions to optimize the intensity,
> duration, and frequency according to patient need. Similar to the
> body of knowledge that has guided decisions on DOT for tuber-
> culosis, efficacy trials should be complemented by outcomes
> data from large-scale DOT-HAART programs and cost-effec-
> tiveness analyses to inform public health decisions regarding
> whether and under what circumstances DOT-HAART should be
> employed. (pp. 176–177)

In London, Lampe et al. (2010) "examined the **association of** self-reported
**physical and psychological symptoms with subsequent virologic
rebound** among [188] patients with viral suppression on combination
[ART] (cART)" (p. 500). "Among this subgroup of HIV patients on successful ART," the investigators found that "physical and psychological
symptoms were common, and were among the strongest predictors of
virologic rebound. The associations appeared largely independent of
various known risk factors for virologic failure" (p. 502). Lampe and colleagues stress that

> an assessment of virologic failure risk that is based solely on lab-
> oratory results, treatment history and adherence may be missing
> an important dimension—information from the patient's per-
> spective that is not captured by these measures. These results
> suggest the importance of ongoing clinical focus on physical and
> psychological symptoms among patients on successful cART, in
> addition to those starting treatment. Simple symptom inquiry
> conducted as part of routine clinical care may be valuable to
> identify patients at risk of future treatment failure, and provide
> opportunity not only for assessing adherence but also for appro-
> priate medical or psychological interventions to address physical
> symptoms and psychological distress. (p. 504)

Carrico, Johnson, Colfax, and Moskowitz (2010) "examined **affective correlates of stimulant use and ART adherence** among HIV-
positive methamphetamine users. . . . [A convenience sample of]

NOTES

122 HIV-positive [MSM] or transgendered individuals on ART who reported using methamphetamine in the past 30 days . . . [was] recruited from the community" (p. 769) in San Francisco. The investigators found that "HIV-specific traumatic stress was consistently and independently associated with more frequent cocaine/crack use (but not with methamphetamine use). Positive affect was independently associated with a decreased likelihood of reporting any injection drug use and an increased likelihood of reporting perfect ART adherence" (p. 769) among methamphetamine users living with HIV. Carrico and colleagues contend that, despite limitations, findings from this study

> may assist with the development of innovative psychological treatments designed to meet the needs of diverse groups of HIV-positive stimulant users on ART. Specifically, findings highlight that <u>interventions designed to reduce HIV-specific traumatic stress as well as enhance positive affect may be efficacious in decreasing stimulant use and improving ART adherence</u>. Future studies should attempt to replicate these findings with larger samples and examine the clinical relevance of interventions designed to improve affect regulation among HIV-positive stimulant users. (p. 776)

COPING, SOCIAL SUPPORT, & QUALITY OF LIFE

"Although IPV [interpersonal violence] is primarily studied among women, men (especially sexual minority men) are also frequently victims of abuse, and sexual minority men with HIV may be particularly vulnerable to abuse and susceptible to adverse health outcomes if abused" (pp. 393–394), according to Pantalone, Hessler, and Simoni (2010), who "examined **mental health pathways between** . . . **IPV** . . . **and health-related outcomes** in [178] HIV-positive sexual minority men engaged with medical care" (p. 387). Study participants were recruited from two urban, public HIV primary care clinics and were diverse with regard to race and ethnicity. The mental health problems that were assessed included anxiety, depression, suicidal ideation, and symptoms of PTSD. The investigators found that

> greater frequency of adult and partner abuse experiences was associated with more frequent or severe mental health problems. Having more mental health problems was, in turn, related to [lower] self-reported HRQOL [health-related quality of life], [lower] self-reported adherence, and [higher] chart-extracted viral load. . . . Those who reported for emergency care were also those who reported experiencing more frequent IPV by non-partners. This was the only direct effect that emerged, and it is

consistent with the results of several large-scale studies of HIV-positive outpatients. . . . [For this reason,] [emergency room] staff should routinely screen for IPV in all HIV patients, irrespective of the presenting problem. (p. 394)

Pantalone and colleagues continue:

As hypothesized, both adult and partner abuse were independently related to mental health problems while controlling for each other. This finding in itself has important clinical implications in terms of the need to assess for all forms of IPV as vulnerability factors for mental disorders, poorer HIV health, and overuse of health care resources. Frequently, the HIV literature focuses on child abuse leading to HIV risk behaviors . . ., which highlights an important but incomplete picture of IPV-health relations. Mental health problems resulting from abuse experiences may be exacerbated by homophobia or anti-HIV attitudes of the perpetrator. . . .

As expected, participants who endorsed greater frequency and severity of mental health problems were those whose health-related outcomes were poorer. It appears clear that violence victimization and mental health problems influence individuals' perceptions of their physical health and their ability to function independently to meet the demands of multiple roles. . . . The final model . . . provid[es] . . . a clear message about the potential benefits of treating mental health problems to improve perceptions of physical health as well as functional capabilities. Interventions that focus on increasing social support and self-care behaviors may be able to improve HRQOL. (p. 394)

Pantalone and colleagues conclude that these results

provide strong support for the contribution of violence exposure and mental health problems to poor health-related outcomes among HIV-positive sexual minority men. Clinical practice implications include provision of more intensive mental health services to patients in order to contain costs associated with physical health problems, which are potentially exacerbated by psychological distress and an IPV history. Also, provider interventions that increase identification of abuse and mental health problems may be needed. Given their social and financial problems, many HIV-positive individuals clearly need referral to social services. However, rather than providing supportive counseling or case management alone, HIV care settings may also wish to offer evidence-based mental health treatments that target specific disorders or symptom clusters. Investigators are

NOTES

encouraged to test and disseminate such <u>interventions</u> in HIV care settings, especially those <u>that combine traditional evidence-based approaches to mental disorders with a specific focus on relevant health-promotion behaviors</u> (Safren et al., 2009[; summarized in the <u>Spring 2009</u> issue of *mental health* **AIDS**]). (p. 395)

Naar-King, Parsons, Murphy, Kolmodin, and Harris (2010) continued their evaluation of data compiled on "a randomized clinical trial compar[ing] . . . Healthy Choices, a four session motivational intervention targeting two of . . . three risk behaviors (HIV medication adherence, sexual risk behavior and substance use)[,] to multidisciplinary specialty care alone" (p. 422; described in the Spring 2010 issue of *mental health* **AIDS**). The trial was conducted among a convenience sample of 186 predominantly African American 16- to 24-year-olds living with HIV drawn from adolescent medicine HIV clinics in five American cities. In this paper, the investigators present "intermediary outcomes available at 3-month follow-up . . . [among] variables proposed to be precursors to behavior change **(motivation, self-efficacy, and depression)**" (p. 422).

Importantly, the **bf youth living with HIV** (YLH) who took part in this study "received the intervention in the real-world setting of adolescent medicine clinics instead of a research venue" (p. 426) and, "of the 94 youth randomly assigned to the treatment condition, 84% received at least one session, 67% received at least two sessions, 56% received at least three sessions, and 49% completed all four sessions" (p. 422). Naar-King and colleagues report that this

brief MI [motivational interviewing] intervention improved depression and also motivation for changing risk behaviors for those who attended at least two MI sessions. This is the first study of a brief intervention to test these important precursors to behavior change in YLH. The intervention effect was strongest for depression . . . [, and s]elf-efficacy, as defined by belief in the ability to avoid risky behaviors in the face of temptation, approached significance for those who received the intervention. It is possible that although MI supports self-efficacy through affirmation of client strengths, <u>confidence to avoid risk in very specific tempting situations may require a more intensive skill-building intervention</u>.

Two-thirds of the sample assigned to the treatment condition received at least two intervention sessions. These youth could not be distinguished from the remaining high-risk youth on any of the baseline variables measured. <u>Increasing access by offering the intervention in the home or community and by including an outreach component may improve intervention retention</u>. . . . <u>Incorporating outreach strategies</u>

within behavior change interventions could not only increase access by providing services in flexible locations, but also by including case-finding approaches. . . .

> Further studies of factors influencing appointment attendance (e.g., motivation and self-efficacy for attending treatment sessions) may elucidate strategies to improve intervention retention.
>
> A limitation of the study is the lack of an attention control. However, standard care in these clinics included significant support services with an average of more than nine visits over a period of 3 months, more than twice what was offered in Healthy Choices. . . .
>
> Results suggest the utility of brief MI delivered in adolescent medicine clinics to improve depression and motivational readiness among youth who access the intervention. Brief MI interventions may be helpful to boost motivation to engage in services offered by multidisciplinary adolescent clinics serving YLH. Interventions that use MI as a precursor to more intensive interventions, such as cognitive-behavioral treatment . . ., are worth further exploration in YLH. (pp. 426–427)

At the other end of the age continuum, "correlations . . . [among] **depression, loneliness, health,** and **HIV/AIDS-related stigma** have been studied, but there is little evaluation of these associations among **HIV-positive adults over the age of 50**," according to Grov, Golub, Parsons, Brennan, and Karpiak (2010), who examined data on "914 New York City-based HIV-positive men and women over the age of 50" (p. 630). The investigators report that "39.1% of participants exhibited symptoms of major depression" (p. 630) and

> controlling for demographic differences and perceived health indicators, higher rates of HIV stigma, and loneliness place older adults at increased risk for major depressive symptoms. . . . [F]or example, every 10-unit increase in loneliness increases the odds of major depressive symptoms by over 80%. Since neither HIV stigma nor loneliness was associated with objective indicators of health (i.e., CD4 count and AIDS diagnosis), the magnitude of these psychosocial factors rather than physical symptoms of disease severity, are primary factors contributing to depression. . . . Although other studies have identified objective indicators of disease progression as significant predictors of depression . . ., these data highlight the importance of looking beyond physical health indicators and focusing efforts to reduce HIV-related stigma and loneliness in order to reduce major depressive symptomatology and improve perceived health among older adults living with

NOTES

HIV. . . . Older HIV-positive adults as they age need to be linked to healthcare, as well as social and emotional support. (p. 637)

In Toronto, Atkins et al. (2010) "examined **the role social support} may play in attenuating the effects of** both **[NP] status and depression on cognitive difficulties.** A total of 357 [male] participants completed a battery of [NP] tests, questionnaires about cognitive difficulties and depression, and an interview that included an assessment of perceived level of social support" (p. 793). Analyses of these data

> revealed that higher levels of cognitive symptom burden were significantly associated with depression . . . while lower levels of cognitive symptom burden were significantly associated with greater social support . . . and higher level of education. . . . There was a significant interaction between [NP] status and depression . . . ; the presence of [NP] impairment with depression was associated with higher levels of cognitive symptom burden. There was also a significant interaction between social support and depression. . . . Interestingly, social support was also associated with a lower cognitive symptom burden for non-depressed individuals living with HIV/AIDS. (p. 793)

Atkins and colleagues believe that these

> findings have important clinical implications for psychological well-being in people with HIV/AIDS. To improve quality of life, it is important to identify individuals who may be depressed and intervene appropriately. Although no evidence supports the hypothesis that depression affects [NP] impairment . . ., depression has been found, both in the present and previous studies, to be associated with higher subjective cognitive symptom burden. . . . This relationship suggests that depression is a key to understand[ing] self-perception of cognitive symptoms. Furthermore, the degree of perceived social support in non-depressed individuals appears to be an important determinant of neurocognitive complaints and is, therefore, a potential target for intervention for individuals with HIV/AIDS who are not depressed. It is important for AIDS organizations and other service providers to recognize the significant protective role of social support on psychological well-being, and be involved in developing programs and activities that promote social support for people living with HIV/AIDS. (p. 799)

ABOUT SUICIDE

SCOPE OF THE PROBLEM

Suicide occurs when a person ends his or her life. It is the 10th leading cause of death among Americans. But suicide deaths are only part of the problem. Suicide attempts impact a larger population—more individuals survive suicide attempts than die. And they are often seriously injured and in need of medical care.

SUICIDE DEATHS IN THE UNITED STATES

- There are far more suicides each year than homicides. In fact, from 2008–2010, the number of suicides has been more than twice that of homicides.
- In 2010, more than 38,000 people died by suicide.

SUICIDE ATTEMPTS IN THE UNITED STATES

- There are an estimated 12 attempted suicides for every one suicide death.
- In 2009, there were an estimated 374,486 people with self-inflicted injuries treated in emergency departments. The number increased to 464,995 in 2010 and 487,770 in 2011.
- The estimated number of people hospitalized for self-inflicted injuries increased from 155,000 in 2009 to 224,000 in 2011.

AGE GROUP DIFFERENCES

- Suicide is the second leading cause of death among 25- to 34-year-olds and the third leading cause of death among 15- to 24-year-olds.
- Suicide among 45- to 54-year-olds is a growing problem; the rate of suicide is higher in this age group than in any other.
- Although older adults engage in suicide attempts less than those in other age groups, they have a higher rate of death by suicide. Over the age of 65, there is one estimated suicide for every 4 attempted suicides compared to 1 suicide for every 100–200 attempts among youth and young adults ages 15–24.

GENDER DISPARITIES

- Men die by suicide four times as often as women and represent 78.8% of all U.S. suicides.
- Women attempt suicide two to three times as often as men.
- Suicide rates for males are highest among those aged 75 and older.
- Suicide rates for females are highest among those aged 45–54.
- Firearms are the most commonly used method of suicide among males.
- Poisoning is the most common method of suicide for females.

Racial and Ethnic Disparities

- The highest suicide rates are among American Indian/Alaskan Natives and Non-Hispanic Whites.
- Asian/Pacific Islanders have the lowest suicide rates among males while Non-Hispanic Blacks have the lowest suicide rate among females.

Risk and Protective Factors

Suicide is a complex human behavior, with no single determining cause. The factors that affect the likelihood of a person attempting or dying by are known as **risk** or **protective factors,** depending on whether they raise or lower the likelihood of suicidal behavior.

Major risk factors for suicide include

- Prior suicide attempt(s)
- Mood disorders
- Substance abuse
- Access to lethal means

Major protective factors include

- Effective mental health care
- Connectedness
- Problem-solving skills

To learn more, *see SPRC's Risk and Protective Factors Resource Sheet.*

Terminology

Suicide

Death caused by self-directed injurious behavior with any intent to die as a result of the behavior.

Note: The term "committed" suicide is discouraged because it connotes the equivalent of a crime or sin. The CDC has also deemed "completed suicide" and "successful suicide" as unacceptable. Preferred terms are "death by suicide" or "died by suicide".

Suicide attempt

A non-fatal self-directed potentially injurious behavior with any intent to die as result of the behavior. A suicide attempt may or may not result in injury.

Suicidal ideation

Thoughts of suicide. These thoughts can range in severity from a vague wish to be dead to active suicidal ideation with a specific plan and intent.

UNINTENTIONAL INJURY

A fatal or nonfatal injury that was unplanned and not intended to happen. Causes include a motor vehicle crash, poisoning, fall, fire, and drowning. Unintentional injuries are sometimes referred to as "accidents," but this term is discouraged since it implies the injury was not preventable.

PREVENTION

Interventions designed to stop suicidal behavior before it occurs. These interventions involve reducing the factors that put people at risk for suicide and suicidal behaviors. They also include increasing the factors that protect people or buffer them from being at risk.

TREATMENT

The care of suicidal people by licensed mental health caregivers, health care providers, and other caregivers with individually tailored strategies designed to change the self-injurious or self-directed violent thoughts, behaviors, mood, environment, or chemistry of individuals that increase the risk for engaging in suicidal behaviors, and help them identify and address their emotional, psychological, and physical needs without engaging in self-destructive behaviors.

POSTVENTION

Actions taken after a suicide has occurred largely to help persons affected by the suicide loss, such as family, friends, and co-workers of the deceased.

REFERENCES

Atkins, J.H., Rubenstein, S.L., Sota, T.L., Rueda, S., Fenta, H., Bacon, J., & Rourke, S.B. (2010). Impact of social support on cognitive symptom burden in HIV/AIDS. *AIDS Care, 22*(7), 793–802.

Brown, L.K., Hadley, W., Stewart, A., Lescano, C., Whiteley, L., Donenberg, G., DiClemente, R., & the Project STYLE Study Group. (2010). Psychiatric disorders and sexual risk among adolescents in mental health treatment. *Journal of Consulting & Clinical Psychology, 78*(4), 590–597.

Carrico, A.W., Johnson, M.O., Colfax, G.N., & Moskowitz, J.T. (2010). Affective correlates of stimulant use and adherence to anti-retroviral therapy among HIV-positive methamphetamine users. *AIDS & Behavior, 14*(4), 769–777.

Elkington, K.S., Bauermeister, J.A., & Zimmerman, M.A. (2010). Psychological distress, substance use, and HIV/STI risk behaviors among youth. *Journal of Youth & Adolescence, 39*(5), 514–527.

Grov, C., Golub, S.A., Parsons, J.T., Brennan, M., & Karpiak, S.E. (2010). Loneliness and HIV-related stigma explain depression among older HIV-positive adults. *AIDS Care, 22*(5), 630–639.

NOTES

Hart, J.E., Jeon, C.Y., Ivers, L.C., Behforouz, H.L., Caldas, A., Drobac, P.C., & Shin, S.S. (2010). Effect of directly observed therapy for highly active antiretroviral therapy on virologic, immunologic, and adherence outcomes: A meta-analysis and systematic review. *Journal of Acquired Immune Deficiency Syndromes, 54*(2), 167–179.

Hurt, C.B., Matthews, D.D., Calabria, M.S., Green, K.A., Adimora, A.A., Golin, C. E., & Hightow-Weidman, L.B. (2010). Sex with older partners is associated with primary HIV infection among men who have sex with men in North Carolina. *Journal of Acquired Immune Deficiency Syndromes, 54*(2), 185–190.

Krug, R., Karus, D., Selwyn, P.A., & Raveis, V.H. (2010). Late-stage HIV/AIDS patients' and their familial caregivers' agreement on the Palliative Care Outcome Scale. *Journal of Pain & Symptom Management, 39*(1), 23–32.

Lampe, F.C., Harding, R., Smith, C.J., Phillips, A.N., Johnson, M., & Sherr, L. (2010). Physical and psychological symptoms and risk of virologic rebound among patients with virologic suppression on antiretroviral therapy. *Journal of Acquired Immune Deficiency Syndromes, 54*(5), 500–505.

McElhiney, M., Rabkin, J., van Gorp, W., & Rabkin, R. (2010). Modafinil effects on cognitive function in HIV+ patients treated for fatigue: A placebo controlled study. *Journal of Clinical & Experimental Neuropsychology, 32*(5), 474–480.

Naar-King, S., Parsons, J.T., Murphy, D., Kolmodin, K., & Harris, D.R. (2010). A multisite randomized trial of a motivational intervention targeting multiple risks in youth living with HIV: Initial effects on motivation, self-efficacy, and depression. *Journal of Adolescent Health, 46*(5), 422–428.

Pantalone, D.W., Hessler, D.M., & Simoni, J.M. (2010). Mental health pathways from interpersonal violence to health-related outcomes in HIV-positive sexual minority men. *Journal of Consulting & Clinical Psychology, 78*(3), 387–397.

Rabkin, J.G., McElhiney, M.C., Rabkin, R., & Ferrando, S.J. (2004). Modafinil treatment for fatigue in HIV+ patients: A pilot study. *Journal of Clinical Psychiatry, 65*(12), 1688–1695.

Rabkin, J.G., McElhiney, M.C., Rabkin, R., & McGrath, P.J. (2010). Modafinil treatment for fatigue in HIV/AIDS: A randomized placebo-controlled study. *Journal of Clinical Psychiatry, 71*(6), 707–715.

Safren, S.A., O'Cleirigh, C., Tan, J.Y., Raminani, S.R., Reilly, L.C., Otto, M.W., & Mayer, K.H. (2009). A randomized controlled trial of cognitive behavioral therapy for adherence and depression (CBT-AD) in HIV-infected individuals. *Health Psychology, 28*(1), 1–10.

Serchuck, L.K., Williams, P.L., Nachman, S., Gadow, K.D., Chernoff, M., & Schwartz, L. (2010). Prevalence of pain and association with psychiatric symptom severity in perinatally HIV-infected children as compared to controls living in HIV-affected households. *AIDS Care*, 22(5), 640–648.

Simioni, S., Cavassini, M., Annoni, J.-M., Abraham, A.R., Bourquin, I., Schiffer, V., Calmy, A., Chave, J.-P., Giacobini, E., Hirschel, B., & Du Pasquier, R.A. (2010). Cognitive dysfunction in HIV patients despite long-standing suppression of viremia. *AIDS*, 24(9), 1243–1250.

Thompson, M.A., Aberg, J.A., Cahn, P., Montaner, J.S.G., Rizzardini, G., Telenti, A., Gatell, J.M., Günthard, H.F., Hammer, S.M., Hirsch, M.S., Jacobsen, D.M., Reiss, P., Richman, D.D., Volberding, P.A., Yeni, P., & Schooley, R.T. (2010). Antiretroviral treatment of adult HIV infection: 2010 recommendations of the International AIDS Society—USA Panel [Review]. *Journal of the American Medical Association*, 304(3), 321–333.

Wong, C.F., Kipke, M.D., Weiss, G., & McDavitt, B. (2010). The impact of recent stressful experiences on HIV-risk related behaviors. *Journal of Adolescence*, 33(3), 463–475.

NOTES

CHAPTER 5

SUBSTANCE USE, ABUSE, AND CO-OCCURRING DISORDERS

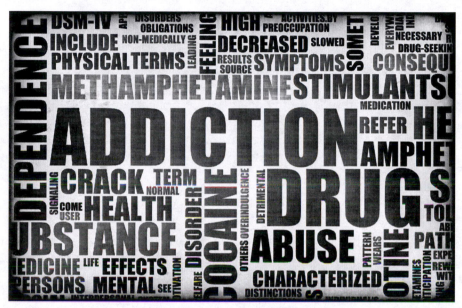

© 2012, kentah, Shutterstock, Inc.

Chapter Objectives

- Describe the continuum of substance use disorders and progression of substance use, abuse, and addiction.
- Describe how substance use disorders are diagnosed.
- Describe the parallels of substance abuse and serious mental illness.
- Discuss the signs, symptoms, and challenges of co-existing conditions.

CASE STUDY

When meeting with the caseworker at the shelter, Tiffany reported she has a son, Caleb, who lives with Tiffany's dad and girlfriend. Tiffany reported that she left Caleb there when he was six months old because she was overwhelmed by taking care of him. Tiffany added that Caleb is now nine months old and is behind developmentally. Tiffany did not disclose that she was abusing a variety of drugs during her pregnancy, including alcohol, painkillers, and marijuana. She did not receive any prenatal care until the end of the pregnancy, which ended with Caleb's premature birth at approximately 33 weeks gestation.

Tiffany reported she has been using drugs and alcohol since she was twelve years old. She and her friends often took alcohol from her father's bar, which he never seemed to notice. By age fourteen, Tiffany was drinking alcohol to get drunk several times a week and started smoking marijuana. She added that when she moved to Texas to live with her mother at age sixteen, she began using her mother's painkillers, then eventually buying them off the street. Tiffany reported that she was sexually assaulted by her stepfather's brother within the first few weeks she lived in Texas. Tiffany did not tell anyone about the assault at that time.

SUBSTANCE ABUSE

This chapter focuses on substance abuse and its impact. Whether a human service professional works in a substance abuse treatment facility or in another type of agency, substance abuse often impacts clients of social service agencies.

The Substance Abuse and Mental Health Services Administration (SAMHSA) sponsors an annual survey, the National Survey on Drug Use and Health (NSDUH). The survey is the primary source of information on the use of illicit drugs, alcohol, and tobacco in the civilian, noninstitutionalized population of the United States aged 12 years or older. The survey interviews approximately 67,500 annually. Below are some statistics found in the 2009 NSDUH report:

- In 2009, 4.3 million persons aged 12 or older (1.7 percent of the population) received treatment for a problem related to the use of alcohol or illicit drugs.
- Slightly more than half of Americans aged 12 or older reported being current drinkers of alcohol in the 2009 survey (51.9 percent). This translates to an estimated 130.6 million people, which is similar to the 2008 estimate of 129.0 million people (51.6 percent).
- In 2009, nearly one quarter (23.7 percent) of persons aged 12 or older participated in binge drinking. This translates to about

59.6 million people. The rate in 2009 is similar to the estimate in 2008. Binge drinking is defined as having five or more drinks on the same occasion on at least 1 day in the 30 days prior to the survey.

- In 2009, an estimated 21.8 million Americans aged 12 or older were current (past month) illicit drug users, meaning they had used an illicit drug during the month prior to the survey interview. This estimate represents 8.7 percent of the population aged 12 or older. Illicit drugs include marijuana/hashish, cocaine (including crack), heroin, hallucinogens, inhalants, or prescription-type psychotherapeutics used nonmedically.

- The rate of current illicit drug use among persons aged 12 or older in 2009 (8.7 percent) was higher than the rate in 2008 (8.0 percent).

- Marijuana was the most commonly used illicit drug. In 2009, there were 16.7 million past month users. Among persons aged 12 or older, the rate of past month marijuana use and the number of users in 2009 (6.6 percent or 16.7 million) were higher than in 2008 (6.1 percent or 15.2 million) and in 2007 (5.8 percent or 14.4 million). (1)

Diagnostic criteria for substance abuse disorders changed with the publication of the 5th edition of the Diagnostic Manual of Mental Disorders (DSM-5) by the American Psychiatric Association.*

Instead of the previous diagnostic categories of Substance Abuse and Substance Dependence, the DSM-5 categorizes substance use disorders on a continuum from mild to severe. Each specific substance is addressed as a distinct disorder. For example, one may be diagnosed with a moderate alcohol use disorder if the individual has four of five symptoms of a substance use disorder in the last twelve months.

The DSM-5 describes eleven criteria which are used in assessing for substance use disorders. The criteria include:

1. The individual may take the substance in larger amounts or over a longer period than was originally intended.
2. The individual may express a persistent desire to cut down or regulate substance use and may report multiple unsuccessful efforts to decrease or discontinue use.
3. The individual may spend a great deal of time obtaining the substance, using the substance, or recovering from its effects.
4. Craving, as manifested by an intense desire or urge for the drug that may occur at any time but is more likely when in an environment where the drug previously was obtained or used.

*American Psychiatric Association. (2013). *Diagnostic and statistical manual of mental disorders* (5th ed.). Washington, DC: Author.

NOTES

Craving has also been shown to involve classical conditioning and is associated with activation of specific reward structures in the brain.

5. Recurrent substance use may result in a failure to fulfill major role obligations at work, school, or home.
6. The individual may continue substance use despite having persistent or recurrent social or interpersonal problems caused or exacerbated by the effects of the substance.
7. Important social, occupational, or recreational activities may be given up or reduced because of substance use. The individual may withdraw from family activities and hobbies in order to use the substance.
8. Recurrent substance use in situations in which it is physically hazardous.
9. The individual may continue substance use despite knowledge of having a persistent or recurrent physical or psychological problem that is likely to have been caused or exacerbated by the substance.
10. Tolerance is signaled by requiring a markedly increased dose of the substance to achieve the desired effect or a markedly reduced effect when the usual dose is consumed. The degree to which tolerance develops depends on the individual.
11. Withdrawal is a syndrome that occurs when blood or tissue concentrations of a substance decline in an individual who had maintained prolonged heavy use of the substance. After developing withdrawal symptoms, the individual is likely to consume the substance to relieve the symptoms. Withdrawal symptoms vary greatly.

The scale of *severity* includes:

- Mild (two or three symptoms)
- Moderate (four or five symptoms)
- Severe (six or more symptoms)

The DSM-5 also lists specifiers that can be used. *Specifiers* include:

- In early remission: the individual has not met any of the criteria for at least three months but less than twelve months.
- In sustained remission: the individual has not met the criteria at any time in the last twelve months.
- On maintenance therapy: the individual is in remission from use but is also on medical maintenance.
- In a controlled environment: these include environments in which individuals are closely supervised, including therapeutic communities, jail, or hospitals.

Individuals may be diagnosed with multiple substance use disorders. For example, if an individual's primary drug of choice is an opioid such as heroin, he/she may be diagnosed with Opioid Use Disorder. If the individual meets six or more symptoms above, he/she would be diagnosed with Severe Opioid Use Disorder. If the individual is currently hospitalized, the specifier of "in a controlled environment" would be added. Therefore, the primary or principal diagnosis is Severe Opioid Use Disorder, in a Controlled Environment. If the individual also reports occasional use of benzodiazepines, a secondary diagnosis of Mild Sedative, Hypnotic, or Anxiolytic Use Disorder could be a secondary diagnosis.

NOTES

CASE EXAMPLE (CAN BE DETACHED TO BE TURNED IN, DISCUSSED IN CLASS)

Gina is a 23-year-old female. She was recently fired from her job waitressing at a restaurant due to missing too much work. She left high school during her junior year and has worked a variety of part-time jobs, usually in the service industry. Gina lives with a friend, Rachel, who is 25 years old. Rachel has two children, ages five and three years of age. Rachel's children currently live with Rachel's mother because of a child protection court order. Rachel and Gina became friends about a year ago when they started partying with the same group of people. Parties always included alcohol and marijuana. Rachel and Gina consume alcohol and marijuana nearly daily. When they "party," now, Rachel and Gina look for opportunities to smoke methamphetamine or snort crack cocaine. These parties occur two or three times per week. Gina smokes marijuana to "come down" from the methamphetamine. Due to limited financial resources, Gina started having sex with her dealer in exchange for marijuana and methamphetamine, something Rachel has been doing since she and Gina met.

QUESTIONS

1. What additional information, if any, do you need to know to make an appropriate diagnosis for Gina and Rachel?

2. Based on the information available, how might you diagnose Gina? Rachel?

(1) Substance Abuse and Mental Health Services Administration. (2010). *Results from the 2009 National Survey on Drug Use and Health: Volume I. Summary of National Findings* (Office of Applied Studies, NSDUH Series H-38A, HHS Publication No. SMA 10-4856Findings). Rockville, MD.

ELECTRONIC ACCESS AND COPIES OF PUBLICATION. This publication may be downloaded from http://www.oas.samhsa.gov. Hard copies may be obtained from http://www.oas.samhsa.gov/copies.cfm. Or please call SAMHSA's Health Information Network at 1-877-SAMHSA-7 (1-877-726-4727) (English and Español).

(2) Source: American Psychiatric Association. (2000). Diagnostic and Statistical Manual of Mental Disorders (4th ed. Text rev.). Washington DC: American Psychiatric Association, p. 197, 199.

CASE EXAMPLE (CAN BE DETACHED TO BE TURNED IN, DISCUSSED IN CLASS)

Trevor is a 16-year-old male. He lives with his parents and attends high school. Trevor is an average student and plays two sports. He is well-liked and has many friends. Trevor began drinking alcohol with his friends when he was 14 years old. Since that time, he and his friends usually drink alcohol on the weekends, at least one night per week. They usually drink at a friend's house whose parents are rarely home on weekend nights. Trevor used to avoid drinking during an athletic season, but due to a recent injury, has decided to drink in-season as well. When Trevor and his friends drink alcohol, Trevor usually drinks to the point of feeling "buzzed," about six beers. Since his injury, Trevor has been drinking eight or nine beers, feeling he has "less to lose" than he did before.

QUESTIONS

1. What additional information, if any, do you need to know to make an appropriate diagnosis for Trevor?

2. Based on the information you do have, how might you diagnose Trevor?

ALCOHOL PRE-TEST

True	False	Question
		Alcoholism only happens to troubled people.
		Females can generally drink more alcohol than males before becoming impaired.
		I cannot be an alcoholic if I don't drink every day.
		Many people consider alcoholism a disease.
		Alcohol consumption by women during pregnancy is safe.
		Children of alcohol and drug addicted parents are up to four times more likely to develop substance abuse and mental health problems than other children.
		Alcohol affects every organ in a drinker's body.
		In 2009, 51.9% of Americans age 12 and older had used alcohol at least once in the 30 days prior to being surveyed by the National Survey on Drug Use and Health.
		Heavy alcohol use can increase risk of certain cancers, stroke, and liver disease.
		In the United States, a "standard" drink is any drink that contains about 0.6 fluid ounces or 14 grams of "pure" alcohol.

ALCOHOL

OVERVIEW

Ethyl alcohol, or ethanol, is an intoxicating ingredient found in beer, wine, and liquor. It is a central nervous system depressant that is rapidly absorbed from the stomach and small intestine into the bloodstream. A standard drink equals 0.6 ounces of pure ethanol, or 12 ounces of beer; 8 ounces of malt liquor; 5 ounces of wine; or 1.5 ounces (a "shot") of 80-proof distilled spirits or liquor (e.g., gin, rum, vodka, or whiskey).

Alcohol affects every organ in the drinker's body and can damage a developing fetus. Intoxication can impair brain function and motor skills; heavy use can increase risk of certain cancers, stroke, and liver disease.

In 2009, 51.9% of Americans age 12 and older had used alcohol at least once in the 30 days prior to being surveyed; 23.7% had binged (5+ drinks within 2 hours); and 6.8% drank heavily (5+ drinks on 5+ occasions). In the 12–17 age range, 14.7% had consumed at least one drink in the 30 days prior to being surveyed; 8.8% had binged; and 2.1% drank heavily. *Source: National Survey on Drug Use and Health (Substance Abuse and Mental Health Administration Web Site).*

In the United States, a "standard" drink is any drink that contains about 0.6 fluid ounces or 14 grams of "pure" alcohol. Although the drinks below are different sizes, each contains approximately the same amount of alcohol and counts as a single standard drink.

A major nationwide survey of 43,000 U.S. adults by the National Institutes of Health shows that only about 2 in 100 people who drink within both the single-day and weekly limits below have alcoholism or alcohol abuse.

"Low risk" is *not* "no risk." Even within these limits, drinkers can have problems if they drink too quickly, have health problems, or are older (both men and women over 65 are generally advised to have no more than 3 drinks on any day and 7 per week). Based on your health and how alcohol affects you, you may need to drink less or not at all.

ALCOHOL ABUSE

The American Medical Association has considered alcoholism a disease since 1956, and yet there has been no universally accepted definition of alcoholism. The DSM-IV-TR is utilized to diagnose alcohol abuse and dependence.

One way to understand alcohol abuse is that it occurs on a continuum. (Insert Alcohol Abuse Continuum Here)

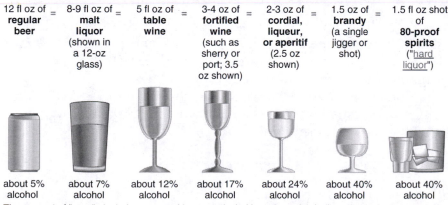

| 12 fl oz of **regular beer** | = | 8-9 fl oz of **malt liquor** (shown in a 12-oz glass) | = | 5 fl oz of **table wine** | ≈ | 3-4 oz of **fortified wine** (such as sherry or port; 3.5 oz shown) | = | 2-3 oz of **cordial, liqueur, or aperitif** (2.5 oz shown) | = | 1.5 oz of **brandy** (a single jigger or shot) | = | 1.5 fl oz shot of **80-proof spirits** ("hard liquor") |

about 5% alcohol — about 7% alcohol — about 12% alcohol — about 17% alcohol — about 24% alcohol — about 40% alcohol — about 40% alcohol

The percent of "pure" alcohol, expressed here as alcohol by volume (alc/vol), varies by beverage.

Source: http://rethinkingdrinking.niaaa.nih.gov/

NOTES

Source: http://www.nida.nih.gov/DrugPages/Alcohol.html

Low-risk drinking limits		MEN	WOMEN
	On any single **DAY**	No more then **4** ⬜⬜⬜⬜ drinks on any **day**	No more then **3** ⬜⬜⬜ drinks on any **day**
		** AND **	** AND **
	Per **WEEK**	No more then **14** ⬜⬜⬜⬜⬜⬜⬜ drinks per **week**	No more then **7** ⬜⬜⬜⬜⬜⬜⬜ drinks per **week**
To stay low risk, keep within BOTH the single-day AND weekly limits.			

WOMEN AND ALCOHOL

Women's drinking patterns are different from men's—especially when it comes to the type of beverage, amounts, and frequency. Women's bodies also react differently to alcohol than men's bodies. As a result, women face particular health risks and realities.

Women should be aware of the health risks associated with drinking alcohol, especially because most women drink at least occasionally, and many women drink a lot.

WHY DO WOMEN FACE HIGHER RISK?

Research shows that women start to have alcohol-related problems at lower drinking levels than men do. One reason is that, on average, women weigh less than men. In addition, alcohol disperses in body water, and pound for pound, women have less water in their bodies than men do. So after a man and woman of the same weight drink the same amount of alcohol, the woman's blood alcohol concentration will tend to be higher, putting her at greater risk for harm. Other biological differences, including hormones, may contribute, as well.

WHAT ARE THE HEALTH RISKS?

LIVER DAMAGE Women who drink are more likely to develop alcoholic hepatitis (liver inflammation) than men who drink the same amount of alcohol. Alcoholic hepatitis can lead to cirrhosis.

HEART DISEASE Chronic heavy drinking is a leading cause of heart disease. Among heavy drinkers, women are more susceptible to alcohol-related heart disease than men, even though women drink less alcohol over a lifetime than men.

BREAST CANCER There is an association between drinking alcohol and developing breast cancer. Women who consume about one drink per day have a 10 percent higher chance of developing breast cancer than women who do not drink at all.

ALCOHOL ABUSE CONTINUUM

No use (1/3 of population)	Low risk use	High risk use "live to use"	Dependence "use to live"	Death
	Have self-imposed rules when drinking	Drink to get drunk	Need alcohol to feel normal, can't get through the day without a drink	Health problems/accidents
	No consequences from drinking	Have consequences such as legal problems, family problems, or loss of a job	Obvious physical problems from drinking, such as weight loss or a sickly look	
	Don't drink to intoxication	Drink to relieve stress or to escape life problems	Psychological dependence. Life centers around alcohol	
	No emphasis on using	Increased frequency in use and tolerance		
	No social problems	Start having physical effects from drinking including hangovers and blackouts		

PREGNANCY Any drinking during pregnancy is risky. A pregnant woman who drinks heavily puts her fetus at risk for learning and behavioral problems and abnormal facial features. Even moderate drinking during pregnancy can cause problems. Drinking during pregnancy also may increase the risk for preterm labor.

Some women should never drink at all, including:

- Anyone under age 21
- Anyone who takes medications that can interact negatively with alcohol
- Anyone who is pregnant or trying to conceive

How much is too much?

A standard drink is roughly 14 grams of pure alcohol, which is found in:

- 12 ounces of beer
- 5 ounces of wine
- 1.5 ounces of distilled spirits

The USDA defines moderate drinking as:

- Up to 1 drink per day for women
- Up to 2 drinks per day for men

At risk

NIAAA also defines how much drinking may put people at risk for developing alcohol dependence.

The Statistics: How often and how much do women drink?

Selected consumption statistics for women and men: U.S. adults 18 years of age and older

	Women	Men
% who had at least I drink in the past year	59.6	71.8
% who had at least I drink in their lifetime, but not in the past year	17.9	16.6
% who had at least I drink in their lifetime	77.5	88.4
% total lifetime abstainers (not even I drink)	22.5	11.6
% of past-year drinkers, by usual number of drinks consumed per drinking day:		
1	48.2	28.7
2	29.9	29.0
3+	21.9	42.3
% of past-year drinkers who drank 4+/5+ drinks on an occasion:		
Never in past year	71.2	56.9
Ever in past year	28.8	43.1
1 to 11 times in past year (< monthly)	14.2	15.3
12+ times in past year (monthly or more often)	14.6	27.8

	Women	Men
% who drank 12+ drinks over the course of the past year	42.1	61.2
% who drank 12+ drinks over the course of some year, but not the past year	13.4	16.6
% who never drank 12+ drinks over the course of any year	44.5	22.2
% of women who had a past-year pregnancy by drinking status:		
Did not drink at all in the past year	41.0	
Drank during the past year, but not at all during pregnancy	49.3	
Drank but in reduced quantities during pregnancy	8.1	
Drank and did not reduce consumption during pregnancy 1.5		

Source: **Wave 1 NESARC.**

Low risk drinking limits are:

Women:
No more than 7 drinks per week and no more than 3 drinks on any single day.

Men:
No more than 14 drinks per week and no more than 4 drinks on any single day.

To stay low risk, you must keep within both the single-day and weekly limits.

SIGNS OF ADOLESCENT SUBSTANCE ABUSE

- Changing circle of friends
- Undergoing emotional highs and lows
- Defying rules and regulations—ex.: going to school "high"
- Showing frustration and giving into peer pressure
- Sleeping more than usual—not sleeping
- Giving many excuses for staying out too late
- Withdrawing from family functions
- Failing to inform parents of significant school events and activities
- Intercepting the mail
- Isolating self (spending a lot of time in their room)
- Selling possessions
- Playing parents against each other
- Weight changes—change in physical appearance and hygiene
- Short tempered—defensive attitude—abusive behavior
- Coming home drunk or high
- Blood shot eyes—unfamiliar smell

Low risk does not mean no risk. Even within these limits, you can have problems if you drink too quickly or have other health issues. Drinking slowly, and making sure you eat enough while drinking, can help minimize alcohol's effects.

For more information please visit:
www.rethinking drinking.niaaa.nih.gov/

- Skipping school—absenteeism—drop extracurricular activities
- Drop in grades
- Suspensions—detentions from school
- Finding drug paraphernalia
- Legal problems

Although some of the behaviors mentioned above are to some extent normal for many adolescents, frequency of occurrence and clustering of these behaviors are indicative of possible substance abuse and needs to be investigated.

STAGES OF ADOLESCENTS USE, ABUSE, AND DEPENDENCY

STAGE 1: Experimental use (treatment—education)
- Occasional
- Low tolerance
- Often unplanned
- Mostly alcohol, some marijuana

STAGE 2: Misuse (treatment—outpatient)
- Increase tolerance
- Money spent
- Develop pattern
- Pride in being able to handle it
- Parents lied to about the extent of use
- Blackouts may begin to occur

STAGE 3: Abuse and Preoccupation (treatment—IOP, or Residential)
- Increase number of time high during the week
- Abusing other drugs
- Being intoxicated becomes common and normal
- May be in legal trouble
- School truancy and trouble with parents over use
- Possible dealing or fronting
- Most non-using friends dropped
- Alcohol and drugs become the center of adolescent activities
- Attempts to cut down or stop to demonstrate control

STAGE 4: Dependency/Addiction (treatment—residential)
- Drinking and/or drug use at school
- Being high was becoming a norm

- Using to face the day
- Adolescent is unable to determine what normal behavior is
- Worsening physical condition (weight loss, frequent illness, poor memory, loss of coordination)
- Very poor academic performance
- Loss of control grows worse

ENABLING BEHAVIORS

Each statement below describes an idea, feeling, attitude, or behavior that can be a small part of the complicated system of enabling: unknowingly helping someone's alcohol/drug problem to continue or get worse. Think about the degree to which each statement applies to your experience of what typically happens when there is someone with a alcohol/drug problem in your community/school.

1. Parents discover supplies of alcohol/drugs but are afraid to say anything to their kids or each other.
2. I think that if I'd been a better parent I could have prevented this; it's my fault.
3. I believe my child couldn't have an alcohol/drug problem because he/she doesn't fit my image of people who do.
4. Parents blame their child's alcohol/drug use on his/her friends.
5. I endure: I think my child will eventually grow out of his/her problem if I'm patient.
6. I excuse my child from participating in the usual family gatherings, or I make excuses for him/her.
7. Parents protect, cover up for, or lie for their child who has a alcohol/drug problem.
8. I no longer trust my child, but I'm afraid to tell them.
9. Parents doubt their own perceptions; they think they may be making something out of nothing.
10. I exert more control ("As long as you're living in this house you'll do what I say").
11. I maintain a "no-talk-rule" by not discussing with other family members painful events, feelings, or the possibility of an alcohol/drug problem in our family.
12. Parents prevent their child from experiencing the consequences of their behavior by "bailing them out" when in trouble with police, school, or others.
13. I'm afraid that if I talk with an adult about a situation that concerns me that he/she will only make the situation worse.
14. I excuse some teens drinking because I know that they have a lot of problems.
15. I excuse some teens drinking because I sometimes drink, myself.
16. I feel that it isn't any of my business if other teens drink.

OTHER FAMILY INFLUENCES ON DRINKING CHOICES

- Parents hold and model low-risk attitudes
- There is a close parent/child relationship
- Parent knows where the child is
- Parents are seen by the child as not too strict but not too lenient
- There is no conflict in message given from time to time or between major message givers.

HOW FAMILIES CAN INFLUENCE DRINKING CHOICES

Family influences that promote the low-risk choice of abstaining	Family influences that promote other low-risk choices
Parent abstain	Parents are low-risk drinkers or abstainers.
Parents do not give alcohol to the child at home.	Parents give alcohol to child at home very infrequently.
Parents clearly communicate expectations for abstinence.	Parents accept low-risk drinking choices by the child but strongly disapprove of high-risk choices.
The child frequently participates in a church or other groups that promote abstinence by members.	The child frequently participates in a church or other groups that are accepting of low-risk drinking choices by members.
The child values doing well at school more than being independent.	The child values doing well at school more than being independent.
The child has age-appropriate limits on socializing, spending money, and work.	The child has age-appropriate limits on socializing, spending money, and work.

Normal adolescent behavior	Drug-affected behavior
FRIENDS	
Some shifting around;	Friends dropped;
Best friend—larger group	Older crowd
Or change of groups;	Vague about names;
Conforms to peer group in manner, dress and values	"junkie" behavior
FAMILY	
Questions rules/regulations;	Hostile to rules/regulations;
Begin to distance self from family;	Breaks curfew, lies, sneaks around, steals, becomes isolated from family; defensive or vague about activities;
Peer group becomes more important;	Extreme lack of respect; Physical or mental violence; very erratic eating habits
Need for privacy, secrecy increases may show lack of respect;	
Some changes in eating habits.	
RELIGION	
Questions parents' religious beliefs; May "try out" other religions	Becomes anti-religion; Uncomfortable talking about it.
SCHOOL	
Increased involvement in social and/or athletic activities;	Decreased involvement;
Academics may or may not be important; going to a school social function;	Failing grades; truancy issues; suspensions or even expulsions;
LEGAL	
May be involved in some minor infractions.	Serious offenses—OWI;
	Auto accidents;
	Thefts; assaults
PHYSICAL & PSYCHOLOGICAL	
Rapid physical growth: fat/thin problem;	Weight loss
Lack of bodily proportion;	Poor health;
Preoccupation with "faults";	Lethargic attitude;
Strong mood swings;	Extreme mood swings;
Time of great energy	Blackouts

NOTES

PROVIDING TO MINORS—KNOW THE LAW, AVOID THE RISK

CONTRIBUTING TO THE DELINQUENCY OF A MINOR
Persons Under Legal Age (PULA) Statute

"It is illegal to sell, give, or otherwise supply alcoholic beverages to any person knowing or having reasonable cause to believe that person to be under legal age."

- **It is illegal to sell, give, or supply alcohol to any person you know or suspect to be under 21.**

"Punishable by a fine of 500–7500 and/or a maximum of five years' imprisonment, depending on whether the alcohol consumption results in a serious injury to any person."

- **The person that provides alcohol to a minor is held legally responsible for that minor's alcohol-related delinquent acts, and any injuries or deaths that result from that minor's acts.**

"It is illegal for those under the legal age to purchase or attempt to purchase, or individually or jointly have alcoholic beverages in their possession or control unless the alcohol was dispensed to a person under legal age within a private home and with the knowledge, presence and consent of that minor's parent or legal guardian."

- **Unless a minor is in the privacy of his own home and the alcohol was provided by his legal guardian, it is illegal for that minor to have alcohol in their possession.**

- **If the minor leaves the home after consuming alcohol, the parent/guardian is then held responsible for any of that minor's actions.**

"It is illegal to sell, dispense, or give to an intoxicated person, or one simulating intoxication, any alcoholic liquor, wine, or beer."

HEALTH EFFECTS OF ALCOHOL

EFFECTS ON THE BRAIN

The **brain does not completely develop until a person is around 21 years** old, which means any brain damage before this age could be permanent (Scholastic Choices, May 2001).

Studies discovered that the hippocampus (the part of the brain that assists with **memory and learning) is about 10% smaller and**

less effective in young adults that were heavy drinkers than in those who were non-drinkers (Scholastic Choices, May 2001).

Individuals who are alcohol dependent show significant impairment in verbal skills on standardized tests (VA Medical Center, Univ. of California, 2001).

EFFECTS ON THE BODY

Each year, **five times as many individuals under 21 die from alcohol overdose than from any other drug,** legal or illegal. Signs of alcohol overdose include: unconsciousness, shallow breathing, vomiting, cardiac arrest, or irregular heartbeat, and low body temperature.

Many **organs are affected more quickly in drinkers under 21,** than in drinkers 21 and older. Rapid damage can occur in the **liver, pancreas, brain, reproductive system, and stomach.**

LIFESTYLE EFFECTS

Individuals under 21 who drink are four times **more likely to develop alcohol dependence** than those who begin drinking at age 21 (NIAAA, 1997).

Young adults who consume alcohol are **more likely to become sexually active at an earlier age,** to have sex more often, and to engage in unprotected sex, placing them at risk for HIV and other sexually transmitted diseases (OIG, 1992).

Individuals under 21 who drink are **7.5 times more likely to use any illicit drug** and **50 times more likely to use cocaine** than their non-drinking peers (CASA, 1994).

Alcohol is associated with the **three leading causes of death** in young adults—accidents, homicides, and suicides (National Center for Substance Abuse at Columbia University, 2003).

ALCOHOL'S TRIP THROUGH THE BODY

Mouth and Esophagus: Alcohol is an irritant to the delicate linings of the throat and food pipe. It burns as it goes down.

Stomach and Intestines: Alcohol has an irritating effect on the stomach's protective lining, resulting in gastric or duodenal ulcers. This condition, if it becomes acute, can cause peritonitis, or perforation of the stomach wall. In the small intestine, alcohol blocks absorption of such substances as thiamine, folic acid, fat, vitamin B1, vitamin B12, and amino acids.

Bloodstream: 95% of the alcohol taken into the body is absorbed into the bloodstream through the lining of the stomach and duodenum. Once in the bloodstream, alcohol quickly goes to every cell and tissue in the body. Alcohol causes red blood cells to clump together in sticky wads, slowing circulation and depriving tissues of oxygen. It also causes anemia by reducing red blood cell production. Alcohol slows the ability of white cells to engulf and destroy bacteria and degenerates the clotting ability of blood platelets.

Pancreas: Alcohol irritates the cells of the pancreas, causing them to swell, thus blocking the flow of digestive enzymes. The chemicals, unable to enter the small intestine, begin to digest the pancreas, leading to acute hemorrhagic pancreatitis. One out of five patients who develop this disease dies during the first attack. Pancreatitis can destroy the pancreas and cause the block of insulin, thus resulting in diabetes.

Liver: Alcohol inflames the cells of the liver, causing them to swell, thus blocking the tiny canal to the small intestine. This prevents the bile from being filtered properly through the liver. Jaundice develops, turning the whites of the eyes and skin yellow. Each drink of alcohol increases the number of liver cells destroyed, eventually causing cirrhosis of the liver. This disease is eight times more frequent among alcoholics than among non-alcoholics.

Heart: Alcohol causes inflammation of the heart muscle. It has a toxic effect on the heart and causes increased amounts of fat to collect, thus disrupting its normal metabolism.

Urinary Bladder and Kidneys: Alcohol inflames the lining of the urinary bladder, making it unable to stretch properly. In the kidneys, alcohol causes increased loss of fluids through its irritating effect.

Sex Glands: Swelling of the prostate gland caused by alcohol interferes with the ability of the male to perform sexually. It also interferes with the ability to climax during intercourse.

Brain: The most dramatic and noticed effect of alcohol is on the brain. It depresses brain centers, progressively producing uncoordination, confusion, disorientation, stupor, anesthesia, coma, death. Alcohol kills brain cells, and brain damage is permanent. Drinking over a period of time causes loss of memory, judgment, and learning ability.

THE "SAFE HOME" HOAX

Through interviews with local teens and parents, investigators learned that the house where Shelby died had a reputation as a "safe home." Says Benito: "Parents in the community told us that the parents allowed what they called 'responsible drinking.' [Parents like these] believe that underage drinking can be done safely; that even if teens overdo it, as they often do, as long as they are being chaperoned and not driving, nothing tragic will happen. They believe kids are going to experiment with drinking anyway, so it may as well happen at home, with adults present." (Jane's father told police he didn't allow other people's children to consume alcohol in his home, although he admitted he allowed his own underage children to drink in moderation.)

As they spoke with the police, the Allens were shocked to discover that although providing alcohol to a minor who was not one's own child was illegal in California, the state provided significant immunity to hosts in this situation through what was known as Civil Code Section 1714, which became law in 1978. When it was enacted, lawmakers felt that too many suits were being filed against deep-pocketed hosts—that guests were overindulging, which led to injury, and then refusing to assume blame. In a nutshell, the code says those who choose to drink too much are responsible for what happens, not those who provide the alcohol.

Currently, 23 states have some degree of social-host immunity that protects those who serve underage guests. At the time of Shelby's death, California was one of only a few states to provide social hosts with nearly full civil-lawsuit protection. It's a stance on responsibility that's totally reasonable, say many—including Patrick Beasley, the Redding attorney retained by the family who hosted Shelby Allen on the night she died.

"If I put a fifth of vodka in front of you, it's your choice [whether] to drink it and how much of it to drink," Beasley says. "Whether or not you abuse it has nothing to do with me."

"Not if the drinker is a kid," Debbie Allen counters. And more and more parents are beginning to agree. "Underage drinking is not a moral, constitutional, or cultural issue," says Cindy Schaider, executive director of the Casa Grande Alliance, a nonprofit drug- and alcohol-abuse prevention coalition in Arizona that, among other things, works to make social hosting for minors a punishable offense. "It's a health and safety issue. Communities are recognizing this, and thus the increased call for these social-host ordinances."

The goal of people who support social-host responsibility is simple: "Homeowners [or renters] can no longer claim they had no idea minors were drinking on their premises. These laws make residents culpable for any underage drinking that goes on in their home and/ or any damage or injury that occurs as a result," says Anthony Wagner, policy and media strategist for the Institute for Public Strategies, a nonprofit public-health-and-safety advocacy group in San Diego. (Wagner has also helped shape and implement social-host ordinances.) "Adults need to understand why underage drinking is dangerous, and that serving liquor to someone under 21 isn't worth what it could end up costing you."

NOTES

NOTES

A DEADLY RITE OF PASSAGE

That's a hard message to get across when teen drinking persists as the great American rite of passage. Consider how it's depicted in movies: From *Sixteen Candles* (released in 1984) to *Superbad* (2007) and beyond, underage drinking has provided decades of coming-of-age-flick entertainment. Generations have giggled over buckets of popcorn as teenagers have vomited on each other, passed out, woken up in strange beds, and seduced one another's best friends, girlfriends, and even parents, only to arrive at the morning after with a hangover, some wild experiences, skyrocketing popularity, and a valuable life lesson learned to boot.

That's the Hollywood version. In real life, the results are too often tragic. According to the Substance Abuse and Mental Health Services Administration (SAMHSA), more than 500 underage drinkers are rushed to ERs in a typical day, and about 5,000 people under 21 die annually of alcohol-related injuries—a number, experts are quick to point out, that is likely to be low because of underreporting.

There's a simple reason why underage drinkers are so likely to be injured or to die: "Kids drink to get drunk," says Frances M. Harding, director of SAMHSA's Center for Substance Abuse Prevention. "They're not having a glass of wine with a meal and enjoying the conversation. They're drinking five drinks or more when they're binge drinking." The landmark College Alcohol Study conducted by the Harvard School of Public Health (a 14-year endeavor involving four national surveys) found that the drinking style of many college students was "one of excess and intoxication." One in five students was a frequent binge drinker, and this group of students consumed three-quarters of the alcohol that all college students drank.

Technically defined as consuming five or more drinks on a single occasion for males and four or more drinks for females, binge drinking can have a devastating impact. "We are prosecuting teenagers who otherwise seem to be good kids for serious crimes all the time, from robberies to rape, and I have to say about 90 percent of these involve alcohol," reports Todd Spitzer, a 20-year law-enforcement veteran (he's been a police officer and a prosecutor) and former state assemblyman who authored a California law enacting tougher penalties for underage DUI offenders. "Kids just do really stupid things when they drink, because their judgment is impaired."

Experts warn that young brains simply cannot process this amount of alcohol. "The brain doesn't stop growing until the mid-20s, and one of the first regions of the brain affected by alcohol—and affected most dramatically—is the area responsible for judgment and decision-making," explains Schaider.

Although binge-drinking behavior is actually down (from 10.7 percent in 2002 to 8.8 percent in 2009 among 12- to 17-year-olds, according to the National Survey on Drug Use and Health), this doesn't mean parents can breathe a sigh of relief. "What concerns me most is the attitude of the parents [toward drinking]," says Daniel G. Amen, M.D., a child psychiatrist, medical director of the Amen Clinics (headquartered in Newport Beach, CA), and coauthor of *Unchain Your Brain: 10 Steps to Breaking the Addictions That Steal Your Life*. "There is a powerful countercultural strain, and one of the ways you see it is the tolerance of 'soft' drugs—like alcohol, prescription medications, and pot. Once you decrease the idea that a drug is dangerous, use of that drug goes up," Dr. Amen says. "If parents think these substances aren't harmful, then they should just see the brain scans. Alcohol decreases functioning and blood flow. When the brain is in this period of intense growth, development is dramatically disrupted. Kids with frequent alcohol use are, quite simply, impaired."

Yet many parents believe drinking alcohol is a relatively safe alternative to drug use, says Harding. In fact, in 2005, the Century Council Survey found that 21 percent of moms of underage girls believed it was OK for teenagers to drink under parental supervision and 20 percent said drinking was a natural part of growing up. "We have to change that outdated way of thinking," insists Schaider. "Social hosting buys into the thinking that kids are going to drink no matter what. But if we educate our kids about the permanent damage alcohol is doing, I am convinced, the kids themselves won't want to drink. If parents were educated about the recent research on drinking, they wouldn't want their kids to drink, either."

The Legal Loophole

Shelby's death compelled Debbie Allen to research what had killed her. "I learned that the party culture had drastically changed since I partied as a teen," she explains. "Kids are drinking differently, and aren't being taught that the way they are drinking can kill them." But what shocked Debbie the most was learning that more and more parents were participating in this dangerous drinking culture by allowing minors to have access to alcohol. Says Debbie: "Shelby lied to us about her whereabouts so she could go to a house where she could 'have fun' experimenting with illegal drinking. She made poor choices, but these poor choices should not have led to her death. Shelby should have known better . . . we all should have. I get it now."

Increasingly, parents who "get" the dangers of underage drinking have had it with parents who don't. Twenty-seven states now have social-host laws on the books. Richard Campbell, a trial lawyer with expertise in social-host cases, knows just how wrong teen drinking can go. He cites a case in Easthampton, MA, in 2007, in which Alexis Garcia, 15, and her best friend shared a bottle of vodka that the pal had received from her dad as a gift. After the two downed it, Lexi went upstairs to take a shower and sober up. She was found facedown in the tub, drowned. He recalls 17-year-old Meaghan Duggan, who, while drinking at a house party in the basement of a close friend's North Andover, MA, home, tripped on a step, suffered a skull fracture, and died as intoxicated underage partiers repeatedly stepped over her body, while the father of the household was fully aware of the underage drinking going on.

As shocking as these cases are, the state often can't file criminal charges, which could lead to jail sentences, against the hosts. Campbell calls civil action, which may provide financial compensation, "the only recourse parents who have lost a child may have. But most of my clients who seek civil damages do so not for the money—most don't care if they ever see a penny. They do it to send a message, to deter other parents who are tempted to throw these kinds of 'safe' drinking parties."

For the Allen family, District Attorney Benito wanted to seek justice for what had unfolded late that December night. He took Shelby's case to a grand jury, and their stance was clear: Go after the parents in the host family. "But legally I couldn't, because by verbalizing the order not to drink (even though alcohol was easily accessible), by making the 911 call, by performing CPR, and also by not being aware of how severe Shelby's condition was, [the parents] were not legally responsible for what occurred," Benito says. "Initially I thought I could not file charges against Jane. But the cell phone texting indicated clearly that she was present the entire time Shelby was dying. And that Shelby died as a direct result of this girl's failure to provide aid." In the legal system, finding failure to provide aid is based on what is called "creating a duty," or responsibility—in this situation, that means providing the illegal substance (liquor) to the point that another person becomes completely at one's mercy: "As a result, in criminal court, you then have the responsibility to at least seek help on this person's behalf," Benito adds.

His decision to file charges of involuntary manslaughter against 16-year-old Jane was not a popular one in the community. "LEAVE HER ALONE," one blogger wrote angrily. Others accused the Allens of trying to find people to blame for their daughter's death and said it was Shelby who had drunk the alcohol that killed her.

"The district attorney made his decision to prosecute Shelby's friend based on his view of the law," Debbie says. "He spent a good deal of time explaining his legal theory to us, and once we understood why charges were appropriate, we supported the prosecution . . . . Our laws say you file in civil court to seek compensation for damages caused by others," she explains, then swallows hard and adds, "and my family has been damaged in ways that cannot be described. My life will never be the same. I still feel like I am made of stone—that's how I've felt since the day Shelby died. It doesn't go away. I have derived what comfort I can from my faith, but what a terrible impact this has had on Tera, on my husband, on our marriage."

Debbie then calmly and methodically recites a list of the specific reasons the Allens filed their civil lawsuit: "The family in question has never been required to tell the truth under oath; the family invited my daughter to their house after midnight when the family had already been drinking; this family provided my daughter with uncontrolled access to a full bar and left her with two other teenagers, knowing they might drink alcohol; a family member saw my daughter become seriously ill to the point where any normal person would have called for emergency medical aid. In my opinion, this family deliberately chose not to call for the medical help that would have saved her life."

Debbie pauses for a moment and then says quietly, "I almost wish this had happened out on the street, because at least there, I think Shelby would have gotten help. A stranger would have at least called 911 for Shelby. A stranger would have tried to contact her parents. My daughter made poor choices that night, but teenagers make poor choices. It's our responsibility as adults to help them survive those poor choices."

In response to critics who say that Jane was too young to know how to handle such a dire situation, Benito reframes the issue: "We weren't asking her to perform heart surgery or CPR; we were simply asking her to tell an adult. Alyssa, a girl of similar age, showed us how to act in this situation. When she saw Shelby's state, she immediately told an adult—an older sister—who called the father. This started the chain reaction to get Shelby help. This was the proper sequence of events. A girl of a similar age did the right thing."

Early in the texting, the moment when Jane described Shelby as "half snoring shaking" marked a critical turning point in the night's events: The forensic pathologist assigned to the case told Benito she'd probably been convulsing at that point. "Had medical help arrived, Shelby could have survived," says Benito.

In November 2009, Jane was acquitted. The Honorable Daniel Flynn ruled that she had not behaved in a criminally negligent way, and found that it was unclear how the second bottle of vodka had been provided for Shelby to fulfill her "unwavering intent" to down 15 vodka shots that night. Despite the outcome, Benito insists that this proceeding did increase awareness about how dangerous binge drinking and social hosting can be—and will continue to. "If one life is saved because of the awareness this raised, it's worth it," he says.

In his statement to the press, Adam Ryan, the attorney who represented the accused teenager during the proceeding, stressed that there was no winner in the case, stating that his client had lost a dear friend and that she would have to live with that loss—and her role in it. He argued that his client had been too young and inexperienced to realize that her friend was in danger of dying from alcohol poisoning.

While the host family cannot comment publicly about Shelby's death for legal reasons, Beasley, who is defending them in the civil suit, insists that his clients' lives have been turned upside down

NOTES

because a "deeply disturbed girl . . . on a suicide mission" was invited to their home for the night—and chose to drink herself to death there. "This case, which is about revenge and money, never should have been litigated," he says. "What happened was a horrible tragedy. I hate this case. But the Allens should have opened their arms to my clients, to their young daughter, who has suffered tremendously over the death of her friend, instead of lashing out vindictively."

"We're not making Shelby out to be a choirgirl," responds Mark R. Swartz, the Gold River, CA, attorney who is representing the Allens this time around. "It's established that no one forced her to drink." Friends and teachers were interviewed after Shelby's death, but no one presented an image of her as a troubled teen. Regardless of Shelby's reputation, Swartz continues, "if she was out of control or drinking too much, it was her friend [Jane's] responsibility to tell the parents what was happening. The father, in particular, should have known better than to leave a group of teenage girls alone with access to a full bar. He should have known what was going on in his own house. And he shouldn't have been allowing access to alcohol to underage kids, especially when he was concerned they were interested in the alcohol."

The Allens were deeply disappointed that there was no finding of criminal responsibility for any of the family members, not even a citation for providing alcohol to a minor. They filed their civil suit against the host family last spring; the trial is set to begin in August. Jane's family has denied all allegations.

The lawsuits don't end there: Beasley, the host family's attorney, has filed a counterclaim against Alyssa, blaming her for the tragedy that unfolded that night, alleging that Alyssa should have sought help for Shelby and, by not doing so, contributed to her death. Alyssa has denied those allegations.

A MOTHER'S MISSION

The Allens say the suit is not about retribution. It's about finding meaning and doing some good in the wake of Shelby's death. The germ of an idea took root in Debbie's mind soon after her loss. What could others learn from this tragedy? How could she help other teens and parents as the legal process took off on its own track? The idea of sharing the sad lessons from that night took shape, and by the time of Shelby's funeral—held the weekend after her death—information about what Debble called "Shelby Rules" was available for mourners after the service. Debble Allen gave her first presentation about alcohol poisoning on January 5, 2009, not quite three weeks after burying her child.

"Life gives you two choices when you suffer a tragedy: Give up or move on. I have a husband and another child to love and take care of I must move on, for their sake if not mine," Debbie says. "But now I also have a mother's passion to educate teens about the dangers of alcohol poisoning amid this new culture of binge drinking—a danger many know nothing about, and a danger my family learned about in the hardest way imaginable. It's not a matter of staying strong; it's a matter of doing what needs to be done, no matter how you are feeling, no matter how sad you are. I believe—and believed almost right away—this is what Shelby would have wanted me to do."

And so Debbie set out to educate students about the dangers of binge drinking and alcohol poisoning through Shelby's Rules, a nonprofit education foundation. "Shelby used to tell me, 'Mom, just tell me how things work. That's how I'm wired,'" Debbie says. "What she meant was, she wasn't going to do or not do something just because I told her my stance on it. She required reasons. Facts. Explanations. I think most kids do.

"If I had told her how alcohol affects the body, how alcohol relaxes every muscle in the body, including the gag reflex, so that if your body is trying to get rid of the booze that's poisoning it, the muscles in the throat may be too slow to respond, and you can choke on your own vomit or not be able to vomit at all . . . if I had explained these specifics to Shelby, she might still be alive."

So, Debbie says, "I explain this stuff to these [other] kids. I admit that I didn't know enough about the dangers of alcohol to properly educate my children about them. I make sure other kids know, 'When in doubt, call 911,' and 'Vomiting = Alcohol poisoning.' " These are two of the key mottoes featured prominently in the materials Debbie hands out at her talks and in the public service messages her organization distributes. She has received letters of appreciation and interest from all over the country—attention sparked in part by the fact that Shelby's uncle, executive producer for the NBC series *ER* at the time, had his niece's story woven into the show's final episode, which aired the spring following Shelby's death.

In over 100 classrooms and auditoriums along the West Coast, Debbie has displayed an 8-ounce water bottle, noting that this was the amount of alcohol that was found in her daughter's body. "I explain that at about a blood alcohol level of 0.16, kids are generally throwing up, and by 0.30, they are passing out. Allowing someone to pass out after drinking and leaving that person to 'sleep it off' may actually be leaving someone to die," says Debbie. "Most kids don't know that the only way to save that person's life if he or she has in fact had too much to drink is to get medical attention immediately." "Shelby's Rules" share specific steps to take: Wake the person up; shake him; pinch him; if he doesn't respond, call 911 and then involve an adult.

The goal, Debbie insists, is not to "teach kids how to drink," as some parents within the community have complained, but to provide kids with an education that will encourage them to take alcohol seriously, hopefully avoid it altogether, and recognize a deadly situation and take the appropriate steps. Debbie takes special pride in the stories she's heard about underage drinkers rescuing their friends from alcohol

NOTES

poisoning—because they knew what to do. "After one presentation I gave in Anderson, [CA], when a teen started vomiting after drinking at a party, his friends immediately marched him home," she recalls. "The boy made it home and collapsed into his mother's arms." His mother then took him to the emergency room, where he was successfully treated for acute alcohol poisoning. "One of the mothers checked to see if those boys were in the group that had seen my presentation, and they were," she reports happily. "It's proof this kind of alcohol education can really save lives."

Debbie often tours with Shelby's best friend, Alyssa—now a college student—who continues to have night-mares about that night. Alyssa, who describes herself as having been "guilt-ridden for months," was cooperative in the investigation of Shelby's death. She also admitted to underage drinking, served her 50 hours of community service with the Shelby's Rules foundation, and made the issue of alcohol poisoning and underage drinking her senior project. Her new-found zero-tolerance perspective on underage drinking, however, has not made her popular with kids her age.

"My stance is that teens shouldn't experiment with alcohol, which means they shouldn't drink at all, because what they wind up doing is seeing how much they can drink before they pass out or get sick. They don't think of alcohol as something that can kill you," Alyssa says. "The kids at our high school, right after Shelby died, were all shocked and kind of scared straight. But that didn't even last very long. Now most of them are drinking just like they did before. One of our friends was talking to me the other day about how wasted she got, how she was throwing up, and I just looked at her like, *Didn't you learn anything from Shelby's death?* Kids just don't get it. They need more information, and they need to hear it more often."

Debbie is also involved in other aspects of the teen binge-drinking issue. She lobbies for tougher underage-drinking and social-host laws. Last spring, she testified for the passage of AB 2486, a California bill seeking to hold adults civilly liable for damages if they knowingly furnish alcohol to underage drinkers in their homes. At the hearing, most-like State Senator Noreen Evans—expressed dismay. "I have to say, I always thought this was the law and I'm just shocked to find out it's not," Evans said, shaking her head. "It should have been the law all along." On August 30, 2010, the bill became state law. A companion amnesty bill—which provides criminal protection for minors who call 911 to assist an underage drinker in difficulty—was signed into law a month later.

As pleased as she is with these results, Debbie Allen's path as an activist has been a fraught one—not just because of the loss she's endured, but also because of the reception her actions have met with. "I've lost good friends as a result of the incident itself and the aftermath," she says, "parents of Shelby's friends—who were friends of mine—who have not provided the support we have asked for: agreement that parents should not allow kids to drink in their homes, or help with our efforts to change laws that provide immunity for parents who do."

This kind of collateral damage doesn't give Debbie even a split second of pause. Her mission is clear. "I've had people say, 'You've turned your whole life over to this issue; it must be very therapeutic for you,' " she says. "Well, it's not therapeutic. Every time I give a presentation, it's painful. My grief has not lessened. In some ways, it has grown as time has passed. No one's child should have to die on a cold bathroom floor while parents sleep warm in beds nearby. I'm determined to save kids' lives. Not my kid's. It's too late for my kid. Other people's kids. *Your* kid."

ILLEGAL DRUGS OF ABUSE

MARIJUANA

Marijuana is the most commonly abused illicit drug in the United States. It is a dry, shredded green and brown mix of flowers, stems, seeds, and leaves derived from the hemp plant *Cannabis sativa*. The main active chemical in marijuana is delta-9-tetrahydrocannabinol, or THC for short.

Marijuana is usually smoked as a cigarette (joint) or in a pipe. It is also smoked in blunts, which are cigars that have been emptied of tobacco and refilled with a mixture of marijuana and tobacco. This mode of delivery combines marijuana's active ingredients with nicotine and other harmful chemicals. Marijuana can also be mixed in food or brewed as a tea. Marijuana smoke has a pungent and distinctive, usually sweet-and-sour odor.

Marijuana intoxication can cause distorted perceptions, impaired coordination, difficulty with thinking and problem solving, and problems with learning and memory. Research has shown that, in chronic users, marijuana's adverse impact on learning and memory can last for days or weeks after the acute effects of the drug wear off. As a result, someone who smokes marijuana every day may be functioning at a suboptimal intellectual level all of the time.

Behavioral interventions, including cognitive-behavioral therapy and motivational incentives (i.e., providing vouchers for goods or services to patients who remain abstinent) have shown efficacy in treating marijuana dependence. Although no medications are currently available, recent discoveries about the workings of the cannabinoid system offer promise for the development of medications to ease withdrawal, block the intoxicating effects of marijuana, and prevent relapse.

The latest treatment data indicate that in 2008 marijuana accounted for 17 percent of admissions (322,000) to treatment facilities in the United States, second only to opiates among illicit substances. Marijuana admissions were primarily male (74 percent), White (49 percent), and young (30 percent were in the 12–17 age range).

Source: http://www.drugabuse.gov/Infofacts/marijuana.html

NOTES

COCAINE

In 2009, 4.8 million Americans age 12 and older had abused cocaine in any form and 1.0 million had abused crack at least once in the year prior to being surveyed. *Source: National Survey on Drug Use and Health (Substance Abuse and Mental Health Administration Web Site).*

One illegal drug of abuse is cocaine, a stimulant. Powder cocaine can be snorted or dissolved in water and then injected. Crack is the street name given to the form of cocaine that has been processed to make a rock crystal, which, when heated, produces vapors that are smoked. The term "crack" refers to the crackling sound produced by the rock as it is heated.

Cocaine is typically ingested by snorting, injecting, and smoking. Snorting is the process of inhaling cocaine powder through the nose, where it is absorbed into the bloodstream through the nasal tissues. Injecting is the use of a needle to insert the drug directly into the bloodstream. Smoking involves inhaling cocaine vapor or smoke into the lungs, where absorption into the bloodstream is as rapid as it is by injection. All three methods of cocaine abuse can lead to addiction and other severe health problems, including increasing the risk of contracting HIV/AIDS and other infectious diseases.

Cocaine creates feelings of increased energy and mental alertness. However, the intensity and duration of cocaine's effects depend on the route of drug administration. The faster cocaine is absorbed into the bloodstream and delivered to the brain, the more intense the high. Injecting or smoking cocaine produces a quicker, stronger high than snorting. On the other hand, faster absorption usually means shorter duration of action: the high from snorting cocaine may last 15 to 30 minutes, but the high from smoking may last only 5 to 10 minutes. In order to sustain the high, cocaine must be administered again. For

© 2012, ejwhite, Shutterstock, Inc.

this reason, cocaine is sometimes abused in binges—taken repeatedly within a relatively short period of time, at increasingly higher doses.

Abusing cocaine has a variety of adverse effects on the body. Cocaine constricts blood vessels, dilates pupils, and increases body temperature, heart rate, and blood pressure. It can also cause headaches and gastrointestinal complications such as abdominal pain and nausea. Because cocaine tends to decrease appetite, chronic users can become malnourished as well. _Source: http://www.drugabuse.gov/ Infofacts/cocaine.html_

When withdrawing from cocaine, a person may experience depression, hypersomnia or insomnia, fatigue, anxiety, irritability, poor concentration, psychomotor retardation, paranoia, and drug craving. Withdrawal from cocaine and other stimulants are not usually associated with medical complications. _Source: Substance Abuse and Mental Health Administration, Detoxification and Substance Abuse Treatment_.

METHAMPHETAMINE

Methamphetamine is a potent and highly addictive psychostimulant According to one national survey, approximately 10 million people in the United States have tried methamphetamine at least once.

Methamphetamine comes in many forms. It can be smoked, snorted, injected, or orally ingested. The preferred method of methamphetamine abuse varies by geographical region and has changed over time. The drug alters mood in different ways, depending on how it is taken. Immediately after smoking the drug or injecting it intravenously, the user experiences an intense rush or "flash" that lasts only a few minutes and is described as extremely pleasurable. Snorting or oral ingestion produces euphoria—a high but not an intense rush. Snorting produces effects within 3 to 5 minutes, and oral ingestion produces effects within 15 to 20 minutes.

As with similar stimulants, methamphetamine most often is used in a "binge and crash" pattern. Because the pleasurable effects of methamphetamine disappear even before the drug concentration in the blood falls significantly—users try to maintain the high by taking more of the drug. In some cases, abusers indulge in a form of binging known as a "run," foregoing food and sleep while continuing abuse for up to several days.

Methamphetamine abuse leads to devastating medical, psychological, and social consequences. Adverse health effects include memory loss, aggression, psychotic behavior, heart damage, malnutrition, and severe dental problems. Methamphetamine abuse also contributes to increased transmission of infectious diseases, such as hepatitis and HIV/ AIDS, and can infuse whole communities with new waves of crime, unemployment, child neglect or abuse, and other social ills. (_Source: http://www.drugabuse.gov/ResearchReports/methamph/methamph3.html_)

METHAMPHETAMINE VS. COCAINE

Stimulant	Stimulant and local anesthetic
Man-made	Plant-derived
Smoking produces a long-lasting high	Smoking produces a brief high
50% of the drug is removed from the body in 12 hours	50% of the drug is removed from the body in 1 hour
Increases dopamine release and blocks dopamine re-uptake	Blocks dopamine re-uptake
Limited medical use	Limited use as a local anesthetic in some surgical procedures

Source: http://www.drugabuse.gov/ResearchReports/methamph/methamph3.html

For example, children who live at or visit drug-production sites or are present during drug production are at risk for:

- Inhalation, absorption, or ingestion of toxic chemicals, drugs, or contaminated foods or drink that may result in respiratory difficulties, nausea, chest pain, eye and tissue irritation, chemical burns, and death;
- Fires and explosions resulting from dangerous methamphetamine production processes;
- Abuse and neglect by parents who often binge on methamphetamine and traumatic consequences that result; and
- Hazardous living conditions (firearms, code violations, poor ventilation, and sanitation). Source: http://www.justice.gov/dea/concern/meth_children.html

While both stimulants, methamphetamine and cocaine are different.

HEROIN

Heroin is an illegal, highly addictive drug. It is both the most abused and the most rapidly acting of the opiates. Heroin is processed from morphine, a naturally occurring substance extracted from the seed pod of certain varieties of poppy plants. It is typically sold as a white or brownish powder or as the black sticky substance known on the streets as "black tar heroin." Although purer heroin is becoming more common, most street heroin is "cut" with other drugs or with substances such as sugar, starch, powdered milk, or quinine. Street heroin

Source: http://www.nida.nih.gov/ResearchReports/Heroin/heroin3.html#short

also can be cut with strychnine or other poisons. Because heroin abusers do not know the actual strength of the drug or its true contents, they are at risk of overdose or death. *Source: http://www.nida.nih.gov/ResearchReports/Heroin/heroin2.html#what*

Heroin is usually injected, sniffed/snorted, or smoked. Typically, a heroin abuser may inject up to four times a day. Intravenous injection provides the greatest intensity and most rapid onset of euphoria (7 to 8 seconds), while intramuscular injection produces a relatively slow onset of euphoria (5 to 8 minutes). When heroin is sniffed or smoked, peak effects are usually felt within 10 to 15 minutes. NIDA researchers have confirmed that all forms of heroin administration are addictive. *Source: http://www.nida.nih.gov/ResearchReports/Heroin/heroin2.html#what*

Heroin abuse has repercussions that extend far beyond the individual user. The medical and social consequences of drug abuse include HIV/AIDS, tuberculosis, fetal effects, crime, violence, and disruptions in family, workplace, and educational environments. Although heroin abuse has trended downward during the past several years, its prevalence is still higher than in the early 1990s. Heroin also is increasing in purity and decreasing in price, which makes it an attractive option for young people. *Source: http://www.nida.nih.gov/ResearchReports/Heroin/Heroin.html*

Opiate withdrawal is rarely fatal. It is characterized by acute withdrawal symptoms which peak 48 to 72 hours after the last opiate dose and disappear within 7 to 10 days, to be followed by a longer term abstinence syndrome of general malaise and opioid craving.

A variety of effective treatments are available for heroin addiction. Treatment tends to be more effective when heroin abuse is identified

NOTES

SHORT- AND LONG-TERM EFFECTS OF HEROIN USE

Short-Term Effects	Long-Term Effects
"Rush"	Addiction
Depressed respiration	Infectious diseases, for example, HIV/AIDS and hepatitis B and C
Clouded mental functioning	Collapsed veins
	Bacterial infections
Nausea and vomiting	Abscesses
Suppression of pain	Infection of heart lining and valves
Spontaneous abortion	Arthritis and other rheumatologic problems

NOTES

early. The treatments that follow vary depending on the individual, but methadone, a synthetic opiate that blocks the effects of heroin and eliminates withdrawal symptoms, has a proven record of success for people addicted to heroin. Other pharmaceutical approaches, such as buprenorphine, and many behavioral therapies also are used for treating heroin addiction. Buprenorphine is a recent addition to the array of medications now available for treating addiction to heroin and other opiates. This medication is different from methadone in that it offers less risk of addiction and can be prescribed in the privacy of a doctor's office. Buprenorphine/naloxone (Suboxone) is a combination drug product formulated to minimize abuse. *Source: http://www. nida.nih.gov/ResearchReports/Heroin/heroin5.html#treatment*

IOWA 2007 NASADAD STATE SNAPSHOT ON METHAMPHETAMINE

2006 DEMOGRAPHICS

- 82.93 White
- 34.95% Between the ages of 25–34
- 57.31% Male
- 42.69% Female

TREATMENT EFFECTIVENESS DATA

Three studies done in <u>Iowa Iowa Adult Methamphetamine Treatment Project - Final Report, 2003; Iowa Outcomes Monitoring System (IOMS) Iowa Project, 2006</u>; and <u>Final Report on the Polk County Adult Drug Court, 2001</u>] demonstrate that treatment for addiction is effective. Key findings are following:

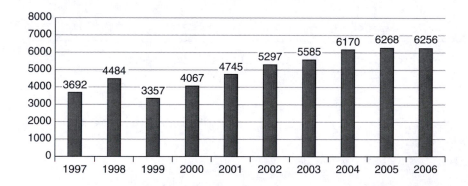

Iowa providers first began noticing methamphetamine use in their client population in 1997.
(Source: Iowa Department of Public Health and Iowa Consortium for Substance Abuse Research and Evaluation).

<u>Treatment is effective in stopping use:</u> The 2003 report found that 71.2% of the clients using methamphetamine remained abstinent six months after treatment. Of those who were abstinent six months post-discharge, 75.4% were abstinent one year after treatment. The 2006 report found that of those who were interviewed six months after their discharge, 54.6% of methamphetamine users were abstinent, 37.6% of marijuana users were abstinent, and 33.6% of those admitted for alcohol abuse were abstinent.

<u>Treatment helps those in recovery stay out of jail.</u> The 2003 report found that 90.4% of methamphetamine clients had not been arrested six months after treatment and 95.7% of methamphetamine clients interviewed one year after treatment had not been arrested during the previous six months. The 2006 study found that in the six months after treatment, 80.8% of methamphetamine users had not been arrested.

<u>Treatment helps people get back to work</u>. The 2003 report found that 54.8% of the methamphetamine clients were working full time six months after treatment while 66.7% were working full time one year after treatment. The 2006 report found that the percentage of those employed full time increased by 16.4% for all clients.

<u>While longer treatment periods improve outcomes, results for clients treated for approximately 60 days or less are still impressive</u>. Through interviews conducted six months after treatment, the 2003 study found that clients who had longer lengths of treatment (more than 90 days) were almost one and a third times more likely to remain abstinent and about one and a half times more likely to be employed full time. The 2006 study found that the methamphetamine client was treated for an average of 87.4 days. In general, clients who were treated for longer periods of time were more likely to be abstinent: 30.0% for 31–60 days, 51.6% for 61–90 days, 51.6% for 91–120 days and 57.8% for more than 120 days.

OTHER STATE ACTIVITIES TO NOTE

- Governors Task Force on Methamphetamine—with specific emphasis by the Governor on methamphetamine treatment.
- Since 2000, Iowa has completed a significant amount of training on best practices to include:
  - Motivational Enhancement/Interviewing
  - Matrix Model
  - NIATx STAR-S1 Grant Recipient
  - SAMHSA Best Practice Tool Kit on Co-Occurring Disorders
- Iowa has invested in research related to treatment outcomes and effectiveness.

NOTES

If additional resources were made available to improve services, the areas in most need of assistance would be:

- Residential and outpatient capacity
- Services for child welfare population or parents of drug endangered children
- Transitional housing
- Wrap-around services
- Staff training
- Sharing of best practices
- Co-Occurring Disorders

LEGAL DRUGS OF ABUSE

HYDROCODONE (TRADE NAMES: VICODIN®, LORTAB®, LORCET®, HYCODAN®, VICOPROFEN®)

Hydrocodone abuse has been escalating in recent years. In 2008, hydrocodone was the most frequently encountered opioid pharmaceutical (37,804 items) in drug evidence submitted to state and local forensic laboratories as reported by the National Forensic Laboratory Information System (NFLIS). During the first six months of 2009, 20,128 hydrocodone items were reported by NFLIS. DEA forensic laboratories identified 473 hydrocodone items/exhibits in 2008 and 294 items/exhibits from January to June 2009. The total number of drug items seized and reported to federal, state, and local laboratories has increased by 109% since 2004.

Hydrocodone is abused for its opioid effects. Widespread diversion via bogus call-in prescriptions, altered prescriptions, theft and illicit purchases from Internet sources are made easier by the present controls placed on hydrocodone products. Hydrocodone pills are the most frequently encountered dosage form in illicit traffic. Hydrocodone is generally abused orally, often in combination with alcohol.

Of particular concern is the prevalence of illicit use of hydrocodone among school-aged children. The 2008 Monitoring the Future Survey reports that 2.9%, 6.7% and 9.7% of 8th, 10th, and 12th graders, respectively, used Vicodin® nonmedically in the previous year. According to the 2008 National Survey on Drug Use and Health (NSDUH), 22,838 people aged 12 and older used hydrocodone for nonmedical purposes in their lifetime.

As with most opiates, abuse of hydrocodone is associated with tolerance, dependence, and addiction. The co-formulation with acetaminophen carries an additional risk of liver toxicity when high, acute doses are consumed. Some individuals who abuse very high doses of

Source: http://www.deadiversion.usdoj.gov/drugs_concern/hydrocodone/hydrocodone.htm

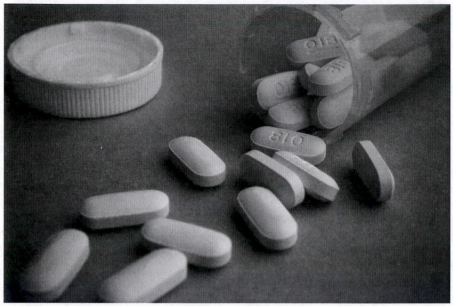

© 2012, Mark Aplet, Shutterstock, Inc.

acetaminophen-containing hydrocodone products may be spared this liver toxicity if they have been chronically taking these products and have escalated their dose slowly over a long period of time.

Every age group has been affected by the relative ease of hydrocodone availability and the perceived safety of these products by medical prescribers. Sometimes viewed as a "white collar" addiction, hydrocodone abuse has increased among all ethnic and economic groups.

OXYCODONE (TRADE NAMES: TYLOX®, PERCODAN®, OXYCONTIN®)

Oxycodone is a schedule II narcotic analgesic and is widely used in clinical medicine. The introduction in 1996 of OxyContin®, commonly known on the street as OC, OX, Oxy, Oxycotton, Hillbilly heroin, and kicker, led to a marked escalation of its abuse as reported by drug abuse treatment centers, law enforcement personnel, and health care professionals. Oxycodone abuse has been a continuing problem in the U.S. since the early 1960s. Oxycodone is abused for its euphoric effects. It is equipotent to morphine in relieving abstinence symptoms from chronic opiate (heroin, morphine) administration.

For this reason, it is often used to alleviate or prevent the onset of opiate withdrawal by street users of heroin and methadone. The large amount of oxycodone (10 to 80 mg) present in controlled release

Source: _http://www.deadiversion.usdoj.gov/drugs_concern/hydrocodone/hydrocodone.htm_
Source: _http://www.deadiversion.usdoj.gov/drugs_concern/oxycodone/summary.htm_

NOTES

formulations (OxyContin®) renders these products highly attractive to opioid abusers and doctor-shoppers. They are abused either as intact tablets or by crushing or chewing the tablet and then swallowing, snorting or injecting. Products containing oxycodone in combination with acetaminophen or aspirin are abused orally. Acetaminophen present in the combination products poses an additional risk of liver toxicity upon chronic abuse.

Every age-group has been affected by the relative prevalence of oxycodone availability and the perceived safety of oxycodone products by professionals. Sometimes seen as a "white-collar" addiction, oxycodone abuse has increased among all ethnic and economic groups.

Oxycodone-containing products are in tablet, capsule, and liquid forms. A variety of colors, markings, and packaging are available. The main sources of oxycodone on the street have been through forged prescriptions, professional diversion through unscrupulous pharmacists, doctors, and dentists, "doctor-shopping," armed robberies, and night break-ins of pharmacies and nursing homes. The diversion and abuse of OxyContin® has become a major public health problem in recent years. In 2008, 13.8 million people aged 12 or older used oxycodone (4.8 million used OxyContin®) for nonmedical use at least once during their lifetime (National Survey on Drug Use and Health, 2008).

BENZODIAZEPINES

The benzodiazepine family of depressants is used therapeutically to produce sedation, induce sleep, relieve anxiety and muscle spasms, and to prevent seizures. In general, benzodiazepines act as hypnotics in high doses, anxiolytics in moderate doses, and sedatives in low doses. Of the drugs marketed in the United States that affect central nervous system function, benzodiazepines are among the most widely prescribed medications. Benzodiazepines with a longer duration of action are utilized to treat insomnia in patients with daytime anxiety. These benzodiazepines include alprazolam (Xanax®), chlordiazepoxide (librium®), clorazepate (Tranxene®), diazepam (Valium®), halazepam (Paxipam®), lorzepam (Ativan®), oxazepam (Serax®), prazepam (Centrax®), and quazepam (Doral®). Clonazepam (Klonopin®), diazepam, and clorazepate are also used as anticonvulsants.

Benzodiazepines are classified as depressants. Repeated use of large doses or, in some cases, daily use of therapeutic doses of benzodiazepines is associated with amnesia, hostility, irritability, and vivid or disturbing dreams, as well as tolerance and physical dependence. The withdrawal syndrome is similar to that of alcohol and may

Source: http://www.justice.gov/dea/concern/b.html#2
Source: http://www.justice.gov/dea/concern/m.html#5

require hospitalization. Abrupt cessation of benzodiazepines is not recommended and tapering-down the dose eliminates many of the unpleasant symptoms.

Individuals who do abuse benzodiazepines often maintain their drug supply by getting prescriptions from several doctors, forging prescriptions, or buying diverted pharmaceutical products on the illicit market. Abuse is frequently associated with adolescents and young adults who take benzodiazepines to obtain a "high." This intoxicated state results in reduced inhibition and impaired judgment. Concurrent use of alcohol or other depressants with benzodiazepines can be life threatening. Abuse of benzodiazepines is particularly high among heroin and cocaine abusers. A large percentage of people entering treatment for narcotic or cocaine addiction also report abusing benzodiazepines.

METHYLPHENIDATE

Methylphenidate, a Schedule II substance, has a high potential for abuse and produces many of the same effects as cocaine or the amphetamines. The primary legitimate medical use of methylphenidate (Ritalin®, Methylin®, Concerta®) is to treat attention deficit hyperactivity disorder (ADHD) in children.

The abuse of this substance has been documented among narcotic addicts who dissolve the tablets in water and inject the mixture. The increased use of this substance for the treatment of ADHD has paralleled an increase in its abuse among adolescents and young adults who crush these tablets and snort the powder to get high. Youngsters have little difficulty obtaining methylphenidate from classmates or friends who have been prescribed it. Binge use, psychotic episodes, cardiovascular complications, and severe psychological addiction have all been associated with methylphenidate abuse.

DISCUSSION QUESTIONS

SUBSTANCE ABUSE SERVICES

Students will respond to the following questions individually and record their responses in a "running journal" which will be turned in for grading. Students will also be divided into small groups of three to four to discuss and then facilitate the responses shared in the small group discussion.

1. What is a recovering alcoholic? How long does recovery take?
2. How have the patterns of drug and alcohol abuse changed over the history of the United States?

NOTES

3. Identify substances discussed in this class, if abused, can result in death. What others substances are you aware of that can lead to death that we did not discuss in class?

4. Which populations or groups of people are at high risk in relation to substance abuse? Why? Which groups create the biggest concern for you? Why?

5. Explain what your understanding is of the differences between primary, secondary, and reactive alcoholism.

6. What are some of the interventions social workers/human service provider's may use in their work with chemically dependent clients?

7. From our discussions in class regarding the harm reduction model, would there be any value in integrating this model in U.S. programs?

8. Can you think of ways in which a generalist social worker/ human service provider with an understanding of substance abuse could be helpful to persons affected by crisis or disaster?

SUBSTANCE ABUSE: *INTERNET RESEARCH EXERCISES*

1. The Substance Abuse and Mental Health Services Administration (http://samhsa.gov/index.aspx) provides information to a variety of audiences.
   a. What are two topics you can browse?
   b. What conferences and events are listed?
   c. What centers and offices are listed on the home page?

2. The National Institutes of Health's National Institute on Drug Abuse has a wealth of resources at http://www.drugabuse.gov/.
   a. What are two audiences this website is trying to reach?
   b. What types of publications are available through this website? Are they any available for free?
   c. List one statistic about alcohol use.

3. Visit the Drug Enforcement Administration's website at http://www.justice.gov/dea.
   a. When was the DEA created?
   b. What is the Drug Schedule? Give at least two examples of drugs on each level of the schedule.
   c. Find the news releases and summarize a new press release.

4. Visit SAMHSA's National Registry of Evidence-based Programs and Practices at http://nrepp.samhsa.gov/.
   a. Search for two interventions related to substance abuse prevention. List them and give a brief description.
   b. Search for two interventions related to substance abuse treatment. List them and give a brief description.

NOTES

OVERVIEW OF CO-OCCURRING DISORDERS

Co-occurring disorders refers to the simultaneous existence of mental disorders and substance abuse or dependence. Clients with co-occurring disorders have at least one disorder of each type which can be established independently of each other. Co-occurring diagnosis is also known as "dual diagnosis."

In the late 1970s, practitioners found that treatment outcomes were dramatically impacted by the combination of substance abuse disorders and mental illness. In the years since, substance abuse treatment programs typically report that 50–75% of their clients have co-occurring disorders. Mental health settings report 20–50% of their clients have co-occurring disorders.

To recover fully, clients need integrated treatment for both conditions. Innovative strategies have emerged for the treatment of co-occurring disorders. The National Association of State Alcohol and Drug Abuse Directors (NASADAD) and the National Association of State Mental Health Program Directors (NASMHPD) developed the Quadrants of Care, a classification system by severity for substance abuse and mental health. The four quadrants for co-occurring disorders are:

- Quadrant I: Less severe mental disorder/less severe substance use disorder
- Quadrant II: More severe mental disorder/less severe substance disorder
- Quadrant III: Less severe mental disorder/more severe substance disorder
- Quadrant IV: More severe mental disorder/more severe substance disorder

Assessment, diagnosis, and treatment are important in the recovery from co-occurring disorders. Assessment gathers a wealth of information. Specifically, assessment should include the client's background, substance use, psychiatric problems, other problem areas, disabilities, strengths, and readiness to change. Diagnosis is based on the DSM-IV-TR. Actions and approaches to treatment are based on assessment and diagnosis. Pharmacological interventions, such as medication for psychiatric disorders, may be a part of treatment. Therefore, collaboration between substance abuse treatment professionals, mental health practitioners and medical professionals is critical.

Substance abuse treatment usually involves Individual therapy, group therapy, education about alcohol and drugs, and participation in a 12-step recovery program such as Alcoholics Anonymous. Treatment for mental illness depends upon the diagnosis. Usually, individual and group therapy is utilized, as well as medication. Many treatment programs also include education and support groups which focus on skills such as communication, problem-solving, and decision making.

SAMHSA reported four key findings from available data about co-occurring disorders:

- Co-occurring disorders are common in the general adult population, although many individuals with co-occurring disorders do not receive treatment.
- Some evidence supports an increased prevalence of people with co-occurring disorders and of more programs for people with co-occurring disorders.
- Rates of mental illness increase as the number of substance use disorders increase, which further complicates treatment.
- Compared to people with only mental illness or substance use disorders, people with co-occurring disorders are more likely to be hospitalized. These rates may be increasing.

CO-OCCURRING MARIJUANA USE AND MENTAL ILLNESS

A number of studies have shown an association between chronic marijuana use and increased rates of anxiety, depression, and schizophrenia. Some of these studies have shown age at first use to be an important risk factor, where early use is related to an increased vulnerability to later problems. However, it is not clear whether marijuana use causes mental problems, exacerbates them, or reflects an attempt to self-medicate symptoms already in existence.

Chronic marijuana use, especially in a very young person, may also be a sign of risk for mental illnesses, including addiction, stemming from genetic or environmental vulnerabilities, such as early exposure to stress or violence. Currently, the strongest evidence links marijuana use and schizophrenia and/or related disorders. High doses of marijuana can produce an acute psychotic reaction; in addition, use of the drug may trigger the onset or relapse of schizophrenia in vulnerable individuals. http://www.drugabuse.gov/Infofacts/marijuana.html

POSTTRAUMATIC STRESS DISORDER (PTSD) AND SUBSTANCE ABUSE

PTSD is one anxiety disorder classified in the DSM-IV-TR. The essential feature of PTSD is exposure to an extreme traumatic stressor involving either

Source: Substance Abuse Treatment for Persons with Co-Occurring Disorders, U.S. Department of Health and Human Services, Substance Abuse and Mental Health Services Administration, 2004.

NOTES

- direct personal experience of an event that involves actual or threatened death or serious injury, or a threat to the physical integrity of another person; or
- learning about unexpected or violent death, serious harm, or threat of death or injury experienced by a family member or other close associate.

The rate of PTSD among people with substance use disorders is 14–34 percent. Among clients in substance abuse treatment, PTSD is two to three time more common in women than in men. 55–99 percent of women with substance abuse problems report a lifetime history of physical and/or sexual abuse. While most women with PTSD and substance use disorders experienced childhood physical or sexual abuse, men with both disorders typically experienced crime victimization or trauma associated with combat. It is also important to recognize that while under the influence of alcohol or drugs, people may be more vulnerable to trauma.

The Chicken or the Egg?

You may be familiar with the riddle, "Which came first, the chicken or the egg?" When it comes to substance abuse and mental illness, you may be wondering, "Which comes first?" To begin understanding the co-occurring nature of these conditions, it may be helpful to review to principles: correlation and causation.

What is the difference between causation and correlation?

One of the most common errors we find in the press is the confusion between *correlation* and *causation* in scientific and health-related studies. In theory, these are easy to distinguish—an action or occurrence can *cause* another (such as smoking causes lung cancer), or it can *correlate* with another (such as smoking is correlated with alcoholism). If one action causes another, then they are most certainly correlated. But just because two things occur together does not mean that one caused the other, even if it seems to make sense.

Unfortunately, our intuition can lead us astray when it comes to distinguishing between causality and correlation. For example, eating breakfast has long been correlated with success in school for elementary school children. It would be easy to conclude that eating breakfast *causes* students to be better learners. It turns out, however, that those who don't eat breakfast are also more likely to be absent or tardy—and it is absenteeism that is playing a significant role in their poor performance. When researchers retested the breakfast theory,

Retrieved from http://stats.org/in_depth/faq/causation_correlation.htm

they found that, independent of other factors, breakfast only helps undernourished children perform better.

Many studies are actually designed to test a correlation, but are suggestive of "reasons" for the correlation. People learn of a study showing that "girls who watch soap operas are more likely to have eating disorders"—a correlation between soap opera watching and eating disorders—but then they incorrectly conclude that watching soap operas *gives* girls eating disorders.

In general, it is extremely difficult to establish causality between two correlated events or observances. In contrast, there are many statistical tools to establish a statistically significant correlation.

There are several reasons why common sense conclusions about cause and effect might be wrong. Correlated occurrences may be due to a common cause. For example, the fact that red hair is correlated with blue eyes stems from a common genetic specification which codes for both. A correlation may also be observed when there is causality behind it—for example, it is well-established that cigarette smoking not only correlates with lung cancer, but actually causes it. But in order to establish cause, we would have to rule out the possibility that smokers are more likely to live in urban areas, where there is more pollution—or any other possible explanation for the observed correlation.

In many cases, it seems obvious that one action causes another. However, there are also many cases when it is not so clear (except perhaps to the already-convinced observer). In the case of soap-opera watching anorexics, we can neither exclude nor embrace the hypothesis that the television is a cause of the problem—additional research would be needed to make a convincing argument for causality. Another hypothesis is that girls inclined to suffer poor body image are drawn to soap operas on television because it satisfies some need related to their poor body image. Yet another hypothesis is that neither causes the other, but rather there is a common trait—say, an overemphasis on appearance by the girls' parents—that causes both an interest in soap operas and an inclination to develop eating disorders. None of these hypotheses are tested in a study that simply asks who is watching soaps and who is developing eating disorders, and finding a correlation between the two.

How, then, does one ever establish causality? This is one of the most daunting challenges of public health professionals and pharmaceutical companies. The most effective way of doing this is through a *controlled study*. In a controlled study, two groups of people who are comparable in almost every way are given two different sets of experiences (such one group watching soap operas and the other game shows), and the outcome is compared. If the two groups have substantially different outcomes, then the different experiences may have caused the different outcome.

NOTES

There are obvious ethical limits of controlled studies—it would be problematic to take two comparable groups and make one smoke while denying cigarettes to the other in order to see if cigarette smoking really causes lung cancer. This is why epidemiological (or observational) studies are so important. These are studies in which large groups of people are followed over time, and their behavior and outcome is also observed. In these studies, it is extremely difficult (though sometimes still possible) to tease out cause and effect, versus a mere correlation.

Typically, one can only establish correlation unless the effects are extremely notable *and* there is no reasonable explanation that challenges causality. This is the case with cigarette smoking, for example. At the time that scientists, industry trade groups, activists and individuals were debating whether the observed correlation between heavy cigarette smoking and lung cancer was causal or not, many other hypotheses were considered (such as sleep deprivation or excessive drinking) and each one dismissed as insufficiently describing the data. It is now a widespread belief among scientists and health professionals that smoking does indeed *cause* lung cancer.

When the stakes are high, people are much more likely to jump to causal conclusions. This seems to be doubly true when it comes to public suspicion about chemicals and environmental pollution. There has been a lot of publicity over the purported relationship between autism and vaccinations, for example. As vaccination rates went up across the United States, so did autism. However, this correlation (which has led many to conclude that vaccination causes autism) has been widely dismissed by public health experts. The rise in autism rates is likely to do with increased awareness and diagnosis, or one of many other possible factors that have changed over the past 50 years.

In general, we should all be wary of our own bias; we like explanations. The media often concludes a causal relationship among correlated observances when causality was not even considered by the study itself. Without clear reasons to accept causality, we should only accept correlation. Two events occurring in close proximity does not imply that one caused the other, even if it seems to makes perfect sense.

Based on what you have learned about this topic and your experiences, answer the following questions:

1. Would you describe the relationship between substance abuse and mental illness as just being *correlation* or do you consider there to be a *causal* relationship? Why?
2. If there is a causal relationship between substance abuse and mental illness, which causes which?

3. "Self-medication" is a commonly used term to describe non-prescription use of substances for the relief or treatment of symptoms or conditions. Give at least three examples of "self-medication."

INTEGRATED APPROACH FOR TREATMENT OF MENTAL ILLNESS AND SUBSTANCE ABUSE

Why Is An Integrated Approach To Treating Severe Mental Illnesses And Substance Abuse Problems So Important?

Despite much research that supports its success integrated treatment is still not made widely available to consumers. Those who struggle both with serious mental illness and substance abuse face problems of enormous proportions. Mental health services tend not to be well prepared to deal with patients having both afflictions. Often only one of the two problems is identified. If both are recognized, the individual may bounce back and forth between services for mental illness and substance abuse, or they may be refused treatment by each of them. Fragmented and uncoordinated services create a service gap for persons with co-occurring disorders.

Providing appropriate, integrated services for these consumers will not only allow for their recovery and improved overall health, but can ameliorate the effects their disorders have on their family, friends, and society at large. By helping these consumers stay in treatment, find housing and jobs, and develop better social skills and judgment, we can potentially begin to substantially diminish some of the most sinister and costly societal problems: crime, HIV/AIDS, domestic violence and more.

There is much evidence that integrated treatment can be effective. For example:

- Individuals with a substance abuse disorders are more likely to receive treatment if they have a co-occurring mental disorder.
- Research shows that when consumers with dual diagnosis successfully overcome alcohol abuse, their response to treatment improves markedly.

With continued education on co-occurring disorders, hopefully more treatments and better understanding are on the way.

WHAT DOES EFFECTIVE INTEGRATED TREATMENT ENTAIL?

Effective integrated treatment consists of the same health professionals working in one setting, providing appropriate treatment for both mental health and substance abuse in a coordinated fashion.

The caregivers see to it that interventions are bundled together; the consumers, therefore, receive consistent treatment, with no division between mental health or substance abuse assistance. The approach, philosophy, and recommendations are seamless. The need to consult with separate teams and programs is eliminated.

Integrated treatment also requires the recognition that substance abuse counseling and traditional mental health counseling are different approaches that must be reconciled to treat co-occurring disorders. It is not enough merely to teach relationship skills to a person with bipolar disorder. They must also learn to explore how to avoid the relationships that are intertwined with their substance abuse.

Providers should recognize that denial is an inherent part of the problem. Patients often do not have insight as to the seriousness and scope of the problem. Abstinence may be a goal of the program but should not be a precondition for entering treatment. If dually diagnosed clients do not fit into local Alcoholics Anonymous (AA) and Narcotics Anonymous (NA) groups, special peer groups based on AA principles might be developed.

Clients with a dual diagnosis have to proceed at their own pace in treatment. An illness model of the problem should be used rather than a moralistic one. Providers need to convey understanding of how hard it is to end an addiction problem and give credit for any accomplishments. Clients should be given opportunities to socialize, have access to recreational activities, and develop peer relationships. Their families should be offered support and education, while learning not to react with guilt or blame buy to learn to cope with two interacting illnesses.

WHAT ARE THE KEY FACTORS IN EFFECTIVE INTEGRATIVE TREATMENT?

There are a number of key factors in an integrated treatment program.

Treatment must be approached in **stages**. First, a *trust* is established between the consumer and caregiver. This helps motivate the consumer to learn the skills for *actively controlling* their illnesses and focus on goals. This helps keep the consumer on track, *preventing relapse*. Treatment can begin at any one of these stages; the program is tailored to the individual.

Assertive outreach has been shown to engage and retain clients at a high rate, while those that fail to include outreach lose clients. Therefore, effective programs, through intensive case management, meeting at the consumer's residence, and other methods of developing a dependable relationship with the client, ensure that more consumers are consistently monitored and counseled.

Effective treatment includes **motivational interventions**, which, through education, support, and counseling, help empower deeply demoralized clients to recognize the importance of their goals and illness self-management.

Of course, counseling is a fundamental component of dual diagnosis services. **Counseling** helps develop positive coping patterns, as well as promotes cognitive and behavioral skills. Counseling can be in the form of individual, group, or family therapy, or a combination of these.

A consumer's **social support** is critical. Their immediate environment has a direct impact on their choices and moods. Therefore, consumers need help strengthening positive relationships and jettisoning those that encourage negative behavior.

Effective integrated treatment programs **view recovery as a long-term, community-based process,** one that can take months or, more likely, years to undergo. Improvement is slow even with a consistent treatment program. However, such an approach prevents relapses and enhances a consumer's gains.

To be effective, a dual diagnosis program must be **comprehensive**, taking into account a number of life's aspects: stress management, social networks, jobs, housing, and activities. These programs view substance abuse as intertwined with mental illness, not a separate issue, and therefore provide solutions to both illnesses simultaneously.

Finally, effective integrative treatment programs must contain elements of **cultural sensitivity and competence** to even lure consumers, much less retain them. Various groups such as African-Americans, homeless, women with children, Hispanics, and other can benefit from services tailored to their particular racial and cultural needs.

HARM-REDUCTION MODEL OF PREVENTION

The harm-reduction model of prevention has the following objectives:

1. To reduce the mortality and morbidity associated with alcohol and drug-related problems.
2. To reduce the rates of abuse of alcohol and drugs.

- Social, cultural, and legislative aspects of prevention are considered in addition to individual responsibility.
- Harm-reduction is a utilitarian approach that lobbies for the greatest good for the greatest number of people.
- Harm-reduction recognizes the indirect consequences of abuse and dependency. (Drunk-driving fatalities, HIV transmission).
- Advocates of a harm-reduction model assume that certain drugs will always be abused. Therefore, programs such as free transportation on college campuses or needle exchanges may be promoted.

McNeece, C.A. & DeNito, D.M. (2005). *Chemical Dependency: A Systems Approach.* Boston: Pearson.

COMMONLY ABUSED DRUGS

Substances: Category and Name	Examples of Commercial and Street Names	DEA Schedule*/ How Administered**	Acute Effects/Health Risks
Tobacco			
Nicotine	Found in cigarettes, cigars, bidis, and smokeless tobacco (snuff, spit tobacco, chew)	Not scheduled/smoked, snorted, chewed	*Increased blood pressure and heart rate/chronic lung disease; cardiovascular disease; stroke; cancers of the mouth, pharynx, larynx, esophagus, stomach, pancreas, cervix, kidney, bladder, and acute myeloid leukemia; adverse pregnancy outcomes; addiction*
Alcohol			
Alcohol (ethyl alcohol)	Found in liquor, beer, and wine	Not scheduled/ swallowed	*In low doses, euphoria, mild stimulation, relaxation, lowered inhibitions; in higher doses, drowsiness, slurred speech, nausea, emotional volatility, loss of coordination, visual distortions, impaired memory, sexual dysfunction, loss of consciousness/increased risk of injuries, violence, fetal damage (in pregnant women); depression, neurologic deficits; hypertension; liver and heart disease; addiction; fatal overdose*
Cannabinoids			
Marijuana	Blunt, dope, ganja, grass, herb, joint, bud, Mary Jane, pot, reefer, green, trees, smoke, sinsemilla, skunk, weed	I/smoked, swallowed	*Euphoria; relaxation; slowed reaction time; distorted sensory perception; impaired balance and coordination; increased heart rate and appetite; impaired learning, memory; anxiety; panic attacks; psychosis/cough; frequent respiratory infections; possible mental health decline; addiction*
Hashish	Boom, gangster, hash, hash oil, hemp	I/smoked, swallowed	
Opioids			
Heroin	*Diacetylmorphine:* smack, horse, brown sugar, dope, H, junk, skag, skunk, white horse, China white; cheese (with OTC cold medicine and antihistamine)	I/injected, smoked, snorted	*Euphoria; drowsiness; impaired coordination; dizziness; confusion; nausea; sedation; feeling of heaviness in the body; slowed or arrested breathing/constipation; endocarditis; hepatitis; HIV; addiction; fatal overdose*
Opium	*Laudanum, paregoric;* big O, black stuff, block, gum, hop	II, III, V/swallowed, smoked	

Substances: Category and Name	Examples of Commercial and Street Names	DEA Schedule*/How Administered**	Acute Effects/Health Risks
Stimulants			
Cocaine	*Cocaine hydrochloride;* blow, bump, C, candy, Charlie, coke, crack, flake, rock, snow, toot	II/snorted, smoked, injected	Increased heart rate, blood pressure, body temperature, metabolism; feelings of exhilaration; increased energy, mental alertness; tremors, reduced appetite; irritability; anxiety; panic; paranoia; violent behavior; psychosis/weight loss; insomnia; cardiac or cardiovascular complications; stroke; seizures; addiction
Amphetamine	*Biphetamine, Dexedrine:* bennies, black beauties, crosses, hearts, LA turnaround, speed, truck drivers, uppers	II/swallowed, snorted, smoked, injected	**Also, for cocaine**—nasal damage from snorting
Methamphetamine	*Desoxyn:* meth, ice, crank, chalk, crystal, fire, glass, go fast, speed	II/swallowed, snorted, smoked, injected	**Also, for methamphetamine**—severe dental problems
Club Drugs			
MDMA (methylenedioxymethamphetamine)	Ecstasy, Adam, clarity, Eve, lover's speed, peace, uppers	I/swallowed, snorted, injected	*MDMA—mild hallucinogenic effects; increased tactile sensitivity; emphatic feelings; lowered inhibition; anxiety; chills; sweating; teeth clenching; muscle cramping/sleep disturbances; depression; impaired memory; hyperthermia; addiction*
Flunitrazepam***	*Rohypnol:* forget-me pill, Mexican Valium, R2, roach, Roche, roofies, roofinol, rope, rophies	IV/swallowed, snorted	*Flunitrazepam—sedation; muscle relaxation; confusion; memory loss; dizziness; impaired coordination/addiction*
GHB***	*Gamma-hydroxybutyrate:* G, Georgia home boy, grievous bodily harm, liquid ectasy, soap, scoop, goop, liquid X	I/swallowed	*GHB—drowsiness; nausea; headache; disorientation; loss of coordination; memory loss/unconsciousness; seizures; coma*
Dissociate Drugs			
Ketamine	*Ketalar SV:* cat Valium, K, Special K, vitamin K	III/Injected, snorted, smoked	*Feelings of being separate from one's body and environment; impaired motor function/anxiety; tremors; numbness; memory loss; nausea*
PCP and analogs	*Phencyclidine;* angel dust, boat, hog, love boat, peace pill	I, II/swallowed, smoked, injected	*Also, for ketamine—analgesia; impaired memory; delirium; respiratory depression and arrest; death*
Salvia divinorum	Salvia, Shepherdess's Herb, Maria Pastora, magic mint, Sally-D	Not scheduled/chewed, swallowed, smoked	*Also, for PCP and analogs—analgesia; psychosis; aggression; violence; slurred speech; loss of coordination; hallucinations*
Dextromethorphan (DXM)	Found in some cough and cold medications: Robotripping, Robo, Triple C	Not scheduled/swallowed	*Also, for DXM—euphoria; slurred speech; confusion; dizziness; distorted visual perceptions*
Hallucinogens			
LSD	*Lysergic acid diethylamide;* acid, blotter, cubes, microdot, yellow sunshine, blue heaven	I/swallowed, absorbed through mouth tissues	*Altered states of perception and feeling; hallucinations; nausea*
Mescaline	Buttons, cactus, mesc, peyote	I/swallowed, smoked	*Also, for LSD and mescaline—increased body temperature, heart rate, blood pressure; loss of appetite; sweating; sleeplessness; numbness; dizziness; weakness; tremors; impulsive behavior; rapid shifts in emotion*
Psilocybin	Magic mushrooms, purple passion, shrooms, little smoke	I/swallowed	*Also, for LSD—Flashbacks, Hallucinogen Persisting Perception Disorder*
			Also, for psilocybin—nervousness; paranoia; panic

Substances: Category and Name	Examples of Commercial and Street Names	DEA Schedule*/ How Administered**	Acute Effects/Health Risks
Other Compounds			
Anabolic steroids	Anadrol, Oxandrin, Durabolin, Depo-Testosterone, Equipoise: roids, juice, gym candy, pumpers	III/injected, swallowed, applied to skin	*Steroids—no intoxication effects*/hypertension; blood clotting and cholesterol changes; liver cysts; hostility and aggression; acne; in adolescents—premature stoppage of growth; in males—prostate cancer, reduced sperm production, shrunken testicles, breast enlargement; in females—menstrual irregularities, development of beard and other masculine characteristics
Inhalants	Solvents (paint thinners, gasoline, glues); gases (butane, propane, aerosol propellants, nitrous oxide); nitrites (isoamyl, isobutyl, cyclohexyl): laughing gas, poppers, snappers, whippets	Not scheduled/inhaled through nose or mouth	*Inhalants (varies by chemical)—stimulation; loss of inhibition; headache; nausea or vomiting; slurred speech; loss of motor coordination; wheezing/cramps; muscle weakness; depression; memory impairment; damage to cardiovascular and nervous systems; unconsciousness; sudden death*
Prescription Medications			
CNS Depressants	For more information on prescription medications, please visit http://www.nida.nih.gov/DrugPages/PrescripDrugsChart.html.		
Stimulants			
Opioid Pain Relievers			

*Schedule I and II drugs have a high potential for abuse. They require greater storage security and have a quota on manufacturing, among other restrictions. Schedule I drugs are available for research only and have no approved medical use; Schedule II drugs are available only by prescription (unrefillable) and require a form for ordering. Schedule III and IV drugs are available by prescription, may have five refills in 6 months, and may be ordered orally. Some Schedule V drugs are available over the counter.

**Some of the health risks are directly related to the route of drug administration. For example, injection drug use can increase the risk of infection through needle contamination with staphylococci, HIV, hepatitis, and other organisms.

***Associated with sexual assaults.

Reprinted from National Institute on Drug Abuse (NIDA). Visit NIDA at www.drugabuse.gov

PRINCIPLES OF DRUG ADDICTION TREATMENT

More than three decades of scientific research show that treatment can help drug-addicted individuals stop drug use, avoid relapse and successfully recover their lives. Based on this research, 13 fundamental principles that characterize effective drug abuse treatment have been developed. These principles are detailed in *NIDA's Principles of Drug Addiction Treatment: A Research-Based Guide*. The guide also describes different types of science-based treatments and provides answers to commonly asked questions.

1. **Addiction is a complex but treatable disease that affects brain function and behavior.** Drugs alter the brain's structure and how it functions, resulting in changes that persist long after drug use has ceased. This may help explain why abusers are at risk for relapse even after long periods of abstinence.

2. **No single treatment is appropriate for everyone.** Matching treatment settings, interventions, and services to an individual's particular problems and needs is critical to his or her ultimate success.

3. **Treatment needs to be readily available.** Because drug-addicted individuals may be uncertain about entering treatment, taking advantage of available services the moment people are ready for treatment is critical. Potential patients can be lost if treatment is not immediately available or readily accessible.

4. **Effective treatment attends to multiple needs of the individual, not just his or her drug abuse.** To be effective, treatment must address the individual's drug abuse and any associated medical, psychological, social, vocational, and legal problems.

5. **Remaining in treatment for an adequate period of time is critical.** The appropriate duration for an individual depends on the type and degree of his or her problems and needs. Research indicates that most addicted individuals need at least 3 months in treatment to significantly reduce or stop their drug use and that the best outcomes occur with longer durations of treatment.

6. **Counseling—individual and/or group—and other behavioral therapies are the most commonly used forms of drug abuse treatment.** Behavioral therapies vary in their focus and may involve addressing a patient's motivations to change, building skills to resist drug use, replacing drug-using activities with constructive and rewarding activities, improving problemsolving skills, and facilitating better interpersonal relationships.

7. **Medications are an important element of treatment for many patients, especially when combined with counseling and other behavioral therapies.** For example, methadone and buprenorphine are effective in helping individuals addicted to heroin or

other opioids stabilize their lives and reduce their illicit drug use. Also, for persons addicted to nicotine, a nicotine replacement product (nicotine patches or gum) or an oral medication (buproprion or varenincline), can be an effective component of treatment when part of a comprehensive behavioral treatment program.

8. **An individual's treatment and services plan must be assessed continually and modified as necessary to ensure it meets his or her changing needs.** A patient may require varying combinations of services and treatment components during the course of treatment and recovery. In addition to counseling or psychotherapy, a patient may require medication, medical services, family therapy, parenting instruction, vocational rehabilitation and/or social and legal services. For many patients, a continuing care approach provides the best results with treatment intensity varying according to a person's changing needs.

9. **Many drug-addicted individuals also have other mental disorders.** Because drug abuse and addiction—both of which are mental disorders—often co-occur with other mental illnesses, patients presenting with one condition should be assessed for the others(s). And when these problems co-occur, treatment should address both (or all), including the use of medications as appropriate.

10. **Medically assisted detoxification is only the first stage of addiction treatment and by itself does little to change long-term drug abuse.** Although medically assisted detoxification can safely manage the acute physical symptoms of withdrawal, detoxification alone is rarely sufficient to help addicted individuals achieve long-term abstinence. Thus patients should be encouraged to continue drug treatment following detoxification.

11. **Treatment does not need to be voluntary to be effective.** Sanctions or enticements from family, employment settings, and/or the criminal justice system can significantly increase treatment entry, retention rates, and the ultimate success of drug treatment interventions.

12. **Drug use during treatment must be monitored continuously, as lapses during treatment do occur.** Knowing their drug use is being monitored can be a powerful incentive for patients and can help them withstand urges to use drugs. Monitoring also provides an early indication of a return to drug use, signaling a possible need to adjust an individual's treatment plan to better meet his or her needs.

13. **Treatment programs should assess patients for the presence of HIV/AIDS, hepatitis B and C, tuberculosis, and other infectious diseases, as well as provide targeted risk-reduction counseling to help patients modify or change behaviors that**

place them at risk of contracting or spreading infectious diseases. Targeted counseling specifically focused on reducing infectious disease risk can help patients further reduce or avoid substance-related and other high-risk behaviors. Treatment providers should encourage and support HIV screening and inform patients that highly active antiretroviral therapy (HAART) has proven effective in combating HIV, including among drug-abusing populations.

NOTES

U.S. Teens Who Currently Use Illicit Drugs or Cigarettes (Past Month Use)

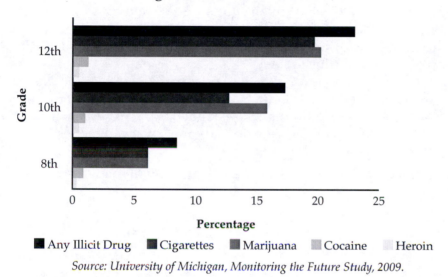

Source: *University of Michigan, Monitoring the Future Study, 2009.*

Dependence on or Abuse of Specific Illicit Drugs in Past Year Among Persons 12 or Older, 2009

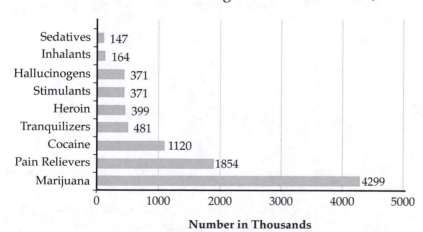

Source: *SAMHSA, 2009 NSDUH*

NOTES

SYNTHETIC DRUGS IN IOWA UPDATE

DCI CRIME LAB: SYNTHETIC DRUG TEST RESULTS

The different compounds discovered through chemical analysis of 459 confirmed synthetic drugs by the DCI Crime Lab since November 2011 totals 18 so far . . . 14 synthetic cannabinoids (a.k.a. fake weed) and 4 synthetic cathinones (a.k.a. bath salts). This compares with 8 explicitly listed synthetic drug compounds in Iowa law (6 cannabinoids and 2 cathinones). Many more samples await testing, and local law enforcement report continued synthetic drug sales.

A legislative proposal to strengthen Iowa law regulating synthetic drugs may potentially cover up to 400 different variations of these compounds. Other prevention efforts are also underway. Anecdotally, substance abuse treatment providers are seeing more client synthetic drug use. The Iowa Department of Public Health has added synthetic drugs to its reporting system.

In addition to Iowa and the District of Columbia, the National Alliance on Model State Drug Laws reports the number of other states passing--or considering passing--synthetic drug law enhancements this year totals 24 on the cannabinoids and 31 on cathinones.

Synthetic Drug Exposure Calls from Iowa Hospitals

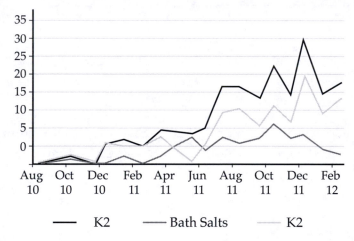

IOWA JCOs: ANECDOTAL REPORTS OF SYNTHETIC DRUG USE

FROM DISTRICT 2:

- In early January a high school girl in Carroll was hospitalized in intensive care in Carroll following her use.
- A 16-year-old male was taken to the emergency room in Marshalltown exhibiting aggressive and erratic behavior. He assaulted staff there, damaged property and urinated around the room. He was hospitalized and eventually ended up in

drug treatment. He admitted using K2 but does not remember the events after his use.

- A young adult male committed suicide with a gun in Lakeview, K2 was found in his pocket, the blood tests have not come back confirming the use yet.
- My staff originally believed the young people were choosing this over street marijuana because it is so difficult to test for and theoretically legal, but my Hamilton Co JCO reported that she was aware of Webster City kids who were out of high school and off probation and attending CC in Ft. Dodge were using it.

FROM A JCO IN POLK COUNTY:

- *I have had 5 of my 30 kids on my caseload test positive for K2. And if I could test more kids more often I would.
- *One young lady was a marijuana smoker. She stopped using marijuana and started using K2 because I was dropping UA's for THC. She was passing out at random places, at school, cell phone store, etc., and throwing up often as well. She was going through all sorts of medical tests for stomach problem and narcolepsy. She generally looked terrible. The doctors were not sure what was wrong, she was being referred to all sorts of specialists. I tested her for K2, and she was positive. She revealed she was using K2 in place of marijuana. She stated to me that almost everyone is using K2.
- *I have another case of possession of synthetics. Juveniles called police after a friend at their house was exhibiting strange behavior, they became concerned and called 911. Child was taken to the hospital after reporting using K2. The charge was dismissed because the PCAO stated the synthetic wasn't tested therefore they could not prove it.
- *Lots of kids have reported using it and freaking out or being very sick from it. I believe we have barely scratched the surface of the K2 and bath salts issue.

FROM ANOTHER JCO IN POLK COUNTY:

- *From a pool of K2 tests we did earlier this year, of some amount like 20 tests, all but 2 were positive. This goes to show the prevalence of this drug.
- *With the difficulty testing for synthetics, both known and unknown/future blends, as well as the prohibitive costs, John Hawkins made a valid point recently that it is behavioral observation that is possibly the best indicator of use. Our contact with clients is possibly the best early-intervention/early-detection of this problem, which has such potential for harm.

Anecdotally, I can only say that use has gone up dramatically in the last year.

NOTES

YSS: SURVEY OF SYNTHETIC CANNABINOID USE BY YOUTH IN TREATMENT

RESIDENTIAL

Summer 2011 when first started seeing it at intake. Current: 14 of 20 (70%).

Female (6 of 6):
1. All six of the girls have used it
2. 1–3 grams......2–3 blunts
3. Experienced hallucinations, paranoia, heard voices, became disoriented and didn't know where they were, seizures
4. Very easy to get from the store and friends

Male (8 of 14):
1. How many have used K2 - 8
2. How much used—1–4 times
3. Effects—Fast heart rate, feel drunk, feel high
4. How easy to get—Very easy
5. Young 13–14 years old.

IOP

- 50% have used.
- Documented 10–15% at intake.
- Tried and preferred over marijuana/higher potency.

MISC

- YSS requested that the UA Company (Dominion Diagnostics, out of Rhode Island) start testing for it. Panel specifically for K2. This UA is being done at Intake to gauge substances used.
- Know of one convenience Story Co. store who is selling it.
- Ordering off the web.

KRATOM

The Iowa DCI Crime Lab confirms one package submission recently tested positive for Kratom (*Mitragyna speciosa korth*), an herbal drug indigenous to Southeast Asia. Other anecdotal reports have been received indicating additional Kratom sales and use in Iowa.

Kratom is promoted as a legal psychoactive product. At low doses, it produces stimulant effects, with users reporting increased alertness, physical energy, talkativeness and sociable behavior. At high doses, opiate, sedative and euphoric effects are reported. Effects occur 5 to 10 minutes after ingestion and last 2 to 5 hours. Acute side effects include nausea, itching, sweating, dry mouth, constipation, increased

Source: DPS/DCI and DEA Drugs/Chemicals of Concern

urination, and loss of appetite. A study in Thailand, where Kratom is illegal, showed Kratom consumption can lead to addiction. Several cases of psychosis were observed in the study, in which Kratom addicts exhibited psychotic symptoms that included hallucinations, delusion and confusion.

IOWA METH LAB TRENDS

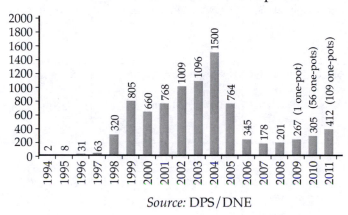

Iowa Meth Lab Incident Response

Source: DPS/DNE

"One pot" labs are more compact than their anhydrous ammonia or red phosphorus counterparts, and typically make smaller amounts of meth. "One pot" labs have been found hidden in backpacks in Iowa. In place of anhydrous ammonia, "one pot" labs use chemicals often contained in fertilizer stakes and cold packs (e.g., ammonium nitrate, ammonium sulfate and sodium hydroxide). These products are sometimes stolen, purchased in large quantities and/or acquired in combination with other meth precursors.

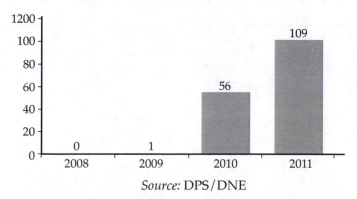

Iowa One Pot Meth Lab Incidents

Source: DPS/DNE

Drug Education Guide

Name	Physical Symptoms	What to Look For	Dangers
ALCOHOL – (beer, wine, liquor)	Intoxication, slurred speech, unsteady walk, relaxation, relaxed inhibition, impaired coordination, slowed reflexes.	Smell of alcohol on clothes or breath, intoxicated behavior, hangover, glazed eyes.	Addiction, accidents as result of impaired ability and judgment, overdose when mixed with other depressants, heart and liver damage.
COCAINE – (coke, rock, crack, base)	Brief intense euphoria, elevated blood pressure & heart rate, restlessness, excitement, feeling of well-being followed by depression.	Glass vials, glass pipe, white crystalline powder, razor blades, syringes, needle marks.	Addiction, heart attack, seizures, lung damage, severe depression, paranoia (see Stimulants).
MARIJUANA – (pot, dope, grass, weed, herb, hash, joint)	Altered perceptions, red eyes, dry mouth, reduced concentration and coordination, euphoria, laughing, hunger.	Rolling papers, pipes, dried plant material, odor of burnt hemp rope, roach clips.	Panic reaction, impaired short term memory, addiction.
HALLUCINOGENS – (acid, LSD, PCP, MDMA, ecstasy, psilocybin mushrooms, peyote)	Altered mood and perceptions, focus on detail, anxiety, panic, nausea, synaesthesia (ex: smell colors, see sounds)	Capsules, tablets, "microdots," blotter squares.	Unpredictable behavior, emotional instability, violent behavior (with PCP)
INHALANTS – (gas, aerosols, glue, nitrites, Rush, White out)	Nausea, dizziness, headaches, lack of coordination and control.	Odor of substance on clothing and breath, intoxication, drowsiness, poor muscular control.	Unconsciousness, suffocation, nausea and vomiting, damage to brain and central nervous system, sudden death.
NARCOTICS – Heroin (junk, dope, Black tar, China white) Demerol, Dilaudid (D's), Morphine, Codeine	Euphoria, drowsiness, insensitivity to pain, nausea, vomiting, watery eyes, runny nose (see Depressants).	Needle marks on arms, needles, syringes, spoons, pinpoint pupils, cold moist skin.	Addiction, lethargy, weight loss, contamination from unsterile needles (hepatitis, AIDS), accidental overdose.
STIMULANTS – (speed, uppers, crank, Bam, black beauties, crystal, dexies, caffeine, nicotine, cocaine, amphetamines)	Alertness, talkativeness, wakefulness, increased blood pressure, loss of appetite, mood elevation.	Pills and capsules, loss of sleep and appetite, irritability or anxiety, weight loss, hyperactivity.	Fatigue leading to exhaustion, addiction, paranoia, depression, confusion, possible hallucinations.
DEPRESSANTS – Barbiturates, Sedatives, Tranquilizers, (downers, tranks, ludes, reds, Valium, yellow jackets, alcohol)	Depressed breathing and heartbeat, intoxication, drowsiness, uncoordinated movements.	Capsules and pills, confused behavior, longer periods of sleep, slurred speech.	Possible overdose, especially in combination w/ alcohol; muscle rigidity; addiction, withdrawal & overdose require medical treatment.

Seven POSSIBLE Symptoms of Drug Involvement

- Change in school or work attendance or performance.
- Alteration of personal appearance.
- Mood swings or attitude changes.
- Withdrawal from responsibilities/family contacts.
- Association with drug-using peers.
- Unusual patterns of behavior.
- Defensive attitude concerning drugs.

CHAPTER 6

CHILD AND DEPENDENT ADULT ABUSE

© 2012, JPagetRFphotos, Shutterstock, Inc.

Chapter Objective

- Discuss issues of child abuse and dependent adult abuse.

NOTES

CASE STUDY

Tiffany's son, Caleb, is nine months old. His development is delayed and he is under the care of a pediatrician for being underweight. Tiffany reported that she did not know she was pregnant until late in the pregnancy and does not know for sure who Caleb's father is. Tiffany's mom helped take care of Caleb until he was one month old, but when her health worsened, the majority of Caleb's care fell to Tiffany. Caleb experienced colic and awoke frequently, leaving Tiffany sleep deprived and frustrated. Tiffany reported she used painkillers to help "mellow" her out when Caleb cried a lot. When Tiffany's friend, Lena, offered for Tiffany and Caleb to move in with her, Tiffany jumped at the idea of having someone around who might help her out. Lena spoiled Caleb by buying him cute outfits and toys. Tiffany knew Lena used methamphetamine often and, when Lena explained that it could help Tiffany deal with Caleb's sleeping schedule, Tiffany agreed to try it out. Lena and Tiffany smoked methamphetamine together in the home several times per week. Tiffany began propping bottles up for Caleb instead of trying to hold him; she would let him cry in his crib behind closed doors and loud music. Tiffany and Lena began a sexual relationship and often had parties at the house.

CHILD ABUSE, DEPENDENT ADULT ABUSE, AND ELDER ABUSE

INFORMATION FOR MANDATORY REPORTERS

Child abuse is an unfortunate social problem that has been around for a large part of our history, and will probably continue to be a part of our society for a much longer period of time. Early cases of child

abuse were initially dealt with under animal protection laws. In Iowa, the state did not "codify" mandatory child abuse reporting laws until 1978. Now, not only locally, but also at the state and national levels, statistics are maintained on confirmed child abuse cases.

Professionals within certain field are mandatory reporters. Some of those professional include daycare providers, school teachers, nursing (medical), social workers, therapists, and counselors to mention a few.

It is important for individuals within these professions and others to be educated and aware of what the process is when reporting alleged or suspected abuse. Most importantly though, is that you as the reporter need to be credible, and that you are not the individual determining if the abuse has actually occurred—you are only the reporter of suspected abuse—not the entity determining if the abuse has or has not occurred.

We need to focus on 6 critical areas when dealing with mandatory reporting and child abuse. Those six areas are:

1. The definition of child abuse according to the Iowa Code
2. To be familiar with and able to identify the categories of child abuse under Iowa law and give an example of each type
3. Be able to describe the physical and behavioral indicators of child abuse
4. Explain the responsibilities of mandatory reporters and the penalties for failure to report
5. Be able to list items that should be in a written child abuse report
6. The ability to recognize the role of human services and law enforcement in dealing with a child abuse report.

Reporting procedures in Iowa are fairly standard, and are similar in most other states. The utmost important thing to remember is to not take matters into your own hands. If imminent danger is present for a child, contact local law enforcement immediately. All other cases, you can call the local DHS (Department of Human Services) office during regular business hours or 1-800-362-2178 within 24 hours of becoming aware of the situation. After making the call, a written report must be filed with the DHS office within 48 hours. Information for the report should include as much factual information that you as the reporter has—but will hopefully include: names, addresses, ages, nature and extent of the injury, who the responsible party might be if other than the parent/caretaker, other information that might be helpful in establishing the cause of the injury, and your name and address.

We also need to be mindful of not only reporting suspected child abuse, but we need to educate individuals on the prevention of child abuse as well. Please refer to Prevent Child Abuse America, www.preventchildabuse.org for additional information. Also, for additional resources, the National Committee to Prevent Child Abuse, www.childabuse.or provides supplemental brochures and educational materials for the public. Some of the examples of brochures

NOTES

include *"What is Shaken Baby Syndrome"*, and *"Understanding How to Eliminate Child Abuse"*.

The Department of Human Services currently has the responsibility to make determinations of abuse in adults 18 years of age and older. The same DHS evaluators also investigate potential child abuse. Also, under Iowa Code, DHS is responsible for investigating allegations of dependent adult abuse as well. Abuse can happen anywhere—private homes, licensed facilities, in the community, etc. Help is available for elder abuse victims, caregivers, and families. More often than not, someone suspects that an older person is in need of assistance or is in an unsafe situation.

What can you do to prevent abuse? Report it!! You can call the same number that is provided for those regarding suspected child abuse which is-1-800-362-2178. Also, if you have concerns regarding potential or suspected abuse taking place within a licensed facility, you can call 1-877-686-0027 to report your concerns. Calls are confidential.

Iowa has a large elderly population, and the need for services is extremely important. Many of the referrals that are brought to the attention of providers are self-neglect cases, suggesting that the elder person/dependent adult is finding it difficult to care for themselves. There is another category of concern regarding elder adults, which is financial exploitation.

Financial exploitation is more than the misuse of the individual's resources, but can directly impact quality of care for the individual's medical, shelter, nutritional needs, etc. to name a few. Unfortunately,

© 2012, PHOTOCREO Michal, Shutterstock, Inc.

we live in a society that does not value our elderly population. Every person, regardless of age, race, sexuality, etc. deserves to be safe from harm. Each year numerous Iowans suffer from abuse—whether it be financial, physical, neglect, emotional, sexual—and sadly—usually at the hands of a family member or family friend. Elder abuse is often times not recognized and is most certainly under reported.

Elder abuse is legally defined in the Iowa code as the mistreatment, neglect, or exploitation of people age 60 or older. It may include physical, sexual, or financial abuse or exploitation. It may also be self-neglect.

Abuse—and what might it look like for and elder adult:

Physical—slapping, pushing, shoving, physical assault
Sexual Offenses—rape, sodomy, unwanted touching, indecent exposure
Financial Exploitation—misuse of funds, property or assets, misuse of the money not directly intended for the adult's benefit.
Neglect—withholding of care by a caregiver
Self-Neglect—exposing self to unsafe condition

What do you need to possibly be looking for? Perhaps injuries that do not fit the explanation that is provided; obvious lack of personal hygiene or medical care; malnourishment, unexplained poverty (bounced checks/overdrawn checking account); behavioral changes such as being withdrawn, timid (which are out of the ordinary for the individual) and perhaps a sense of increased anxiety or depression. These symptoms are not to say that abuse is occurring, but they certainly deserve some attention.

Abuse can be brought on due to stress, mental or physical limitation, alcohol and drug problems, gambling concerns, emotional problems—or perhaps just from a lack of understanding, information, knowledge or resources.

If nothing else—report it!

CHILD ABUSE: A GUIDE FOR MANDATORY REPORTERS

To make a report of suspected child abuse, contact your local Department of Human Services office during regular office hours. You may also make reports at any time by calling the toll-free 24-hour hotline:

CHILD ABUSE OVERVIEW

Child abuse is not a new phenomenon. The abuse and neglect of children has been documented for more than two thousand years. However, attempts to prevent child abuse are relatively new.

The first documented legal response to child abuse in the United States occurred in 1874. The New York Society for the Prevention of Cruelty to Animals pleaded in court to have an eight-year-old child

NOTES

removed from her abusive and neglectful environment. Since there were no child abuse laws, the Society argued that the child was, in fact, an animal, and should be provided the same protection as other animals. During the last few decades of the 1800s, societies to protect children from cruelty were formed in many states.

The next movement to protect children came as the result of several pediatricians publishing articles about children suffering multiple fractures and brain injuries at the hands of their caretakers. In 1961, Dr. C. Henry Kempe, then president of the American Academy of Pediatrics, held a conference on the "battered child syndrome," in which he outlined a "duty" to the child to prevent "repetition of trauma." The Battered Child Syndrome Conference resulted in many states passing laws to protect children from physical abuse.

Child abuse is now recognized as a problem of epidemic proportions. Child abuse has serious consequences that may remain as indelible pain throughout the victim's lifetime. The violence and negligence of parents and caretakers serve as a model for children as they grow up. The child victims of today, without protection and treatment, may become the child abusers of tomorrow.

As with any social issue, child abuse is a problem for the entire community. Achieving the goals of protective services requires the coordination of many resources. Each professional group and agency involved with a family assumes responsibility for specific elements of the child protective service process.

NATIONAL DATA Nationally, the 2007 "Child Maltreatment Report," published by the U.S. Department of Health and Human Services Children's Bureau, indicates that an estimated 3.2 million reports of child abuse involving 5.8 million children were made to child protection agencies that year, and that approximately 62% were accepted for investigation or assessment.

One-fourth of the investigations and assessments (25%) confirmed child abuse. There were an estimated 794,000 victims of child abuse nationwide. The rate of victimization was 10.6 per 1,000 children. The highest victimization rates were for the birth to age 3 group (16.5 per 1,000 children). There was no prior history of victimization for 75% of all victims.

National studies continue to indicate that only about one-third of maltreated children are reported to child protection agencies. Significant numbers of victims remain unidentified without protection and treatment.

In 1985, the U.S. Surgeon General declared family violence to be a national epidemic. At that time, an estimated 3.3 million children were exposed to violence by a family member against a mother or female caretaker. The U.S. Advisory Board on Child Abuse and Neglect found domestic violence to be the single major precursor to child abuse and neglect fatalities in the United States. Child abuse is 15 times more likely to occur in homes where adult domestic violence is present.

According to the *Effective Intervention in Domestic Violence & Child Maltreatment Cases: Guide for Policy and Practice*, published by the National Council of Juvenile and Family Court Judges in 1999, "domestic violence perpetrators do not victimize only adults. Recent reviews of more than two decades of studies have revealed that in families where women are abused, many of their children also are maltreated.

According to the Iowa Attorney General's Office, Crime Victim Assistance Division, from January 1995 through April 2009, 193 Iowans have been killed in domestic abuse homicides. During that period:

- 124 women were killed by their spouse, former spouse, boy-friend, or intimate partner;
- 23 men were killed by their partners;
- 46 bystanders were killed, including 20 children;
- 151 minor children survived the murder of their mother or father; and
- 62 children were present at the scene of a parent's murder.

Although many adults believe they have protected their child from exposure to domestic violence, 80% to 90% of children in those homes can give detailed descriptions of the violence experienced in their families. (Doyne, S., Bowermasyer, J., & Meloy, R. (1999). "Custody Disputes Involving Domestic Violence: Making Children's Needs a Priority," *Juvenile & Family Court Journal*, 50, (2)).

The U.S. Advisory Board on Child Abuse suggests that domestic violence may be the single major precursor to child fatalities in this country.

Varying by samples selected and types of data gathered, the majority of these studies have found that a substantial proportion, ranging from 30 to 60 percent, of battered mothers' children also are maltreated. Children who are abused physically or sexually or witness violence tend to exhibit more developmental, cognitive, emotional, and social behavior problems, including depression and increased aggression, than other children."

IOWA RESPONSE Iowa's child abuse reporting law, Iowa Code sections 232.67 through 232.75, was initially enacted in 1978 and has been amended several times since then. The intent of the law is to identify children who are victims of abuse. The law also provides for a professional assessment to determine if abuse has occurred. Accompanying the assessment are protective services designed to protect, treat, and prevent further maltreatment.

The purpose of the Iowa law is to provide the greatest possible protection to children by encouraging the reporting of suspected child abuse. The state respects the bond between parent and child. However, the state does assert the right to intervene for the general welfare of the child when there is a clear and present danger to the child's

NOTES

health, welfare, and safety. The state does not intend to interfere with reasonable parental discipline and child-rearing practices that are not injurious to the child.

According to Iowa statute, the Department of Human Services (DHS) has the responsibility to assess reports of suspected child abuse. DHS is the agency designated by law to receive reports of suspected child abuse and neglect.

In calendar year 2008, DHS accepted 23,236 reports for assessment. After completing the assessment of the allegations, DHS confirmed that abuse occurred in 7,981 (34%) of the assessed reports. There were 11,003 child victims named in the confirmed reports. Some children suffered multiple types of abuse or repeat maltreatment. These results represent a rate of 15.6 per 1,000 Iowa children abused for 2008.

DHS works closely with physicians, nurses, educators, mental health practitioners, law enforcement agencies, and the judiciary. These parties are involved in the identification, reporting, assessment, and treatment of cases of child maltreatment.

IOWA CONFIRMED CHILD ABUSE IN CALENDAR YEAR 2006–2008

Type of abuse	Percentage of Total Confirmed or Founded Abuse		
	2006	2007	2008
Denial of critical care	77.2%	78.87%	79.4%
Physical abuse	10.0%	9.35%	10.8%
Presence of illegal drugs	7.2%	6.63%	3.86%
Sexual abuse	4.1%	3.81%	3.86%
Cohabitation with registered sex offender	0.7%	0.84%	1.11%
Manufacturing or possession of danger-ous substance with intent to manufacture	0.5%	0.34%	0.67%
Mental injury	0.1%	0.12%	0.20%
Child prostitution	0.0%	0.0%	0.0%
Bestiality in the pres-ence of a minor	0.0%	0.0%	0.0%

Source: DHS Division of Results-Based Accountability reports of child abuse allegations that were confirmed or founded in calendar years 2006, 2007, and 2008. (Note: A victim may have suffered more than one type of abuse.)

Ultimately, children can be kept safer from abuse and neglect through increased community ownership, responsibility, and involvement. One entity (whether legislators, DHS, physicians, educators, or local law enforcement) alone cannot eliminate "child abuse." The safety of children depends upon how well communities support families, organize basic systems, and make inclusive decisions about available resources.

Partnerships that involve parents, neighbors, and grassroots community groups, in addition to public agencies and non-profit organizations, create community ownership, responsibility, and involvement. The vision of partnerships has evolved with the realization that "one size does not fit all." Through partnerships, its citizens define a community's needs, and services can be tailored to the particular needs and strengths of individual communities.

The child abuse reporting law is only one type of Iowa statute designed to deal with child abuse. Juvenile justice laws authorize the court to provide protection for children through supervision in their own homes or in substitute care. Criminal laws are separate from the child abuse reporting and juvenile justice laws. Criminal laws provide for prosecution of alleged perpetrators in cases where a criminal act has been committed.

AM I A MANDATORY REPORTER OF CHILD ABUSE?

Iowa law defines classes of people who <u>must</u> make a report of child abuse within 24 hours when they reasonably believe a child has suffered abuse. These "mandatory reporters" are professionals who have frequent contact with children, generally in one of six disciplines:

<u>Health</u>	<u>Education</u>	<u>Child care</u>
<u>Mental health</u>	<u>Law enforcement</u>	<u>Social work</u>

As outlined in Iowa Code section 232.69, the following classes of people are mandatory reporters when they examine, attend, counsel, or treat a child in the scope of professional practice or in their employment responsibilities:

- All licensed physicians and surgeons.
- Physician assistants.
- Dentists.
- Licensed dental hygienists.
- Optometrists.
- Podiatrists.
- Chiropractors.
- Residents or interns in any of the professions listed above.
- Registered nurses.
- Licensed practical nurse.

NOTES

- Basic and advanced emergency medical care providers.
- A social worker.
- An employee or operator of a public or private health care facility as defined in Iowa Code section 135C.1.
- A certified psychologist.
- A licensed school employee, certified paraeducator, or holder of a coaching authorization issued under Iowa Code section 272.31.
- An employee or operator of a licensed child care center, registered child care home, Head Start program, Family Development and Self-Sufficiency Grant program under Iowa Code section 217.12, or Healthy Opportunities for Parents to Experience Success—Healthy Families Iowa program under Iowa Code section 135.106.
- An employee or operator of a licensed substance abuse program or facility licensed under Iowa Code Chapter 125.
- An employee of an institution operated by DHS listed in Iowa Code section 218.1.
- An employee or operator of a juvenile detention or juvenile shelter care facility approved under Iowa Code section 232.142.
- An employee or operator of a foster care facility licensed or approved under Iowa Code Chapter 237.
- An employee or operator of a mental health center.
- A peace officer.
- A counselor or mental health professional.
- An employee or operator of a provider of services to children funded under a federally approved Medicaid home- and community-based services waiver.

The employer or supervisor of a person who is a mandatory reporter shall not apply a policy, work rule, or other requirement that interferes with the person making a report of child abuse.

Clergy members are not considered to be mandatory reporters unless they are functioning as social workers, counselors, or another role described as a mandatory reporter. If a member of clergy provides counseling services to a child, and the child discloses an abuse allegation, then the clergy member is mandated to report as a counselor. (The counseling is provided to a child during the scope of the reporter's profession as a counselor, not clergy.)

HEALTH   Health service professionals play many roles in the recognition and treatment of child abuse, including the recognition of the abuse, reporting the suspected abuse, crisis intervention, and long-term treatment.

Health services personnel are often the first line of defense in the early detection of child abuse. Most health professionals who treat children are required to be mandatory reporters of child abuse.

Health care professionals are often called upon to work collaboratively with many other disciplines, including social work, education, law enforcement, and the courts to ensure a multi-disciplinary approach to the recognition and treatment of child abuse.

A health care practitioner may, if medically indicated, take or cause to be taken, a radiological examination, physical examination, or other medical test of the child or take photographs, which would provide medical indications for the child abuse assessment.

A physician has the authority to keep a child in custody without a court order and without the consent of a parent, guardian, or custodian, provided that the child is in a circumstance or condition that presents an imminent danger to the child's life or health. However, the physician must orally notify the court within 24 hours. The ability to take or keep a child in custody is unique to physicians and peace officers.

EDUCATION Educators may spend more hours per day with children than their families. That's why the role of educators is vital in the mandatory reporting process. All licensed school employees, teachers, coaches and paraeducators are mandatory reporters.

The involvement of educators in the reporting of child abuse is mandated or supported by federal standards and regulations and state laws, policies and procedures. Each of these government levels provides authority for, encourages, or mandates educator involvement in the reporting process by stating what is required of the educator and how that obligation is to be fulfilled.

The primary authority at the federal level is the Federal Family Education Rights and Privacy Act (FERPA) of 1974. FERPA, which governs the release of information from school records, does not bar the reporting of suspected child abuse by educators.

In the majority of cases, educators will be relying not on school records, but on their own personal knowledge and observations when reporting child abuse. Because no school records are involved in these cases, FERPA does not apply.

In a small number of cases, it may be necessary to consult school records to determine whether a report of child abuse should be made. Ordinarily parental consent is required before information contained in school records can be released. However, there are exceptions that can apply in cases of child abuse.

Some local school systems and boards of education have enacted school policies and procedures regarding child abuse reporting. The policies and procedures support state law with regard to reporting and often provide internal mechanisms to be followed when a report of child abuse is made.

Local school policy may specify that parents be notified when the school makes a report of child abuse. If so, notify DHS of that local policy when making the report of child abuse.

NOTES

Sometimes local procedure may require that administrative staff be notified when a report of child abuse is made and a copy of the written report be filed.

CHILD CARE Child care providers play a critical role in keeping children safe. It is very important for them to report when they suspect child abuse. Child care providers include child care staff, foster parents, and residential care personnel. All of these people are mandatory reporters. A child care provider who suspects that a child has been abused should report that to DHS and to the licensing worker.

MENTAL HEALTH Mental health professionals are often trusted with intimate information about children and families. This makes their role critical when reporting child abuse. All counseling providers, even those who are self-employed, are mandatory reporters of child abuse in regard to the child they counsel.

LAW ENFORCEMENT Law enforcement officers play a very important role in protecting our children from child abuse. Law enforcement officers are seen as a symbol of public safety. They are in an excellent position to raise community awareness about child abuse.

Law enforcement officers often encounter situations that involve child abuse. For example, on domestic calls or during drug arrests the officer may learn of information that constitutes an allegation of child abuse. Children residing in homes where methamphetamine is being manufactured or where precursors are present constitutes an allegation of child abuse as well as possible criminal charges. Law enforcement is mandated to report to DHS.

Law enforcement officers who suspect child abuse in the line of duty are required to report that abuse to the Department of Human Services as soon as they suspect it. Law enforcement officers need to follow the same procedures as all mandatory reporters in reporting child abuse.

Law enforcement and child protective services may need to work together. Sometimes child protective service workers must visit isolated, dangerous locations and deal with unstable, violent, or substance abusing individuals.

Generally, child protective service workers do not have on-site communications (radio, car phone, etc.), weapons, or special training in self-protection. It is often necessary for law enforcement personnel to accompany child protective workers to conduct their assessment. Failure to have proper backup may have unfortunate consequences to both the child protection worker and the child that may have been abused.

Law enforcement has the power to arrest and to enforce any standing orders of the court. When it is necessary to remove a child from the child's home, law enforcement officers are often called upon for assistance. Law enforcement has the general authority to take custody of children.

Law enforcement is often able to react to emergency situations faster than child protective service. Law enforcement is also available 24 hours a day, while the child protection worker after hour response is limited in some communities.

OTHERS REQUIRED TO REPORT Some employers may have specific policies that require certain training and reporting procedures regarding child abuse for their staff, even when they are not by law considered mandatory reporters. Reporters who by law are not considered mandatory reporters will be considered permissive reporters regardless of the employer's requirements.

Iowa Administrative Code 441–175.23(2) mandates certified adoption investigators and DHS income maintenance workers to report suspected abuse. Income maintenance workers and certified adoption investigators are "mandated," not mandatory reporters. As such, they are not required to make a written report, although they may do so if they wish. They receive the same information and notices as permissive reporters. They are not entitled to written notification that the assessment has been completed nor to a copy of information placed on the Registry.

How do I report child abuse?

According to Iowa Code section 232.70, if you are a mandatory reporter of child abuse and you suspect a child has been abused, you need to report it to the Department of Human Services. The law requires you to report suspected child abuse to DHS orally within 24 hours of becoming aware of the situation. You must also make a report in writing within 48 hours after your oral report. The employer or supervisor of a person who is a mandatory or permissive reporter shall not apply a policy, work rule, or other requirement that interferes with the person making a report of child abuse.

As a mandatory reporter, you are also required to make an **oral report to law enforcement** if you have reason to believe that immediate protection of the child is necessary.

The law requires the reporting of suspected child abuse. It is not the reporter's role to validate the abuse. The law does not require you to have proof that the abuse occurred before reporting. The law clearly specifies that reports of child abuse must be made when the person reporting "reasonably believes a child has suffered abuse."

Reports are made in terms of the child's possible condition, not in terms of an accusation against parents. A report of child abuse is not an accusation, but a request to determine whether child abuse exists and begin the helping process.

Making a report of child abuse may be difficult. You may have doubts about whether the circumstances merit a report, how the parents will react, what the outcome will be, and whether or not the report

NOTES

will put the child at greater risk. The best way to minimize the difficulty of reporting is to:

- Be knowledgeable about the reporting requirements, and
- Be aware of the Department's intake criteria and the response that is initiated by making a report.

Within 24 hours of receiving your report, you will be orally notified whether or not the report has been accepted or rejected. Within five working days, you will also be sent form 470-3789, *Notice of Intake Decision,* indicating whether the report of child abuse was accepted or rejected.

REPORTING PROCEDURES If you see a child that is in **imminent danger,** immediately contact **law enforcement,** to provide immediate assistance to the child. Law enforcement is the only profession that can take a child into custody in that situation. After you have notified law enforcement, then call DHS.

To report a suspected case of child abuse:

- Call your county DHS office during regular business hours.
- Outside of regular business hours, please call 1-800-362-2178.
- Then, follow up by making a written report.

Oral and written reports should contain the following information, if it is known:

- The names and home address of the child and the child's parents or other persons believed to be responsible for the child's care.
- The child's present whereabouts.
- The child's age.
- The nature and extent of the child's injuries, including any evidence of previous injuries.
- The name, age, and condition of other children in the same household.
- Any other information that you believe may be helpful in establishing the cause of the abuse or neglect to the child.
- The identity of the person or persons responsible for the abuse or neglect to the child.
- Your name and address.

A sample copy of form 470-0665, *Report of Suspected Child Abuse,* is included at the end of this Guide. This form is available from the DHS website (http://www.dhs.state.ia.us). This specific form is not required, but you may use it as a guide in making a report of child abuse.

If you suspect sexual abuse of a child under the age of 12 by a non-caretaker, you are required by law to make a report of child abuse to DHS. If the child is aged 12 or older, you may report the sexual abuse by a non-caretaker but you are not required by law to do so.

DHS must report all sexual abuse allegations to law enforcement within 72 hours.

WAIVER OF CONFIDENTIALITY The issues of confidentiality and privileged communication are often areas of concern for mental health and health service professionals. Rules around confidentiality and privileged communication are waived during the child abuse assessment process (once a report of child abuse becomes a case).

Iowa Code section 232.71B indicates that the Department may request information from any person believed to have knowledge of a child abuse case. County attorneys, law enforcement officers, social services agencies, and all mandatory reporters (whether or not they made the report of suspected abuse) are obligated to cooperate and assist with the child abuse assessment upon the request of the Department.

Confidentiality is waived in Iowa Code section 232.74, which reads:

> Sections 622.9 (on communication between husband and wife) and 622.10 (on communication in professional confidence) and any statute or rule of evidence which excludes or makes privileged the testimony of health practitioners or mental health professionals as to confidential communications do not apply to evidence regarding a child's injuries or the cause of the injuries in any judicial proceeding, civil or criminal, resulting from a report of child abuse.

Physician privilege is waived in cases of suspected child abuse. Physicians are allowed to share whatever information is necessary with the Department of Human Services to facilitate a thorough assessment.

It is a good idea to let your clients know your status as a child abuse reporter at the onset of treatment. This will help establish an open relationship and minimize the client's feelings of betrayal if a report needs to be made. Making a child abuse referral does not necessarily mean that your relationship with the child and family will end, especially when you are able to support the family during the assessment process.

When possible, discuss the need to make a child abuse report with the family. However, be aware that there are certain situations where if the family is warned about the assessment process, the child may be at risk for further abuse, or the family may leave with the child.

In situations where you are not required to make a child abuse report, ethically you need to address these concerns in a therapeutic setting. Refer to your Professional Code of Ethics for further clarification on issues surrounding child abuse.

IMMUNITY FROM LIABILITY Iowa Code section 232.73 provides immunity from any civil or criminal liability which might otherwise be incurred when a person participates in good faith in:

- Making a report, photographs, or x-rays,
- Performing a medically relevant test, or
- Assisting in an assessment of a child abuse report.

NOTES

A person has the same immunity with respect to participation in good faith in any judicial proceeding resulting from the report or relating to the subject matter of the report.

As used in this section and section 232.77, "medically relevant test" means a test that produces reliable results of exposure to cocaine, heroin, amphetamine, methamphetamine, or other illegal drugs, or their combinations or derivatives, including a drug urine screen test.

SANCTIONS FOR FAILURE TO REPORT CHILD ABUSE Iowa Code section 232.75 provides for civil and criminal sanctions for failing to report child abuse. Any person, official, agency, or institution required by this chapter to report a suspected case of child abuse who knowingly and willfully fails to do so is guilty of a simple misdemeanor.

Any person, official, agency, or institution required by Iowa Code section 232.69 to report a suspected case of child abuse who knowingly fails to do so, or who knowingly interferes with the making of such a report in violation of section 232.70, is civilly liable for the damages proximately caused by such failure or interference.

SANCTIONS FOR REPORTING FALSE INFORMATION The act of reporting false information regarding an alleged act of child abuse to DHS or causing false information to be reported, knowing that the information is false or that the act did not occur, is classified as simple misdemeanor under Iowa Code section 232.75, subsection 3.

If DHS receives a fourth report which identifies the same child as a victim of child abuse and the same person as the alleged abuser or which is from the same person, and DHS determined that the three earlier reports were entirely false or without merit, DHS may:

- Determine that the report is again false or without merit due to the report's spurious or frivolous nature.
- Terminate its assessment of the report.
- Provide information concerning the reports to the county attorney for consideration of criminal charges.

INDICATORS OF POSSIBLE CHILD ABUSE The following physical and behavioral indicators are listed as signs of possible child abuse for you to consider in making your report. These indicators need to be evaluated in the context of the child's environment. The presence of one or more of these symptoms does not necessarily prove abuse. These lists are examples and are not all-inclusive.

PHYSICAL INDICATORS

- Bruises and welts on the face, lips, mouth, torso, back, buttocks, or thighs in various stages of healing
- Bruises and welts in unusual patterns reflecting the shape of the article used (e.g., electric cord, belt buckle) or in clusters indicating repeated contact

- Bruises on infant, especially facial bruises
- Subdural hematomas, retinal hemorrhages, internal injuries
- Cigarette burns, especially on the soles, palms, backs or buttocks
- Immersion burns (sock-like, glove-like, doughnut-shaped) on buttocks or genitalia
- Burns patterned like an electric element, iron or utensil
- Rope burns on arms, legs, neck or torso
- Fractures of the skull, nose, ribs or facial structure in various stages of healing
- Multiple or spiral fractures
- Unexplained (or multiple history for) bruises, burns or fractures
- Lacerations or abrasions to the mouth, frenulum, lips, gums, eyes or external genitalia
- Bite marks or loss of hair
- Speech disorders, lags in physical development, ulcers
- Asthma, severe allergies or failure to thrive
- Consistent hunger, poor hygiene, inappropriate dress
- Consistent lack of supervision; abandonment
- Unattended physical or emotional problems or medical needs
- Difficulty in walking or sitting
- Pain or itching in the genital area
- Bruises, bleeding or infection in the external genitalia, vaginal or anal areas
- Torn, stained or bloody underclothing
- Frequent urinary or yeast infections
- Venereal disease, especially in pre-teens
- Pregnancy
- Substance abuse—alcohol or drugs
- Positive test for presence of illegal drugs in the child's body

BEHAVIOR INDICATORS

- Afraid to go home; frightened of parents
- Alcohol or drug abuse
- Apprehensive when children cry, overly concerned for siblings
- Begging, stealing or hoarding food
- Behavioral extremes, such as aggressiveness or withdrawal
- Complaints of soreness, uncomfortable movement
- Constant fatigue, listlessness or falling asleep in class
- Delay in securing or failure to secure medical care
- Delinquent, runaway or truant behaviors
- Destructive, antisocial or neurotic traits, habit disorders
- Developmental or language delays

- Excessive seductiveness or promiscuity
- Extended stays at school (early arrival and late departure)
- Extreme aggression, rage, or hyperactivity
- Fear of a person or an intense dislike of being left with someone
- Frequently absent or tardy from school or drops out of school or sudden school difficulties
- History of abuse or neglect provided by the child
- Inappropriate clothing for the weather
- Massive weight change
- Indirect allusions to problems at home such as, "I want to live with you"
- Lack of emotional control, withdrawal, chronic depression, hysteria, fantasy or infantile behavior
- Lags in growth or development
- Multiple or inconsistent histories for a given injury
- Overly compliant, passive, undemanding behavior; apathy
- Poor peer relationships; shunned by peers
- Poor self-esteem, self-devaluation, lack of confidence or self-destructive behavior
- Role-reversal behavior or overly dependent behavior; states there is no caretaker
- Suicide attempts
- Unusual interest in or knowledge of sexual matters, expressing affection in inappropriate ways
- Wary of adult contacts, lack of trust, uncomfortable with or threatened by physical contact or closeness

WHAT IS CHILD ABUSE UNDER IOWA LAW?

DHS has the legal authority to conduct an assessment of child abuse when it is alleged that:

- The victim is a child.
- The child is subjected to one or more of the nine categories of child abuse defined in Iowa Code section 232.68:

  - <u>Physical abuse</u>
  - <u>Mental injury</u>
  - <u>Sexual abuse</u>
  - <u>Denial of critical care</u>
  - <u>Child prostitution</u>
  - <u>Presence of illegal drugs</u>
  - <u>Manufacturing or possession of a dangerous substance</u>
  - <u>Bestiality in the presence of a minor</u>
  - <u>Allows access by a registered sex offender</u>

- The abuse is the result of the acts or omissions of the person responsible for the care of the child.

CHILD A **child** is defined in Iowa Code section 232.68 as any person under the age of 18 years.

The victim of child abuse is a person under the age of 18 who has suffered one or more of the categories of child abuse as defined in Iowa law (physical abuse, mental injury, sexual abuse, denial of critical care, child prostitution, presence of illegal drugs, manufacturing or possession of a dangerous substance or bestiality in the presence of a minor.

CARETAKER A perpetrator of child abuse must be a **person responsible for the care of a child**. **A person responsible for the care of a child** is defined in Iowa Code section 232.68 as:

a. Parent, guardian, or foster parent.
b. A relative or any other person with whom the child resides and who assumes care or supervision of the child, without reference to the length of time or continuity of such residence.
c. An employee or agent of any public or private facility providing care for a child, including an institution, hospital, health care facility, group home, mental health center, residential treatment center, shelter care facility, detention center, or child care facility.
d. Any person providing care for a child, but with whom the child does not reside, without reference to the duration of the care.

A person who assumes responsibility for the care or supervision of the child may assume such responsibility through verbal or written agreement, or implicitly through the willing assumption of the caretaking role.

Perpetrators of child abuse come from all walks of life, races, religions, and nationalities. They come from all professions and represent all levels of intelligence and standards of living. There is no single social strata free from incidents of child abuse.

Abusive parents may show disregard for the child's own needs, limited abilities, and feelings. Many abusive parents believe that children exist to satisfy parental needs and that the child's needs are unimportant. Children who don't satisfy the parent's needs may become victims of child abuse.

Sexual abusers may have deviant personality traits and behaviors that can result in sexual contact with a child. Sexual abuse perpetrators sometimes use threats, bribery, coercion or force to engage a child in sexual activity. They violate the trust that a child inherently places in them for care and protection, and exploit the power and authority of their position as a trusted caretaker in order to sexually misuse a child. Often the child is threatened or warned "not to tell," creating a conspiracy of silence about the abuse.

NOTES

EDUCATORS AS CARETAKERS Normally teachers are not considered caretakers in the teaching and supervising of children. **Note:** If there is an accusation of child abuse (physical abuse, sexual abuse or child prostitution) by an employee in the school district, every school district will have policies and procedures in place which they will follow.

Iowa Code section 280.17 requires that "board of directors of a public school and the authorities in control of a nonpublic school prescribe procedures, in accordance with the guidelines contained in the model policy developed by the Department of Education in consultation with the Department of Human Services, and adopted by the Department of Education, for handling reports of child abuse, alleged to have been committed by an employee or agent of the public or nonpublic school."

The jurisdiction established by 281 Iowa Administrative Code 102.3, for reports of child abuse alleged to have been committed by an employee or agent of a public or nonpublic school, is "acts of the school employee on school grounds, on school time, on a school-sponsored activity, or in a school-related context."

There are times when an educator may be in the role of a caretaker and outside the jurisdiction of the school. For example, a teacher could be considered a caretaker if the teacher is responsible for supervising a child on an overnight trip.

DHS will review reports of child abuse alleged to have been committed by an employee or agent of a public or nonpublic school to determine if a joint assessment with school investigative personnel is appropriate. Where jurisdiction is unclear or there are other extenuating circumstances, DHS may initiate an assessment.

CHILDREN AS CARETAKERS Children are sometimes caretakers for other children and may be responsible for abusing a child in their care. Children may be in a caretaker role, for example, as a baby-sitter. An adult caretaker may be considered responsible if they delegated care responsibilities to an inappropriate minor caregiver.

A mandatory reporter who suspects that abuse has occurred when one child is caring for another is required by law to make a child abuse report. DHS will then determine if any action should be taken.

PHYSICAL ABUSE "Physical abuse" is defined as any non-accidental physical injury, or injury which is at variance with the history given of it, suffered by a child as the result of the acts or omissions of a person responsible for the care of the child.

Common indicators could include unusual or unexplained burns, bruises, or fractures. Health services personnel should be especially alert to cases of child abuse where inconsistent histories are presented.

Inconsistent histories can take the form of an explanation that does not fit the degree or type of injury to the child, or where the story or explanation of the injury changes over time.

Some indicators of child abuse are not visible on the child's body. Many times there are no physical indicators of abuse. A child's behavior can change as a result of abuse. Health services personnel need to be alert to possible behavioral indicators of abuse and if they believe those to be present, they are required to make a report. Behavioral indicators include behaviors such as:

- Extreme aggression.
- Withdrawal.
- Seductive behaviors.
- Being uncomfortable with physical contact or closeness.

MENTAL INJURY "Mental injury" is defined as any mental injury to a child's intellectual or psychological capacity as evidenced by an observable and substantial impairment in the child's ability to function within the child's normal range of performance and behavior as the result of the acts or omissions of a person responsible for the care of the child, if the impairment is diagnosed and confirmed by a licensed physician or qualified mental health professional as defined in Iowa Code section 622.10.

Examples of mental injury may include:

- **Ignoring** the child and failing to provide necessary stimulation, responsiveness, and validation of the child's worth in normal family routine.
- **Rejecting** the child's value, needs, and request for adult validation and nurturance.
- **Isolating** the child from the family and community; denying the child normal human contact.
- **Terrorizing** the child with continual verbal assaults, creating a climate of fear, hostility, and anxiety, thus preventing the child from gaining feelings of safety and security.
- **Corrupting** the child by encouraging and reinforcing destructive, antisocial behavior until the child is so impaired in socio-emotional development that interaction in normal social environments is not possible.
- **Verbally assaulting** the child with constant, excessive name-calling, harsh threats, and sarcastic put downs that continually "beat down" the child's self-esteem with humiliation.
- **Overpressuring** the child with subtle but consistent pressure to grow up fast and to achieve too early in the areas of academics, physical or motor skills, or social interaction, which leaves the child feeling that he or she is never quite good enough.

NOTES

SEXUAL ABUSE "Sexual abuse" is defined as the commission of a sexual offense with or to a child pursuant to Iowa Code Chapter 709, Iowa Code section 726.2, or Iowa Code section 728.12, subsection 1, as a result of the acts or omissions of the person responsible for the care of the child.

Notwithstanding Iowa Code section 702.5, the commission of a sexual offense under this paragraph includes any sexual offense referred to in this paragraph with or to a person under the age of 18 years.

There are several sub-categories of sexual abuse:

- First degree sexual abuse
- Second degree sexual abuse
- Third degree sexual abuse
- Detention in a brothel
- Lascivious acts with a child
- Indecent exposure
- Assault with intent to commit sexual abuse
- Indecent contact with a child
- Lascivious conduct with a minor
- Incest
- Sexual exploitation by a counselor or therapist
- Sexual exploitation of a minor
- Sexual misconduct with offenders and juveniles
- Invasion of privacy-nudity

Behavioral indicators of sexual abuse could include things such as excessive knowledge of sexual matters beyond their normal developmental age or seductiveness. Physical indicators of sexual abuse could include things such as bruised or bleeding genitalia, venereal disease, or even pregnancy.

DENIAL OF CRITICAL CARE "Denial of critical care" is defined as the failure on the part of a person responsible for the care of a child to provide for the adequate food, shelter, clothing or other care necessary for the child's health and welfare when financially able to do so or when offered financial or other reasonable means to do so.

Note: What most people think of as an issue of "neglect" is covered under the child abuse category of "denial of critical care."

A parent or guardian legitimately practicing religious beliefs who does not provide specified medical treatment for a child for that reason alone shall not be considered abusing the child. However, this does not preclude a court from ordering that medical service be provided to the child where the child's health requires it.

Denial of critical care includes the following eight sub-categories:

- **Failure to provide adequate food and nutrition** to such an extent that there is danger of the child suffering injury or death.
- **Failure to provide adequate shelter** to such an extent that there is danger of the child suffering injury or death.
- **Failure to provide adequate clothing** to such an extent that there is danger of the child suffering injury or death.

- **Failure to provide adequate health care** to such an extent that there is danger of the child suffering serious injury or death.

- **Failure to provide the mental health care** necessary to adequately treat an observable and substantial impairment in the child's ability to function.

- **Gross failure to meet the emotional** needs of the child necessary for normal development evidenced by the presence of an observable and substantial impairment in the child's ability to function within the normal range of performance and behavior.

- **Failure to provide proper supervision** of a child which a reasonable and prudent person would exercise under similar facts and circumstances, to such an extent that there is danger of the child suffering injury or death.

This definition includes cruel and undue confinement of a child and the dangerous operation of a motor vehicle when the person responsible for the care of the child is driving recklessly or driving while intoxicated with the child in the vehicle.

Other situations that fall under this subcategory include:

- Illegal drug usage by the caretaker of a child

  When you make an allegation of denial of critical care because a child lacks proper supervision due to illegal drug usage by a caretaker you may be asked questions to help DHS determine the type of drug and the degree of risk to the child.

  Some illegal drugs may have a greater impact on the supervision abilities of the caretaker than others. For example, methamphetamine usage by a child's caretaker has inherent risks to the child given the known effects of methamphetamines. DHS will consider the known effect of the drug named and other information to assess risk to the child's safety.

- Children home alone

  DHS receives many inquiries each year regarding when a child can be left home alone safely. Iowa law does not define an age that is appropriate for a child to be left alone. Each situation is unique. Examples of questions to help determine whether there are safety concerns for the child include:

  - Does the child have any physical disabilities?
  - Could the child get out of the house in an emergency?
  - Does the child have a phone and know how to use it?
  - Does the child know how to reach the caretaker?
  - How long will the child be left home alone?
  - Is the child afraid to be left home alone?
  - Does the child know how to respond to an emergency such as fire or injury?

NOTES

- Lice and truancy

  Head lice and truancy are often reported as child abuse allegations. However, the endangerment does not generally rise to the level that must be present to constitute a child abuse allegation.

  If other conditions are present or the situation poses a risk to the child's health and welfare, it should be reported as child abuse. Even if the report is rejected for assessment, other services may be offered to the child and family.

- **Failure to respond to the infant's life-threatening conditions** by failing to provide treatment which in the treating physician's judgment will be most likely to be effective in ameliorating or correcting all conditions.

This subcategory or the denial of critical care abuse type is also known as "withholding of medically indicated treatment." The type of treatments included are appropriate nutrition, hydration, and medication.

The term does not include the failure to provide treatment other than appropriate nutrition, hydration and medication to an infant when, in the treating physician's medical judgment, any of the following circumstances apply:

- The infant is chronically and irreversibly comatose.
- The provision of treatment would merely prolong dying, not be effective in ameliorating or correcting all of the infant's life-threatening conditions, or otherwise be futile in terms of the survival of the infant.
- The provision of the treatment would be virtually futile in terms of the survival of the infant and the treatment itself under the circumstances would be inhumane.

CHILD PROSTITUTION "Child prostitution" is defined as the acts or omissions of a person responsible for the care of a child which allow, permit, or encourage the child to engage in acts prohibited pursuant to Iowa Code section 725.1. Notwithstanding Iowa Code section 702.5, acts or omissions under this paragraph include an act or omission referred to in this paragraph with or to a person under the age of 18 years.

Note: "Prostitution" is defined as a person who sells or offers for sale the person's services as a partner in a sex act, or who purchases or offers to purchase such services.

PRESENCE OF ILLEGAL DRUGS "Presence of illegal drugs" is defined as occurring when an illegal drug is present in a child's body as a direct and foreseeable consequence of the acts or omissions of the person responsible for the care of the child.

Iowa Code section 232.77 states that, "If a health practitioner discovers in a child physical or behavioral symptoms of the effect of exposure to cocaine, heroin, amphetamine, methamphetamine, or other illegal drugs or combination or derivatives thereof, which were not prescribed by a health practitioner, or if the health practitioner has determined through examination of the natural mother of the child that the child was exposed in utero, the health practitioner may perform or cause to be performed a medically relevant test as defined section 232.73, on the child. The practitioner shall report any positive results of such a test on the child to the department. The department shall begin an assessment pursuant to section 232.71B upon receipt of such a report."

"Illegal drugs" are defined as cocaine, heroin, amphetamine, methamphetamine, other illegal drugs (including marijuana), or combinations or derivatives of illegal drugs which were not prescribed by a health practitioner.

Examples of situations that may result in a determination of this type of abuse:

- An infant is born with illegal drugs present in the infant's system as determined by a medical test. The illegal drugs were present in the infant's body due to the illegal drug usage by the mother before the baby's birth.
- A three-year-old child tests positive for illegal drugs due to exposure to the illegal drugs when the child's caretakers used illegal drugs in the child's home.

MANUFACTURING OR POSSESSION OF A DANGEROUS SUBSTANCE "Manufacturing or possession of a dangerous substance" is defined in Iowa Code section 232.2, subsection 6, paragraph p, as occurring when the person responsible for the care of a child:

- Has manufactured a dangerous substance in the presence of the child, or
- Knowingly allows the manufacture of a dangerous substance by another person in the presence of a child, or
- Possesses a product containing ephedrine, its salts, optical isomers, salts of optical isomers, or pseudoephedrine, its salts, optical isomers, salts of optical isomers, with the intent to use the product as a precursor or an intermediary to a dangerous substance in the presence of the child.

For the purposes of this definition, "in the presence of a child" means the manufacture or possession occurred:

- In the physical presence of a child, or
- In a child's home, on the premises, or in a motor vehicle located on the premises, or

NOTES

- Under other circumstances in which a reasonably prudent person would know that the manufacture or possession may be seen, smelled, or heard by a child.

Iowa Code section 232.2, subsection 6, paragraph p, defines "dangerous substance" as:

- Amphetamine, its salts, isomers, or salts of its isomers.
- Methamphetamine, its salts, isomers, or salts of its isomers.
- A chemical or combination of chemicals that poses a reasonable risk of causing an explosion, fire, or other danger to the life or health of people who are in the vicinity while the chemical or combination of chemicals is used or is intended to be used in any of the following:
  - The process of manufacturing an illegal or controlled substance.
  - As a precursor in the manufacturing of an illegal or controlled substance.
  - As an intermediary in the manufacturing of an illegal or controlled substance.

Note: DHS must report this type of allegation to law enforcement, as this is a criminal act.

BESTIALITY IN THE PRESENCE OF A MINOR Bestiality in the presence of a minor is defined as the commission of a sex act with an animal in the presence of a minor as defined in Iowa Code section 717C.1 by a person who resides in a home with a child, as the result of the acts or omissions of a person responsible for the care of the child. **Note:** DHS must report this type of allegation to law enforcement, as this is a criminal act.

ALLOWS ACCESS BY A REGISTERED SEX OFFENDER It is child abuse if a caretaker-knowingly allows unsupervised access to a child by a registered sex offender or allows a registered sex offender to have custody or control of a child up to age 14 or a child up to age 18 if the child has a mental or physical disability. The exceptions are if the registered sex offender is the caretaker' spouse or is a minor child of the caretaker. **Note:** DHS must report this type of allegation to law enforcement, as this is a criminal act under child endangerment.

HOW DOES DHS RESPOND?

A DHS child abuse assessment consists of the following processes:

- Intake
- Case assignment
- Evaluation of the alleged abuse

- Determining if abuse occurred
- Placing a report on the Child Abuse Registry
- Assessment of family strengths and needs
- Preparing forms and reports

INTAKE The purpose of intake is to obtain information to ensure that reports of child abuse meeting the criteria for assessment are accepted and reports that do not meet the legal requirements are appropriately rejected. DHS policy is to accept a report when there is insufficient information to reject it.

The first step in this process is to initiate safeguards for children who are at risk or have been abused. DHS staff will ask questions of the reporter, record necessary information, and discern between significant and extraneous information.

Information gathered at intake includes:

- The allegation of child abuse
- The identify and location of the child, parents or caretakers
- The safety of and risk to the child
- The identity and location of the person allegedly responsible for the abuse
- That person's access to children
- Information regarding the mandatory reporter

The supervisor is responsible for ensuring that accurate information is documented.

While it is helpful to be familiar with child abuse definitions to make a report, knowing the definitions and terminology is not essential. DHS will determine the type of abuse being alleged. It may be possible to make reasonable inferences that would cause a report to be accepted for assessment based upon the description of what occurred, so detail and accurate information is essential.

You may be contacted when:

- Your initial report is made through a written report of child abuse.
- Any of the information in your initial report is unclear or incomplete.
- Information in your initial report is called into question once the assessment is initiated.
- The written report you submit contains new or different information from that provided in your oral report of child abuse.

REPORTS FROM MULTIPLE REPORTERS When more than one mandatory reporter reasonably suspects abuse involving the same incident, the mandatory reporters, may jointly make a written report to DHS.

NOTES

When more than one reporter separately makes a report of suspected child abuse on the same incident, and the first report is currently being assessed, DHS will advise the subsequent reporters that the report of child abuse they are making has already been accepted as a case.

TIME FRAME FOR DECIDING WHETHER TO ACCEPT A REPORT FOR ASSESSMENT The DHS decision on whether to accept or reject a report of child abuse is to be made within a **1-hour or 12-hour** time frame from receipt of the report, depending on the information which is provided and the level of risk to the child:

- When a report indicates that the child has suffered a "**high-risk**" injury or there is an **immediate threat** to the child, the Department acts immediately to address the child's safety. The decision to accept the report of child abuse is made within **one hour** from receipt of the report.

- When the report **does not meet the criteria** to be accepted, such as the person alleged responsible is not a caretaker, but the report alleges the child is at **high risk**, DHS still acts immediately to address the child's safety (by calling law enforcement, for example). A supervisor reviews and approves the decision to reject the report of child abuse within **one hour** from receipt of the report.

- When a report indicates that the child has been abused, but it is not considered a "high risk" injury or there is **no immediate threat** to the child, DHS still acts promptly. The decision to accept the report of child abuse and supervisory approval on that decision are made within **12 hours** from receipt of the report.

- When the report **does not meet the criteria** to be accepted, such as the person alleged responsible is not a caretaker, and the report alleges the child is not considered to be at "high risk," a supervisor reviews and approves the decision to reject the report of child abuse within **12 hours** from receipt of the report.

ACCEPTED INTAKES When your report meets the criteria for assessment, DHS will inform you that the report of child abuse has been accepted as a case within 24 hours of receiving the report. DHS may provide this oral notification at the time that the report is made if the report is accepted immediately.

If your report is not accepted immediately because further consultation is required with a supervisor, you will be informed that further consultation is needed before a decision can be made, and someone will be calling you back with the decision.

REJECTED INTAKES DHS must obtain sufficient information to be able to determine if a report meets the intake criteria. A supervisor reviews the report and makes the final determination about rejecting the report for assessment.

If your report is rejected, DHS will:

- Contact law enforcement if a child's safety appears to be in jeopardy.
- Orally notify you that the report has been rejected within 24 hours of receipt.
- Send you a written notice indicating the decision to reject the report within five working days of its receipt, using form 470-3789, *Notice of Intake Decision*, which includes instructions on what to do if you disagree with the decision.
- Provide a copy of intake information to the county attorney within five working days of its receipt.

You will be advised that:

- The report is being rejected for one or more of the following reasons:
  - The reported victim is not a child.
  - The person alleged to have abused the child is not a caretaker.
  - The reported abuse does not fall within the definition of child abuse.
- The report will be screened for a possible "child in need of assistance" assessment to determine if juvenile court action is necessary. The family may apply for services through DHS if there is a founded child abuse report or a juvenile court order.
- You may inform the family of services available in the community.

When intake information does not meet the legal definition of child abuse, but a criminal act to a child is alleged, DHS refers the report to the appropriate law enforcement agency.

If the intake information alleges sexual abuse of a child by a person who is not a "caretaker," DHS refers the report to law enforcement verbally and also submits the referral information in writing within 72 hours of receiving the report.

The local DHS assessment unit keeps a copy of intake information for reports of child abuse that have been rejected for six months, then destroys it.

Rejected intake information is not considered "child abuse information." It is governed by the same provisions of confidentiality as DHS service case records. If a subject of a report requests information about a rejected intake involving the subject, DHS will provide a copy of the rejected intake to the subject, if it is available, after removing the name of the reporter.

If you become aware of new information after your report has been rejected, make a new report to DHS.

Case assignment   When a report indicates that the child has suffered a "high risk" injury or there is an immediate threat to the child, DHS must act immediately to address the child's safety. The case must be assigned **immediately**.

When a report indicates that the child has been abused but it is not considered a "high risk" injury or there is no immediate threat to the child, DHS must still act promptly. The case must be assigned within **12 hours from receipt of the report**.

The primary purpose of the assessment is to take action to protect and safeguard the child by evaluating the safety of and risk to the child named in the report and any other children in the same home as the parents or other person responsible for their care.

If DHS staff believe at any time during the assessment that there is an immediate threat because of abuse, they will immediately contact the proper authorities and communicate these concerns. This may include any or all of the following:

- Law enforcement
- Juvenile court
- Physicians

DHS staff have contact with the family in all assessments. Other assessment activities vary, depending upon the evaluation of the child's safety and the family's strengths and needs.

Evaluation of the alleged abuse   During the evaluation process, DHS gathers information about the allegations of child abuse, as well as the strengths and needs of the family, through:

- Observing the alleged child victim
- Interviewing subjects of the report and other sources
- Gathering documentation
- Evaluating the safety of and risk to the child

Observation of the Alleged Child Victim   The purpose of observation of the alleged victim is to address the safety of the child and determine if the child has visible symptoms of abuse. Careful and timely observation of the child is most relevant to physical abuse allegations. Observation may also be relevant in assessments involving allegations of denial of critical care, particularly failure to provide adequate food, shelter, or clothing.

Requirements for observations depend on the level of risk to the child posed by the allegation, as follows:

- <u>1 hour</u> when the report involves an immediate threat or high risk to the child's safety.
- <u>24 hours</u> when the report doesn't involve immediate threat or high risk to the child but the person alleged responsible has access to the child.
- <u>96 hours</u> when the report doesn't involve an immediate threat or high risk to the child and the person alleged responsible clearly does not have access to the child.

Whenever possible, the child protection worker attempts to observe and interview the child named in the report when interviewing the parents. When the worker must observe and interview a child named in the report away from the parental home, attempts are made to obtain parental consent.

Interviews with Subjects of the Report and Other Sources **DHS** staff interview the child to gather information not only regarding the abuse allegations, but also about the child's immediate safety, the risk of abuse, the parents, the person allegedly responsible for the abuse, and the family.

Other siblings may be interviewed to determine if they have experienced abuse, to evaluate their vulnerability, to gather corroborating information regarding the alleged child victim, and to gather information to assist in the risk assessment.

During an assessment, DHS may interview parents who are not alleged to have abused the child to find out what they know about the alleged abuse, gather information related to the risk of abuse; and determine their capacity to protect the child.

Iowa law requires that the person allegedly responsible for abuse be offered an opportunity (when the person's whereabouts are known) to be interviewed and respond to the allegations, but the person may decline the interview. The information is used to determine if abuse occurred, as well as to measure the risk this person may present to the alleged victim, other children, or others residing in the household.

DHS may contact and interview other people who may have relevant information to share regarding the report of the alleged abuse and the assessment of the safety of and risk to the child. During an assessment, physicians are asked to contact DHS immediately when:

- The parents or caretakers fail to take the child to the scheduled appointment.
- There is any confirmation or evidence of physical abuse.
- The child has other medical conditions that require immediate medical attention.

NOTES

Professional consultation may be sought, including the use of multi-disciplinary teams, or child protection assistance teams or child protection centers when a determination is needed which is outside the Department's professional scope. For example, a worker may be able to identify a child who is underweight, but "failure to thrive" is a diagnosis that only a physician can make.

Multidisciplinary teams consist of professionals practicing in medicine, public health, mental health, social work, child development, education, law, juvenile probation, law enforcement, nursing, domestic violence and substance abuse counseling.

These teams function as an advisory and consultation group to aid child protection workers in resolving issues related to a case during the assessment phase. They may also assist in identifying treatment plans. Counties or multi-county areas with 50 or more reports of child abuse annually are required to develop multidisciplinary teams.

Child protection assistance teams are convened by the county attorney and involve DHS, law enforcement and the county attorney to consult on cases involving a forcible felony against a child younger than age 14 by a person responsible for the care of the child and child sexual abuse. The team may consult with other professionals in specified disciplines.

The county attorney is to establish a team for each county unless two or more county attorneys agree to establish a single team for a multicounty area. The team may consult with or include juvenile court officers, medical and mental health professions, physicians or other hospital-based health professions, court appointed special advocates, guardian ad litem and members of a multidisciplinary team created by DHS for child abuse assessments.

DHS has established agreements with multiple child protection centers across the state of Iowa. These centers assist child protection workers in assessment of reports of child abuse. In most cases, these centers provide medical evaluations and psychosocial assessments of the victim when there are allegations of sexual abuse or serious physical abuse.

Other evaluative information is sometimes obtained through textbooks, scholarly journals, or other publications.

GATHERING DOCUMENTATION Documentation gathered during the assessment process is used to assist in determining if the information contained with the report of child abuse is accurate, to complete the assessment of family strengths, and developing a plan of action.

Iowa Code section 232.71B indicates that any mandatory reporter, the county attorney, any law enforcement agency, and any social service agency in the state shall cooperate and assist in the assessment upon the request of the DHS.

In addition to information gathered through interviews, the child protective worker may take photographs or secure photographs taken by others to show injuries to the child or to document conditions in the household. Common sources for photographic documentation are police departments and hospitals.

DHS by law may request the criminal history of a person alleged to be responsible for abuse. Information suggesting that a record check is advisable may include allegations of sexual abuse, domestic violence, or abuse of alcohol or other drugs.

DHS may use medical reports and records that are relevant to the report of child abuse, including X-rays, findings of physical or sexual abuse examinations, reports from interviews and examinations at a child protection center and medically relevant tests related to the presence of illegal drugs within a child's body.

DHS may use audiotapes, videotapes, and other electronic recording media to document observations or conversations.

EVALUATION OF THE SAFETY OF AND RISK TO THE CHILD The evaluation of a child's safety is an ongoing activity that continues during the entire assessment process. A safety analysis focuses on the current situation. A child is considered "safe" when the evaluation of all available information leads to the conclusion that the child will not be abused in the current living arrangement.

If a child is determined not to be safe, DHS takes action to address safety concerns. This may include (but is not limited to) any of the following active steps:

- Provision of family preservation services.
- Provision of family centered services.
- Removal of a child from the home.
- Placement of child with relatives.
- Removal of person allegedly responsible for the abuse from the home.

The assessment of the risk of abuse to the child is based on the following factors:

- Severity of the incident or condition.
- Chronicity of the incident or condition.
- The child's age, medical condition, mental and physical maturity, and functioning.
- Attitude of the person allegedly responsible for the abuse regarding its occurrence.
- Current resources, services, and supports available to the family that can meet the family's needs and increase protection for the child.
- Special events, situations, or circumstances that may have created immediate stress, tension, or anxiety in the family or household.
- Access of the person allegedly responsible for the abuse to the child.
- Willingness and ability of the parent, or caretaker not responsible for the abuse, to protect the child from further abuse.

NOTES

DETERMINATION IF ABUSE OCCURRED After gathering necessary information from observations, interviews and documentation, and after assessing the credibility of subjects of the report, collateral contacts and information, DHS must determine whether or not abuse occurred. Each category or subcategory of child abuse requires that specific criteria be met in order to conclude that abuse occurred.

This determination is based on a "preponderance" of credible evidence, defined as greater than 50% of the credible evidence gathered. The child protective worker must make one of the following conclusions regarding a report of child abuse:

- **Not confirmed:** Based on the credible evidence gathered, DHS determines that there is not a preponderance of available credible evidence that abuse did occur.
- **Confirmed (but not placed on the Child Abuse Registry):** Based on a preponderance of all of the credible evidence available to DHS, the allegation of abuse is confirmed; however, the abuse will not be placed on the Child Abuse Registry.
- **Founded:** Based on a preponderance of credible evidence available to DHS, the allegation of abuse is confirmed and it is the type of abuse that requires placement on the Child Abuse Registry.

DETERMINATION IF REPORT IS PLACED ON THE CHILD ABUSE REGISTRY After a decision is made that a report of child abuse is confirmed, DHS makes a determination about whether the report must be placed on the Child Abuse Registry.

When a report of child abuse is placed on the Child Abuse Registry, the child's name, the names of the child's parents, and the name of the perpetrator of the abuse are all entered into the Registry. Placing the name of a person responsible for the abuse of a child on the Registry may affect employment, registration, and licensure opportunities for that person.

"Founded" reports must be placed on the Child Abuse Registry. A report that is not confirmed cannot be placed on the Registry. A report of child abuse that is confirmed must be placed on the Registry as a founded report under any of the following circumstances:

- **Physical abuse**, when one or more of the following criteria are met:
  - The injury was not minor.
  - The injury was not isolated.
  - The injury is likely to reoccur.
- **Denial of critical care** by:
  - Failure to provide adequate food and nutrition.
  - Failure to provide adequate shelter.

- Failure to provide adequate health care.
- Failure to provide adequate mental health care.
- Gross failure to meet emotional needs.
- Failure to respond to an infant's life-threatening condition.
- Failure to provide proper supervision, **when** one or more of the following criteria are met:
  - The risk of injury was not minor.
  - The risk of injury was not isolated.
  - The risk of injury is likely to reoccur.
- Failure to provide adequate clothing, **when** one or more of the following criteria are met:
  - The risk of injury was not minor.
  - The risk of injury was not isolated.
  - The risk of injury is likely to reoccur.
- **Mental injury**.
- **Presence of illegal drugs.**
- **Child prostitution.**
- **Sexual abuse committed by a person age 14 or older** at the time of the abuse.
- **Manufacturing or possession of dangerous substances with the intent to use the product as a precursor or intermediary.**
- **Bestiality in the presence of a minor.**
- **Allows access by a registered sex offender**

Also, the report shall be **founded** when:

- The case was referred for juvenile or criminal court action. DHS may recommend court action for an adjudication, removal, or redisposition on an existing court case.
- Within 12 months of the report, the county attorney or juvenile court initiated **court action that resulted in an adjudication or criminal conviction.** (This could result in change in determination of placement on the Registry for a report not previously placed on the Registry.)
- The same person has been confirmed responsible for abuse in the **last 18 months**. If there is any prior report, the current assessment will be placed on the Registry if abuse is confirmed, because the abuse occurrence was not isolated.
- The person responsible for the abuse **continues to pose a danger** to the child named or another child. This is determined by assessing if the abuse was minor, isolated, and unlikely to reoccur. If the incident does not meet these three criteria, then the person may continue to pose a danger to the child named or to another child and the incident will be placed on the Registry.

NOTES

In summary, all confirmed reports of abuse will be placed on the Registry as founded reports except for:

- Denial of critical care through failure to provide proper supervision, when the endangerment of the child was minor, isolated and unlikely to reoccur.
- Denial of critical care through failure to provide adequate clothing, when the endangerment of the child was minor, isolated and unlikely to reoccur.
- Physical abuse, when the injury to the child was minor, isolated and unlikely to reoccur.

ASSESSMENT OF FAMILY'S STRENGTHS AND NEEDS The assessment process requires an evaluation of the family's functioning, strengths, and needs. The family's participation is essential. Information is gathered from family members to identify strengths, possible rehabilitation needs of the child and family, and develop the plan of action. The process usually includes a visit to the home.

As part of the evaluation of the family functioning, the Department gathers information on:

- Home environment
- Parent or caretaker characteristics
- Child characteristics
- Domestic violence and substance abuse
- Social and environmental characteristics

PREPARATION OF REPORTS AND FORMS There are several reports and forms which are generated as a result of an assessment being initiated providing notification and other relevant information to reporters, subjects of the report, the county attorney and juvenile court.

- **Notice of Intake Decision**

  The *Notice of Intake Decision* provides written notification to all mandatory and permissive reporters about whether or not a report of child abuse was accepted or rejected for assessment. This form is completed and mailed to the reporter within five working days of the receipt of a report.

- **Parental Notification**

  The *Parental Notification* form provides written notice to the parents of a child who is the subject of a child abuse assessment within five working days of commencing an assessment. Both custodial and noncustodial parents are notified if their whereabouts are known. DHS is required by law to issue this notification. Only the court may waive issuance of the notice.

- **Child Protective Assessment Summary**

The *Child Protective Services Assessment Summary* provides documentation of efforts to assess the abuse allegations and to assess the child and family functioning. The *Child Protective Services Assessment Summary* is available to the mandatory reporter who made the report, upon request. The custodial and noncustodial parents are provided a copy of the summary at the completion of the assessment. The safety and risk assessment can be released only with the permission of the subjects.

The Summary includes report and disposition information divided in several sections.

- **Abuse reported.** This section includes the allegations reported, including the name of the child subject, the person alleged to be responsible, and the type of abuse reported; and any additional allegations received while the assessment is being conducted.

- **Assessment of child safety.** This section includes an assessment of the immediate safety of the child, actions taken to address safety issues, and an assessment of future risk to the child.

- **Summary of contacts.** This section includes family and child identification, with a list of household members by name, and relationship to one another. It describes the date and time the child subject was observed; the rationale for using confidential access, if applicable; and the physical evidence pertaining to the abuse allegations. It identifies those interviewed (by name, date, and time), including collateral contacts and a summary of their remarks.

This section describes DHS efforts to locate and interview the person alleged to be responsible for the abuse and the documents DHS requested and examined pertaining to the abuse allegations. It includes information about all previous confirmed incidents of child abuse (both founded and confirmed not placed on Registry) involving any subjects of the current assessment and relevant information from any previous DHS contact with the child or family.

- **Determination as to whether abuse occurred.** This section includes documentation to support whether abuse did or did not occur; the identification of the type of abuse that occurred, if any, and its severity or significance; and the identification of the child and the person responsible for the abuse.

- **Rationale for placement or non-placement on the Registry.** This section specifies why the report is or is not being placed on the Child Abuse Registry. Specific circumstances that require placement of the report on the Registry are documented.

- **Recommendation for juvenile court action.** This section contains specific recommendations to the county attorney regarding the initiation (or continuation) of juvenile court action, along with the rationale to support the recommendation.
- **Recommendation for criminal court action.** This section contains specific recommendations to the county attorney regarding the initiation of any criminal prosecution and rationale for this recommendation, reference to any joint assessment with law enforcement, and the current status of a criminal investigation, when charges have already been filed.

- **Notice of Child Abuse Assessment**
  The *Notice of Child Abuse Assessment* is issued to the parents, guardians, custodians of the child, noncustodial parent, child, person alleged to be responsible for the abuse, as well as the mandatory reporter, when applicable, a facility administrator and other child protection workers who assisted in completing the assessment, if any. The *Notice*:
  - Indicates that the assessment process is concluded and whether the allegations of abuse were founded, confirmed or not confirmed.
  - Lists the recommendation for services and juvenile or criminal court.
  - Provides information regarding confidentiality provisions related to child abuse assessment information and how to request an appeal hearing.
  - Provides information on how to obtain copies of the *Child Protective Assessment Services Summary*. Mandatory reporters may use the notice form to request a copy of the written summary of the assessment of their allegations of abuse.

WHAT HAPPENS AFTER THE ASSESSMENT?

By the close of the child protective assessment process, the child protection worker will determine the family's eligibility and need for services. The eligibility for services is based on age of the child, the risk of abuse or reabuse, and the finding of child abuse assessment. DHS provides protective services to abused and neglected children and their families without regard to income when there is a founded child abuse report or with a court order. Community resources provide rehabilitative services for the prevention and treatment of child abuse to children and families.

SERVICE RECOMMENDATIONS AND REFERRALS During or at the conclusion of a child abuse assessment, the department may recommend information, information and referral, community care referral, or services provided by the department. If it is believed that treatment services are necessary for the protection of the abused child or other children in the home, juvenile court intervention shall be sought.

- **Information or information and referral.** Families with children of any age that have confirmed or not confirmed abuse and low risk of abuse shall be provided either information and referral or information when:
  - No service needs are identified, and the worker recommends no service; or
  - Service needs are identified, and the worker recommends new or continuing services to the family to be provided through informal supports; or.
  - Service needs are identified, and the worker recommends new or continuing services to the family to be provided through community agencies.
- **Referral to community care.** With the exception of families of children with an open department service case, court action pending, or abuse in an out-of-home setting, a referral to community care shall be offered to:
  - Families with children whose abuse is not confirmed that have moderate to high risk of abuse when service needs are identified and the worker recommends community care.
  - Families with children that have confirmed but not founded abuse and moderate or high risk of abuse when service needs are identified and the worker recommends community care.
  - Families with children with founded abuse, a victim child six years of age or older, and a low risk of repeat abuse when service needs are identified and the worker recommends community care.

Note: "Community care" means child and family-focused services and supports provided to families referred from the department. Services shall be geared toward keeping the children in the family safe from abuse and neglect; keeping the family intact; preventing the need for further intervention by the department, including removal of the child from the home; and building ongoing linkages to community-based resources that improve the safety, health, stability, and well-being of families served.

- **Referral for department services.** Families with children that have founded abuse and moderate to high risk of abuse and families with victim children under age six that have founded abuse and low risk of abuse shall be offered department services on a voluntary basis.

NOTES

- The worker shall recommend new or continuing treatment services to the family to be provided by the department, either directly or through contracted agencies.
- Families refusing voluntary services shall be referred for a child in need of assistance action through juvenile court.

DHS services such as homemaker services, parenting classes, respite child care, foster care, financial assistance, psychological and psychiatric services, and sexual abuse treatment may be provided and may be provided without court involvement if the parent consents to services. Other interventions can be ordered by a court.

Juvenile court intervention may be sought in order to intervene on an emergency basis to place the child in protective custody by removing the child from the home or by seeking adjudication of the child to place the child under the protective supervision of the juvenile court with the child remaining in the care and custody of the parent.

The child protective assessment worker continuously evaluates the safety and risk to the child while conducting the assessment of allegations of abuse. The assessment worker may consider alternatives to the removal of a child if the child would be provided adequate protection. Options may include:

- Bringing protective relatives to the child's home while the parents leave the home.
- Initiating public health nurse or visiting nurse services.
- Initiating homemaker services or family-centered services.
- Implementing intensive services, such as family preservation.
- Placing the child in voluntary foster or shelter care.
- Placing the child voluntarily with relatives or friends.
- Obtaining a court order requiring that the person responsible for the abuse leave the home, when other family members are willing and able to adequately protect the child.

When the juvenile court orders the person alleged responsible for the abuse to vacate the child's residence, a child in need of assistance petition must be filed within three days. If there are concerns about the person having contact with the child following the person's removal from the home, a "no contact" order through the county attorney may be requested.

REMOVAL OF A CHILD Iowa laws provide for a child to be placed in protective custody in various situations. DHS does not have a statutory authority to simply "remove" a child from a parent or other caretaker. The procedures for a child to be placed in protective custody are outlined in Iowa Code sections 272.78 through 232.79A.

Assessment workers do not have the legal authority to remove children from their home without a court order or parental consent.

Only a peace officer or a physician treating a child may remove a child without a court order if the child's immediate removal is necessary to avoid imminent danger to the child's life or health. There are four legal procedures for the emergency temporary removal of a child:

- Emergency removal by an ex parte court order
- Emergency removal of the child by a peace officer
- Emergency removal of the child by a physician
- With parent's consent

REMOVAL BY EX PARTE COURT ORDER   A child may be taken into custody following the issuance of an **ex parte court order** pursuant to Iowa Code section 232.78, which states:

1. The juvenile court may enter an ex parte order directing a peace officer or a juvenile court officer to take custody of a child before or after the filing of a petition under Chapter 232 provided all of the following apply:
   a. The person responsible for the care of the child is absent, or though present, was asked and refused to consent to the removal of the child and was informed of an intent to apply for an order under this section, or there is reasonable cause to believe that a request for consent would further endanger the child, or there is reasonable cause to believe that a request for consent will cause the parent, guardian, or legal custodian to take flight with the child.
   b. It appears that the child's immediate removal is necessary to avoid imminent danger to the child's life or health. The circumstances or conditions indicating the presence of such imminent danger shall include but are not limited to any of the following:
      (1) The refusal or failure of the person responsible for the care of the child to comply with the request of a peace officer, juvenile court officer, or child protection worker for such person to obtain and provide to the requester the results of a physical or mental examination of the child. The request for a physical examination of the child may specify the performance of a medically relevant test.
      (2) The refusal or failure of the person responsible for the care of the child or a person present in the person's home to comply with a request of a peace officer, juvenile court officer, or child protection worker for such a person to submit to and provide to the requester the results of a medically relevant test of the person.
   c. There is not enough time to file a petition and hold a hearing under [Iowa Code] section 232.95.

NOTES

    d. The application for the order includes a statement of the facts to support the findings specified in paragraphs a, b, and c.

2. The person making the application for an order shall assert facts showing there is reasonable cause to believe that the child cannot either be returned to the place where the child was residing or placed with the parent who does not have physical care of the child.

3. Except for good cause shown or unless the child is sooner returned to the place where the child was residing or permitted to return to the child care facility, a petition shall be filed under this chapter within three days or the issuance of the order.

4. The juvenile court may enter an order authorizing a physician or hospital to provide emergency medical or surgical procedures before the filing of a petition under Chapter 232 provided:

    a. Such procedures are necessary to safeguard the life and health of the child; and

    b. There is not enough time to file a petition under this chapter and hold a hearing as provided in section 232.95.

5. The juvenile court, before or after the filing of a petition under Chapter 232, may enter an ex parte order authorizing a physician or hospital to conduct an outpatient physical examination of a child, or authorizing a physician . . ., a psychologist . . ., or a community mental health center . . . to conduct an outpatient mental examination of a child, if necessary to identify the nature, extent, and cause of injuries to the child, provided all the following apply:

    a. The parent, guardian, or legal custodian is absent, or though present, was asked and refused to provide written consent to the examination.

    b. The juvenile court has entered an ex parte order directing the removal of the child from the child's home or a child care facility under this section.

    c. There is not enough time to file a petition and to hold a hearing as provided in section 232.98.

6. Any person who may file a petition under Chapter 232 may apply for an order for temporary removal, or the court on its own motion may issue such an order. An appropriate person designated by the court shall confer with a person seeking the removal order, shall make every reasonable effort to inform the parent or other person legally responsible for the child's care of the application, and shall make such inquiries as will aid the court in disposing of such application.

    The person designated by the court shall file with the court a complete written report providing all details of the designee's conference with the person seeking the removal order, the designee's efforts to inform the parents or other person legally responsible for the child's care of the application, any inquiries made by the designee to aid the court in disposing of the application, and all information the designee communicated to the court. The report shall be filed within five days of the date of the removal order.

If the court does not designate any appropriate person who performs the required duties, notwithstanding section 234.39 or any other provision of law, the child's parent shall not be responsible for paying the cost of care and services for the duration of the removal order.

7. Any order entered authorizing temporary removal of a child must include both of the following:
   a. A determination made by the court that continuation of the child in the child's home would be contrary to the welfare of the child. Such a determination must be made on a case-by-case basis. The grounds for the court's determination must be explicitly documented and stated in the order. However, preserving the safety of the child must be the court's paramount consideration. If imminent danger to the child's life or health exists at the time of the court's consideration, the determination shall not be a prerequisite to the removal of the child.
   b. A statement informing the child's parent that the consequences of a permanent removal may include termination of the parent's rights with respect to the child.

If deemed appropriate by the court, upon being informed that there has been an emergency removal or keeping of a child without a court order, the court may enter an order in accordance with section 232.78.

REMOVAL OF A CHILD BY A PEACE OFFICER OR A PHYSICIAN A child may be taken into custody without a court order pursuant to Iowa Code section 232.79, which indicates that:

1. A peace officer or juvenile court officer may take a child into custody, a physician treating a child may keep the child in custody, or a juvenile court officer may authorize a peace officer, physician, or medical security personnel to take a child into custody, without a court order as required under section 232.78 and without the consent of a parent, guardian, or custodian provided that both of the following apply:
   a. The child is in a circumstance or condition that presents an imminent danger to the child's life or health.
   b. There is not enough time to apply for an order under section 232.78.
2. If a person authorized by this section removes or retains custody of a child, the person shall:
   a. Bring the child immediately to a place designated by the rules of the court for this purpose, unless the person is a physician

NOTES

treating the child and the child is or will presently be admitted to a hospital.

b. Make every reasonable effort to inform the parent, guardian, or custodian of the whereabouts of the child.

c. In accordance with court-established procedures, immediately orally inform the court of the emergency removal and the circumstances surrounding the removal.

d. Within 24-hours of orally informing the court of the emergency removal in accordance with paragraph "c," inform the court in writing of the emergency removal and the circumstances surrounding the removal.

3. Any person, agency, or institution acting in good faith in the removal or keeping of a child pursuant to this section, and any employer of or person under the direction of such a person, agency, or institution, shall have immunity from any civil or criminal liability that might otherwise be incurred or imposed as the result of such removal or keeping.

4. a. When the court is informed that there has been an emergency removal or keeping of a child without a court order, the court shall direct the department of human services or the juvenile probation department to make every reasonable effort to communicate immediately with the child's parent or parents or other person legally responsible for the child's care.

Upon locating the child's parent or parents or other person legally responsible for the child's care, the department of human services or the juvenile probation department shall, in accordance with court-established procedures, immediately orally inform the court. After orally informing the court, the department of human services or the juvenile probation department shall provide to the court written documentation of the oral information.

b. The court shall authorize the department of human services or the juvenile probation department to cause a child thus removed or kept to be returned if it concludes there is not an imminent risk to the child's life and health in so doing.

If the department of human services or the juvenile probation department receives information which could affect the court's decision regarding the child's return, the department of human services or the juvenile probation department, in accordance with court established procedures, shall immediately orally provide the information to the court. After orally providing the information to the court, the department of human services or the juvenile probation department shall provide to the court written documentation of the oral information.

If the child is not returned, the department of human services or the juvenile probation department shall forthwith cause a petition to be filed within three days after the removal.

    c. If deemed appropriate by the court, upon being informed that there has been an emergency removal or keeping of a child without a court order, the court may enter an order in accordance with section 232.78.

  5. When there has been an emergency removal or keeping of a child without a court order, a physical examination of the child by a licensed medical practitioner shall be performed within 24-hours of such removal, unless the child is returned to the child's home within 24-hours of the removal.

A child without adult supervision may be taken into custody pursuant to Iowa Code section 232.79A, which indicates that:

> If a peace officer determines that a child does not have adult supervision because the child's parent, guardian, or other person responsible for the care of the child has been arrested and detained or has been unexpectedly incapacitated, and that no adult who is legally responsible for the care of the child can be located within a reasonable period of time, the peace officer shall attempt to place the child with an adult relative of the child, an adult person who cares for the child, or another adult person who is known to the child. The person with whom the child is placed is authorized to give consent for emergency medical treatment of the child and shall not be held liable for any action arising from giving the consent.

> Upon the request of the peace officer, the Department shall assist in making the placement. The placement shall not exceed a period of 24-hours and shall be terminated when a person who is legally responsible for the care of the child is located and takes custody of the child.

> If a person who is legally responsible for the care of the child cannot be located within the 24-hour period or a placement in accordance with this section is unavailable, the provisions of section 232.79 shall apply. If the person with whom the child is placed charges a fee for the care of the child, the fee shall be paid from funds provided in the appropriation to the Department for protective child care.

REMOVAL WITH PARENT'S CONSENT A parent, guardian, or custodian may voluntarily consent to placement of a child in foster care. Voluntary placement must be for less than a 30-day period. Court action will be sought if the child can not be returned home.

    A voluntary placement may be appropriate when the need for placement is expected to be short-term, such as during the parent's illness or for crisis intervention. When a parent must be out of the home for a time-limited period, make every effort to help the family find relatives or friends who can assume temporary responsibility for the child as an alternative to foster care placement.

JUVENILE COURT HEARINGS Juvenile court hearings are held when children are removed from their parent's custody or when treatment or DHS supervision of abused or neglected children is necessary because the parents are unwilling or unable to provide such treatment or supervision.

Parents are notified immediately if their child is placed in other care. A petition for a hearing must be filed with the juvenile court within three days of the removal of a child from a parent's care. A juvenile court hearing is held promptly in order to review the need for continued protection of the child through shelter care. Parents are provided the opportunity at the shelter care hearing to present evidence that their child can be returned home without danger of injury or harm.

The court ensures that the parent's and the children's rights will be protected. An attorney will be appointed to represent the child's best interest in these cases. The attorney representing the child is called the guardian ad litem. The court may also appoint a court-appointed special advocate (CASA) to assist in informing the court regarding child's progress and recommendations.

The parents have a right to legal counsel. If they cannot afford an attorney, the court will appoint one.

Additional hearings are held if the court determines that the child needs its protection. At each hearing, the court reviews the efforts of the parents to remedy problems and the services arranged for or provided by DHS to help the parents and children.

CHILD IN NEED OF ASSISTANCE A child in need of assistance is defined in Iowa Code section 232.2, subsection 6, as: an unmarried child:

a. Whose parent, guardian or other custodian has abandoned or deserted the child.

b. Whose parent, guardian, other custodian, or other member of the household in which the child resides has physically abused or neglected the child, or is imminently likely to abuse or neglect the child.

c. Who has suffered or is imminently likely to suffer harmful effects as a result of either of the following:
   (1) Mental injury caused by the acts of the child's parent, guardian, or custodian.
   (2) The failure of the child's parent, guardian, custodian, or other member of the household in which the child resides to exercise a reasonable degree of care in supervising the child.

d. Who has been, or is imminently likely to be, sexually abused by the child's parent, guardian, custodian, or other member of the household in which the child resides.

e. Who is in need of medical treatment to cure, alleviate, or prevent serious injury or illness and whose parent, guardian or custodian is unwilling or unable to provide such treatment.

f. Who is in need of treatment to cure or alleviate serious mental illness or disorder, or emotional damage as evidenced by severe anxiety, depression, withdrawal, or untoward aggressive behavior toward self or others and whose parent, guardian, or custodian is unwilling to provide such treatment.

g. Whose parent, guardian, or custodian fails to exercise a minimal degree of care in supplying the child with adequate food, clothing, or shelter and refuses other means made available to provide such essentials.

h. Who has committed a delinquent act as a result of pressure, guidance, or approval from a parent, guardian, custodian, or other member of the household in which the child resides.

i. Who has been the subject of or a party to sexual activities for hire or who poses for live display or for photographic or other means of pictorial reproduction or display which is designated to appeal to the prurient interest and is patently offensive; and taken as a whole, lacks serious literary, scientific, political or artistic value.

j. Who is without a parent, guardian, or other custodian.

k. Whose parent, guardian, or other custodian, for good cause desires to be relieved of the child's care and custody.

l. Who for good cause desires to have the child's parents relieved of the child's care and custody.

m. Who is in need of treatment to cure or alleviate chemical dependency and whose parent, guardian, or custodian is unwilling or unable to provide such treatment.

n. Whose parent's or guardian's mental capacity or condition, imprisonment, or drug or alcohol abuse results in the child not receiving adequate care.

o. In whose body there is an illegal drug present as a direct and foreseeable consequence of the acts or omissions of the child's parent, guardian, or custodian. The presence of the drug shall be determined in accordance with a medically relevant test as defined in section 232.73.

p. Whose parent, guardian, or custodian does any of the following: Unlawfully manufactures a dangerous substance in the presence of a child. Knowingly allows such manufacture by another person in the presence of a child, or in the presence of a child possesses a product containing ephedrine, its salts, optical isomers, salts of optical isomers, or pseudoephedrine, its salts, optical isomers, salts of optical isomers, with the intent to use the product as a precursor or an intermediary to a dangerous substance.

(1) For the purposes of this paragraph "p," "in the presence of a child" means the physical presence of a child during the

manufacture or possession, the manufacture or possession occurred in a child's home, on the premises, or in a motor vehicle located on the premises, or the manufacture or possession occurred under other circumstances in which a reasonably prudent person would know that the manufacture or possession may be seen, smelled, or heard by a child.

(2) For the purpose of this paragraph "p," "dangerous substance" means any of the following:

   (a) Amphetamine, its salts, isomers, or salts of its isomers.

   (b) Methamphetamine, its salts, isomers, or salts of its isomers.

   (c) A chemical or combination of chemicals that poses a reasonable risk of causing an explosion, fire, or other danger to the life or health of persons who are in the vicinity while the chemical or combination of chemicals is used or is intended to be used in any of the following:

     (i) The process of manufacturing an illegal or controlled substance.

     (ii) As a precursor in the manufacturing of an illegal or controlled substance.

     (iii) As an intermediary in the manufacturing of an illegal or controlled substance.

q. Who is a newborn infant whose parent has voluntarily released custody of the child in accordance with Chapter 233.

HOW IS CHILD ABUSE INFORMATION TREATED?

Iowa Code section 235A.15 provides that confidentiality of child abuse information shall be maintained, except as specifically authorized.

Under Iowa law, "child abuse information" includes any or all of the following data maintained by DHS in a manual or automated data storage system and individually identified:

- Report data, including information pertaining to an assessment of an allegation of child abuse in which DHS has determined the alleged abuse meets the definition of child abuse.

- Assessment data, including information pertaining to the DHS evaluation of a family.

- Disposition data, including information pertaining to an opinion or decision as the occurrence of child abuse.

Note: Iowa Code section 232.71B, subsection 2, directs that DHS shall not reveal the identity of the reporter of child abuse in the written notification to parents or otherwise.

The Department shall withhold the name of the person who made the report of suspected child abuse. Only the court may allow the release of that person's name.

PROTECTIVE DISCLOSURE Iowa Code allows for DHS to disclose that an individual is listed on the child abuse registry, the dependent adult abuse registry or is required to register for the sexual offender registry when it is necessary for the protection of a child. The disclosure can only be made to persons who are subjects of a child abuse assessment.

DISPOSITION OF REPORTS Iowa law limits access to child abuse information to specific individuals and entities depending on placement of the Child Abuse Registry. All subjects of the report and their attorneys have access to:

- Information contained within the Child Protective Services Assessment Summary.
- Correspondence or written information that pertains to *Child Protective Services Assessment Summary*.

A copy of the entire *Child Protective Services Assessment Summary* is automatically provided to subjects, including but not limited to the custodial and noncustodial parents.

If a person with access to the *Child Protective Services Assessment Summary* as a result of the current assessment does not have access to all information listed from previous summaries, the inaccessible information is deleted before providing the summary to that person.

Note: The safety assessment, safety plan, and family risk assessment are considered assessment data, and its dissemination by law is more restrictive.

A person who is the subject of a child abuse report may also receive a copy of the *Child Protective Services Assessment Summary* for that report by submitting a request to the Department. Subjects may use either the *Request for Child Abuse Information* or the Notice of Child Abuse Assessment to make this request.

Mandatory reporters may request a founded report using either form. They will receive a *Notice of Child Abuse Assessment* when the assessment report is completed as the reporter of the abuse. Mandatory reporters may also request founded reports when they are providing care or treatment to a child victim, their families or the person responsible for the abuse.

All other requesters must use the *Request for Child Abuse Information* to request a copy of the assessment report.

REQUESTS FOR CORRECTION AND APPEALS A subject (child, parent, guardian or legal custodian, alleged perpetrator) who feels there is incorrect or erroneous information contained in the *Child Protective Services Assessment Summary*, or who disagrees with its conclusions, may request a correction of the report.

The subject must submit a written request within six months of the completion of the *Child Protective* must submit a written request

NOTES

within six months of the completion of the *Child Protective Assessment Summary*. Requests must be sent to:

Appeals Section
1305 E Walnut St, 5th Floor
Des Moines, Iowa 50319-0114

An administrative hearing and or a prehearing is then scheduled. At the evidentiary hearing, the matter will be heard before an administrative law judge. The administrative law judge may also uphold, modify, or overturn the finding.

A requester who is not satisfied with the decision of the administrative law judge may appeal the matter the district court.

ACCESS TO CHILD ABUSE INFORMATION Another function of the Child Abuse Registry is approval of the dissemination of child abuse information to persons authorized to receive this information. Iowa Code section 235A.17 indicates that an authorized recipient of child abuse information shall not redisseminate the information to anyone else.

Access to child abuse information is authorized for:

- Subjects of a report (child, parent, guardian or legal custodian, alleged perpetrator)
- The attorney for any subject
- An employee or agent of DHS who is responsible for assessment of the report of child abuse
- Other DHS personnel when necessary for the performance of their official duties and functions
- The mandatory reporter who reported the abuse
- The county attorney
- The juvenile court

Access to child abuse information is also authorized to persons involved in an assessment of child abuse (such as a health practitioner or mental health professional, a law enforcement officer, or a multidisciplinary team).

Access to certain child abuse information is authorized to individuals, agencies, or facilities providing care to a child named in a report that includes:

- A facility licensing authority
- A person or agency responsible for the care of a child victim or perpetrator
- An administrator of a psychiatric medical institution
- An administrator of a child foster care facility
- An administrator of a registered or licensed child care facility

- The superintendent of the Iowa Braille and Sightsaving School
- The superintendent of the School for the Deaf
- An administrator of a community mental health center
- An administrator of an agency providing services under a county management plan
- An administrator of a facility or program operated by the state, city or county providing direct care to children for applicant and employee record checks
- An administrator of an agency providing Medicaid home- and community-based waiver services for applicant and employee record checks
- An administrator of a child care resource and referral agency under contract with DHS
- An administrator of a hospital for applicant and employee record checks

Access to child abuse information is also authorized under some circumstances related to judicial and administrative proceedings, such as:

- The juvenile court
- A juvenile court officer
- A Court appointed special advocate
- An expert witness at any stage of an appeal hearing
- A district court
- A probation or parole officer
- An adult correctional officer
- Each board of examiners and licensing board
- A court or agency hearing an appeal for correction of child abuse information
- The Department of Justice for review by the prosecutor's review committee or the commitment of sexually violent predators

Access to certain child abuse information is also authorized to others under certain circumstances, including:

- A person conducting bona fide child abuse research
- DHS personnel for official duties
- A DHS employee for record checks of state operated institutions employees
- A DHS registration or licensing employee
- A DHS adoption worker
- The attorney for DHS
- A certified adoption investigator

- A certified adoption worker
- A child protection agency from another state for investigative, treatment or adoptive or foster care placement services
- Foster care review boards, or to conduct a record check evaluation
- The Board of Educational Examiners
- A legally authorized protection and advocacy agency
- The Iowa Board for the Treatment of Sexual Offenders
- A licensed child placing agency for adoptive placement
- The superintendent or designee of school district, or authorities for a nonpublic school, for employee and volunteer record checks
- Department of Inspections and Appeals for applicants for employment

CIVIL AND CRIMINAL LIABILITY REGARDING CHILD ABUSE INFORMATION

According to Iowa Code section 235A.20, any aggrieved person may institute a civil action for damages under Iowa Code Chapter 669 or 670 or to restrain the dissemination of child abuse information in violation of Iowa Code Chapter 232.

Any recipient proven to have disseminated child abuse information or to have requested and received such information in violation of Chapter 232, shall be liable for actual damages and exemplary damages for each violation. The recipient shall also be liable for court costs, expenses, and reasonable attorney's fees incurred by the party bringing the action.

The same penalties apply to any employee of the Department who knowingly destroys investigation or assessment data, except in accordance with rules established for retention of child abuse information under Iowa Code section 235A.18.

Also, according to Iowa Code section 235A.21, the following people are guilty of a serious misdemeanor under the Iowa criminal code:

- Any person who willfully requests, obtains, or seeks to obtain child abuse information under false pretenses.
- Any person who willfully communicates or seeks to communicate child abuse information to any agency or person except in accordance with Iowa Code sections 235A.15 and 235A.17.
- Any person connected with any research authorized pursuant to Iowa Code section 235A.15 who willfully falsifies child abuse information or any records relating to child abuse information.

Any person who knowingly, but without criminal purpose, communicates, or seeks to communicate child abuse information except in accordance with sections 235A.15 and 235A.17 shall be guilty of a simple misdemeanor.

WHAT TRAINING DO MANDATORY REPORTERS NEED?

Mandatory reporters are required by law to complete two hours of training during their first six months of employment and two hours every five years thereafter.

The 2001 Iowa General Assembly established the requirement for the creation of a panel for the "review and approval" of mandatory reporter training curricula. The Director of the Department of Public Health convened a panel to satisfy the mandate of the legislation.

People who work in position classifications that under law make the person a mandatory reporter of child or dependent adult abuse but do not have a mandatory reporter training curriculum approved by a licensing or examining board must acquire training approved by the panel. The website for information is (http://www.idph.state. ia.us/dir_off/abuseeducation/default.htm).

Mandatory report training curricula must be approved by the Abuse Education Review Panel to satisfy the Iowa Code mandated training requirement. Licensed professionals are required to complete training that is required and approved by their respective licensing and examining boards or approved by the Abuse Education Review Panel.

Iowa Code subsection 232.69(3) states that:

a. For the purposes of this section, "licensing board" means an examining board designated in [Iowa Code] section 147.13, the Board of Educational Examiners created in [Iowa Code] section 272.2, or a licensing board as defined in [Iowa Code] section 272C.1.
b. A person required to make a report under subsection 1, other than a physician whose professional practice does not regularly involve providing primary health care to children, shall complete two hours of training relating to the identification and reporting of child abuse within six months of initial employment or self-employment involving the examinations, attending, counseling, or treatment of children, on a regular basis.

    Within one month of initial employment or self-employment, the person shall obtain a statement of the abuse reporting requirements from the person's employer or, if self-employed, from the department. The person shall complete at least two hours of additional child abuse identification and reporting training every five years.
c. If the person is an employee of a hospital or similar institution, or of a public or private institution, agency, or facility, the employer shall be responsible for obtaining the child abuse identification and reporting training.

    If the person is self-employed, employed in a licensed or certified profession, or employed by a facility or program that is subject to licensure, regulation, or approval by a state agency, the person shall obtain the child abuse identification and reporting training as provided in paragraph "d."

d. The person may complete the initial or additional training requirements as part of any of the following that are applicable to the person:

   (1) A continuing education program required under [Iowa Code] Chapter 272C and approved by the appropriate licensing or examining board.

   (2) A training program using a curriculum approved by the abuse education review panel established by the Director of Public Health pursuant to [Iowa Code] section 135.11.

   (3) A training program using such an approved curriculum offered by the Department of Human Services, the Department of Education, an area education agency, a school district, the Iowa Law Enforcement Academy, or a similar public agency.

e. A licensing board with authority over the license of a person required to make a report shall require as a condition of licensure that the person is in compliance with the requirements for abuse training under this subsection. The licensing board shall require the person upon licensure renewal to accurately document for the licensing board the person's completion of the training requirements.

   However, the licensing board may adopt rules providing for waiver or suspension of the compliance requirements, if the waiver or suspension is in the public interest, applicable to a person who is engaged in active duty in the military service of this state or of the United States, to a person for whom compliance with the training requirements would impose a significant hardship, or to a person who is practicing a licensed profession outside this state or is otherwise subject to circumstances that would preclude the person from encountering child abuse in this state.

f. For persons required to make a report who are not engaged in a licensed profession that is subject to the authority of a licensing board but are employed by a facility or program subject to licensure, registration, or approval by a state agency, the agency shall require as a condition of renewal of the facility's or program's licensure, registration, or approval, that such persons employed by the facility or program are in compliance with the training requirements of this section.

g. For peace officers, the elected or appointed official designated as the head of the agency employing the peace office shall ensure compliance with the training requirements of this section.

h. For persons who are employees of state departments and political subdivisions of the state, the department director or the chief administrator of the political subdivision shall ensure the persons' compliance with the training requirements of this section.

REVIEW QUESTIONS

You have been provided with all of the information necessary to carry out all duties and responsibilities required of a mandatory reporter of child abuse. The following review questions are provided to emphasize key points in this Guide.

Q) *In what year was the child abuse reporting law initially enacted?*

A) 1978

Q) *What is the purpose of the child abuse reporting law?*

A) The child abuse reporting law is to provide protection to children by encouraging the reporting of suspected abuse.

Q) *Which state agency is responsible for providing protective services to children?*

A) The Department of Human Services.

Q) *Who are mandatory reporters of child abuse?*

A) Professionals who have frequent contact with children in the course of their work are considered to be mandatory reporters.

Q) *What fields are mandatory reporters typically employed in?*

A) Health, law enforcement, child care, education, mental health, and social work.

Q) *What training is required for mandatory reporters of child abuse?*

A) All mandatory reporters are required to complete two hours of approved training relating to the identification and reporting of child abuse within six months of initial employment or self-employment. All mandatory reporters are also required to complete at least two hours of additional child abuse identification and reporting training every five years.

Q) *What is the definition of child by Iowa law?*

A) Any person under the age of 18 years.

Q) *Who are typical perpetrators of child abuse?*

A) Perpetrators of child abuse come from all walks of life, races, religions, and nationalities.

Q) *When does DHS have the legal authority to conduct assessments of child abuse?*

A) When the victim is a child, the alleged victim is subjected to one or more of the eight categories of child abuse, and the abuse is the result of the acts or omissions of the person responsible for the care of the child.

NOTES

Q) *Who are people "responsible for the care of a child"?*

A) • A parent, guardian, or foster parent.
   • A relative or any other person with whom the child resides, and who assumes care or supervision of the child, without reference to the length of time or continuity of such residence.
   • An employee or agent of any public or private facility providing care for a child, including an institution, hospital, health care facility, group home, mental health center, residential treatment center, shelter care facility, detention center, or child care facility.
   • Any person providing care for a child, but with whom the child does not reside, without reference to the duration of the care.

A person who assumes responsibility for the care or supervision of a child may assume this responsibility through verbal or written agreement, or implicitly through the willing assumption of the caretaking role.

Q) *When is an educator considered a caretaker for a child?*

A) A teacher could be assessed as a person responsible for child abuse if the teacher is acting in a caretaking role, for example having supervision responsibilities for a child on an overnight trip.

Q) *Can children be in a caretaker role?*

A) Yes, a child can be a person responsible for abuse when the child is acting in a caretaker role for another child, such as a baby-sitting situation.

Q) *What are the nine categories of child abuse?*

A) 1. Physical abuse
   2. Sexual abuse
   3. Child prostitution
   4. Mental injury
   5. Denial of critical care
   6. Presence of illegal drugs
   7. Manufacturing or possession of a dangerous substance
   8. Bestiality in the presence of a minor
   9. Allows access by a registered sex offender

Q) *What is the definition of physical abuse?*

A) Any non-accidental physical injury, or injury which is at variance with the history given of it, suffered by a child as the result of the acts or omissions of a person responsible for the care of the child.

Q) *What is the definition of mental injury?*

A) Any mental injury to a child's intellectual or psychological capacity, as evidenced by an observable and substantial impairment in the child's ability to function within the child's normal range of performance and behavior, as the result of the acts or omissions of a person responsible for the care of the child, if the impairment is diagnosed and confirmed by a licensed physician or qualified mental health professional.

Q) *What are some examples of mental injury?*

A) • Ignoring the child and failing to provide necessary stimulation, responsiveness, and validation of the child's worth in normal family routine.

• Rejecting the child's value, needs, and requests for adult validation and nurturance.

• Isolating the child from the family and community; denying the child normal human contact.

• Terrorizing the child with continual verbal assaults, creating a climate of fear, hostility, and anxiety and preventing the child from gaining feelings of safety and security.

• Corrupting the child by encouraging and reinforcing destructive, antisocial behavior until the child is so impaired in socioemotional development that interaction in normal social environments is not possible.

• Verbally assaulting the child with constant, excessive name-calling, harsh threats, and sarcastic put-downs that continually "beat down" the child's self-esteem with humiliation.

• Overpressuring the child with subtle but consistent pressure to grow up fast and to achieve too early in the areas of academics, physical/motor skills, and social interaction, which leaves the child feeling that he or she is never quite good enough.

Q) *What is the definition of sexual abuse?*

A) The commission of a sexual offense with or to a child as a result of the acts or omissions of the person responsible for the care of the child. The commission of a sexual offense includes any sexual offense with or to a person under the age of 18 years.

Q) *What is the definition of denial of critical care?*

A) The failure on the part of a person responsible for the care of a child to provide for the adequate food, shelter, clothing or other care necessary for the child's health and welfare when financially able to do so or when offered financial or other reasonable means to do so.

Q) *What are the eight subcategories of denial of critical care?*

A) 1. Failure to provide adequate food and nutrition.
2. Failure to provide adequate shelter.

NOTES

3. Failure to provide adequate clothing.
4. Failure to provide adequate health care.
5. Failure to provide mental health care.
6. Gross failure to meet emotional needs.
7. Failure to provide proper supervision.
8. Failure to respond to an infant's life-threatening condition.

Q) *What questions are helpful in determining if a child should be left home alone?*

A) • Does the child have any physical, mental, or emotional disabilities?
   • Could the child get out of the house alone in an emergency and have a safe place to go?
   • Does the child have a phone and know how to use it?
   • Does the child know how to reach the child's caretaker?
   • How long will the child be left home alone?
   • Is the child afraid to be left home alone?
   • Does the child know how to respond to an emergency such as fire or injury?

Q) *What is the definition of child prostitution?*

A) Child prostitution is the acts or omissions of a person responsible for the care of a child which allow, permit, or encourage the child to engage in acts of prostitution when the child is under the age of 18 years.

Q) *What is the definition of presence of illegal drugs?*

A) Presence of illegal drugs is when an illegal drug is present in a child's body as a direct and foreseeable consequence of the acts or omissions of the person responsible for the child's care.

Q) *What is the definition of manufacturing or possession of a dangerous substance?*

A) The person responsible for the care of a child manufactured a dangerous substance or, in the presence of the child, possesses a product containing ephedrine, its salts, optical isomers, salts of optical isomers, or pseudoephedrine, its salts, optical isomers, salts of optical isomers with the intent to use the product as a precursor or an intermediary to a dangerous substance.

Q) *What are the time frames a mandatory reporter must follow when making a report of child abuse?*

A) If you suspect a child has been abused, you need to report it orally to DHS within 24 hours of becoming aware of the situation. Within 48 hours after that, you need to make a written report to DHS.

Q) *What should you do if you see a child that is in imminent danger?*

A) Immediately contact law enforcement, then contact DHS.

Q) *What information should be in any oral or written reports of child abuse?*

A) • The names and home address of the child and the child's parents or other persons believed to be responsible for the child's care.
   • The child's present whereabouts.
   • The child's age.
   • The nature and extent of the child's injuries including any evidence of previous injuries.
   • The name, age, and condition of other children in the same household.
   • Any other information that you believe may be helpful in establishing the cause of the abuse or neglect to the child.
   • The identity of the person or persons responsible for the abuse or neglect to the child.
   • Your name and address.

Q) *How should a mandatory reporter deal with confidentiality issues?*

A) Rules around confidentiality and privileged communication are waived during the assessment process.

Q) *Are mandatory reporters liable for any damages occurring because of a report of child abuse?*

A) No, Iowa law states that any person participating in good faith in making a report of child abuse shall have immunity from any civil or criminal liability which might otherwise be incurred or imposed. The person shall have the same immunity with respect to participation in good faith in any judicial proceeding resulting from the report or relating to the subject matter of the report.

Q) *What happens if a mandatory reporter fails to make a report of child abuse?*

A) Under Iowa law there are civil and criminal sanctions for failing to report child abuse. Any person, official, agency or institution, who knowingly and willfully fails to make a report of child abuse or who knowingly interferes with the making of such a report is guilty of a simple misdemeanor and is civilly liable for the damages proximately caused by such failure or interference.

Q) *What happens if someone knowingly makes a false report of child abuse?*

A) A person who reports or causes to be reported to DHS false information regarding an alleged act of child abuse, knowing that the information is false or that the act did not occur, commits a simple misdemeanor.

NOTES

If DHS receives more than three reports from the same person or which identify the same child as a victim of child abuse or the same person as the alleged abuser, and DHS determines the reports to be entirely false or without merit, DHS shall provide information concerning the reports to the county attorney for consideration of criminal charges.

Q) *What is involved in a child abuse assessment?*

A) A child abuse assessment consists of:
- Intake
- Case assignment
- Evaluation of the alleged abuse
- Determination of whether abuse occurred
- Decision on placing a report on the Child Abuse Registry
- Assessment of family's strengths and needs
- Preparation of reports and forms

Q) *When are head lice or truancy appropriate for a child abuse assessment?*

A) The endangerment caused by head lice or truancy does not generally rise to the level that must be present in order to constitute a child abuse allegation. If other conditions are present or the situation poses a risk to the child's health and welfare, it should be reported as child abuse. Even if the report is rejected for assessment, other services may be offered to the child and family.

Q) *What is the mandatory reporter's role in the observation of a child during the assessment process?*

A) When the observation of a child needs to take place at the school or in a child care facility, the administrator of the facility or school is required by law to provide the child protection worker with confidential access to the child.

Q) *Who will know the name of the person making a report of child abuse?*

A) DHS will safeguard the reporter's identity during the assessment process. However, the reporter should be aware that continued confidentiality cannot be guaranteed if the report results in juvenile, civil, or criminal court action.

Q) *Who will be interviewed during a child abuse assessment?*

A) Interviews whenever possible will be conducted with:
- The alleged child victim
- The parents and other adults in the household
- The alleged perpetrator
- Collateral sources, witnesses, or other parties with information

Q) *What types of information may be gathered during a child abuse assessment?*

A) Documentation gathered may include, but is not limited to, descriptions, photographs, medical reports and records, reports from child protection centers, and any other pertinent reports, such as mental health center evaluations, treatment records, criminal records, law enforcement reports, and audio and video tapes.

Q) *What are child protection centers?*

A) There are several child protection centers throughout the state. These centers assist child protection workers in assessing some reports of child abuse. In most cases, these centers provide medical evaluation and psychosocial assessments of the victim when there are allegations of sexual abuse.

Q) *What is the role of multidisciplinary teams?*

A) Multidisciplinary teams, exist in counties that have more than 50 reports of child abuse annually. These teams function as an advisory and consultation group to aid child protection workers in resolving issues related to a case during the assessment process.

Q) *What are the conclusions of an assessment based on?*

A) The conclusions of an assessment are based on an evaluation of all of the information gathered during the assessment, including physical evidence, documentary evidence, observations, and interviews of the victim, perpetrator and others.

Q) *What are the conclusions a child protective worker may reach at the completion of an assessment?*

A) At the completion of the assessment, the worker must make one of the following conclusions: Abuse is not confirmed, abuse is confirmed (but not placed on the Child Abuse Registry), or abuse is founded (confirmed and placed on the Child Abuse Registry).

Q) *What do the conclusions mean?*

A) <u>Not confirmed</u> means that, based on the credible evidence gathered, the Department determined that there was not a preponderance of evidence that abuse did occur.

<u>Confirmed</u> (but not placed on the Child Abuse Registry) means that, based on a preponderance of all of the credible evidence available to the Department, the allegation of abuse is confirmed; however, the abuse will not be placed on the Child Abuse Registry.

<u>Founded</u> (confirmed and placed on the Child Abuse Registry) means that, based on a preponderance of all of the credible evidence available to the Department, the allegation of abuse is confirmed and it is placed on the Child Abuse Registry.

NOTES

Q) *What types of abuse are confirmed but not placed on the Child Abuse Registry?*

A) This applies only to two types of abuse, a physical abuse where the injury was nonaccidental and minor, isolated, and unlikely to reoccur and denial of critical care (lack of proper supervision or lack of adequate clothing) where the risk to the child's health and welfare was minor, isolated and is unlikely to reoccur.

If the abuse was minor, isolated, and unlikely to reoccur the abuse may not be placed on the Registry.

Q) *What types of abuse are founded and placed on the Child Abuse Registry?*

A) Most confirmed reports are placed on the registry as founded reports. This includes:

- All cases referred for juvenile or criminal court action
- Physical abuse when the injury was not minor or isolated or is likely to reoccur
- All mental injury
- All sexual abuse unless the perpetrator is under the age of 14 and does not pose a danger to other children
- Denial of critical care when the injury was not minor, or isolated or is likely to reoccur
- All child prostitution
- All presence of illegal drugs
- When the perpetrator continues to pose a threat; or a prior confirmed abuse incident occurred
- Manufacturing or possession of a dangerous substance
- Bestiality in the presence of a minor
- Allows access by a registered sex offender

Q) *What does a "preponderance" of the evidence mean?*

A) A preponderance of the evidence is defined as greater than 50% of the evidence gathered.

Q) *What notifications can the mandatory reporter expect to receive from DHS?*

A) Oral notification of intake decision within 24 hours of making the report, written notification of intake decision sent within 5 working days, outcome notification of assessment sent within 20 working days, and a copy of the founded abuse report if requested.

Q) *When do parents receive notification that a child abuse assessment is being conducted?*

A) Written notification will be given to custodial and noncustodial parents within five working days that an assessment is being conducted.

Q) *Who receives notification that the assessment is completed and what the outcome is?*

A) Notification of the completion of the assessment and the outcome will be given to juvenile court, the county attorney, all subjects of the report (the alleged child victim, custodial and noncustodial parents, and the alleged perpetrator), and the mandatory reporter.

Q) *Do mandatory reporters receive a copy of the assessment report automatically?*

A) No, the report is automatically provided to juvenile court, the county attorney, the child, and the custodial and non-custodial parent.

Q) *How do mandatory reporters receive a copy of the assessment report?*

A) Mandatory reporters may request child abuse information regarding a specific report. Any request should be made using the *Request for Child Abuse Information* form provided by DHS or the *Notice of Child Abuse Assessment* that is sent to the mandatory reporter when the assessment is completed.

Q) *What is the Child Abuse Registry?*

A) The Child Abuse Registry was established by Iowa law and is maintained by the Department of Human Services. The Child Abuse Registry serves several functions. It gathers information about child abuse cases in Iowa, records repeat occurrences of child abuse, records dissemination of child abuse, collects information for appeals, and provides background checks for certain professionals.

Q) *How long are the subjects of a founded abuse report on the Registry?*

A) Subjects of a founded abuse reports are placed on the Registry for ten years from the most recent report.

Q *Who has access to child abuse information?*

A) Iowa law states that the DHS shall not reveal the identity of the reporter of child abuse in the written notification to parents or otherwise. Only the court may require DHS to release the reporter's name. The reporter's name could be released during other judicial actions. The information on the Child Abuse Registry is confidential and can be accessed by authorized entities, agencies or individuals specified in law.

Q) *Who can take protective custody of a child?*

A) Iowa law provides juvenile court with the ability to enter an "ex parte order" directing a peace officer to take custody of a child. When the child is in a circumstance or condition that presents an imminent danger to the child's life or health, and there isn't time to file for a court order, the law provides for a peace officer to take

NOTES

NOTES

a child into custody or a physician treating a child to keep the child in custody without the consent of the parent, guardian, or custodian.

Q) *When does juvenile court become involved?*

A) Juvenile court hearings are held when children are removed from their parents' custody, or when treatment or state supervision of abused or neglected children is necessary because the parents are unwilling or unable to provide such treatment or supervision.

Q) *When are people responsible for abuse criminally prosecuted?*

A) Criminal prosecution of a person responsible for child abuse is at the discretion of the county attorney.

Q *When does law enforcement become involved in a child abuse assessment?*

A) Law enforcement may become involved in a child abuse assessment at any time. Cases of child prostitution, homicide, sexual abuse and severe trauma require a joint assessment by law enforcement personnel and the DHS.

SAFE HAVEN FOR NEWBORNS

What is the Safe Haven Act?

Iowa has joined 30 other states in creating safe havens for infants. The Newborn Safe Haven Act (Iowa Code Chapter 233) is a law that allows parents (or another person who has the parent's authorization) to leave an infant up to 14 days old at a hospital or health care facility without fear of prosecution for abandonment.

What Is a Safe Haven?

A "safe haven" is an institutional health facility, which is defined according to the Act to be:

- A "hospital" as defined in Iowa Code section 135B.1, including a facility providing medical or health services that is open 24 hours per day, 7 days per week and is a hospital emergency room; or

- A "health care facility" as defined in Iowa Code section 135C.1, including a residential care facility, a nursing facility, an intermediate care facility for persons with mental illness, or an intermediate care facility for persons with mental retardation.

Immunity

The Act provides immunity from prosecution for abandonment for a parent (or a person acting with the parent's authorization) who leaves an infant at a hospital or health care facility.

The Act provides immunity from civil or criminal liability for hospitals, health care facilities, and persons employed by those facilities that perform reasonable acts necessary to protect the physical health and safety of the infant.

More Information   You can get more information by:

- Going to the Department's web site at:
  http://www.dhs.state.ia.us/safehaven/safehaven.asp

- Reading the Safe Haven Act, Iowa Code Chapter 233.
  The Code of Iowa is available at public libraries or on line at:
  http://www.legis.state.ia.us/IowaLaw.html

NEWBORN INFANT CUSTODY RELEASE PROCEDURES (NEWBORN SAFE HAVEN ACT)

233.1 Newborn **safe haven** Act—definitions.

233.2 Newborn infant custody release procedures.

233.3 Immunity.

233.4 Rights of parents.

233.6 Education and public information.

REPORT OF SUSPECTED CHILD ABUSE

This form may be used as the written report which the law requires all mandated reporters to file with the Department of Human Services following an oral report of suspected child abuse. If your agency has a report form or letter format which includes all of the information requested on this form, you may use the agency format in place of this form.

Fill in as much information under each category as is known. Submit the completed form to the local office of the Department of Human Services <u>within 48 hours</u> of oral report.

FAMILY INFORMATION

Name of child		Age		Date of birth
Address		City		State
Phone	School			Grade level
Name of parent or guardian			Phone (*if different from child's*)	
Address (*if different from child's*)				

OTHER CHILDREN IN THE HOME

NAME	BIRTH DATE	CONDITION

INFORMATION ABOUT SUSPECTED ABUSE

In this section, indicate the date of suspected abuse; the nature, extent and cause of the suspected abuse; the persons thought to be responsible for the suspected abuse; evidence of previous abuse; and other pertinent information needed to conduct the assessment. Use the back of this form if necessary to complete the information requested above and to identify individuals who have been informed of the child abuse report, such as building administrator, supervisor, etc.

REPORTER INFORMATION

Name and title or position		
Office address		
Phone	Relationship to child	
Names of other mandatory reporters who have knowledge of the abuse		
Signature of reporter	Date	

DEPENDENT ADULT ABUSE OVERVIEW

"Dependent adult" abuse allegations involve people who are aged 18 or over and are incapable of adequate self care due to physical or mental conditions and require assistance from other people. Dependent adults may be elderly or may have diminished physical or mental capacities that prevent them from meeting their own needs adequately.

Researchers estimate that only 1 in 14 incidents of elder abuse actually come to the attention of law enforcement or human service agencies. Elder abuse is one of the most under-recognized and under-reported social problems in the United States. It is far less likely to be reported than child abuse because of the lack of public awareness. Nationally, it is estimated that over 55% of elder abuse is due to self-neglect. Such abuse can happen anywhere . . . in private homes, at health care facilities and in the community at large.

Iowa has an increasing proportion of people who are aged 60 or over. The number of persons 80 or over is increasing more rapidly than any other age group. Iowa's proportion of older adults in the population exceeds that of the United States as a whole. Nationwide, Iowa ranks:

2nd   in the percentage of persons over age 85
2nd   in the percentage of persons over age 75
3rd   in the percentage of persons over age 65
4th   in the percentage of persons over age 60

In 1993, the Department of Elder Affairs, Iowa State University, and area agencies on aging conducted a statewide needs assessment of non institutionalized Iowans aged 60 to 104. In general, older people in Iowa appear to be doing fairly well, but there are also large numbers who are vulnerable and at risk.

About half of the people in the study lived alone, a trend that is likely to continue into the next century. Those living alone more likely to be older women with lower incomes. The older a woman becomes in our society, the more likely she is to live alone.

Health problems that occur when an elderly person lives alone are more likely to create problems for independent living. While many family and friends provide strong support systems for the elderly, many people who live alone have no one to help them and must rely on the provision of services or on paid assistance. In fact, the data shows that much of the assistance the elderly are receiving is coming from professionals. The elderly who are living alone must have services available to them in order to maintain their independence.

NOTES

Dependent adults also include those who have diminished physical or mental capacity. People who have a diminished ability to protect themselves and are dependent on others for basic needs are particularly vulnerable to mistreatment, physical violence, threats of assault, verbal abuse, financial exploitation, physical or emotional neglect, and sexual abuse. Iowa has a sizable population of adults who are dependent but are not elderly.

IOWA RESPONSE Iowa Code Section 235B, "Dependent Adult Abuse," took effect on January 1, 1983, and has been amended yearly since then. This law authorizes the Department of Human Services (DHS) to accept reports of suspected dependent adult abuse, evaluate those reports, complete an assessment of needed services, make referrals for services, and maintain a central registry of abuse information.

DHS has legal authority to conduct evaluations and assessments of alleged dependent adult abuse that occurs in the community when it is alleged that:

- The victim meets the definition of being a dependent adult, and
- The victim suffers one or more of the five categories of abuse or neglect, and
- The abuse or neglect occurred as a result of the acts or omissions of a responsible caretaker or of the dependent adult.

DHS conducts approximately 1600 evaluations of dependent adult abuse annually.

Under Iowa Code Chapter 235E, the Department of Inspections and Appeals is now responsible for accepting reports of suspected dependent adult abuse in the following facilities and for completing evaluations of these reports:

- Health care facilities licensed in Iowa Code section 135C.1,
- Hospitals defined in Iowa Code section 135B.1,
- Elder group homes defined in Iowa Code section 231B.1,
- Assisted living programs certified in Iowa Code section 231C.3, and
- Adult day services programs defined in Iowa Code section 231D.1.

Additionally, dependent adult abuse may be a crime. Often the evaluating worker and law enforcement work together. Criminal laws provide for the prosecution of alleged perpetrators in cases where a criminal act has been committed.

Other laws provide other means of protection for dependent adults, including substitute decision makers and, when necessary, the involuntary commitment of adults for substance abuse or mental health reasons.

Services can be provided for dependent adults. However all adults have a right to self-determination. This means that the dependent adult can refuse services unless a court determines that the person is not competent to make decisions or is threatening his or her own life or that of others.

Iowa Code section 235B.4 creates a central registry in DHS to provide a single source for the statewide collection, maintenance, and dissemination of dependent adult abuse information. The Central Abuse Registry includes report data, investigative data, and disposition data relating to reports of dependent adult abuse. The purpose of the Registry is to:

- Facilitate the identification of victims or potential victims of dependent adult abuse by making available a single, statewide source of dependent adult data.
- Facilitate research on dependent adult abuse by making available a single, statewide source of dependent adult abuse data.
- Provide maximum safeguards against the unwarranted invasions of privacy that such a registry might otherwise entail.

The Registry issues an annual report on its administrative operation, including information as to the number of requests for dependent adult abuse data, the proportion of requests attributable to each type of authorized access, the frequency and nature of irregularities, and other pertinent matters.

Am I a mandatory reporter of dependent adult abuse?

Iowa Code sections 235B.3(2) and 235E.2 require all of the following people to report suspected dependent adult abuse to the Department of Human Services or the Department of Inspections and Appeals if the person in the course of employment examines, attends, counsels, or treats a dependent adult and reasonably believes the dependent adult has suffered abuse:

- A member of the staff of a community mental health center
- A staff member or employee of a health care facility defined in Iowa Code 135C.1; hospital as defined in Iowa Code 135B; elder group home as defined in Iowa Code 231B.1; assisted living program certified under Iowa Code 231C.3, or adult day services programs defined in Iowa Code 231D.1
- A peace officer
- An in-home homemaker-home health aide
- A person employed as an outreach person
- A health practitioner, as defined in Iowa Code section 232.68

NOTES

- A member of the staff or an employee of a community supervised apartment living arrangement, sheltered workshop, or work activity center
- A social worker
- A certified psychologist
- A care review committee member assigned to an elder group home pursuant to Iowa Code Chapter 231B

NOTE: **Any** other person who believes that a dependent adult has suffered abuse **may** make a report of the suspected abuse to DHS. Mandatory reporters may also report suspected abuse **outside** the scope of their professional practice, as **permissive** reporters. An employee of a financial institution may report suspected financial exploitation of a dependent adult.

HOW DO I REPORT DEPENDENT ADULT ABUSE?

441 Iowa Administrative Code 176.4(235B) and 176.5(235B)
Iowa Code Section 235B.3 requires that if you are a mandatory reporter of dependent adult abuse, and you suspect a dependent adult has been abused, you must report it to DHS. Iowa Code Section 235E.2 requires that if the abuse occurred in a health care facility, hospital, elder group home, assisted living or adult day services program, you should report it to the Department of Inspections and Appeals (DIA). Make the report to DHS or DIA by telephone or by other means.

Both the DHS Central Abuse Registry and DHS local offices accept reports from any person who believes dependent adult abuse has occurred. DHS maintain a toll-free telephone line 1-800-362-2178, which is available on a 24-hour-a-day, seven-day-a-week basis. Any person may use this number to report cases of suspected dependent adult abuse. All authorized persons may also use this number for obtaining dependent adult abuse information. DIA can be contacted at 1-877-686-0027.

If you have reason to believe that immediate protection for the dependent adult is advisable, also make an oral report to the appropriate law enforcement agency. A county attorney or law enforcement agency that receives a report of dependent adult abuse must refer it to DHS.

You must also make a report in writing within 48 hours after your oral report. You may use DHS form 470-2441, **Suspected Dependent Adult Abuse Report**, or a format you develop that meets the requirements listed below, based on 441 Iowa Administrative Code 176.5(235B). See the end of this handbook for a sample of form 470-2441.

If you are a staff member or employee, you must also immediately notify the person in charge or the person's designated agent. "Immediately" means within 24 hours from the time the mandatory reporter

Intake Numbers for Reporting Abuse

Area 1: Sioux City
Phone: 712-255-2699
Fax: 712-255-2676

Area 2: Waterloo
Phone: 319-291-2441
Fax: 319-291-2619

Area 3: Dubuque
Phone: 888-583-1039
Local: 563-1039
Fax: 563-557-9177

Area 4: Ames
Phone: 866-474-5366
Local: 268-7000
Fax: 515-268-7019

Area 5: Council Bluffs
Phone: 877-683-0323
Fax: 712-328-4878

Area 6: Des Moines
Phone: 515-283-9110
Fax: 515-283-7912

Area 7: Cedar Rapids
Phone: 319-892-5055
Fax: 319-362-2565

Area 8: Davenport
Phone: 888-270-3864
Fax: 563-326-8240

Less than fulltime offices

Map of Iowa counties with intake numbers:

Lyon 60, Osceola 72, Dickinson 30, Emmet 32, Kossuth 55, Winnebago 95, Worth 98, Mitchell 66, Howard 45, Winneshiek 96, Allamakee 3

Sioux 84, O'Brien 71, Clay 21, Palo Alto 74, Hancock 41, Cerro Gordo 17, Floyd 34, Chickasaw 19, Fayette 33, Clayton 22

Plymouth 75, Cherokee 18, Buena Vista, Pocahontas 76, Humboldt 46, Wright 99, Franklin 35, Butler 12, Bremer 9, Winneshiek

Woodbury 97, Ida 47, Sac 81, Calhoun 13, Webster 94, Hamilton 40, Hardin 42, Grundy 38, Black Hawk 7, Buchanan 10, Delaware 28, Dubuque 31

Monona 67, Crawford 24, Carroll 14, Greene 37, Boone 8, Story 85, Marshall 64, Tama 86, Benton 6, Linn 57, Jones 53, Jackson 49

Harrison 43, Shelby 83, Audubon 5, Guthrie 39, Dallas 25, Polk 77, Jasper 50, Poweshiek 79, Iowa 48, Johnson 52, Cedar 16, Clinton 23

Pottawattamie 78, Cass 15, Adair 1, Madison 61, Warren 91, Marion 63, Mahaska 62, Keokuk 54, Washington 92, Muscatine 70, Scott 82

Mills 65, Montgomery 69, Adams 2, Union 88, Clarke 20, Lucas 59, Monroe 68, Wapello 90, Jefferson 51, Henry 44, Louisa 58, Des Moines 29

Fremont 36, Page 73, Taylor 87, Ringgold 80, Decatur 27, Wayne 93, Appanoose 4, Davis 26, Van Buren 89, Lee 56

NOTES

suspects abuse of a dependent adult. The employer or supervisor of a mandatory abuse reporter shall not apply any policy, work rule, or other requirement that interferes with the person making a report of dependent adult abuse or that results in the failure of another person to make the report.

If you are a staff member or employee of a facility or program licensed or certified by the DIA, you must immediately notify the person in charge or the person's designated agent, who then makes the report to the DIA, within 24 hours, unless the person you are to report directly to is the person you suspect of abusing the dependent adult.

REPORT REQUIREMENTS Include in your report the following information, or as much of it as you are able to furnish:

- The names and home addresses of the dependent adult, relatives, caretakers, and other people believed to be responsible for the dependent adult's care.
- The dependent adult's present whereabouts, if not the same as the address given.
- The reason the adult is believed to be dependent.
- The dependent adult's age.
- The nature and extent of the adult abuse, including evidence of previous adult abuse.
- Information concerning the suspected adult abuse of other dependent adults in the same residence.
- Other information that you believe might be helpful in establishing the cause of the abuse or the identity of the people responsible for the abuse or helpful in assisting the dependent adult.
- Your name and address.

A report that meets the criteria will be accepted whether or not it contains all of the information listed.

CONFIDENTIALITY AND IMMUNITY FROM LIABILITY Iowa Code section 235B.3, states in subsections 7 through 10:

The department shall inform the appropriate county attorneys of any reports of dependent adult abuse. The department may request information from any person believed to have knowledge of a case of dependent adult abuse. The person, including but not limited to a county attorney, a law enforcement agency, a multidisciplinary team, or a social services agency in the state shall cooperate and assist in the evaluation upon the request of the department. County attorneys and appropriate law enforcement agencies shall also take any other lawful action necessary or advisable for the protection of the dependent adult.

A person participating in good faith in reporting or cooperating with or assisting the department in evaluating a case of dependent adult abuse has immunity from liability, civil or criminal, which might otherwise be incurred or imposed based upon the act of making the report or giving the assistance. The person has the same immunity with respect to participating in good faith in a judicial proceeding resulting from the report or cooperation or assistance or relating to the subject matter of the report, cooperation, or assistance.

It shall be unlawful for any person or employer to discharge, suspend, or otherwise discipline a person required to report or voluntarily reporting an instance of suspected dependent adult abuse pursuant to subsection 2 or 4, or cooperating with, or assisting the department of human services in evaluating a case of dependent adult abuse, or participating in judicial proceedings relating to the reporting or cooperation or assistance based solely upon the person's reporting or assistance relative to the instance of dependent adult abuse. A person or employer found in violation of this subsection is guilty of a simple misdemeanor.

A person required by this section to report a suspected case of dependent adult abuse who knowingly and willfully fails to do so commits a simple misdemeanor. A person required by this section to report a suspected case of dependent adult abuse who knowingly fails to do so or who knowingly interferes with the making of a dependent adult abuse report or applies a requirement that results in a failure to make a report, is civilly liable for the damages proximately caused by the failure.

INDICATORS OF POSSIBLE DEPENDENT ADULT ABUSE The following physical, behavioral, and environmental indicators are listed as signs of possible dependent adult abuse for you to consider in making your report. These lists are examples and are not all-inclusive.

Environment

- No food in the house or rotted, infested food
- Lack of proper food storage
- Special dietary foods not available
- Inadequate cooking facilities or equipment
- Clothes extremely dirty or uncared for
- Not dressed appropriately for the weather
- Inadequate or ill fitting clothing, not dressing
- Wearing all of one's clothing at once
- Unvented gas heaters, chimney in poor repair
- No fuel for heating or fuel stored dangerously
- Lack of water or contaminated water
- Gross accumulation of garbage, papers, and clutter
- Lack of access to essential rooms
- Lack of access to community resources
- Lives on the street
- Large number of pets with no apparent means of care

- Structure dilapidated or in poor repair
- Fallen steps, high grass, rotted porch, leaking roof
- Utilities cut off or lack of heat in winter
- Doors or windows made out of cardboard
- Sudden withdrawals or closing out of bank accounts
- No TV, radio, telephone, newspapers, magazines

- No income, unpaid bills
- Out of money by second week of the month
- Income does not meet monthly expenditures
- Signs checks over to others
- Sudden change in money management habits
- No friends or family visits
- No means of transportation
- Not physically able to get out and shop, pay bills, etc.

Physical Condition

- Lack of medical care
- Lack of personal cleanliness and grooming, body odors
- Swollen eyes or ankles, decayed teeth or no teeth
- Bites, fleas, sores, lesions, lacerations
- Multiple or repeated or untreated injuries
- Injuries incompatible with explanation
- Bruises, broken bones or burns

- Untreated pressure sores
- Signs of confinement (tied to furniture, locked in a room, etc.)
- Obesity, malnourishment or dehydration
- Tremors
- Difficulty in communication
- Broken glasses frames or lenses
- Drunk, overly medicated
- Lying in urine, feces, old food
- No use of limbs, lack of mobility

Behavior

- Intentional physical self-abuse, suicidal statements
- Persistent liar
- Does not follow medication directions
- Refuses needed medical attention
- Refuses to accept services offered by others
- Threatens or attacks others physically or verbally
- Refuses to accept presence of visitor
- Refuses to open door
- In total darkness
- Denies obvious problems (medical conditions, etc.)

- Refuses to discuss the situation
- Lack of trust in family as well as in others
- Refuses to take medication
- Denies any wrong-doing, medically or otherwise
- Unjustified pride in self-sufficiency
- Procrastination
- Turns off hearing aid
- Hallucinations, confusion or delusions
- Disorientation as to place and time
- Forgetfulness, losing things, not shutting stove off
- Loneliness, anger, or fearfulness

- Increased depression, anxiety or hostility
- Withdrawn, reclusive, suspicious, timid, unresponsive
- Diminished mental capacity
- Vague health complaints
- Longing for death

WHAT IS DEPENDENT ADULT ABUSE UNDER IOWA LAW?

There are two laws, Iowa Code Chapter 235B for dependent adults in the community and Iowa Code Chapter 235E for dependent adults who live in facilities. "Facilities" include health care facilities defined in Iowa Code section 135C.1, hospitals defined in Iowa Code, section 135B.1, elder group homes defined in Iowa Code section 231B.1, assisted living programs defined in Iowa Code section 231C.1, and adult day services programs defined in Iowa Code section 231D.1.

DEFINITIONS USED BY DHS As defined in Iowa Code section 235B.2, "dependent adult abuse" includes five categories of abuse as the result of the willful or negligent acts or omissions of a caretaker:

- Financial exploitation
- Physical abuse (including assault and unreasonable confinement or punishment)
- Sexual abuse
- Sexual exploitation by a caretaker
- Denial of critical care (which may also be committed by the dependent adult)

VICTIM To be accepted for evaluation, a report must concern a dependent adult. Iowa Code section 235B.2 defines "dependent adult" as a person 18 years of age or older who is:

- Unable to protect the person's own interests or unable to adequately perform or obtain services necessary to meet essential human needs.
- As a result of a physical or mental condition that requires assistance from another.

Dependent adult abuse does not include allegations involving:

- Domestic abuse in a situation where the victim is not "dependent."
- People who are legally incarcerated in a penal setting, either in a local jail or in the custody of the Department of Corrections.

PERSON RESPONSIBLE FOR ABUSE Iowa Code section 235B.2 defines "caretaker" as a related or nonrelated person who has the responsibility for the protection, care, or custody of a dependent adult as a result of

NOTES

NOTES

assuming the responsibility voluntarily, by contract, through employment, or by the order of the court.

Financial exploitation "Financial exploitation" means the act or process of:

- Taking unfair advantage of a dependent adult or the adult's physical or financial resources for one's own personal or pecuniary profit without the informed consent of the dependent adult, including theft.
- By the use of undue influence, harassment, duress, deception, false representation, or false pretenses.
- As a result of the willful or negligent acts or omissions of a caretaker.

Physical abuse

"Physical abuse" means one of the following, as a result of the willful or negligent acts or omissions of a caretaker:

- Physical injury to a dependent adult
- Injury to a dependent adult which is at a variance with the history given
- Unreasonable confinement of a dependent adult
- Unreasonable punishment of a dependent adult
- Assault of a dependent adult

"An assault" is committed by a caretaker when, without justification, the person does any of the following:

- Any act which is intended to cause pain or injury to, or which is intended to result in physical contact which will be insulting or offensive to another, coupled with the apparent ability to execute the act.
- Any act, which is intended to place another in fear of immediate physical contact, which will be painful, injurious, insulting, or offensive, coupled with the apparent ability to execute the ace.
- Intentionally points any firearm toward another, or displays in a threatening manner any dangerous weapon toward another.

However, the act shall not be considered an assault when the person doing the act and the other person are voluntary participants in a sport, social or other activity that is not in itself criminal, and the act:

- Is a reasonably foreseeable incident of that sport or activity, and
- Does not create an unreasonable risk of serious injury or breach of the peace,
- Note that there does not have to be an injury to constitute physical abuse.

SEXUAL ABUSE "Sexual abuse" means the commission of a sexual offense under Iowa Code Chapter 709 or Iowa Code section 726.2 with or against a dependent adult as a result of the willful or negligent acts or omissions of a caretaker. "Sexual abuse" includes the following subcategories:

- First degree sexual abuse
- Second degree sexual abuse
- Third degree sexual abuse
- Detention in a brothel
- Indecent exposure
- Assault with intent to commit sexual abuse and incest
- Sexual exploitation by a counselor or therapist
- Sexual exploitation of a dependent adult by a caretaker
- Invasion of privacy, nudity
- Incest

SEXUAL EXPLOITATION BY A CARETAKER "Sexual exploitation by a care-taker" means any consensual or nonconsensual sexual conduct with a dependent adult. This includes but is not limited to kissing; touching the clothed or unclothed inner thigh, breast, groin, buttock, anus, pubes, or genitals; or a sex act as defined in section 702.17.

Sexual exploitation also includes the transmission, display, or taking of electronic images of the unclothed breast, groin, buttock, anus, pubes, or genitals of a dependent adult by a caretaker for a purpose not related to treatment or diagnosis or as part of an ongoing assessment, evaluation, or investigation.

Sexual exploitation does not include touching which is part of a necessary examination, treatment, or care by a caretaker acting within the scope of the practice or employment of the caretaker; the exchange of a brief touch or hug between the dependent adult and a caretaker for the purpose of reassurance, comfort, or casual friendship; or touching between spouses.

DENIAL OF CRITICAL CARE "Denial of critical care" means the deprivation of the minimum food, shelter, clothing, supervision, physical or mental health care, or other care necessary to maintain a dependent adult's life or health, as a result of the willful or negligent acts or omissions of a caretaker. This includes the following sub-categories:

- Denial of or failure to provide adequate food
- Denial of or failure to provide adequate shelter
- Denial of or failure to provide adequate clothing
- Denial of or failure to provide adequate medical care
- Denial of or failure to provide adequate mental health care
- Denial of or failure to meet emotional needs necessary for normal functioning

NOTES

- Denial of or failure to provide proper supervision
- Denial of or failure to provide adequate physical care

NOTE: Denial of critical care may also be the deprivation of the minimum food, shelter, clothing, supervision, physical or mental health care, and other care necessary to maintain a dependent adult's life or health as a result of the acts or omissions of the dependent adult. (This includes the sub-categories listed above.)

Dependent adult abuse does **not** include the following circumstances:

- The dependent adult declines medical treatment because the dependent adult holds a belief or is an adherent of a religion whose tenets and practices call for reliance on spiritual means in place of reliance on medical treatment.
- The dependent adult's caretaker declines such treatment acting in accordance with the dependent adult's stated or implied consent, if the dependent adult holds a belief or is an adherent of a religion whose tenets and practices call for reliance on spiritual means in place of reliance on medical treatment.
- The dependent adult or the dependent adult's next of kin or guardian requests withholding or withdrawal of health care from a dependent adult who is terminally ill, in the opinion of a licensed physician, pursuant to the applicable procedures under Iowa Code Chapters 125, 144A, 222, 229, or 633.

DEFINITIONS USED BY DIA DIA evaluates reports of abuse in health care facilities, hospitals, assisted living programs, elder group homes, and adult day services programs.

As defined by Iowa code Section 235E.1, "dependent adult abuse" includes the following as a result of the willful misconduct or gross negligence or reckless acts or omissions of a caretaker, taking into account the totality of the circumstances.

- Physical abuse
- Sexual abuse
- Sexual exploitation by a caretaker
- Financial exploitation
- Neglect

VICTIM To be accepted for evaluation, a report must concern a dependent adult. "Dependent adult" means a person 18 years of age or older whose ability to perform the normal activities of daily living or to provide for the person's own care or protection is impaired, either temporarily or permanently.

PERSON RESPONSIBLE FOR ABUSE The abuse must have occurred as a result of actions taken by a "caretaker" who is a staff member of a facility or program and who provides care, protection, or services to a dependent adult voluntarily, by contract, through employment, or by order of the court.

PHYSICAL ABUSE "Physical abuse" means one of the following, as a result of the willful misconduct or gross negligence or reckless acts or omissions of a caretaker, taking into account the totality of the circumstances:

- Physical injury
- Injury which is at a variance with the history give of the injury
- Unreasonable confinement
- Unreasonable punishment
- Assault that involved the breach of skill, care, and learning ordinarily exercised by a caretaker in similar circumstances.

"Assault" means the commission of (1) any act that is generally intended to cause pain or injury to a dependent adult, or is generally intended to result in physical contact that would be considered by a reasonable person to be insulting or offensive or (2) any act that is intended to place another in fear of immediate physical contact that will be painful, injurious, insulting or offensive, coupled with the apparent ability to execute the act.

SEXUAL ABUSE "Sexual abuse" means the commission of a sexual offense under Iowa Code chapter 709 or section 726.2 with or against a dependent adult. This includes the following sub-categories:

- First degree sexual abuse
- Second degree sexual abuse
- Third degree sexual abuse
- Detention in a brothel
- Indecent exposure
- Assault with intent to commit sexual abuse and incest
- Sexual exploitation by a counselor or therapist
- Invasion of privacy, nudity
- Incest

SEXUAL EXPLOITATION BY A CARETAKER "Sexual exploitation by a caretaker" means any consensual or nonconsensual sexual conduct with a dependent adult. This includes but is not limited to kissing; touching of the clothed or unclothed breast, groin, buttock, anus, pubes, or genitals; or a sex act as defined in Iowa Code section 702.17.

NOTES

"Sexual exploitation" also includes the transmission, display, or taking of electronic images of the unclothed breast, groin, buttock, anus, or pubes that is not related to treatment or diagnosis or part of an ongoing investigation.

"Sexual exploitation" does not include touching that is part of a necessary examination, treatment, or care by a caretaker acting within the scope of the practice or employment of the caretaker; the exchange of a brief touch or hug between the dependent adult and a caretaker for the purpose of reassurance, comfort, or casual friendship; or touching between spouses or domestic partners in an intimate relationship.

FINANCIAL EXPLOITATION "Exploitation" means a caretaker who knowingly obtains, uses, endeavors to obtain to use, or who misappropriates, a dependent adult's funds, assets, medications, or property with the intent to temporarily or permanently deprive a dependent adult of the use, benefit, or possession of the funds, assets, medication, or property for the benefit of someone other than the dependent adult.

NEGLECT "Neglect" means the deprivation of the minimum food, shelter, clothing, supervision, physical or mental health care, or other care necessary to maintain a dependent adult's life or physical or mental health.

Dependent adult abuse in health care facilities, assisted living programs, elder group homes, and adult day service programs does not include the following circumstances:

- The dependent adult declines medical treatment because the adult holds a belief or is an adherent of a religion whose tenets and practices call for reliance on spiritual means in place of reliance on medical treatment.
- The dependent adult's caretaker declines medical treatment acting in accordance with the dependent adult's stated or implied consent.
- A dependent adult or the adult's next of kin or guardian requests withholding or withdrawing of health care from the adult who is terminally ill, in the opinion of a licensed physician, pursuant to the applicable procedures under Iowa Code chapters 125, 144A, 222, 229, or 633.

REPORT CONCLUSIONS DIA has three possible outcomes in a dependent adult abuse evaluation:

- **Founded:** It is determined by a preponderance of evidence (more than 50%) that abuse has occurred. Information on founded reports is maintained on the Central Abuse Registry for ten years and then sealed.

- **Unfounded:** It is determined by a preponderance of evidence (more than 50%) that abuse has not occurred. Information on unfounded reports is destroyed five years from the date they were unfounded.
- **Confirmed, not registered:** It is determined by a preponderance of evidence (more than 50%) that abuse has occurred. When physical abuse or denial of critical care by a caretaker is determined to be minor, isolated and unlikely to reoccur, the report is maintained for five years and then destroyed, unless a subsequent report is founded.

If there is a subsequent report committed by the same caretaker within five years of the nonregistered report, it also may be considered minor, isolated, and unlikely to reoccur depending on the circumstances. These reports are called "assessments" rather than "evaluations." The subsequent reports will be kept for ten years and then sealed.

HOW DOES DHS RESPOND?

441 Iowa Administrative Code 176.6(235B)
Immediately upon receipt of a report of dependent adult abuse, DHS shall:

- Make an oral report to the Central Abuse Registry.
- Forward a copy of the report to the Registry.
- Notify the local county attorney of the receipt of the report.
- Commence an appropriate evaluation or assessment.

Upon receipt of a report of suspected dependent adult abuse, the Central Abuse Registry searches its records. If Registry records reveal any previous report of dependent adult abuse involving the same adult or any other pertinent information with respect to the same adult, the Registry immediately notifies the appropriate DHS office or law enforcement agency of that fact.

The primary purpose of the evaluation or assessment is the protection of the dependent adult named in the report. The evaluation or assessment shall include all of the following:

- Identification of the nature, extent, and cause of the adult abuse, if any, to the dependent adult named in the report.
- The identification of the person or persons responsible for the adult abuse.
- A determination of whether other dependent adults in the same residence have been subjected to adult abuse.
- A critical examination of the residential environment of the dependent adult named in the report, and the dependent

adult's relationship with caretakers and other adults in the same residence.

- A critical explanation of all other pertinent matters.

The DHS process of evaluating reports of dependent adult abuse is as follows:

- Intake
- Appropriate evaluation or assessment
  - Contact with the dependent adult at the person's residence or at a care or training program
  - Interview with the alleged perpetrator
  - Obtaining information from subjects of the report and other relevant parties
- Documentation of conclusions and recommendations for services or court action
- Documentation of evaluation through completion of reports
- Completion of required correspondence to subjects and mandatory reporters

Reports of suspected abuse are rejected for evaluation or assessment for the following reasons:

- The subject of the report is not a dependent adult.
- The alleged perpetrator is not a caretaker.
- The allegations do not constitute abuse.
- The information provided is insufficient to suspect abuse.
- The information is provided in duplicative or in addition to a previous report.
- The report was referred to the Department of Inspections and Appeals.

You will be notified whether or not your report is accepted for evaluation or assessment.

EVALUATION OR ASSESSMENT DHS may request information from any person believed to have knowledge of a case of dependent adult abuse. This includes but is not limited to a county attorney, a law enforcement agency, a multidisciplinary team, a social services agency in the state, or any person who is required to report dependent adult abuse, whether or not the person made the specific dependent adult abuse report.

The person **shall cooperate and assist** in the evaluation upon the request of DHS. County attorneys, law enforcement agencies, multidisciplinary teams, and social services agencies in the state shall cooperate and assist in the evaluation or assessment upon the request of DHS. County attorneys and law enforcement agencies shall also take any other lawful action necessary or advisable for the protection of the dependent adult.

With the consent of the dependent adult or caretaker, the evaluation or assessment may, when appropriate, include a visit to the residence of the dependent adult named in the report and an examination of the dependent adult.

If permission to enter the residence and to examine the dependent adult is refused, the district court may authorize DHS to enter the dependent adult's residence and to examine the dependent adult to make an evaluation or assessment, upon a showing of probable cause that the dependent adult has been abused. A court may also authorize DHS to gain access to the financial records of the dependent adult upon a showing of probable cause that the dependent adult has been financially exploited.

DHS transmits a copy of its evaluation or assessment report, including actions taken or contemplated, to the Registry within 20 regular working days after it receives the adult abuse report, unless the Registry grants an extension of time for good cause.

Upon completion of the report, **all subjects and mandatory reporters are notified in writing** of the conclusions of the evaluation or assessment report.

BOARDING HOMES 2009 Iowa Acts, Senate File 484, section 5
DIA registers boarding homes and DHS evaluates allegations of abuse in boarding homes, through a coordinated interagency approach. The composition of the multidisciplinary team depends on the allegations and discoveries made during an evaluation or assessment of abuse or violation of registration.

DHS and DIA may participate in a investigation composed of employees from the State Fire Marshall, the Division of Criminal Investigation of the Department of Public Safety, the Workforce Development Department, the Civil Rights Commission, or other local, state, or federal agencies.

REPORT CONCLUSIONS The conclusion of the investigation is based on an evaluation of all of the information gathered during the investigation. There are three possible outcomes in a dependent adult evaluation or assessment:

- Founded: It is determined by a preponderance of evidence (more than 50%) that abuse has occurred. These are the only reports that are listed on the Central Abuse Registry. (See Retention of Records.)

- Unfounded: It is determined by a preponderance of evidence (more than 50%) that abuse has not occurred.

- Confirmed, not registered: It is determined by a preponderance of evidence (more than 50%) that the physical abuse or denial of critical care by a caretaker has occurred, but the abuse is determined to be minor, isolated, and unlikely to reoccur.

WHAT HAPPENS AFTER THE EVALUATION?

Based on the evaluation, DHS completes an assessment of services needed by a dependent adult believed to be the victim of abuse, the dependent adult's family, or a caretaker. In some situations there are treatment services that are available and may be offered to assist the dependent adult.

DHS does not have independent legal authority to compel the acceptance of protective services. Adults have constitutional rights that guarantee certain freedoms. Adults have a right to self-determination and have the right to voluntarily accept services or to decline or refuse them. DHS strives to balance a person's right to personal freedom with the need to protect dependent adults who are unable to protect themselves.

Upon voluntary acceptance of the offer of services, DHS makes referrals or may provide necessary protective services to eligible dependent adults, their family members, and caretakers. The following services may be offered and provided without regard to income: dependent adult protection, social casework, adult day care, adult support, transportation, and family planning.

LAW ENFORCEMENT INTERVENTION Iowa Code section 235B.3A gives the following responsibilities to law enforcement officers:

If a peace officer has reason to believe that dependent adult abuse, which is criminal in nature, has occurred, the officer shall use all reasonable means to prevent further abuse, including but not limited to any of the following:

1. If requested, remaining on the scene as long as there is a danger to the dependent adult's physical safety without the presence of a peace officer, including but not limited to staying in the dwelling unit, or if unable to remain at the scene, assisting the dependent adult in leaving the residence and securing support services or emergency shelter services.
2. Assisting the dependent adult in obtaining medical treatment necessitated by the dependent adult abuse, including providing assistance to the dependent adult in obtaining transportation to the emergency room of the nearest hospital.
3. Providing a dependent adult with immediate and adequate notice of the dependent adult's rights. The notice shall consist of handing the dependent adult a copy of the following written statement, requesting the dependent adult to read the card and asking the dependent adult whether the dependent adult understands the rights:

    a. You have the right to ask the court for the following help on a temporary basis:

       (1) Keeping the alleged perpetrator away from you, your home, and your place of work.

       (2) The right to stay at your home without interference from the alleged perpetrator.

       (3) Professional counseling for you, your family, or household members, and the alleged perpetrator of the dependent adult abuse.

    b. If you are in need of medical treatment, you have the right to request that the peace officer present assist you in obtaining transportation to the nearest hospital or otherwise assist you.

    c. If you believe that police protection is needed for your physical safety, you have the right to request that the peace officer present remain at the scene until you and other affected parties can leave or safety is otherwise ensured.

The notice shall also contain the telephone number of the local emergency shelter services, support services, or crisis lines operating in the area.

COURT ACTION DHS transmits a copy of the report of its evaluation or assessment to the local county attorney. The county attorney notifies the DHS local office of any actions or contemplated actions with respect to a suspected case of adult abuse.

    When a dependent adult is the victim of a criminal act by the caretaker, the caretaker may be criminally charged for maltreatment of the dependent adult. Some examples are:

Neglect or abandonment of a dependent person	Iowa Code 726.3
Wanton neglect of a dependent adult	Iowa Code 726.8(1)
Nonsupport of a dependent adult	Iowa Code 726.8(2)
Assault (various forms)	Iowa Code 708
Sexual abuse (various forms)	Iowa Code 709
Incest	Iowa Code 726.2
Dependent adult abuse (various forms)	Iowa Code 235B.20

When there is no way to protect a dependent adult adequately with voluntary services, the district court may be petitioned to intervene on behalf of the dependent adult. The district court can be petitioned to do any of the following:

- Authorize the provision of protective services to a dependent adult who is in need of services but lacks the capacity to consent to receipt of those services.
- Enjoin a caretaker from interfering with the provision of protective services to a dependent adult who is in need of such services and consents to the receipt of those services.

NOTES

- Restrain a caretaker from abusing a dependent adult.
- Order the provision of the following to a dependent adult who has been the victim of dependent adult abuse when the dependent adult lacks capacity to consent to the receipt of services or is subject to an immediate threat to the person's health and safety, or when the dependent adult's abuse results in irreparable harm to the person's physical or financial resources or property:
  - Removal of the dependent adult to safer surroundings
  - Provision of medical services to the dependent
  - Provision of other needed services to the dependent adult

When DHS determines that the best interests of the dependent adult require court action, DHS may initiate action for:

- The appointment of a guardian or conservator, or
- The admission or commitment to an appropriate institution or facility, pursuant to the applicable procedures under Iowa Code Chapters 125, 222, 229, or 633.

When DHS determines a dependent adult is suffering from abuse which represents an immediate danger to the health or safety of the dependent adult and results in irreparable harm to the dependent adult or the physical or financial resources or the dependent adult, and the adult lacks the capacity to consent to receive services, DHS will petition the court to order any of the following:

- Remove the dependent adult to safer surroundings;
- Order the provision of medical services;
- Order the provision of available services, including emergency services; or
- Terminate a guardianship or conservatorship.

The county attorney shall assist DHS in the preparation of the necessary papers to initiate the action, and shall appear and represent DHS at all district court proceedings. DHS assists the district court during all stages of court proceedings involving a suspected case of adult abuse.

In every case involving adult abuse substantiated by DHS that results in a judicial proceeding on behalf of the dependent adult, the court shall appoint legal counsel to represent the dependent adult in the proceedings. The court may also appoint a guardian ad litem to represent the dependent adult when necessary to protect the dependent adult's best interests. The same attorney may be appointed to serve both as legal counsel and as guardian ad litem.

Before legal counsel or a guardian ad litem is appointed pursuant to 1983 Iowa Acts, chapter 153, section 4, the court shall require the dependent adult to complete under oath a detailed financial statement. If, on the basis of that financial statement, the court deems that the dependent adult or the legally responsible person is able to bear all or a portion of the cost of the legal counsel or guardian ad litem, the court shall so order. When the dependent adult or the legally responsible person is unable to bear the cost of the legal counsel or guardian ad litem, the expense shall be paid out of the court expense fund.

SUBSTANCE ABUSE COMMITMENT Either the county attorney or an interested person may commence proceedings under Iowa Code Chapter 125 for the involuntary commitment of a substance abuser to a facility. Proceedings begin with the filing of a verified application with the clerk of the district court of the county where the respondent is presently located or which is the respondent's place of residence.

The application must:

- State that the applicant believes the respondent is a chronic substance abuser
- State other pertinent facts
- Be accompanied by one or more or the following:
  - A written statement of support by a physician
  - One or more supporting affidavits
  - Other corroborative information

An attorney is appointed to represent the respondent. The court orders a hearing and an examination. The court may issue an order for immediate custody if the respondent is believed to be a danger to self or others.

A commitment hearing is held. The respondent's welfare is paramount. If the evidence is clear and convincing, a complete evaluation is ordered. The evaluating facility must report to the court whether the respondent:

- Does not require further treatment, or
- Requires full-time (inpatient) treatment, or
- Requires out patient treatment, or
- Needs treatment but is not responding to the treatment provided

Further hearings can order continued treatment if warranted.

MENTAL HEALTH COMMITMENT Any interested person may commence proceedings under Iowa Code Chapter 229 for the involuntary hospitalization of a person. Proceedings are begun by filing a verified application with the clerk of the district court of the county where the respondent is presently located, or which is the respondent's place of residence. The application must:

- State that the applicant believes the respondent is seriously mentally impaired
- State other pertinent facts

NOTES

- Be accompanied by one or more of the following:
  - A written statement of support by a physician
  - One or more supporting affidavits
  - Other corroborative information

An attorney is appointed to represent the respondent. The court orders a hearing and an examination. The court may issue an order for immediate custody if the respondent is believed to be a danger to self or others.

A commitment hearing is held. The respondent's welfare is paramount. If the evidence is clear and convincing, a complete evaluation is ordered.

The evaluating facility must report to the court whether the respondent:

- Does not require further treatment, or
- Requires full-time (inpatient) treatment, or
- Requires outpatient treatment, or
- Needs treatment but is not responding to the treatment provided

Further hearings can order continued treatment if warranted.

CONSERVATORSHIP A "conservatorship" is a court-authorized relationship under Iowa Code sections 633.566–633.667 whereby one person assumes the responsibility for the custody and control of the property of another. The person to whom custody of the property is awarded is called a "conservator." The person over whose property custody is granted is called a "ward."

The appointment of a conservator means that the ward is either under legal age or by reason of mental, physical, or other incapacity is unable to make or carry out important decisions concerning the ward's **financial** affairs. It does not mean that the ward is of unsound mind.

A petition for the appointment of a conservator of the property of a dependent adult may be sought to protect the property of the dependent adult if the protective concern is based on an imminent danger to that person's property. In the absence of legal action, no person has the right to manage the property of an adult contrary to the adult's consent.

A conservator must do all of the following:

- Take possession of the ward's property and protect and preserve it, invest it prudently, and account for it.
- Maintain a complete list of all receipts and disbursements.
- Within 60 days of appointment, file an initial report and inventory of the property of the ward in the conservator's possession or of which the conservator has knowledge.

- File with the court the following reports containing full itemized accounting and a list of all assets:
  - An annual report filed within 30 days of the anniversary date of the conservator's appointment.
  - A final report filed at the termination of the conservatorship.

Failure to file a required report is a breach of the conservator's duty to the ward and to the court. If the ward's will comes into the conservator's hands, it must be delivered to the court for safekeeping.

A conservator has these general powers:

- Collect, receive and receipt for any property or income of the ward, including Social Security or Veterans Benefits.
- Sell or transfer perishable personal property or personal property having an established market value.
- Receive additional property from any source.
- Make payments to the ward or to others for the benefit of the ward.
- After obtaining a court order the conservator may:
  - Invest and reinvest the funds of the ward.
  - Sell, lease or mortgage real estate.
  - Do any other thing the court determines to be in the ward's best interest.

GUARDIANSHIP When the concern is for the dependent adult's life, rather than the adult's property, a person may seek guardianship appointment to provide for the legal sanction of moving the adult or protecting the adult. In the absence of such legal action, no one has the right to physically relocate an adult against the adult's will. The appointment of a guardian, authorized under Iowa Code sections 633.552–633.565, does not constitute an adjudication that the ward is of unsound mind.

The following conditions must be verified before filing a guardianship petition:

- The dependent adult is incompetent to make decisions regarding the adult's person.
- A qualified professional has written a document clearly stating that the dependent adult is incompetent to make decisions regarding the adult's person and the reasons for this.
- A qualified person has agreed to act as the guardian if appointed.

A guardian may be granted the following powers and duties, which may be exercised without prior court approval:

- Providing for the care, comfort and maintenance of the ward, including the appropriate training and education to maximize the ward's potential.

NOTES

- Taking reasonable care of the ward's clothing, furniture, vehicle and other personal effects.
- Assisting the ward in developing maximum self-reliance and independence.
- Ensuring the ward receives necessary emergency medical services.
- Ensuring the ward receives professional care, counseling, treatment or services as necessary.
- Any other powers or duties the court may specify.

A guardian may be granted the following powers, which may be exercised only upon court approval:

- Changing the ward's permanent residence at the guardian's request, if the proposed new residence is more restrictive of the ward's liberties than the current residence.
- Arranging the provisions of major elective surgery or any other non-emergency major medical procedure.
- Consent to the withholding or withdrawal of life-sustaining procedures in accordance with Iowa Code Chapter 144A.

The court may take into account all available information concerning the capabilities of the ward and any additional evaluation deemed necessary. The court may direct that the guardian have only a specially limited responsibility for the ward. If so, the court shall state those areas of responsibility that shall be supervised by the guardian. The ward shall retain all others. The court may alter the respective responsibilities of the guardian and the ward after notice to the ward and an opportunity to be heard.

A guardian must file the following reports with the court:

- An initial report within 60 days of appointment.
- An annual report within 30 days of the anniversary date of the appointment.
- A final report within 30 days of the event causing termination.

HOW IS DEPENDENT ADULT ABUSE INFORMATION HANDLED?

Iowa Code section 235B.6 provides that confidentiality of dependent adult information shall be maintained, except as specifically authorized. DHS must withhold the name of the person who made the report of suspected dependent adult abuse. Only the court or the Central Abuse Registry may allow the release of that person's name.

RETENTION OF RECORDS Information on all **founded** reports (whether evaluated by DHS or by DIA) is maintained on the Central Abuse

Registry for 10 years and then sealed. Exception: When the dependent adult is responsible for self-denial of critical care, DHS keeps the report in the local office, not on the Central Registry. These are called "assessments" rather than "evaluations."

Information on DHS-evaluated reports that are **confirmed, not registered is** maintained in the local office for 5 years and then destroyed, unless a subsequent report is founded. If there is a subsequent report committed by the same caretaker within 5 years, the original report will be kept in the local office and sealed 10 years after the subsequent report.

Information on **unfounded** reports is destroyed 5 years from the date they were unfounded.

Reports that are **rejected** for evaluation or assessment are kept in the local office for 3 years and then expunged.

ACCESS TO INFORMATION Access to "founded" or "unfounded" dependent adult abuse information is authorized to:

- "Subjects" of a report (the adult victim, the guardian or legal custodian of the adult victim, and the alleged perpetrator) or the attorney for any subject.
- An employee or agent of DHS responsible for investigating an abuse report.
- DHS personnel as necessary for the performance of their official duties.
- The mandatory reporter who reported the abuse.
- The long-term care resident's advocate.
- Multidisciplinary teams.

Access to "founded" dependent adult abuse information (not to "unfounded" information) is also authorized to:

- People involved in an investigation of dependent care, including a health practitioner or mental health professional, a law enforcement officer, a multidisciplinary team.
- Individuals, agencies, or facilities providing care to a dependent adult named in a report under some circumstances. This includes a facility licensing authority, a person or agency responsible for the care of a dependent adult victim or perpetrator, a DHS registration or licensing employee, or a person providing care to an adult who is regulated by DHS, and the legally authorized protection and advocacy agency.
- Judicial and administrative proceedings under some circumstances. This may include district court, a court or administrative agency hearing an appeal for correction of dependent adult abuse information, an expert witness at any stage of an appeal

NOTES

hearing, and a court or administrative agency making an unemployment compensation determination.

- A person conducting bona fide dependent adult abuse research.
- DHS personnel, a person or agency under contract with DHS to carry out the duties of the Registry, or the attorney for DHS.
- The Department of Justice.
- A legally constituted adult protection agency from another state for investigative or treatment purposes.
- A health care facility administrator or designee.
- State or local substitute decision maker.
- A nursing student program administrator and to the Board of Education for abuse background checks.

To request dependent adult abuse information, complete form 470-0612, *Request for Dependent Adult Abuse Registry Information*. A sample of this form is included at the end of this handbook. Send this form to the local DHS office or to the Central Abuse Registry at the following address: DHS Central Abuse Registry, 1305 E Walnut St, 5th Floor, Des Moines, Iowa 50319-0114

A person who would not otherwise have access to dependent adult abuse information, may request this information on an individual who agrees to authorize this information for the purpose of a background check. This can be accomplished by completing form 470-4531, *Authorization for Release of Dependent Adult Abuse Information*. A sample of this form is included at the end of this handbook.

The form must be completed as follows:

- The person requesting the information must complete and sign the top section of the form, and
- The person authorizing the background check must sign in the middle section.

Dependent adult abuse information is limited to whether or not there is a record of the person being checked as having been found to have abused a dependent adult. The person requesting the information will fax or mail the form to the Central Abuse Registry. The address and fax number are at the top of the form. DHS will perform the background check and fax or mail it back to the requester.

REQUEST FOR CORRECTION OR EXPUNGEMENT OF ABUSE INFORMATION A subject of a dependent adult abuse report who feels there is incorrect or erroneous information contained in the evaluation or assessment report, or who disagrees with the conclusions of the report, may request correction of the report.

To request a correction of a report, a person must file a written statement to the effect that the information referring to the person is in whole or in part erroneous with DHS within six months of the date of the notice of the results of the evaluation. Submit to: DHS Appeals Section, 1305 E Walnut St, 5th Floor, Des Moines, Iowa 50319-0114

The local office social worker or the social worker's supervisor may wish to review the report, along with any additional information the requester provides. They may uphold, modify or overturn the original funding. A requester not satisfied with the local office review may request an administrative appeal hearing.

The administrative law judge may uphold, modify, or overturn the finding. DHS may defer the hearing until the conclusion of a court case relating to the information or findings.

If the requester is not satisfied with the decision of the administrative law judge, the matter may be appealed to the district court. The decision resulting from the hearing may be appealed to the court of Polk County or to the court of the district in which the person resides.

Iowa Code section 235B.10 provides in subsections 4, 5, and 6 that:

Upon the request of the appellant, the record and evidence in such cases shall be closed to all but the court and its officers, and access to the record and evidence shall be prohibited unless otherwise ordered by the court. The clerk shall maintain a separate docket for such actions. A person other than the appellant shall not permit a copy of the testimony or pleadings or the substance of the testimony or pleadings to be made available to any person other than a party to the action or the party's attorney. Violation of the provisions of this subsection shall be a public offense punishable under section 235B.12.

If the Registry corrects or eliminates information as requested or as ordered by the court, the Registry shall advise all persons who have received the incorrect information of the fact. Upon application to the court and service of notice on the Registry, an individual may request and obtain a list of all persons who have received dependent adult abuse information referring to that individual.

In the course of any proceeding provided for by this section, the identity of the person who reported the disputed information and the identity of any person who has been reported as having abused an adult may be withheld upon a determination by the registry that disclosure of the person's identity would be detrimental to the person's interest.

WHAT TRAINING DO MANDATORY REPORTERS NEED?

Iowa Code section 235B.16 requires that a mandatory reporter whose work involves the examination, attending, counseling, or treatment of adults on a regular basis shall:

NOTES

- Obtain a statement of the abuse reporting requirements from the person's employer (or from DHS, if self-employed) within one month of initial employment or self-employment.
- Complete two hours of training relating to the identification and reporting of dependent adult abuse within six months of initial employment (or self-employment).
- Complete at least two hours of additional dependent adult abuse identification and reporting training every five years.

NOTE: These requirements do not apply to a physician whose professional practice does not regularly involve providing primary health care to adults.

If the person is an employee of a hospital or similar public or private facility, the employer is responsible for providing the training. To the extent that the employer provides approved training on the employer's premises, the hours of training completed by employees shall be included in the calculation of nursing or service hours required to be provided to a patient or resident per day.

If the person is self-employed, employed in a licensed or certified profession, or employed by a facility or program that is subject to licensure, regulation, or approval by a state agency, the person shall obtain the training as part of:

- A continuing education program required under Iowa Code chapter 272C and approved by the applicable licensing board,
- A training board using a curriculum approved by the abuse education review panel established by the Director of Public Health, or
- A training program using such an approved curriculum offered by the Department of Human Services, the Department of Aging, the Department of Inspection and Appeals, the Iowa Law Enforcement Academy, or a similar public agency.

A person required to complete both child abuse and dependent adult abuse mandatory reporter training may complete the training through a program that combines child abuse and dependent adult abuse curricula and thereby meet both training requirements simultaneously. The person may satisfy the combined requirements through completion of a two-hour training program, if the training curriculum is approved by the applicable licensing or examining board or by the abuse education review panel established by the Department of Public Health.

Related provisions of Iowa Code section 235B.10 require:

- The Department of Aging in cooperation with the Department of Human Services shall conduct a public information and education program. The elements and goals of the program include but are not limited to:

- Informing the public regarding the laws governing dependent adult abuse and the reporting requirements for dependent adult abuse.

- Providing caretakers with information regarding services to alleviate the emotional, psychological, physical, or financial stress associated with the caretaker and dependent adult relationship.

- Affecting public attitudes regarding the role of the dependent adult in society.

- The Department of Human Services, in cooperation with the Department of Aging and the Department of Inspections and Appeals, shall institute a program of education and training for persons, including members of provider groups and family members, who may come in contact with dependent adult abuse. The program shall include but is not limited to Instruction regarding recognition of dependent adult abuse and the procedure for the reporting of suspected abuse.

- The content of the continuing education required pursuant to Iowa Code Chapter 272C for a licensed professional providing care or service to a dependent adult shall include, but is not limited to, the responsibilities, obligations, powers, and duties of a person regarding the reporting of suspected dependent adult abuse, and training to aid the professional in identifying instances of dependent adult abuse.

- The Department of Inspections and Appeals shall provide training to investigators regarding the collection and preservation of evidence in the case of suspected dependent adult abuse.

- For the purposes of this subsection, "licensing board" means an examining board designated in Iowa Code section 147.13, the Board of Educational Examiners created in Iowa Code section 272.2, or a licensing board as defined in Iowa Code section 272C.1.

- A licensing board with authority over the license of a person required to report cases of dependent adult abuse pursuant to Iowa Code section 235B.3 shall require as a condition of licensure that the person be in compliance with the requirements for abuse training under this subsection. The licensing board shall require the person upon licensure renewal to accurately document for the licensing board the person's completion of the training requirements.

  However, the licensing board may adopt rules providing for waiver or suspension of the compliance requirements, if the waiver of suspension is in the public interest, applicable to a person who is engaged in active duty in the military service

NOTES

of this state or the United States, to a person for whom compliance with the training requirements would impose a significant hardship, or to a person who is practicing a licensed profession outside this state or is otherwise subject to circumstances that would preclude the person from encountering dependent adult abuse in this state.

- For persons required to report cases of dependent adult abuse pursuant to Iowa Code section 235B.3, who are not engaged in a licensed profession that is subject to the authority of a licensing board but are employed by a facility or program subject to licensure, registration, or approval by a state agency, the agency shall require as a condition of the renewal of the facility's or program's licensure, registration, or approval, that such persons employed by the facility or program are in compliance with the training requirements of this subsection.

- For peace officers, the elected or appointed official designated as the head of the agency employing the peace officer shall ensure compliance with the training requirements of this subsection.

- For mandatory reporters who are employees of state departments and political subdivisions of the state, the department director or the chief administrator of the political subdivision shall ensure the person's compliance with the training requirements of this subsection.

SUSPECTED DEPENDENT ADULT ABUSE REPORT

This form may be used as the written report that mandatory reporters file with the Department of Human Services following an oral report of suspected dependent adult abuse. See page 2 for instructions.

There are three criteria for a dependent adult abuse referral:
(1) A dependent adult.   (2) Abuse as defined in Iowa Code 235B.   (3) A caretaker, if applicable.

REPORT INFORMATION

Name of Dependent	Phone ( )	Birth Date	
Street	City	State	Zip Code

1. Person is a dependent adult because:

2. Type of abuse noted:

❑ Denial of care by dependent adult him/herself

❑ Physical injury   ❑ Financial exploitation   ❑ Denial of care by caretaker
❑ Sexual offense   ❑ Unreasonable punishment   ❑ Unreasonable confinement

Information about suspected abuse: (Incidents, previous abuse, person responsible for abuse, name and address of guardian, etc.)

3. Caretaker: (Omit if deprivation is by the dependent adult.)

Name	Phone ( )		
Street	City	State	Zip Code

Person is a caretaker because:

REPORTER INFORMATION

Name	Position	Relationship to Adult
Office Address		Phone ( )
Names of other mandatory reporters who have knowledge of the abuse		
Signature of Reporter		Date

INSTRUCTIONS FOR COMPLETING FORM 470–2441, SUSPECTED DEPENDENT ADULT ABUSE REPORT

⇨ The mandatory reporter who has made the initial oral report of suspected abuse to the Department of Human Services prepares this form.

⇨ Submit this form <u>within 48 hours </u>of the oral report to the Protective Service Unit that will be conducting the evaluation or assessment.

⇨ If the oral report was not accepted for evaluation or assessment, this form is not necessary.

⇨ If your agency has a report form or letter format that includes all of the information requested on this form, you may use the agency format in place of form 470–2441.

Use the space below if there is not enough space for all pertinent information on the front of this form. You can attach collateral reports or other information to the form.

REQUEST FOR DEPENDENT ADULT ABUSE REGISTRY INFORMATION

To request information about dependent adult abuse, complete this form and mail it to:
Central Abuse Registry, Iowa Department of Human Services, 1305 E Walnut, Des Moines, Iowa 50319-0114. Note: Information will be released only to people who have access to it under Iowa Code section 235B.6.

Criminal Penalties (235B.12)

1. Any person who willfully requests, or seeks to obtain dependent adult abuse information under false pretenses, or who willfully communicates or seeks to communicate dependent adult abuse information to any agency or person except in accordance with section 235B.6 and 235B.8, or any person connected with any research authorized pursuant to section 235B.6 who willfully falsifies dependent adult abuse information or any records relating thereto, is guilty of a serious misdemeanor. Any person who knowingly, but without criminal purposes, communicates or seeks to communicate dependent adult abuse information except in accordance with section 235B.6 and 235B.8 shall be guilty of a simple misdemeanor.
2. Any responsible grounds for belief that a person has violated any provision of this chapter shall be grounds for the immediate withdrawal of any authorized access such person might otherwise have to dependent adult abuse information.

Redissemination of Dependent Adult Abuse Information (235B.8)

1. A recipient of dependent adult abuse information authorized to receive the information shall not redisseminate the information, except that redissemination shall be permitted when all of the following conditions apply:
   a. The redissemination is for official purposes in connection with prescribed duties or, in the case of a health practitioner, pursuant to professional responsibilities.
   b. The person to whom such information would be redisseminated would have independent access to the same information under section 235B.6.
   c. A written record is made of the redissemination, including the name of the recipient and the date and purpose of the redissemination.
   d. The written record is forwarded to the registry within thirty days of the redissemination.

Name of person making request:	Office phone:
Office address:	
Position and basis for authorization (Code 235B.6):	

Information requested concerning (name—first, middle, last):	Social security number:	Birth date:
Maiden name or alias (if applicable): Address:		

What information is requested:	

Date	Signature		
To be completed by Registry personnel	Date:	
❑ Request approved by:		
❑ Request denied because:		
Information released:		

AUTHORIZATION FOR RELEASE OF DEPENDENT
ADULT ABUSE INFORMATION

This form must be used to authorize release of dependent adult abuse information when the person requesting the information does not have independent access to it in Iowa law. Complete a separate form for each person about whom information is requested. Send the original to the Central Abuse Registry, Iowa Department of Human Services, 1305 E Walnut Street, 5th Floor, Des Moines, IA 50319-0114 or fax to 515-242-6884.

To be completed by the person requesting information:			
Requester			
Address			
City	State	Zip Code	Phone Number

The information concerns:

Name (first, middle initial, last)			
Maiden Name or Alias (if applicable)		Birth Date	Social Security Number
Address			
City	State	Zip Code	County

What is the purpose of your request for dependent adult abuse information?

I have read and understand the legal provisions for handling dependent adult abuse information that are printed on the second page of this form

Signature	Date

To be completed by the person authorizing the Department of Human Services to release dependent adult abuse information:

Signature	Date

To be completed by the Central Abuse Registry or designee:

☐ The person named above is listed on the Dependent Adult Abuse Registry as having abused a dependent adult.

☐ The person named above is not listed on the Dependent Adult Abuse Registry as having abused a dependent adult.

☐ This request for information is denied because the form is incomplete.

Signature	Date

Comments

LEGAL PROVISIONS FOR THE HANDLING OF DEPENDENT ADULT ABUSE

Redissemination of Dependent Adult Abuse Information, Iowa Code 235B.8

A person, agency, or other recipient of dependent adult abuse information shall not redisseminate this information. However, redissemination is permitted when all of the following conditions apply:

- The redissemination is for official purposes in connection with prescribed duties or, in the case of a health practitioner, pursuant to professional responsibilities.
- The person to whom the information would be redisseminated would have independent access to the same information under Iowa Code section 235B.6.
- A written record is made of the redissemination, including the name of the recipient and the date and purpose of the redissemination.
- The written record is forwarded to the Registry within 30 days of the redissemination.

Criminal Penalties, Iowa Code 235B.12

Any person is guilty of a criminal offense when the person:

- Willfully requests, obtains, or seeks to obtain dependent adult abuse information under false pretense.
- Willfully communicates or seeks to communicate dependent adult abuse information to any agency or person except in accordance with Iowa Code sections 235B.6 through 235B.8.
- Is connected with any research authorized pursuant to Iowa Code section 235B.6 and willfully falsifies dependent adult abuse information or any records relating to dependent adult abuse.

Upon conviction for each offense, the person shall be punished by a fine of up to $1,000 or imprisonment for not more than two years, or by both fine and imprisonment.

Any person who knowingly, but without criminal purposes, communicates, or seeks to communicate dependent adult abuse information except in accordance with Iowa Code sections 235B.6 and 235B.8 shall be fined not more than $100 or be imprisoned not more than ten days for each such offense.

AUTHORIZATION FOR RELEASE OF CHILD ABUSE INFORMATION

This form must be used to authorize release of child abuse information when the person requesting that the information does not have independent access to it in Iowa law. Complete a separate form for each person about whom information is requested. Send the original to the Central Abuse Registry, Iowa Department of Human Services, 401 SW 7th Street, Suite G, Des Moines, Iowa, 50309-3574.

PART A: *To be completed by the person requesting information.*			
1.	Requester		
	Address		
	City	State	Zip Code	Phone Number ( )
2.	The information concerns:		
	Name (first, middle initial, last)		
	Maiden Name or Alias (if applicable)	Birth Date	Social Security Number
	Address		
	City	State	Zip Code	County
3.	What is the purpose of your request for dependent adult abuse information?		
4.	I have read and understand the legal provisions for handling dependent adult abuse information that are printed on the second page of this form.		
	Signature	Date	

PART B: *To be completed by the person authorizing the Department of Human Services to release dependent adult abuse information.*

I understand that my signature authorizes the requester to receive information to verify whether I am named on the child Abuse Registry in a child abuse report as having abused a child (Iowa Code 235A.15). To the best of my knowledge, all or part of the information contained in Part A of this form is correct.

Signature	Date

PART C: To be completed by the Central Abuse Registry or designee.

1. ☐ The person named above is listed on the Dependent Adult Abuse Registry as having abused a dependent adult.
2. ☐ The person named above is not listed on the Dependent Adult Abuse Registry as having abused a dependent adult.
3. ☐ This request for information is denied because the form is incomplete.

Signature	Date

Comments

LEGAL PROVISIONS FOR THE HANDLING OF CHILD ABUSE INFORMATION

Redissemination of Child Abuse Information (Iowa Code 235A.17)

A person, agency, or other recipient of child abuse information shall not redisseminate this information. However, redissemination is permitted when all of the following conditions apply:

- The redissemination is for official purposes in connection with prescribed duties or, in the case of a health practitioner, pursuant to professional responsibilities.
- The person to whom the information would be redisseminated would have independent access to the same information under Iowa Code Section 235A.15.
- A written record is made of the redissemination, including the name of the recipient and the date and purpose of the redissemination.
- The written record is forwarded to the Registry within 30 days of the redissemination.

Criminal Penalties (Iowa Code 235A.21)

- Any person is guilty of a criminal offense when the person:
  - Willfully requests, obtains, or seeks to obtain child abuse information under false pretense.
  - Willfully communicates or seeks to communicate child abuse information to any agency or person except in accordance with Iowa Code Sections 235A.15 and 235A.17.
  - Is connected with any research authorized pursuant to Iowa Code Section 235A.15 and willfully falsifies child abuse information or any records relating to child abuse.
- Upon conviction for each offense, the person shall be punished by a fine of up to $1,000 or imprisonment for not more than two years, or by both fine and imprisonment.
- Any person who knowingly, but without criminal purposes, communicates or seeks to communicate child abuse information except in accordance with Iowa Code Sections 235A.15 and 235A.17 shall be fined not more than $100 or be imprisoned not more than ten days for each such offense.
- Any reasonable grounds for belief that a person has violated any provision of Iowa Code Chapter 235A shall be grounds for the immediate withdrawal of any authorized access that the person might otherwise have to child abuse information.

THE ADVERSE CHILDHOOD EXPERIENCES (ACE) STUDY

ABOUT THE STUDY: WHAT EVERYONE SHOULD KNOW!

Over 17,000 Kaiser Permanente members voluntarily participated in a study to find out about how stressful or traumatic experiences during childhood affect adult health. After all the identifying information about the patients was removed, the Centers for Disease Control and Prevention processed the information the patients provided in their questionnaires,

HERE'S WHAT WE LEARNED:

Many people experience harsh events in their childhood. 63% of the people who participated in the study had experienced at least one category of childhood trauma. Over 20% experienced 3 or more categories of trauma which we call Adverse Childhood Experiences (ACEs).

- 11% experienced emotional abuse.
- 28% experienced physical abuse.
- 21% experienced sexual abuse.
- 15% experienced emotional neglect.
- 10% experienced physical neglect.
- 13% witnessed their mothers being treated violently.
- 27% grew up with someone in the household using alcohol and/or drugs.
- 19% grew up with a mentally-ill person in the household.
- 23% lost a parent due to separation or divorce.
- 5% grew up with a household member in jail or prison.

ACEs seem to account for one-half to two-thirds of the serious problems with drug use. They increase the likelihood that girls will have sex before reaching 15 years of age, and that boys or young men will be more likely to impregnate a teenage girl.

Adversity in childhood causes mental health disorders such as depression, hallucinations and post-traumatic stress disorders.

The more categories of trauma experienced in childhood, the greater the likelihood of experiencing:

- alcoholism and alcohol abuse
- chronic obstructive pulmonary disease (COPD)
- depression
- fetal death
- poor health-related quality of life

- illicit drug use
- ischemic heart disease (IHD)
- liver disease
- risk for intimate partner violence
- multiple sexual partners
- sexually transmitted diseases (STDs)
- smoking
- obesity
- suicide attempts
- unintended pregnancies

IF YOU EXPERIENCED CHILDHOOD TRAUMA, YOU'RE NOT ALONE.
Talk with your family health practitioner about what happened to you when you were a child. Ask for help.

For more information about the ACE Study, email carolredding@ acestudy.org, visit www.acestudy.org, or the Centers for Disease Control and Prevention at: http://www.cdc.gov/NCCDPHP/ACE/

ADVERSE CHILDHOOD EXPERIENCES (ACEs)

A NEW WAY OF UNDERSTANDING ADULT HEALTH RISKS IN IOWA

Most folks intuitively know that childhood experiences shape adult lives. But a new line of research is greatly expanding our understanding of this process—documenting how nurturing, stable environments help children develop the cognitive and emotional skills and robust sense of self they need to thrive as adults.

The research, coming this year to Iowa, also shows how negative experiences can derail those processes, leading to a host of health problems and risk behaviors in adulthood.

Adverse childhood experiences, or ACEs, are broadly defined as incidents during childhood that harm social, cognitive and emotional functioning. Frequent or prolonged exposure to such events creates toxic stress that damages the architecture of the developing brain.

The negative outcomes are serious. On the health side, they include diabetes, hypertension and heart disease, depression, morbidity and early death. On the risky-behavior side, they include smoking, over-eating, alcoholism and drug use.

Evidence shows that the more ACEs a person experiences, the more likely poor health outcomes become. Ongoing research by the Centers for Disease Control finds that, worst case, trauma in childhood could take as many as 20 years off life expectancy.

NOTES

Adverse childhood experiences don't guarantee bad outcomes for adults, but they increase the odds of struggle. And they are largely preventable.

WHAT ARE ADVERSE CHILDHOOD EXPERIENCES?

ACES are incidents that dramatically upset the safe, nurturing environments children need to thrive.

The original, seminal ACEs work, conducted from 1995 to 1997 by investigators Robert Anda and Vincent Felitti, included surveys of more than 17,000 Kaiser Permanente HMO members about their childhood exposure to nine different adverse experiences:

- Recurrent physical abuse
- Recurrent emotional abuse
- Contact sexual abuse
- An alcohol and/or drug abuser in the household
- An incarcerated household member
- Someone in the household who is chronically depressed, mentally ill, institutionalized or suicidal
- Mother is treated violently
- One or no parents
- Emotional or physical neglect

Those results, combined with the findings of physical exams and ongoing tracking of members' health experiences, strongly documented the link between adverse childhood experiences and negative health and behavioral outcomes later in life.

LEARNING ABOUT ACEs IN IOWA

Iowa advocates are just starting to explore the prevalence of ACEs, but we already know the Iowa adult population has health problems strongly associated with ACEs in national studies. In 2010, an estimated:

- 66% (1,534,756) of Iowans were overweight or obese
- 8% (173,877) had been told they were diabetic, and another 6% (122,236) prediabetic
- 8% (178,514) had cardiovascular disease
- 16% (373,256) were current smokers, and 23% (542,497) former smokers
- 5% (120,555) were heavy drinkers, and 17% (391,803) binge drinkers[1]

These health outcomes are costly. Estimates attributed $738 million in Iowa health care costs to adult obesity in 2003, with almost 50 percent of those costs paid by Medicare ($165 million) and Medicaid ($198 million).[2] Chronic cardiovascular health conditions cost Iowans an estimated $1.34 billion annually.[3] The total cost of diabetes in Iowa exceeds $1.5 billion a year.[4]

Long term, one of the most important ways to contain health costs is not by finding cheaper ways to treat such conditions, but preventing them in the first place. Preventing or mitigating the effects of ACEs is one place to start.

To document ACEs in the Iowa population, health planners this year added specific ACEs-related questions to an annual state health survey conducted by the CDC. The Behavioral Risk Factor Surveillance System is a timely and accurate source of Iowa data on health risk behaviors, preventive-health practices, and health-care access, primarily related to chronic disease and injury. Responses on ACEs will be available for analysis in fall 2013.

WHY ARE ADVERSE CHILDHOOD EXPERIENCES SO DAMAGING?
TOXIC STRESS

Extensive research on the biology of stress shows that healthy development can be derailed by excessive or prolonged activation of the body's stress response systems, with damaging effects on learning, behavior and health.

Learning to cope with stress is an important part of child development. When we are threatened, our bodies prepare us to respond by increasing our heart rate, blood pressure and stress hormones, such as cortisol. When a young child's stress response systems are activated within an environment of supportive adult relationships, these physiological effects are buffered and brought back down to baseline. The result is the development of healthy stress response systems.

Toxic stress occurs when a child experiences strong, frequent and/or prolonged adversity—physical or emotional abuse, chronic neglect, caregiver substance abuse or mental illness, exposure to violence and/or the accumulated burdens of family economic hardship—without adequate adult support.

The prolonged activation of stress response systems disrupts the development of brain architecture and other organs and increases the risk for stress-related disease and cognitive impairment. The more adverse experiences in childhood, the greater the likelihood of developmental delays and later health problems, including heart disease, diabetes, substance abuse and depression.

Source: From the Harvard Center for the Developing Child, http://developingchild.harvard.edu/topics/science_of_early_childhood/toxic_stress_response/

NOTES

THE MORE ACES, THE HIGHER THE RISK OF POOR ADULT OUTCOMES

Anda and Felitt's work on ACEs has helped build a new understanding of the cumulative effect of adverse experiences on human development. The likelihood of risky behavior or poor health outcomes increases substantially with the number of ACEs reported, as demonstrated in the chart below.

Outcome	No ACEs	1–3 ACEs	4–8 ACEs
Heart disease	1 in 14	1 in 7	1 in 6
Smoker	1 in 16	1 in 9	1 in 6
Alcoholic	1 in 69	1 in 9	1 in 6
Suicide attempt	1 in 96	1 in 10	1 in 5
IV-drug user	1 in 480	1 in 43	1 in 30

THE GOOD NEWS? WE KNOW HOW TO REDUCE DAMAGE FROM TOXIC STRESS

The most effective prevention is to reduce young children's exposure to extremely stressful conditions, such as recurrent abuse, chronic neglect, caregiver mental illness or substance abuse, violence and/or repeated conflict.

Research shows that, even under stressful conditions, supportive, responsive relationships with caring adults as early in life as possible can prevent or reverse the damaging effects of toxic stress response.

Source: From "The High Cost of Adverse Childhood Experiences," PowerPoint, Washington State Family Policy Council (2007).

There are increasingly sophisticated interventions to help families stabilize themselves. We also know there are factors that can minimize the damage from ACEs:

- Caring relationships with parents, extended family and other caring adults
- Good health and a history of adequate development
- Good peer relationships
- Hobbies and interests
- Active coping style
- Positive self-esteem
- Good social skills
- Internal focus of control
- Easy temperament
- Balance between seeking help and seeking autonomy

WHAT'S NEXT FOR IOWA?

The experience of other states tells us that Iowa-specific ACEs data will offer a powerful new way to structure state and local planning around human-service systems.

Washington State's ACEs work "invited people to rethink their mental models on how to solve child and family problems, but also social problems like child abuse, domestic violence, substance abuse," said Laura Porter, director of the Washington Family Policy Council, a cabinet-level organization of local public health and safety networks in that state.

Advocates there report programs are better positioned to support children's healthy reactions to trauma. For example, Washington's crisis nurseries--serving children who have been referred from Child Protective Services--have implemented programs to teach these young children how to calm and sooth themselves through play.

Iowa-specific ACEs information could lead to similar, concrete changes in programs and policies here. For example, advocates might use the data to:

- Increase policymakers' understanding of the prevalence of ACES in order to inform policy decisions, such as Iowa's mental-health redesign.
- Integrate trauma-informed professional development across all state departments and systems serving families.

Source: From "Adverse Childhood Experiences in Wisconsin: Findings from the 2010 Behavioral Risk Factor Survey," Children's Trust Fund, Children's Hospital and Health System and the Child Abuse Prevention Fund.

NOTES

- Infuse high-quality, evidence-based practices into family-based programming
- Improve the effectiveness of public-health awareness campaigns by refining their messages based on ACEs information.
- Promote early intervention and identification of ACEs through universal screening or assessment within family-serving systems.

This is an exciting opportunity for Iowans who care about the well-being of our citizens. How to respond to this new information on ACEs is a topic requiring broad input at the state and local levels, among the public and private sectors, and from families, policymakers, health-care providers and educators.

That kind of statewide conversation can deliver on the promise of ACEs to address adversity in the lives of Iowa children and prevent their clear and long-term impacts.

ENDNOTES:

1. Data from Behavioral Risk Factor Surveillance System (BRFSS) annual report for Iowa, 2010.
2. Finkelstein EA, Fiebelkorn IC, Wang G. State-level estimates of annual medical expenditures attributable to obesity. Obesity Research. 2004; 12 (1):18–24.
3. Milken Institute, An Unhealthy America: The Economic Impact of Chronic Disease, October 2007.
4. "Combined State Sheets." Juvenile Diabetes Research Foundation, 2010. http://advocacy.jdrf.org/files/General_Files/Advocacy/2010/ CombinedStateSheets4.05.10.pdf. The American Diabetes Association estimates that a third of these costs are indirect, such as lost work productivity, and two-thirds are the direct result of medical bills.

THE RELATIONSHIP OF ADVERSE CHILDHOOD EXPERIENCES TO ADULT MEDICAL DISEASE, PSYCHIATRIC DISORDERS, AND SEXUAL BEHAVIOR: IMPLICATIONS FOR HEALTHCARE

"In my beginning is my end"
T.S. Eliot, *Four Quartets*[1]

INTRODUCTION

Biomedical researchers increasingly recognize that childhood events, specifically abuse and emotional trauma, have profound and enduring effects on the neuroregulatory systems mediating medical illness as well as on behavior from childhood into adult life. Our understanding of the connection between emotional trauma in childhood and the pathways to pathology in adulthood is still being formed as neuroscientists begin to describe the changes that take place on the molecular level as a result of events that occurred decades earlier.

The turning point in modern understanding of the role of trauma in medical and psychiatric pathology is commonly credited to Freud, who studied patients of the French neurologist, Charcot, attributing their unusual behavior to histories of trauma rather than to underlying biomedical pathology[2]. The writings of Freud and Breuer as well as Janet represented a departure from the traditional view that mental illness and unexplained medical disease were the result of divine retribution or demonic possession, instead revealing that they were strongly associated with a history of childhood abuse[3].

The focus of this chapter will be an examination of the relationship between traumatic stress in childhood and the leading causes of morbidity, mortality, and disability in the United States: cardiovascular disease, chronic lung disease, chronic liver disease, depression and other forms of mental illness, obesity, smoking, and alcohol and drug abuse. To do this, we will draw on our experience with the Adverse Childhood Experiences (ACE) Study, a major American epidemiological study providing retrospective and prospective analysis in over 17,000 individuals of the effect of traumatic experiences during the first eighteen years of life on adolescent and adult medical and psychiatric disease, sexual behavior, healthcare costs, and life expectancy.[4]

NOTES

The ACE Study is an outgrowth of repeated counterintuitive observations made while operating a major weight loss program that uses the technique of supplemented fasting, which allows non-surgical weight reduction of approximately three hundred pounds (135 Kg) per year. Unexpectedly, our Weight Program had a high dropout rate, limited almost exclusively to patients successfully losing weight. Exploring the reasons underlying the high prevalence of patients inexplicably fleeing their own success in the Weight Program ultimately led us to recognize that weight loss is often sexually or physically threatening and that certain of the more intractable public health problems like obesity were *also* unconscious, or occasionally conscious, compensatory behaviors which were put in place as solutions to problems dating back to the earliest years, but hidden by time, by shame, by secrecy, and by social taboos against exploring certain areas of life experience. It became evident that traumatic life experiences during childhood and adolescence were far more common than generally recognized, were complexly interrelated, and were associated decades later in a strong and proportionate manner with outcomes important to medical practice, public health, and the social fabric of the nation. In the context of everyday medical practice, we came to recognize that the earliest years of infancy and childhood are not lost but, like a child's footprints in wet cement, are often life-long.

The findings from the ACE Study provide a remarkable insight into how we become what we are as individuals and as a nation. They are important medically, socially, and economically. Indeed, they have given us reason to reconsider the very structure of medical, public health, and social services practices in America.

OUTLINE OF THE ACE STUDY AND ITS SETTING

The Adverse Childhood Experiences (ACE) Study was carried out in Kaiser Permanente's Department of Preventive Medicine in San Diego, in collaboration with the US Centers for Disease Control and Prevention (CDC). This particular Department of Preventive Medicine provided an ideal setting for such collaboration because for many years we have carried out detailed biomedical, psychological, and social (biopsychosocial) evaluations of over 50,000 adult Kaiser Health Plan members a year. The CDC contributed the essential skill sets for study design and massive data management required for meaningful interpretation of clinical observations.

Kaiser Health Plan patients are middle-class Americans; all have high quality health insurance. In any 4-year period, 81% of adult Plan members in San Diego choose to come in for comprehensive medical evaluation. We asked 26,000 consecutive adults coming through the Department if they would help us understand how childhood events might affect adult health status. The majority agreed and, after certain exclusions for incomplete data and duplicate participation, the ACE

Study cohort had over 17,000 individuals. The Study was carried out in two waves, to allow midpoint correction.

The participants were 80% white including Hispanic, 10% black, and 10% Asian; 74% had attended college; their average age was 57. Almost exactly half were men, half women. This is a solidly middle-class group from the 7th largest city in the United States; it is not a group that can be dismissed as atypical, aberrant, or 'not in my practice'. Disturbingly, it is us—a point not to be overlooked when considering the problems of translating the Study's findings into action.

Eight categories of adverse childhood experiences (ACEs) were studied in the first wave; two categories of neglect were added in the second wave. We empirically selected these categories because of their discovered high prevalence in the Weight Program. Their prevalence in a general, middle-class population was also unexpectedly high. We created for each individual an ACE Score, a count of the number of *categories* of adverse childhood experience that had occurred during the first eighteen years of life. ACE Score does not tally incidents within a category. The scoring system is simple: the occurrence during childhood or adolescence of any one category of adverse experience is scored as one point. There is no further scoring for multiple incidents within a category; thus, an alcoholic and a drug user within a household score the same as one alcoholic; multiple sexual molestations by multiple individuals are totaled as one point. If anything, this would tend to understate our findings. The ACE Score therefore can range from 0 to 8 or 10, depending on the data being from Wave 1 or Wave 2. Specifics of the questions underlying each category are detailed in our original article.[4]

Only one third of this middle-class population had an ACE Score of 0. If any one category was experienced, there was 87% likelihood that at least one additional category was present. One in six individuals had an ACE Score of 4 or more, and one in nine had an ACE Score of 5 or more. Thus, every physician sees several high ACE Score patients each day. Typically, they are the most difficult patients of the day. Women were 50% more likely than men to have experienced five or more categories of adverse childhood experiences. We believe that here is a key to what in mainstream epidemiology appears as women's natural proneness to ill-defined health problems like fibromyalgia, chronic fatigue syndrome, obesity, irritable bowel syndrome, and chronic non-malignant pain syndromes. In light of our findings, we now see these as medical constructs, artifacts resulting from medical blindness to social realities and ignorance of the impact of gender.

Somewhat surprisingly, the ACE categories turned out to be approximately equal to each other in impact; an ACE Score of 4 thus consists of *any* four of the categories. The categories do not occur randomly; the number of individuals with high ACE Scores is distinctly higher than if the categories exist independently of each other.[5] The

NOTES

ten reference categories experienced during childhood or adolescence are as below, with their prevalence in parentheses:

- Abuse
1. emotional—recurrent threats, humiliation (11%)
2. physical—beating, not spanking (28%)
3. contact sexual abuse (28% women, 16% men; 22% overall)

- Household dysfunction
1. mother treated violently (13%)
2. household member was alcoholic or drug user (27%)
3. household member was imprisoned (6%)
4. household member was chronically depressed, suicidal, mentally ill, or in psychiatric hospital (17%)
5. not raised by both biological parents (23%)

- Neglect
1. physical (10%)
2. emotional (15%)

The essence of the ACE Study has been to match retrospectively, approximately a half century after the fact, an individual's current state of health and well-being against adverse events in childhood (the ACE Score), and then to follow the cohort forward to match ACE Score prospectively against doctor office visits, ER visits, hospitalization, pharmacy costs, and death. We recently have passed the fourteen-year mark in the prospective arm of the Study.

FINDINGS:

We will illustrate with a sampling from our findings in the ACE Study the long-lasting, strongly proportionate, and often profound relationship between adverse childhood experiences and important categories of emotional state, health risks, disease burden, sexual behavior, disability, and healthcare costs—decades later.

PSYCHIATRIC DISORDERS

The relationship between ACE Score and self-acknowledged chronic depression is illustrated in Fig. 1A[6]. Should one doubt the reliability of self-acknowledged chronic depression, there is a similar but stronger relationship between ACE Score and later suicide attempts as shown in the exponential progression of Fig. 1B[7]. The p value of all graphic depictions herein is .001 or lower.

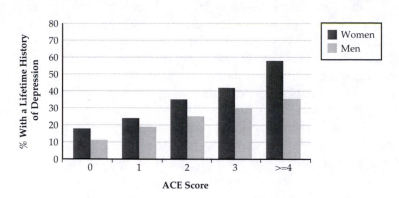

Fig. 1A

Childhood Experiences
Underlie Suicide Attempts

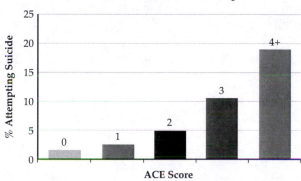

Fig. 1B

ACE Score and Rates of
Antidepressant Prescriptions
approximately 50 years later

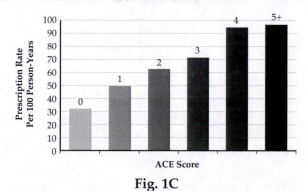

Fig. 1C

NOTES

One continues to see a proportionate relationship between ACE Score and depression by analysis of prescription rates for antidepressant medications after a ten-year prospective follow-up, now approximately fifty to sixty years after the ACEs occurred[8]. (Fig. IC). It would appear that depression, often unrecognized in medical practice, is in fact common and has deep roots, commonly going back to the developmental years of life.

An analysis of population attributable risk (that portion of a problem in the overall population whose prevalence can be attributed to specific risk factors) shows that 54% of current depression and 58% of suicide attempts in women can be attributed to adverse childhood experiences. Whatever later factors might trigger suicide, childhood experiences cannot be left out of the equation. Seeman, McEwen, et al[9] have described this general concept of background burden as allostatic load.

A similar relationship exists between ACE Score and later hallucinations, shown in Fig. 1D. Lest one reasonably suspect that, at ACE Score 7 or higher, people will likely be using street drugs or alcohol to modulate their feelings, and that *these* might be the cause of hallucinations, we have corrected for alcohol and drug use and find the same relationship exists.[10]

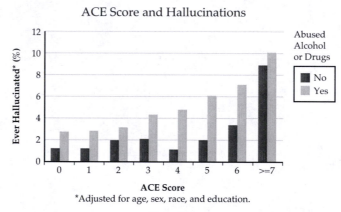

ACE Score and Hallucinations

*Adjusted for age, sex, race, and education.

Fig. 1D

Clinicians treating somatization or disorders with no clear medical etiology, as well as those dreading such patients, will find Fig. 1E of special interest. Indeed, this figure exemplifies our observation in the Weight Program that what one sees, the presenting problem, is often only the marker for the real problem, which lies buried in time, concealed by patient shame, secrecy, and sometimes amnesia—and frequent clinician discomfort. Amnesia, usually considered a theatrical device of Hollywood movies of the 1940s, is in fact alive and well, though unrecognized, in everyday medical practice. In our

Weight Program, we found 12% of the participants were partially or sometimes totally amnestic for a period of their lives, typically the few years before weight gain began. In the ACE Study, we found that there was a distinct relationship of ACE Score to impaired memory of childhood, and we understand this phenomenon to be reflective of dissociative responses to emotional trauma.[11] (Fig. 1F)

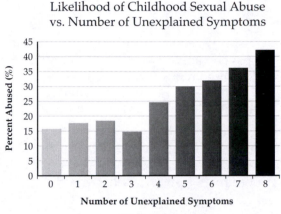

Fig. 1E

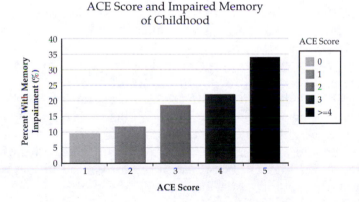

Fig. 1F

All told, it is clear that adverse childhood experiences have a profound, proportionate, and long-lasting effect on emotional state, whether measured by depression or suicide attempts, by protective unconscious devices like somatization and dissociation, or by self-help attempts that are misguidedly addressed solely as long-term health risks—perhaps because we physicians are less than comfortable acknowledging the manifest short-term benefits these "health risks" offer to the patient dealing with hidden trauma.

HEALTH RISKS

The most common contemporary health risks are smoking, alcoholism, illicit drug use, obesity, and high-level promiscuity. Though widely understood to be harmful to health, each is notably difficult to give up. Conventional logic is not particularly useful in understanding this apparent paradox. As though opposing forces are not known to exist commonly in biological systems, little consideration is given to the possibility that many long-term health risks might *also* be personally beneficial in the short term. For instance, American Indians understood the psychoactive benefits of nicotine for centuries with their peace pipe, before its risks were recognized. We repeatedly hear from patients of the benefits of these "health risks." Indeed, relevant insights are even built into our language: "Have a smoke, relax." "Sit down and have something to eat. You'll feel better." Or, need 'a fix', referring to intravenous drug use. Conversely, the common reference to "drug abuse" serves to conceal the short-term functionality of such behavior. It is perhaps noteworthy that the demonized street drug, crystal meth, is the very compound that was introduced in pure form and reliable dosage in 1940 as one of the first prescription antidepressants in the United States: methamphetamine.

In the ACE Study, we found strong, proportionate relationships between the number of categories of adverse childhood experience (ACE Score) and the use of various psychoactive materials or behaviors. The saying, "It's hard to get enough of something that *almost* works." provides insight. Three common categories of what are usually termed addictions (the unconscious compulsive use of psychoactive agents) are illustrated in this section. Self-acknowledged current smoking[12,13] (Fig. 2A), self-defined alcoholism[4,6,14] (Fig. 2B), and self-acknowledged injection drug use[15] (Fig. 2C) are strongly related in a proportionate manner to our several specific categories of adverse experiences during childhood. Additionally, we found that poor self-rated job performance correlates with ACE Score[16]. (Fig. 2C)

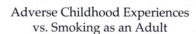

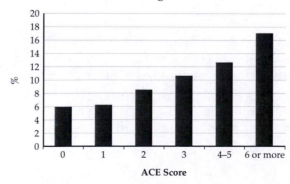

Fig. 2A

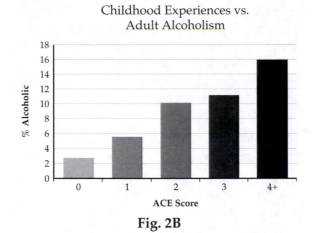

Childhood Experiences vs. Adult Alcoholism

Fig. 2B

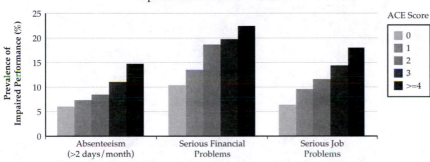

ACE Score and Indicators of Impaired Worker Performance

Fig. 2C

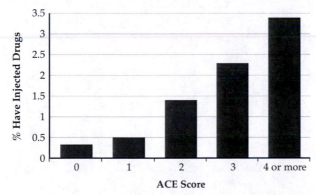

ACE Score vs. Intravenous Drug Use

Fig. 2D

The relationship of ACE Score to IV drug use is particularly striking, given that male children with ACE Score 6 or more have a 4,600% increased likelihood of later becoming an injection drug user, compared to an ACE Score 0 male child; this moves the probability from an arithmetic to an exponential progression. Relationships of

NOTES

this magnitude are rare in epidemiology. This, coupled with related information, suggests that the basic cause of addiction is predominantly experience-dependent during childhood and not substance-dependent. This challenge to the usual concept of the cause of addictions has significant implications for medical practice and for treatment programs.[17]

SEXUAL BEHAVIOR

Using teen pregnancy and promiscuity as measures of sexual behavior, we found that ACE Score has a proportionate relationship to these outcomes. (Fig. 3A, 3B.) So too does miscarriage of pregnancy, indicating the complexity of the relationship of early life psychosocial experience to what are usually considered purely biomedical outcomes.[18]

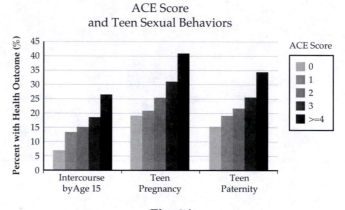

Fig. 3A

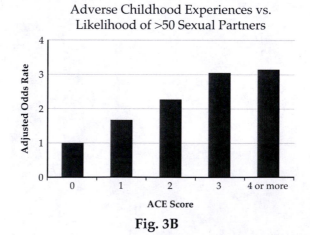

Fig. 3B

MEDICAL DISEASE

We found in the ACE Study that biomedical disease in adults has a significant relationship to adverse life experiences in childhood. The implication of this observation that life experience can transmute into organic disease over time is a profound change from an earlier era when infectious diseases like rheumatic fever or polio, or nutritional deficiency like pellagra, would come to mind as the main medical link between childhood events and adult disease. In spite of this change in our understanding of the etiology of biomedical outcomes, we find no evidence that there has been a change in the frequency of overall adverse childhood experiences in various age cohorts spanning the twentieth century.[19]

Four examples of the links between childhood experience and adult biomedical disease are the relationship of ACE Score to liver disease[20] (Fig. 4A), chronic obstructive pulmonary disease or COPD[21] (Fig. 4B), coronary artery disease or CAD[22] (Fig. 4C), and autoimmune disease.[23] The data for CAD show the effect of ACE Score after correcting for, or in the absence of, the conventional risk factors for coronary disease like hyperlipidemia, smoking, etc.

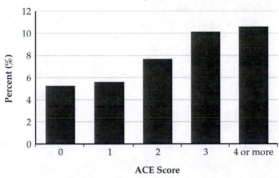

Fig. 4A

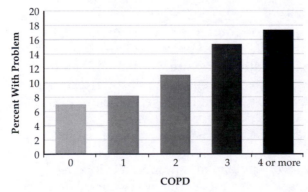

Fig. 4B

ACEs Increase Likelihood of Heart Disease

- Emotional abuse   1.7x
- Physical abuse   1.5x
- Sexual abuse   1.4x
- Domestic violence   1.4x
- Mental illness   1.4x
- Substance abuse   1.3x
- Household criminal   1.7x
- Emotional neglect   1.3x
- Physical neglect   1.4x

Fig. 4C

Certain of these relationships of childhood experience to later biomedical disease might initially be thought to be straightforward, for instance assuming that COPD or CAD are merely the obvious outcomes of cigarette smoking. In this case, one might reasonably assume that the total relationship of adverse childhood experience to later biomedical disease lies in the observation that stressful early life experience leads to a coping behavior like smoking, which becomes the mechanism of biomedical damage. While this hypothesis is true, it is incomplete; the actual situation is more complex. For instance, in our analysis published in *Circulation*,[22] we found that there was a strong relationship of ACE Score to coronary disease, *after* correcting for all the conventional risk factors like smoking, cholesterol, etc. This illustrates that adverse experiences in childhood are related to adult disease by two basic etiologic mechanisms:

- conventional risk factors that actually are attempts at self-help through the use of agents like nicotine with its documented, multiple psychoactive benefits, in addition to its now well-recognized cardiovascular risks, and
- the effects of chronic stress as mediated through the mechanisms of chronic hypercortisolemia, pro-inflammatory cytokines, and other stress responses on the developing brain and body systems, dysregulation of the stress response, and pathophysiological mechanisms yet to be discovered.

A public health paradox is implicit in these observations. One sees that certain common public health problems, while indeed that, are often also unconsciously attempted solutions to major life problems harkening back to the developmental years. The idea of the problem being the solution, while understandably disturbing to many, is certainly in keeping with the fact that opposing forces routinely co-exist in biological systems. Understanding that it is hard to give up something that almost works, particularly at the behest of well-intentioned people who have little understanding of what has gone on, provides us a new way of understanding treatment failure in addiction programs where typically the attempted solution rather than the core problem is being addressed.

HEALTHCARE COSTS

At the fourteen-year point in the prospective arm of the Study, we have only begun to analyze pharmacy data. Given the average age of our cohort, we are now looking at prescription drug use fifty to sixty years after the fact. Prescription costs are an increasingly significant portion of rapidly rising national healthcare expenditures in the United States. The relationship of ACE Score to antidepressant prescription rates has already been shown in Fig. 1C. Below, in Fig. 5A and 5B, we show the relationship of adverse childhood experiences to the decades-later use of anti-psychotic and anxiolytic medications.[8] Analyses of the relationships of ACE Score to doctor office visits, Emergency Department visits, hospitalization, and death are in progress. The economic effect of Fig. 1E will be intuitively obvious to practitioners who have observed that multi-volume patients commonly do not have a unifying diagnosis underlying all the medical attention. Rather, they have a multiplicity of symptoms: illness, but not disease.

Kirkengen has more fully discussed the nature, origins, and often-unwitting medical creation of this complex phenomenon in her book, *Inscribed Bodies*.[24] The 2000 Nobelist in Economics, James Heckman, has grasped the enormity of the economic and social consequences of the long-term effects of adverse childhood experiences and has written perceptively on the subject.[25]

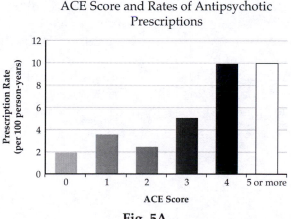

Fig. 5A

NOTES

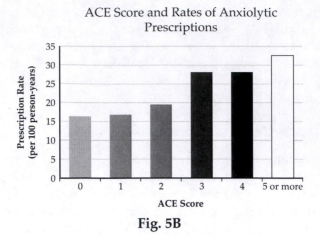

Fig. 5B

Life expectancy

Although we have not yet begun our prospective analysis of adult death rates as they may be related to adverse childhood experiences, a suggestive insight can be provided by use of the null hypothesis. Using the null hypothesis, we might propose that if there is *no* relationship of ACE Score to ultimate mortality, then we ought to be able to predict certain expected findings and consequently test for them. Thus, if there is no relationship of ACE Score to adult mortality, the age distribution of Kaiser Health Plan members choosing to come in for comprehensive medical evaluation ought to be independent of ACE Score. In Fig. 6A, we see that the age distribution for ACE Score 0 individuals is what one would expect: old people are more likely to come in for comprehensive medical evaluation than are young people, and intermediate age quantiles have the expected relative proportionality. However, at ACE Score 2, what had been the most common age quantile has become the least common, and what had been the least common has become the most common. At ACE Score 4, the initially most common age quantile has almost disappeared. We anticipate that, when our prospective analysis of death rates is completed, it will illustrate convincingly that there is an increasing death rate as the ACE Score increases. Certainly, this would be the expected continuation of our findings that ACE Score is strongly related first to health risks, then to disease, then to one outcome of disease: death.

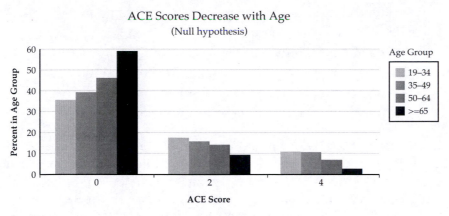

Fig. 6A

Reasonably, one might challenge this interpretation of selective attrition by hypothesizing that our patients are progressively so humiliated by exposure of their increasing ACE Scores that they are subsequently avoiding necessary medical care. Such an hypothesis is not supported by our findings. Some years ago we had on site for six months a psychoanalytically-trained psychiatrist who saw selected high ACE Score patients immediately after their comprehensive medical evaluation, rather than after referral to psychiatry. An anonymous questionnaire, returned by 81% of the patients he saw, showed that his hour-long interview was overwhelmingly interpreted by patients as highly desirable and appreciated. Talking about the worst secret of one's life with an experienced person, being understood, and coming away feeling still accepted as a human being, seems to be remarkably important and beneficial, perhaps not unlike the role of Confession in the Roman Catholic Church, a technique whose persistence over nearly two millennia suggests it has functional benefit to those involved in its use.

IMPLICATIONS FOR HEALTHCARE

We have made a limited but instructive attempt to integrate the ACE Study findings into clinical practice. At Kaiser Permanente's high-volume Department of Preventive Medicine in San Diego, we have used what we learned to expand radically the nature of our Review of Systems (ROS) and Past History questionnaire. We have now asked routinely of over 440,000 adult individuals undergoing comprehensive medical evaluation a number of questions of newly discovered relevance, the following of which are a sample:

- Have you ever been a combat soldier?
- Have you ever lived in a war zone?
- Have you been physically abused as a child?

NOTES

- Have you been sexually molested as a child or adolescent?
- Have you ever been raped?
- Who in your family has been murdered?
- Who in your family has had a nervous breakdown?
- Who in your family has been a suicide?
- Who in your family has been alcoholic or a drug user?

Such questions have been accepted by patients in the context of a well-devised medical questionnaire that is filled out at home. Examiners have learned that the most productive response to a *Yes* answer is, "I see that you have. . . . Tell me how that has affected you later in your life." While not a simple transition for staff, and one requiring an organized training effort, the transition has been effective and with measured benefits. An independent organization carried out a neural network analysis—an artificial intelligence approach to mathematical modeling and data mining—of the data from over 100,000 patient evaluations (2 years' work) using this new approach: a truly biopsychosocial approach to comprehensive medical evaluation. Surprisingly, a 35% reduction in doctor office visits (DOVs) was found in the year subsequent to evaluation, compared to the year before. Additionally, analysis showed an 11% reduction in Emergency Department (ED) visits and a 3% reduction in hospitalizations. This change was dramatically and unexpectedly different from a much smaller, 700-patient evaluation carried out 20 years earlier when we worked in the more usual biomedical mode. That earlier approach provided a net 11% reduction in DOVs compared to the antecedent year, in spite of a 14% referral rate. No evaluation was made then of ED visits or hospitalization. Finally, we found that the unexpectedly notable reductions in DOVs and ED visits totally disappeared in the second year after comprehensive evaluation, when there was a reversion to prior baseline. While the underlying biopsychosocial information was present in charts with laser-printed clarity, it was almost never integrated into subsequent medical visits. Interpreting the basis of this major reduction in doctor office visits was not within the purview of the ACE Study design, but the impression of the clinicians seeing these patients is that it represents the benefit of having, through a comprehensive medical history, the worst secrets of one's life understood by another, and still being accepted as a human being. The Swiss psychologist, Alice Miller, describes this as the role of 'the enlightened witness'.[26]

If these first year results are replicable, and we believe they should be, the implications for primary medical care are those of a paradigm shift. While offering tremendous opportunity, paradigm shifts are resisted. The philosopher, Eric Hoffer, has discussed this problem in his book, *The Ordeal of Change*.[27] Jeffrey Masson, in *Assault on Truth*[28] describes the enormous social pressures on Freud to recant his interpretation of his findings of traumatic sexual experiences in childhood as being valid. Louise De Salvo points out in *Virginia Woolf*[29] how literary commentators almost uniformly avoid discussing the themes of incest in Woolf's work in favor of erudite discussions of her style and literary techniques.

If treatment implications of what we found in the ACE Study are far-reaching, the problems of integrating this information into clinical practice are absolutely daunting. Simply put, it is easier for all of us to deal with the presenting symptom of the moment than to attempt to understand it in the full context of the patient, particularly when that full context involves thematic material of child abuse and household dysfunction that is usually protected by social taboos against exploring these areas of human experience. Though the proposed approach demonstrably would save time and money in the long run, most of us operate in the short run, and respond to valid forces that are both external and internal.

The very nature of the material in the ACE Study is such as to make most of us uncomfortable. Why would a physician or leader of any major health agency want to leave the familiarity of traditional biomedical disease and enter this area of threatening uncertainty that none of us have been trained to deal with? As physicians, we typically focus our attention on tertiary consequences, far downstream, while the primary causes are well protected by time, social convention, and taboo. We have often limited ourselves to the smallest part of the problem, that part in which we are erudite and comfortable as mere prescribers of medication or users of impressive technologies. Thus, although the ACE Study and its fifty-some publications have generated significant intellectual interest in North America and Europe during the past dozen years, its findings are only beginning to be translated into significant clinical or social action. The reasons for this are important to consider if this information is to be converted into meaningful social and medical opportunity.

Conclusion

The influence of childhood experience, including often-unrecognized traumatic events, is as powerful as Freud and his colleagues originally described it to be. These influences are long-lasting, and neuroscientists are now describing the intermediary mechanisms that develop as a result of these stressors. Unfortunately, and in spite of these findings, the biopsychosocial model and the bio-medical model of psychiatry remain at odds rather than taking advantage of the new discoveries to reinforce each other.

Many of our most intractable public health problems are the result of compensatory behaviors like smoking, overeating, and alcohol and

NOTES

drug use which provide immediate partial relief from the emotional problems caused by traumatic childhood experiences. The chronic life stress of these developmental experiences is generally unrecognized and hence unappreciated as a second etiologic mechanism. These experiences are lost in time and concealed by shame, secrecy, and social taboo against the exploration of certain topics of human experience.

The findings of the Adverse Childhood Experiences (ACE) Study provide a credible basis for a new paradigm of medical, public health, and social service practice that would start with comprehensive biopsychosocial evaluation of all patients at the outset of ongoing medical care. We have demonstrated in our practice that this approach is acceptable to patients, affordable, and beneficial in multiple ways. The potential gain is huge. So too is the likelihood of clinician and institutional resistance to this change. Actualizing the benefits of this paradigm shift will depend on first identifying and resolving the various bases for resistance to it. In reality, this will require far more planning than would be needed to introduce a purely intellectual or technical advance. However, our experience suggests that it can be done.

REFERENCES

1. Eliot, TS. *Four Quartets*. Harcourt, Brace, and World. New York, 1943.
2. Breuer, J. and Freud, S. *Studies on Hysteria*. [1893—95] in Standard Edition, vol. 2, trans. Strachey, J. Hogarth Press. London, 1955.
3. Ibid.
4. Felitti VJ, Anda RF, Nordenberg D, Williamson DF, Spitz AM, Edwards V, Koss MP, Marks IS. The relationship of adult health status to childhood abuse and household dysfunction. *American Journal of Preventive Medicine*. 1998; 14: 245–58.
5. Doug M, Anda RF, Felitti, VJ, Dube SR, Williamson DF, Thompson TJ, Loo CM. Giles WH. The interrelatedness of multiple forms of childhood abuse, neglect, and household dysfunction. *Child Abuse and Neglect*. 2004; 28: 771–784.
6. Anda RF, Whitfield CL, Felitti VJ, Chapman D, Edwards VJ, Dube SR, Williamson DF. Alcohol-impaired parents and adverse childhood experiences: the risk of depression and alcoholism during adulthood. *Psychiatric Services,* 2002; 53: 1001–1009.
7. Dube SR, Anda RF, Felitti VJ, Chapman D, Williamson DF, Giles WH. Childhood abuse, household dysfunction and the risk of attempted suicide throughout the life span: Findings from the Adverse Childhood Experiences Study. *Journal of the American Medical Association*. 2001; 286: 3089–3096.

8. Anda RF, Brown DW, Felitti VJ, Bremner JD, Dube SR, Giles WH. The Relationship of Adverse Childhood Experiences to Rates of Prescribed Psychotropic Medications in Adulthood. *American Journal of Preventive Medicine,* 2007; 32: 389–94.

9. Seeman T, McEwen B, Rowe J, Singer B. Allostatic load as a marker of cumulative biological risk. *Proceedings of the National Academy of Sciences.* 2001; 98: 4770–4775.

10. Whitfield CL, Dube SR, Felitti VJ, Anda RP. Adverse Childhood Experiences and Subsequent Hallucinations. *Child Abuse & Neglect.* 2005; 29: 797–810.

11. Anda RF, Felitti VJ, Walker J, Whitfield CL, Bremner JD, Perry BD, Dube SR, Giles WH, The Enduring Effects of Abuse and Related Adverse Experiences in Childhood: A Convergence of Evidence from Neurobiology and Epidemiology. *European Archives of Psychiatry and Clinical Neurosciences.* 2006; 256: 174–186.

12. Anda RF, Croft JB, Pelitti VJ, Nordenberg D, Giles WH, Williamson DF, Giovino GA. Adverse childhood experiences and smoking during adolescence and adulthood. *Journal of the American Medical Association.* 1999; 282: 1652–1658.

13. Edwards VJ, Anda RF, Gu D, Dube SR, Felitti VJ. Adverse childhood experiences and smoking persistence in adults with smoking-related symptoms and illness. *The Permanente Journal.* 2007; 11: 5–13.

14. Dube SR., Miller JW, Brown DW, Giles WH, Felitti VJ, Dong M, Anda RF. Adverse Childhood Experiences and the Association with Ever Using Alcohol and Initiating Alcohol Use During Adolescence. *Journal of Adolescent Health.* 2006; 38: 444. e1–10.

15. Dube SR, Anda RF, Felitti VJ, Chapman DP, Giles WH. Childhood Abuse, Neglect, and Household Dysfunction and the Risk of Illicit Drug Use: The Adverse Childhood Experiences Study. *Pediatrics.* 2003; 111: 564–572.

16. Anda RF, Fleisher VI, Felitti VJ, Edwards VJ, Whitfield CL, Dube SR, Williamson DF. Childhood Abuse, Household Dysfunction, and Indicators of Impaired Worker Performance in Adulthood. *The Permanente Journal.* 2004; 8: 30–38.

17. Felitti VJ. Ursprünge des Suchtverhaltens—Evidenzen aus einer Studie zu belastenden Kindheitserfahrungen. *Praxis der dinclerpsychologie and Kinderpsychiatrie.* 2003; 52: 547–559.

18. Hillis SD, Anda RF, Dube SR, Felitti VJ, Marchbanks PA, Marks JS. The Association Between Adolescent Pregnancy, Long-Term Psychosocial Outcomes, and Fetal Death. *Pediatrics.* 2004; 113: 320–7.

19. Dube SR., Felitti VJ, Dong M, Giles WH, Anda RF. The Impact of Adverse Childhood Experiences on Health Problems: Evidence from Four Birth Cohorts Dating Back to 1900. *Preventive Medicine.* 2003; 37: 268–77.

NOTES

NOTES

20. Dong M, Dube SR, Felitti VJ, Giles WH, Anda RF. Adverse Childhood Experiences and Self-reported Liver Disease: New Insights into a Causal Pathway. *Archives of Internal Medicine*. 2003; 163: 1949–1956.

21. Anda RF, Brown DW, Dube SR, Bremner JD, Felitti VJ, Giles WH. The Relationship of Adverse Childhood Experiences to the Prevalence, Incidence of Hospitalization, and Rates of Prescription Drug Use of Obstructive Pulmonary Disease in a Cohort of Adults. *American Journal of Preventive Medicine*. 2009 (in press)

22. Dong M, Giles WH, Felitti VJ, Dube, SR, Williams JE, Chapman DP, Anda RF. Insights into causal pathways for ischemic heart disease: Adverse Childhood Experiences Study. *Circulation*. 2004; 110: 1761–1766.

23. Dube S, Fairweather D, Pearson W, Felitti V, Anda R, Croft J. Cumulative Childhood Stress and Autoimmune Diseases in Adults. *Psychosomatic Medicine*. 2009; 71: 243–250.

24. Kirkengen, AL. *Inscribed Bodies*. Kluwer Academic Publishers. Dordrecht, 2001.

25. Heckman J, Knudsen E, Cameron J, Shonkoff J. Economic, Neurobiological, and Behavioral Perspectives on Building America's Future Workforce. *Proceedings of the National Academy of Sciences*. 2006; 103:10155–10162.

26. Miller, Alice. *The Body Never Lies*. W. W. Norton. New York, 2006.

27. Hoffer, Eric. *The Ordeal of Change*. Harper and Row. New York, 1959.

28. Masson JM. *Assault on Truth*. Farrar, Straus, and Giroux. New York, 1984.

29. De Salvo, Louise. *Virginia Woolf: The impact of childhood sexual abuse on her life and work*. Beacon Press. Boston, 1989.

CHAPTER 7

AT-RISK POPULATIONS

© 2012, LeventeGyori, Shutterstock, Inc.

Chapter Objectives

- Discuss issues confronting a variety of at-risk populations.

CASE STUDY

Tiffany reported that her father is not speaking to her because of her recent relationship with another woman, Lena. Tiffany added that her father's girlfriend "walked in" on Tiffany and Lena, leading to an angry and violent confrontation between Tiffany, Lena, and Tiffany's father. Tiffany explained that her father confronted Lena and Tiffany in their home after he had been drinking. He was physically violent to Tiffany and threatened to show Lena "what sex was supposed to be like." Tiffany reported that her father grew up in a traditional Irish Catholic family and believed that same-sex relationships were wrong.

Generalist practice theory directs social workers to develop intervention plans based on a careful assessment of the individual client within the totality of her or his life. Social workers also need to take into consideration the client's age, ethnicity, and gender when developing plans for chemically dependent clients.

When people abuse alcohol or other substances as a reaction to grief or the overwhelming trauma of disaster or war, this seems understandable to society. Less well understood are the socioeconomic stressors that also exist. Often times alcohol or drugs are used, even if temporary, to reduce pain—which could be the pain of being poor.

WOMEN AND CHILDREN

Among the most vulnerable populations in United States are addicted women and their children. Findings from the 2000 National Household Survey on Drug Use demonstrate that a small percentage of women than men use alcohol, engage in binge drinking, or use alcohol heavily, yet women and their children are at risk.

It is estimated that only a small portion of addicted women receive services. The reasons for this vary, but include the outmoded societal attitude that it is acceptable for men to drink to excess, but for women, especially mothers, to do so is immoral.

Turnbull's (1998, 2001) research suggests:

- That women who were depressed often self-medicated with alcohol, thus becoming more depressed (alcohol depresses the central nervous system).
- Suicide ideation and marital disruption were sometimes present at the point at which the women sought treatment.
- Early treatment of depression might decrease the occurrence of alcohol dependence and associated risks.

Some women need counseling, probably with a female social worker, that focuses on childhood or current experiences with violence and victimization. Family and couple therapy is helpful to many women, as is parent training, given the guilt that addicted women experience because of their failures in this area.

Rhodes and Johnson (1994) found that teaching women to accept that alcohol has taken power over their lives, which is a tenet of alcoholics anonymous and may be more useful with men—is potentially devastating to women. Instead, they encourage the use of empowerment approaches, helping the women to acquire competence and self-esteem.

Then, because addicted women are less likely to have health insurance, substance abuse intervention is needed in the places such women frequent: shelters, public health departments and possible jails.

Health care systems tend to be particularly punitive toward homeless women because they lack health insurance. If inpatient addiction care can be obtained, women's guilt may be compounded by the need to place their children in foster care. Group homes or community centers can sometimes be found that will offer nurturing post-hospital care for recovering mother and their children. Such facilities locally would include the Area Substance Abuse Council's—Heart of Iowa Program and the Amethyst House.

Another area we need to pay close attention to for women and their children is Fetal Alcohol Syndrome—FAS—which is currently being described as being on the spectrum of Fetal Alcohol. The name was given to describe the abnormalities in children that can result from consumption of alcohol during pregnancy. This actually places both the mother and the unborn child at risk.

Some the abnormalities that accompany Fetal Alcohol Syndrome might be:

- Growth deficiencies
- Mental retardation (intellectual disabilities)
- Characteristic facial features
- Cleft palate
- Small brain development
- Behavioral problems

Recognizing that some unborn children will be damaged by even a very small amount of alcohol, many physicians are recommending complete abstinence during pregnancy.

YOUTHS

Adolescents and young adults frequently use even abuse drugs and alcohol as a part of their developmental process. While this doesn't necessarily lead to adult dependency, it may be associated with unsafe sexual activity leading to sexually transmitted diseases/infections such as HIV/AIDS, and/or pregnancy, car accidents, drowning, and illegal activities.

NOTES

NATIVE AMERICANS

We have discussed that racism and poverty can be factors in substance abuse. Native American women belong to several at-risk groups and perhaps, not surprisingly, they have a higher rate of children born with Fetal Alcohol Syndrome.

HISPANIC AMERICANS

The Hispanic population in the United States according the last census is increasing more rapidly than most other population cohorts. The youth rate of illicit drug and alcohol use is lower that of many other populations, it is still a concern however to the families.

Melvin Delgado, a social worker, suggests that we need to look at culture-specific services for Hispanic families and he identifies five areas:

1. Ceremonial use/religious prohibition
2. Heritage viewed with pride or a deficit?
3. What language/dialect is being used?
4. How does the individual's network view drinking or substance use?
5. Prior assistance in any form?

AFRICAN AMERICANS

Ethnic sensitivity acquires new dimensions when the client is African American. Few black Americans, regardless of education or socioeconomic status have escaped the experience of racism, of being treated with unequal status. Sensitivity to this component permits the social worker to help the substance dependent client understand how alcoholism contributes to his or her own experiences of oppression.

LGBT

The government statistical reports cited for other groups record no data regarding alcohol and drug use by gay men or lesbian women. The absence of reliable data does not eliminate the possibility that "oppression of gay men and lesbian women and subculture support of drinking could produce higher rates of alcoholism among them.

Series: Issue Briefs
Author(s): Child Welfare Information Gateway
Year Published: 2011

[1]In this issue brief, the terms "disproportionality" and "overrepresentation" are used interchangeably to refer to the proportion of ethnic or racial groups of children in child welfare compared to those groups on the general population. "Disparity" refers to the more global condition of disproportionality or overrepresentation.

Internalized homophobia results in tremendous anxiety and self-hatred, sometimes assuaged by alcoholism." (Anderson, 1995, p.205)

ADDRESSING RACIAL DISPROPORTIONALITY IN CHILD WELFARE

PREVALENCE

A significant amount of research has documented the overrepresentation[1] of certain racial and ethnic groups, including African-Americans and Native Americans, in the child welfare system when compared with their representation in the general population (e.g., McRoy, 2005; Derezotes, Poertner, & Testa, 2005; Hill, 2005, 2006; Casey-CSSP Alliance for Racial Equity, 2006; Overrepresentation of minority youth in care, 2008). While the extent of this overrepresentation varies significantly across different regions of the country, it exists at some level in virtually every locality.

At the same time, research from the first three National Incidence Studies of Child Abuse and Neglect (NIS) found no relationship between race and the incidence of child maltreatment after controlling for poverty and other risk factors (Sedlak & Broadhurst, 1996). Instead, incidence of child abuse and neglect was associated with poverty, single parenthood, and certain other related factors. However, the most recent NIS (NIS-4) indicated that Black children experience maltreatment at higher rates than White children in several categories of maltreatment. The study's authors suggest that the findings are at least partly a consequence of the greater precision of the NIS-4 estimates and partly due to the enlarged gap between Black and White children in economic well-being, since socioeconomic status is the strongest predictor of maltreatment rates (Sedlak, McPherson, & Das, 2010).

How extensive is overrepresentation of certain groups in child welfare compared to the general population of children? Statistics from the U.S. Census Bureau's (2009) *2008 American Community Survey* and from the U.S. Department of Health and Human Services (U.S. HHS, 2009a) Adoption and Foster Care Analysis and Reporting System (AFCARS) for 2008 give some idea of the extent of the disparity, using the example of foster care. (See Table 1.)

The AFCARS figures for 1998 through 2008 show a drop in the percentage of African-American children in foster care, although a large disparity remains when compared with figures for White children. For the first year for which the percentages were provided, 1998, African-American children constituted 43 percent of those in foster care. By 2008, that percentage had dropped to 31 percent.[2]

---

[2]The most recent AFCARS numbers, for FY 2009, show that African-American children make up 30 percent of those in foster care (see www.acf.hhs.gov/programs/cb/stats_research/afcars/tar/report17.htm).

Table 1   Race/ethnicity of children in total population vs. in foster care in 2008.

Race/ethnicity	Percentage of total child population*	Percentage of children in foster care**
American Indian/Alaskan Native	1%	2%
Asian	4%	1%
African-American	14%	31%
Hispanic	22%	20%
White, non-Hispanic	56%	40%

*U.S. Census Bureau's *2008 American Community Survey*, which provides statistics on children and youth under 18 as 1-year estimates.

**U.S. Department of Health and Human Services' (2009) AFCARS data for FY 2008, which provides statistics on children and youth in the child welfare system up to age 20 (although only 5 percent are 18+ years) on September 30, 2008. The two columns of percentages show the disparity between each race's representation in the general population vs. its representation in the foster care population. Note that this does not show each group's representation in the child welfare system as a whole, just representation in out-of-home care.

While these national statistics provide some idea of the extent of the overrepresentation, they do not show the wide discrepancies in population numbers among States and even within States. For example, while Native American children constitute 2 percent of the foster care population nationally, they are overrepresented in States where there are larger Native American populations, such as Hawaii (10.5 percent), Minnesota (8.2 percent), and South Dakota (7.9 percent) (Hill, 2005). Jurisdictions need to gather and evaluate their own statistics to identify what groups are over- or underrepresented and where the disproportionality occurs (e.g., reporting, screening, placement) in order to determine the best way to address the problem.[3]

Disproportionality can also indicate the disparate outcomes, services, and treatment that children and families of color experience while interacting with the child welfare system.[4] For instance, while the average stay in foster care for White children at the end of FY 2003 was approximately 24 months, the average length of stay for African-American children at the same time was more than 40 months (Stoltzfus, 2005). Some of this disparity may be attributed to the trend for African-American children to spend more time in foster care with relatives, but that practice does not account for the enormity of the

[3]A number of jurisdictions have begun to assess and address disproportionality. For instance, read *Places to Watch: Promising Practices to Address Racial Disproportionality in Child Welfare Services* (Casey-CSSP Alliance for Racial Equity, 2006) or view *Racial Equity: Recent State Legislative Initiatives* (National Conference of State Legislatures, 2007).

[4]The phrase "of color" refers to non-White or nonmajority race or ethnicity.

gap. Another example of the disparity in services is found in the underrepresentation of Asian children in foster care. One might conclude from their low representation in the child welfare system that some Asian children and families may not be identified as needing services.

The Child and Family Services Reviews

As early as the first round of the Child and Family Services Reviews (CFSRs), numerous State Final Reports noted the problem of disproportionality in the child welfare system and reported on issues that may intensify or cause the overrepresentation of minority groups.[5] For example, at least 25 State first-round Final Reports identified gaps in culturally appropriate services, and at least 24 State Final Reports indicated that language differences are a barrier to services, case planning, investigations, or training. Only 38 percent of States received a positive rating on the CFSR indicator regarding whether a State's recruitment efforts for foster and adoptive parents reflect the racial and ethnic diversity of children in need of out-of-home care (U.S. HHS, n.d.).

In the second round of CFSRs, only 14 of 41 States received a positive rating on the item regarding State efforts to recruit and retain resource parents who reflect the racial and ethnic diversity of the foster care population in that State.[6] For the States that received a rating of "Strength" for this CFSR item, a number of strategies were cited that accounted for the States' success in recruiting a diverse foster and adoptive parent population. Some of these promising practices included a pilot program targeting prospective parents of Native American descent (North Dakota), a program that used children's zip codes as one factor in matching them with resource families (Idaho), and the compilation and analysis of demographic data on families who had adopted and families underrepresented in the pool of prospective parents (Ohio).

[5]The CFSRs are designed to enable the Children's Bureau of the U.S. Department of Health and Human Services to ensure that State child welfare agency practice is in conformity with Federal child welfare requirements, to determine what is actually happening to children and families as they are engaged in State child welfare services, and to assist States in enhancing their capacity to help children and families achieve positive outcomes. For more information about the CFSR process, visit the Children's Bureau website.

[6]At the time of this report, Round 2 Final Reports were available for only 41 States. Ratings on Item 44 (The State has in place a process for ensuring the diligent recruitment of potential foster and adoptive families that reflect the ethnic and racial diversity of children in the State for whom foster and adoptive homes are needed) were found by perusing each of those reports, which could be located through a search function on the Children's Bureau website.

SOCIAL READJUSTMENT RATING SCALE (SRRS)

Thomas H. Holmes & Richard H. Rahe (developers)

The following instrument is based on the premise that good and bad events in one's life can increase stress levels and make one more susceptible to illness and mental health problems.

ASSESSMENT

1.	Death of a spouse	100	22. Change in responsibilities at work	29
2.	Divorce	73	23. Son or daughter leaving home	29
3.	Marital separation	65	24. Trouble with in-laws	29
4.	Jail term	63	25. Outstanding personal achievements	28
5.	Death of a close family member	63	26. Wife begins or stops work	26
6.	Personal injury or illness	53	27. Begin or end school	26
7.	Marriage	50	28. Change in living conditions	25
8.	Fired at work	47	29. Revision of personal habits	24
9.	Marital reconciliation	45	30. Trouble with boss	23
10.	Retirement	45	31. Change in work hours or conditions	20
11.	Change in health of family member	44	32. Change in residence	20
12.	Pregnancy	40	33. Change in school	20
13.	Sex difficulties	39	34. Change in recreation	19
14.	Gain of a new family member	39	35. Change in religious activities	19
15.	Business readjustment	39	36. Change in social activities	18
16.	Change in financial state	38	37. Loan less than $50,000	17
17.	Death of a close friend	37	38. Change in sleeping habits	16
18.	Change to different line of work	36	39. Change in no. of family get togethers	15
19.	Change in no. of arguments with spouse	35	40. Change in eating habits	15
20.	Mortgage over $50,000	35	41. Vacation	13
			42. Holidays	12
21.	Foreclosure of mortgage	30	43. Minor violations of laws	11

SCORING

Each event should be considered if it has taken place in the last 12 months. Add values to the right of each item to obtain the total score.

Your susceptibility to illness and mental health problems:

Low	≤ 149
Mild	= 150–200
Moderate	= 200–299
Major	≥ 300

FOR MORE INFORMATION

Here are some helpful resources:

American Association for Geriatric Psychiatry
7910 Woodmont Avenue, Suite 1050
Bethesda, MD 20814-3004
1-301-654-7850
www.aagpgpa.org

American Psychological Association
750 First Street, NE
Washington, DC 20002-4242
1-800-374-2721 (toll-free)
1-202-336-6123 (TDD/TTY)
www.apa.org

Depression and Bipolar Support Alliance
730 North Franklin Street, Suite 501
Chicago, IL 60654-7225
1-800-826-3632 (toll-free)
www.dbsalliance.org

National Alliance on Mental Illness
3803 North Fairfax Drive, Suite 100
Arlington, VA 22203
1-800-950-6264 (toll-free)
1-703-524-7600
www.nami.org

National Institute of Mental Health
6001 Executive Boulevard
Room 8184, MSC 9663
Bethesda, MD 20892-9663
1-866-615-6464 (toll-free)
1-866-415-8051 (TTY/toll-free)
www.nimh.nih.gov

National Library of Medicine MedlinePlus
www.medlineplus.gov

Mental Health America
2000 North Beauregard Street
6th Floor
Alexandria, VA 22311
1-800-969-6642 (toll-free)
1-800-433-5959 (TTY/toll-free)
www.nmha.org

National Suicide Prevention Lifeline
1-800-273-8255 (toll-free/24 hours a day)
1-800-799-4889 (TTY/toll-free)

For more information on health and aging, contact:

National Institute on Aging Information Center
P.O. Box 8057
Gaithersburg, MD 20898-8057
1-800-222-2225 (toll-free)
1-800-222-4225 (TTY/toll-free)
www.nia.nih.gov
www.nia.nih.gov/Espanol

NOTES

ALZHEIMER'S DISEASE

Alzheimer's disease is an irreversible, progressive brain disease that slowly destroys memory and thinking skills, and eventually even the ability to carry out the simplest tasks. In most people with Alzheimer's, symptoms first appear after age 60.

Alzheimer's disease is the most common cause of dementia among older people. Dementia is the loss of cognitive functioning—thinking, remembering, and reasoning—to such an extent that it interferes with a person's daily life and activities. Estimates vary, but experts suggest that as many as 5.1 million Americans may have Alzheimer's.

Alzheimer's disease is named after Dr. Alois Alzheimer. In 1906, Dr. Alzheimer noticed changes in the brain tissue of a woman who had died of an unusual mental illness. Her symptoms included memory loss, language problems, and unpredictable behavior. After she died, he examined her brain and found many abnormal clumps (now called amyloid plaques) and tangled bundles of fibers (now called neurofibrillary tangles). Plaques and tangles in the brain are two of the main features of Alzheimer's disease. The third is the loss of connections between nerve cells (neurons) in the brain.

Alzheimer's Disease Education & Referral (ADEAR) Center
A Service of the National Institute on Aging
National Institutes of Health
U.S. Department of Health and Human Services

CHANGES IN THE BRAIN IN ALZHEIMER'S DISEASE

Although we still don't know what starts the Alzheimer's disease process, we do know that damage to the brain begins as many as 10 to 20 years before any problems are evident. Tangles begin to develop deep in the brain, in an area called the entorhinal cortex, and plaques form in other areas. As more and more plaques and tangles form in particular brain areas, healthy neurons begin to work less efficiently. Then, they lose their ability to function and communicate with each other, and eventually they die. This damaging process spreads to a nearby structure, called the hippocampus, which is essential in forming memories. As the death of neurons increases, affected brain regions begin to shrink. By the final stage of Alzheimer's, damage is widespread and brain tissue has shrunk significantly.

VERY EARLY SIGNS AND SYMPTOMS Memory problems are one of the first signs of Alzheimer's disease. Some people with memory problems have a condition called amnestic mild cognitive impairment (MCI). People with this condition have more memory problems than normal for people their age, but their symptoms are not as severe as those with Alzheimer's. More people with MCI, compared with those without MCI, go on to develop Alzheimer's.

Other changes may also signal the very early stages of Alzheimer's disease. For example, brain imaging and biomarker studies of people with MCI and those with a family history of Alzheimer's are beginning to detect early changes in the brain like those seen in Alzheimer's. These findings will need to be confirmed by other studies but appear promising. Other recent research has found links between some movement difficulties and MCI. Researchers also have seen links between some problems with the sense of smell and cognitive problems. Such findings offer hope that some day we may have tools that could help detect Alzheimer's early, track the course of the disease, and monitor response to treatments.

MILD ALZHEIMER'S DISEASE As Alzheimer's disease progresses, memory loss continues and changes in other cognitive abilities appear. Problems can include getting lost, trouble handling money and paying bills, repeating questions, taking longer to complete normal daily tasks, poor judgment, and small mood and personality changes. People often are diagnosed in this stage.

MODERATE ALZHEIMER'S DISEASE In this stage, damage occurs in areas of the brain that control language, reasoning, sensory processing, and conscious thought. Memory loss and confusion increase, and people begin to have problems recognizing family and friends. They may be unable to learn new things, carry out tasks that involve multiple steps

NOTES

(such as getting dressed), or cope with new situations. They may have hallucinations, delusions, and paranoia, and may behave impulsively.

SEVERE ALZHEIMER'S DISEASE By the final stage, plaques and tangles have spread throughout the brain and brain tissue has shrunk significantly. People with severe Alzheimer's cannot communicate and are completely dependent on others for their care. Near the end, the person may be in bed most or all of the time as the body shuts down.

WHAT CAUSES ALZHEIMER'S

Scientists don't yet fully understand what causes Alzheimer's disease, but it is clear that it develops because of a complex series of events that take place in the brain over a long period of time. It is likely that the causes include genetic, environmental, and lifestyle factors. Because people differ in their genetic make-up and lifestyle, the importance of these factors for preventing or delaying Alzheimer's differs from person to person.

THE BASICS OF ALZHEIMER'S Scientists are conducting studies to learn more about plaques, tangles, and other features of Alzheimer's disease. They can now visualize plaques by imaging the brains of living individuals. They are also exploring the very earliest steps in the disease process. Findings from these studies will help them understand the causes of Alzheimer's.

One of the great mysteries of Alzheimer's disease is why it largely strikes older adults. Research on how the brain changes normally with age is shedding light on this question. For example, scientists are learning how age-related changes in the brain may harm neurons and contribute to Alzheimer's damage. These age-related changes include atrophy (shrinking) of certain parts of the brain, inflammation, and the production of unstable molecules called free radicals.

GENETICS In a very few families, people develop Alzheimer's disease in their 30s, 40s, and 50s. Many of these people have a mutation, or permanent change, in one of three genes that they inherited from a parent. We know that these gene mutations cause Alzheimer's in these "early-onset" familial cases. Not all early-onset cases are caused by such mutations.

Most people with Alzheimer's disease have "late-onset" Alzheimer's, which usually develops after age 60. Many studies have linked a gene called APOE to late-onset Alzheimer's. This gene has several forms. One of them, APOE ε4, increases a person's risk of getting the disease. About 40 percent of all people who develop late-onset Alzheimer's carry this gene. However, carrying the APOE ε4 form of the gene does not necessarily mean that a person will develop Alzheimer's disease, and people carrying no APOE ε4 forms can also develop the disease.

Most experts believe that additional genes may influence the development of late-onset Alzheimer's in some way. Scientists around the world are searching for these genes. Researchers have identified variants of the SORL1, CLU, PICALM, and CR1 genes that may play a role in risk of late-onset Alzheimer's. For more about this area of research, see the **Alzheimer's Disease Genetics Fact Sheet,** available at *www.nia.nih.gov/Alzheimers/Publications/geneticsfs.htm.*

LIFESTYLE FACTORS A nutritious diet, physical activity, social engagement, and mentally stimulating pursuits can all help people stay healthy. New research suggests the possibility that these factors also might help to reduce the risk of cognitive decline and Alzheimer's disease. Scientists are investigating associations between cognitive decline and vascular and metabolic conditions such as heart disease, stroke, high blood pressure, diabetes, and obesity. Understanding these relationships and testing them in clinical trials will help us understand whether reducing risk factors for these diseases may help with Alzheimer's as well.

HOW ALZHEIMER'S DISEASE IS DIAGNOSED

Alzheimer's disease can be definitively diagnosed only after death by linking clinical course with an examination of brain tissue and pathology in an autopsy. But doctors now have several methods and tools to help them determine fairly accurately whether a person who is having memory problems has "possible Alzheimer's disease" (dementia may be due to another cause) or "probable Alzheimer's disease" (no other cause for dementia can be found). To diagnose Alzheimer's, doctors:

- ask questions about the person's overall health, past medical problems, ability to carry out daily activities, and changes in behavior and personality
- conduct tests of memory, problem solving, attention, counting, and language
- carry out medical tests, such as tests of blood, urine, or spinal fluid
- perform brain scans, such as computerized tomography (CT) or magnetic resonance imaging (MRI)

These tests may be repeated to give doctors information about how the person's memory is changing over time.

Early diagnosis is beneficial for several reasons. Having an early diagnosis and starting treatment in the early stages of the disease can help preserve function for months to years, even though the underlying disease process cannot be changed. Having an early diagnosis also helps families plan for the future, make living arrangements, take care of financial and legal matters, and develop support networks.

In addition, an early diagnosis can provide greater opportunities for people to get involved in clinical trials. In a clinical trial, scientists test drugs or treatments to see which are most effective and for whom they work best. (See the box, at right, for more information.)

HOW ALZHEIMER'S IS TREATED

Alzheimer's disease is a complex disease, and no single "magic bullet" is likely to prevent or cure it. That's why current treatments focus on several different aspects, including helping people maintain mental function; managing behavioral symptoms; and slowing, delaying, or preventing the disease.

HELPING PEOPLE WITH ALZHEIMER'S MAINTAIN MENTAL FUNCTION Four medications are approved by the U.S. Food and Drug Administration to treat Alzheimer's. Donepezil (Aricept®), rivastigmine (Exelon®), and galantamine (Razadyne®) are used to treat mild to moderate Alzheimer's (donepezil can be used for severe Alzheimer's as well). Memantine (Namenda®) is used to treat moderate to severe Alzheimer's. These drugs work by regulating neurotransmitters (the chemicals that transmit messages between neurons). They may help maintain thinking, memory, and speaking skills, and help with certain behavioral problems. However, these drugs don't change the underlying disease process and may help only for a few months to a few years.

MANAGING BEHAVIORAL SYMPTOMS Common behavioral symptoms of Alzheimer's include sleeplessness, agitation, wandering, anxiety, anger, and depression. Scientists are learning why these symptoms occur and are studying new treatments—drug and non-drug—to manage them. Treating behavioral symptoms often makes people with Alzheimer's more comfortable and makes their care easier for caregivers.

SLOWING, DELAYING, OR PREVENTING ALZHEIMER'S DISEASE Alzheimer's disease research has developed to a point where scientists can look beyond treating symptoms to think about addressing the underlying disease process. In ongoing clinical trials, scientists are looking at many possible interventions, such as cardiovascular and diabetes treatments, antioxidants, immunization therapy, cognitive training, and physical activity.

SUPPORTING FAMILIES AND CAREGIVERS

Caring for a person with Alzheimer's disease can have high physical, emotional, and financial costs. The demands of day-to-day care, changing family roles, and difficult decisions about placement in a care facility can be hard to handle. Researchers are learning a lot about Alzheimer's caregiving, and studies are helping experts develop new ways to support caregivers.

Becoming well-informed about the disease is one important long-term strategy. Programs that teach families about the various stages of Alzheimer's and about flexible and practical strategies for dealing with difficult caregiving situations provide vital help to those who care for people with Alzheimer's.

Developing good coping skills and a strong support network of family and friends also are important ways that caregivers can help themselves handle the stresses of caring for a loved one with Alzheimer's disease. For example, staying physically active provides physical and emotional benefits.

Some Alzheimer's caregivers have found that participating in a support group is a critical lifeline. These support groups allow caregivers to find respite, express concerns, share experiences, get tips, and receive emotional comfort. The Alzheimer's Association, Alzheimer's Disease Centers, and many other organizations sponsor in-person and online support groups across the country. There are a growing number of groups for people in the early stage of Alzheimer's and their families. Support networks can be especially valuable when caregivers face the difficult decision of whether and when to place a loved one in a nursing home or assisted living facility. For more information about at-home caregiving, see **Caring for a Person with Alzheimer's Disease: Your Easy-to-Use Guide from the National Institute on Aging** at *www.nia.nih.gov/Alzheimers/Publications/CaringAD*.

NOTES

ADVANCING OUR UNDERSTANDING

Thirty years ago, we knew very little about Alzheimer's disease. Since then, scientists have made many important advances. Research supported by NIA and other organizations has expanded knowledge of brain function in healthy older people, identified ways we might lessen normal age-related declines in mental function, and deepened our understanding of the disease. Many scientists and physicians are now working together to untangle the genetic, biological, and environmental factors that, over many years, ultimately result in Alzheimer's. This effort is bringing us closer to the day when we will be able to manage successfully or even prevent this devastating disease.

FOR MORE INFORMATION

To learn about support groups, services, research centers, research studies, and publications about Alzheimer's disease, contact the following resources:

Alzheimer's Disease Education and Referral (ADEAR) Center
P.O. Box 8250
Silver Spring, MD 20907-8250
1-800-438-4380 (toll-free)
www.nia.nih.gov/Alzheimers

The National Institute on Aging's ADEAR Center offers information and publications for families, caregivers, and professionals on diagnosis, treatment, patient care, caregiver needs, long-term care, education and training, and research related to Alzheimer's disease. Staff members answer telephone, email, and written requests and make referrals to local and national resources. The ADEAR website provides free, online publications in English and Spanish; email alert and online *Connections* newsletter subscriptions; an Alzheimer's

disease clinical trials database; the Alzheimer's Disease Library database; and more.

Alzheimer's Association
225 N. Michigan Avenue, Floor 17
Chicago, IL 60601-7633
1-800-272-3900 (toll-free)
1-866-403-3073 (TDD/toll-free)
www.alz.org

Alzheimer's Foundation of America
322 Eighth Avenue, 7th Floor
New York, NY 10001
1-866-AFA-8484 (1-866-232-8484; toll-free)
www.alzfdn.org

Eldercare Locator
1-800-677-1116 (toll-free)
www.eldercare.gov

Family Caregiver Alliance
180 Montgomery Street, Suite 1100
San Francisco, CA 94104
1-800-445-8106 (toll-free)
www.caregiver.org

NIHSeniorHealth
www.nihseniorhealth.gov/ alzheimersdisease/toc.html

MAJOR DEPRESSIVE EPISODE AND TREATMENT FOR DEPRESSION AMONG VETERANS AGED 21 TO 39

IN BRIEF

- An estimated 9.3 percent of veterans aged 21 to 39 (312,000 persons) experienced at least one major depressive episode (MDE) in the past year
- Among veterans aged 21 to 39 with past year MDE, over half (51.7 percent) reported severe impairment in at least one of four role domains (i.e., home management, work, close relationships with others, and social life), and nearly one quarter (23.5 percent) reported very severe impairment in at least one of the domains
- More than half (59.6 percent) of veterans aged 21 to 39 who experienced past year MDE received treatment for depression in the past year

Recent research indicates that an estimated 25 to 30 percent of the veterans of the wars in Iraq and Afghanistan have reported symptoms of a mental disorder or cognitive condition.[7,8] Untreated mental

© 2012, David Lee, Shutterstock, Inc.

[7] Seal, K. H., Bertenthal, D., Miner, C. R., Sen, S., & Marmar, C. (2007). Bringing the war back home: Mental health disorders among 103,788 US veterans returning from Iraq and Afghanistan seen at Department of Veterans Affairs facilities. *Archives of Internal Medicine, 167*, 476–482.

[8] Tanielian, T., & Jaycox, L. H. (Eds.). (2008). *Invisible wounds of war: Psychological and cognitive injuries, their consequences, and services to assist recovery* (MG-720-CCF). Santa Monica, CA: Rand Corporation. [Available at *http://www.rand.org/multi/military/veterans/*]

http://www.oas.samhsa.gov/2k8/veteransDepressed/veteransDepressed.htm

health problems can result in long-term negative consequences for the affected individuals, their families, their communities, and our Nation as a whole.

The National Survey on Drug Use and Health (NSDUH) includes questions about military veteran status, major depressive episode (MDE),[9] and treatment for depression. This issue of *The NSDUH Report* examines data from veterans aged 21 to 39, an age group that includes veterans with relatively recent service. The report provides data on

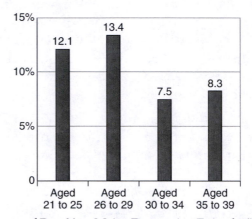

Figure 1: Percentages of Past Year Major Depressive Episode (MDE) among Veterans Aged 21 to 39, by Age Group: 2004 to 2007

Age Group	Percent
Aged 21 to 25	12.1%
Aged 26 to 29	13.4%
Aged 30 to 34	7.5%
Aged 35 to 39	8.3%

Figure 2: Percentages of past year major depressive episode (mde) among veterans aged 21 to 39, by age group: 2004 to 2007

Source: SAMHSA, 2004–2007 NSDUHs.

[9] The National Survey on Drug Use and Health (NSDUH) defines lifetime and past year major depressive episode (MDE) using the diagnostic criteria in the 4th edition of the *Diagnostic and Statistical Manual of Mental Disorders* (DSM-IV), which specifies a period of 2 weeks or longer during which there is either depressed mood or loss of interest or pleasure and at least four other symptoms that reflect a change in functioning, such as problems with sleep, eating, energy, concentration, and self-image. In assessing MDE, no exclusions were made for MDE caused by medical illness, bereavement, or substance use disorders.

the prevalence of past year MDE, levels of impairment resulting from MDE as measured by the Sheehan Disability Scale (SDS),[10] average number of days of the inability to carry out normal activities due to MDE, and past year treatment for MDE. It should be noted that the NSDUH does not collect data to determine whether or not veterans served in combat or in which conflicts they served. All findings presented in this report are based on combined 2004 to 2007 NSDUH data.

NOTES

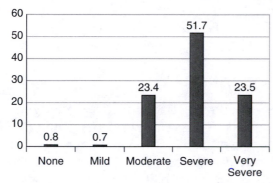

Figure 3: Overall Severity of Role Impairment* among Veterans Aged 21 to 39 Who Experienced Past Year Major Depressive Episode (MDE)**: 2004 to 2007

* See End Note 4.
** Due to rounding, percentages do not total 100 percent.

Severity	Percent
None	0.8%
Mild	0.7%
Moderate	23.4%
Severe	51.7%
Very Severe	23.5%

Figure 4: Overall Severity of Role Impairment* Among Veterans Aged 21 to 39 Who Experienced Past Year Major Depressive Episode (MDE)**: 2004 to 2007

Source: SAMHSA, 2004–2007 NSDUHs.

[10] The Sheehan Disability Scale (SDS) measures the impact of MDE on a person's life. The SDS asks adults aged 18 or older to give a rating of 0 to 10 (with 10 being the highest) for the level of impairment caused by the disorder in each of four role domains: (1) home management, (2) work, (3) close relationships with others, and (4) social life. Respondents with unknown severity of SDS role impairment data or for whom particular activities were not applicable were excluded.

NOTES

WHAT PERCENTAGE OF VETERANS AGED 21 TO 39 EXPERIENCED PAST YEAR MDE?

An annual average of 9.3 percent of veterans in this age group (an estimated 312,000 persons) experienced at least one MDE in the past year. The rate of past year MDE was higher among veterans aged 21 to 25 and those aged 26 to 29 (12.1 and 13.4 percent, respectively) than among veterans aged 30 to 34 and those aged 35 to 39 (7.5 and 8.3 percent, respectively) (Figure 1).

Female veterans were twice as likely as their male counterparts to have experienced past year MDE (16.6 vs. 8.0 percent). Rates for past year MDE were similar among black, white, and Hispanic veterans aged 21 to 39 (9.6, 9.2, and 8.5 percent, respectively).

HOW DID PAST YEAR MDE AFFECT VETERANS?

Almost all (99.2 percent) veterans aged 21 to 39 with past year MDE reported having experienced some level of resulting impairment in one or more of the role domains of home management, work, close relationships with others, and social life (Figure 2). Over half (51.7 percent) reported severe impairment in at least one of these role domains, and nearly one quarter (23.5 percent) reported very severe impairment in at least one of the domains.

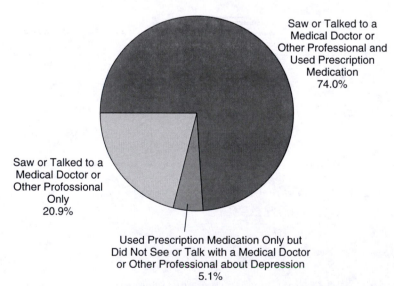

Figure 5: Percentages of Type of Treatment Received for Depression in the Past Year among Veterans Aged 21 to 39 Who Experienced Past Year MDE and Who Received Treatment for Depression in the Past Year: 2004 to 2007

Treatment received	Percent
Used Prescription Medication Only but Did Not See or Talk with a Medical Doctor or Other Professional about Depression	5.1%
Saw or Talked to a Medical Doctor or Other Professional Only	20.9%
Saw or Talked to a Medical Doctor or Other Professional and Used Prescription Medication	74.0%

Figure 6: Percentages of Type of Treatment Received for Depression in the Past Year among Veterans Aged 21 to 39 Who Experienced Past Year MDE and Who Received Treatment for Depression in the Past Year: 2004 to 2007

Source: SAMHSA, 2004–2007 NSDUHs.

Severe or very severe impairment in role functioning was reported by 55.4 percent of these veterans for home management, 41.3 percent for ability to work, 50.4 percent for close relationships with others, and 57.7 percent for social life.

Overall, those veterans with past year MDE who reported any impairment in any domain of role functioning were unable to carry out normal activities on an average of 57.4 days in the past year; those who reported a very severe impairment were unable to carry out normal activities on an average of 120.0 days in the past year.

HOW MANY WERE TREATED FOR DEPRESSION AND WHAT TYPE OF TREATMENT DID THEY RECEIVE?

More than half (59.6 percent) of veterans aged 21 to 39 who experienced past year MDE received treatment for depression in the past year. Among those who received treatment for depression, 74.0 percent saw or talked to a medical doctor or other health professional about depression and used prescription medication for depression, 20.9 percent saw or talked to a medical doctor or other health professional about depression but did not use a prescription medication for depression, and 5.1 percent used prescription medication for depression but did not see or talk with a medical doctor or other professional about depression in the past year (Figure 3).[11]

[11] Information to fully determine how these individuals could have taken prescription medication without seeing a doctor or health professional was not collected. It is possible that this group includes persons who last saw or spoke to a doctor or other professional about depression more than a year ago yet took prescription medication for MDE during the past year.

NOTES

DISCUSSION

With the recent combat deployments in Iraq and Afghanistan, treating the mental health care needs of veterans will be a continuing challenge for the mental health care system for years to come. Identifying and understanding the mental health service needs of service men and women, including the need for appropriate medical and therapeutic services, are a critical part of facilitating veterans' successful re-entry into civilian life and to reducing the long-term negative consequences of depression and other mental and emotional problems for veterans, their families, and their communities.

SUGGESTED CITATION

Substance Abuse and Mental Health Services Administration, Office of Applied Studies. (November 6, 2008). *The NSDUH Report—Major Depressive Episode and Treatment for Depression among Veterans Aged 21 to 39.* Rockville, MD.

SAMHSA NEWS RELEASE

FEMALE VETERANS AGED 20–39 LESS LIKELY TO USE MOST HARMFUL SUBSTANCES THAN MALE COUNTERPARTS

According to a new spotlight by the Substance Abuse and Mental Health Services Administration (SAMHSA), female veterans aged 20–39 are far less likely to engage in binge drinking or the use of substances such as cigarettes and illicit drugs than male veterans of the same age group.

The differences were most pronounced in terms of binge drinking—drinking five or more drinks on the same occasion. While 22.9 percent of female veterans reported binge drinking in the past month, 43.2 percent of male veterans in this age group had engaged in it within the same period.

There was also a significant difference in the levels of substance abuse between female and male veterans age 20–39 regarding illicit drug use. While 13.1 percent of male veterans used illicit drugs in the past month only 9.6 percent of female veterans used drugs.

Similarly there was a significant difference in cigarette use levels. Past month cigarette use for males was 40.9 percent, while it was 33.4 percent for female veterans.

However, male and female levels of past month non medical use of prescription drugs such as pain relievers, tranquilizers, stimulants,

http://www.samhsa.gov/newsroom/advisories/1011101504.aspx

or sedatives was not much different—about 4 percent for male veterans and approximately 3.5 percent for female veterans

"The nation's service women and men have sacrificed much for their country and the nation must do everything it can to provide comprehensive health care to meet their behavioral health needs and those of their families," said SAMHSA Administrator Pamela S. Hyde, J.D. "Although this survey finds some striking differences in the levels of substance use among female and male veterans, it is important to remember that many female veterans may have other critical behavioral health care needs due to the unique conditions they may have experienced during their service. Thus it is essential that comprehensive behavioral health care services are provided to meet the challenges facing all veterans."

Female veterans aged 20–39 less likely to use most substances than male counterparts, was developed as part of the agency's strategic initiative on data, outcomes, and quality—an effort to inform policy makers and service providers on the nature and scope of behavioral health issues. It is drawn from SAMHSA's 2009 National Survey on Drug Use and Health (NSDUH). The survey collects data by administering questionnaires to a representative sample of the population through face-to-face interviews at their places of residence.

HOMELESSNESS AMONG VETERANS

While the number of Veterans experiencing homelessness has been declining over the past two years, 107,000 former service men and women were homeless on a given night in 2009 as estimated by the VA. Sixty-one percent of homeless Veterans are between ages 35 and 54. Though 96 percent of homeless Veterans are male, the number of female Iraq and Afghanistan Veterans experiencing homelessness is increasing as is the number of homeless Veterans who have dependent children.

In general, Veterans have high rates of Post-Traumatic Stress Disorder, traumatic brain injury, and sexual trauma, which can lead to higher risk for homelessness. About half of homeless Veterans have serious mental illness and 70 percent have substance abuse problems. Half of homeless Veterans have histories of involvement with the legal system. Veterans are more likely to live outdoors—unsheltered—and experience long-term, chronic homelessness.

OPENING DOORS: HOMELESSNESS AMONG YOUTH

While the exact number of youth experiencing homelessness is difficult to determine given varying definitions of homelessness and the age range considered as youth, the most recent information from the Dept. of Education reports 52,950 unaccompanied homeless youth were supported through school-based programs in 2008–09. According to HUD data, 22,631 young people who live on their own used emergency or transitional housing services in 2009. It is widely agreed this is a serious undercount as unaccompanied youth are often unconnected to services or shelters.

Youth often leave home as a result of a severe family conflict which might include physical and/or sexual abuse. One quarter of former foster youth experience homelessness within four years of exiting foster care. Too often, youth are separated from other family members when shelter policies force older adolescent males to be housed in adult shelters.

http://www.usich.gov/usich_resources/fact_sheets/opening_doors_homelessness_among_veterans/
http://www.usich.gov/usich_resources/fact_sheets/opening_doors_homelessness_among_youth/

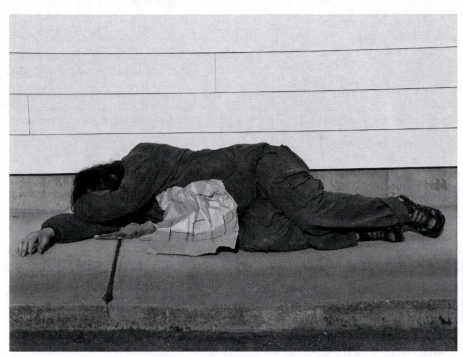

© 2012, agsandrew, Shutterstock, Inc.

Research shows a high prevalence of depression, suicide initiations, and other mental health disorders among youth who are homeless. Chronic physical health conditions are common as are high rates of substance abuse disorders. Many youth who become homeless have histories of academic difficulties including suspension and expulsion. Homeless youth engage in risky behaviors and have high rates of prior arrests and convictions.

More needs to be known about the costs associated with youth homelessness but we know that high rates of medical and behavioral health care and incarceration are costly. These costs compound over a lifetime as today's homeless youth become tomorrow's homeless adults.

HOMELESSNESS AMONG FAMILIES

Millions of hard-working, responsible families are at risk of losing their homes as a result of job losses, reduction in working hours, or low wages. Medical crises can also lead to homelessness due to an inability to work and the financial cost of care.

http://www.usich.gov/usich_resources/fact_sheets/opening_doors_homelessness_among_families_fact_sheet/

Over the course of 2009, more than half a million individuals in families needed emergency shelter or transitional housing. At least 300,000 were under the age of 18, according to HUD reports. The Department of Education reported a 20 percent increase over the previous year in the number of students enrolled in public schools for 2008–09 who are experiencing homelessness. Families experiencing homelessness are usually headed by a single woman who is, on average, in her late 20s with two children, one or both under the age of six. Among mothers with children experiencing homelessness, more than 80 percent had previously experienced domestic violence.

Children in families experiencing homelessness have high rates of acute and chronic health problems and the majority has been exposed to violence. These children are also more likely to have emotional and behavioral problems. The long-term effects of homelessness on a child's school performance appear significant and long-lasting.

There are significant costs associated with family homelessness including the high cost of housing a family in emergency shelter or transitional housing as well as the strains on the education, health care, and child welfare systems.

Sharayna: A Young Woman Who Experienced Homelessness and How She Turned Her Life Around

Among the 9,000 people across the country who participated in the development of *Opening Doors*, Sharayna, a young woman from Columbus who suffered years of abuse and lived on the streets, had a chance to share her perspective with federal officials during the process. With the help of the Coalition for Homelessness and Housing in Ohio's Youth Empowerment Program (YEP), she has turned her life around. Her perspective was so important; she was highlighted in *Opening Doors*.

Sharayna first arrived in Columbus, Ohio at 16, fleeing a history of parental abuse, mental illness, and the drug trade. During her adolescence, she moved around from one relative to another in Buffalo, NY and Columbus, but each time there continued to be more obstacles, more unstable living conditions, and dwindling funds to get by. She arrived in Columbus for the final time at 18 to get a fresh start away from the drug trade she was involved in, but had no identification, social security card, or birth certificate. She ended up homeless.

She stayed on the streets, at the local homeless shelter when there was room, and in cars. Because of the trauma of an unstable and abusive childhood, she was plagued by mental health issues that became

http://www.usich.gov/media_center/success_stories/sharayna/

barriers to her stability. Desperate for money, she agreed to steal a car for someone and was arrested. Upon hearing the details of Sharayna's mental health problems and history of abuse and homelessness, the court ordered her into counseling and mental health treatment and she was released into a shelter.

It was at the shelter that she met Angela Lariviere, founder of YEP, which specializes in assisting unaccompanied youth who are homeless and not eligible for other state resources. Sharayna was enrolled in YEP's pilot Youth Housing Program, and has continued to receive mental health counseling and earned her high school diploma. Although every day is a struggle, Sharayna has remained stably housed and healthy for the past 22 months while working with the YEP program. She has also enrolled in the local community college and just recently moved into her own apartment.

Sharayna continues to be involved as an advocate and advisor to YEP, working with the Youth Mental Health Committee, Supportive Employment Group and Housing Committee. She volunteers three days a week at YEP, determined to give back to the program that turned her life around and continues to assist her in so many ways. Most importantly, Sharayna now knows that she is not forgotten: "I now see that a whole mass of adults in my community and my government are working to help youth like me, and that there are adults who really care."

In June 2010, her commitment and the success of YEP, led her and Angela to attend the launch of *Opening Doors* at the White House. Sharayna's success is proof that interventions in and a focus on the lives of youth like Sharayna can produce sustainable outcomes and help vulnerable youths escape homelessness.

HOW MANY PEOPLE EXPERIENCE HOMELESSNESS?

Many people call or write the National Coalition for the Homeless to ask about the number of homeless people in the United States. There is no easy answer to this question and, in fact, the question itself is misleading. In most cases, homelessness is a temporary circumstance—not a permanent condition. A more appropriate measure of the magnitude of homelessness is the number of people who experience homelessness over time, not the number of "homeless people."

Studies of homelessness are complicated by problems of definitions and methodology. This fact sheet describes definitions of homelessness, methodologies for counting homeless people, recent estimates of homelessness, and estimates of the increase in homelessness over the past two decades. Additional resources for further study are also provided.

http://www.nationalhomeless.org/factsheets/How_Many.html

Definitions and Statistics

As a result of methodological and financial constraints, most studies are limited to counting people who are in shelters or on the streets. While this approach may yield useful information about the number of people who use services such as shelters and soup kitchens, or who are easy to locate on the street, it can result in underestimates of homelessness. Many people who lack a stable, permanent residence have few shelter options because shelters are filled to capacity or are unavailable. A recent study conducted by the U.S. Conference of Mayors found that 12 of the 23 cities surveyed had to turn people in need of shelter away due to a lack of capacity. Ten of the cities found an increase in households with children seeking access to shelters and transitional housing while six cities cited increases in the numbers of individuals seeking these resources (U.S. Conference of Mayors, 2007).

On an average night in the 23 cities surveyed, 94 percent of people living on the streets were single adults, 4 percent were part of families and 2 percent were unaccompanied minors. Seventy percent of those in emergency shelters were single adults, 29 percent were part of families and 1 percent were unaccompanied minors. Of those in transitional housing, 43 percent were single adults, 56 percent were part of families, and 1 percent were unaccompanied minors. Those who occupied permanent supportive housing were 60 percent single adults, 39.5 percent were part of families, and .5 percent were unaccompanied minors (U.S. Conference of Mayors, 2008).

The average length of stay in emergency shelter was 69 days for single men, 51 days for single women, and 70 days for families. For those staying in transitional housing, the average stay for single men was 175 days, 196 days for single women, and 223 days for families. Permanent supportive housing had the longest average stay, with 556 days for single men, 571 days for single women, and 604 days for women (U.S. Conference of Mayors, 2008). The homeless population is estimated to be 42 percent African-American, 39 percent white, 13 percent Hispanic, 4 percent Native American and 2 percent Asian, although it varies widely depending on the part of the country. An average of 26 percent of homeless people are considered mentally ill, while 13 percent of homeless individuals were physically disabled (U.S. Conference of Mayors, 2008). Nineteen percent of single homeless people are victims of domestic violence while 13 percent are veterans and 2 percent are HIV positive. Nineteen percent of homeless people are employed (U.S. Conference of Mayors, 2008).

In addition, a study of homelessness in 50 cities found that in virtually every city, the city's official estimated number of homeless people greatly exceeded the number of emergency shelter and transitional housing spaces (National Law Center on Homelessness and Poverty, 2004). Moreover, there are few or no shelters in rural areas of the United States, despite significant levels of homelessness

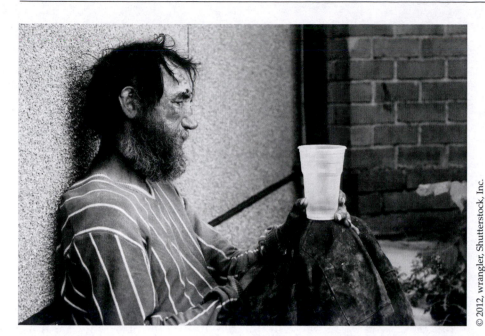

(Brown, 2002). The Council for Affordable and Rural Housing estimates that about nine percent of the nation's homeless are in rural areas (The Council for Affordable and Rural Housing). As a result of these and other factors, many people in homeless situations are forced to live with relatives and friends in crowded, temporary arrangements. People in these situations are experiencing homelessness, but are less likely to be counted. For instance, of the children and youth identified as homeless by the Department of Education in FY2000, only 35% lived in shelters; 34% lived doubled-up with family or friends, and 23% lived in motels and other locations. Yet, these children and youth may not immediately be recognized as homeless and are sometimes denied access to shelter or the protections and services of the McKinney-Vento Act (U.S. Department of Education).

METHODOLOGY

Researchers use different methods to measure homelessness. One method attempts to count all the people who are literally homeless on a given day or during a given week (**point-in-time counts**). A second method of counting homeless people examines the number of people who are homeless over a given period of time (**period prevalence counts**).

Choosing between point-in-time counts and period-prevalence counts has significant implications for understanding the magnitude and dynamics of homelessness. The high turnover in the homeless population documented by recent studies (see below) suggests that many more people experience homelessness than previously thought and that

NOTES

most of these people do not remain homeless. Because point-in-time studies give just a "snapshot" picture of homelessness, they only count those who are homeless at a particular time. Over time, however, some people will find housing and escape homelessness while new people will lose housing and become homeless. Systemic social and economic factors (prolonged unemployment or sudden loss of a job, lack of affordable housing, domestic violence, etc.) are frequently responsible for these episodes of homelessness. Point-in-time studies do not accurately identify these intermittently homeless people, and therefore tend to overestimate the proportion of people who are so-called "chronically homeless"—particularly those who suffer from severe mental illness and/or addiction disorders and therefore have a much harder time escaping homelessness and finding permanent housing. For these reasons, point-in-time counts are often criticized as misrepresenting the magnitude and nature of homelessness.

There is another important methodological issue that should be considered. Regardless of the time period over which the study was conducted, many people will not be counted because they are not in places researchers can easily find. This group of people, often referred to as "the unsheltered" or "hidden" homeless, frequently stay in automobiles, camp grounds, or other places that researchers cannot effectively search. For instance, a national study of formerly homeless people found that the most common places people who had been homeless stayed were vehicles (59.2%) and makeshift housing, such as tents, boxes, caves, or boxcars (24.6%) (Link et al., 1995). This suggests that homeless counts may miss significant numbers of people who are homeless, including those living in doubled-up situations.

NATIONAL ESTIMATES OF HOMELESSNESS

There are several national estimates of homelessness. Many are dated, or based on dated information. For all of the reasons discussed above, none of these estimates is the definitive representation of "how many people are homeless." In a recent approximation USA Today estimated 1.6 million people unduplicated persons used transitional housing or emergency shelters. Of these people, approximately 1/3 are members of households with children, a nine percent increase since 2007. Another approximation is from a study done by the National Law Center on Homelessness and Poverty which states that approximately 3.5 million people, 1.35 million of them children, are likely to experience homelessness in a given year (National Law Center on Homelessness and Poverty, 2007).

These numbers, based on findings from the National Law Center on Homelessness and Poverty, Urban Institute and specifically the National Survey of Homeless Assistance Providers, draw their estimates from a study of service providers across the country at two different times of the year in 1996. They found that, on a given night in October, 444,000 people (in 346,000 households) experienced homelessness—which translates to 6.3% of the population of people living in poverty. On a given night in February, 842,000 (in 637,000 households) experienced homelessness—which translates to almost 10% of the population of people living in poverty. Converting these estimates into an annual projection, the numbers that emerge are 2.3 million people (based on the October estimate) and 3.5 million people (based on the February estimate). This translates to approximately 1% of the U.S. population experiencing homelessness each year, 38% (October) to 39% (February) of them being children (Urban Institute 2000).

It is also important to note that this study was based on a national survey of service providers. Since not all people experiencing homelessness utilize service providers, the actual numbers of people experiencing homelessness are likely higher than those found in the study. Thus, we are estimating on the high end of the study's numbers: 3.5 million people, 39% of which are children (Urban Institute 2000).

In early 2007, the National Alliance to End Homelessness reported a point-in-time estimate of 744,313 people experiencing homelessness in January 2005.

IS HOMELESSNESS INCREASING?

One limited measure of the growth in homelessness is the increase in the number of shelter beds over time. A 1991 study examined homelessness "rates" (the number of shelter beds in a city divided by the city's population) in 182 U.S. cities with populations over 100,000. The study found that homelessness rates tripled between 1981 and 1989 for the 182 cities as a group (Burt, 1997).

A 1997 review of research conducted over the past decade (1987–1997) in 11 communities and 4 states found that shelter capacity more than doubled in 9 communities and 3 states during that time period (National Coalition for the Homeless, 1997). In two communities and two states, shelter capacity tripled over the decade.

These numbers are useful for measuring the growth in demand for shelter beds (and the resources made available to respond to that growth) over time. They indicate a dramatic increase in homelessness in the United States over the past two decades. Additionally, in the U.S. Conference of Mayors report from 2008, 19 of the 25 cities reported an increase in homelessness from 2007. More specifically, 16 cities reported an increase in the number of homeless families.

Also, due to the recent foreclosures crisis, homelessness has been on the rise. In the U.S. Conference of Mayor's 2008 Report, 12 of the 25 cities surveyed reported an increase in homelessness due to foreclosures and another 6 didn't have enough data to be sure. Thirteen of these cities had adopted policies to deal with the recent increase in victims of the housing crisis, but 10 cities had not implemented new policies.

NOTES

CONCLUSION

By its very nature, homelessness is impossible to measure with 100% accuracy. More important than knowing the precise number of people who experience homelessness is our progress in ending it. Recent studies suggest that the United States generates homelessness at a much higher rate than previously thought. Our task in ending homelessness is thus more important now than ever.

HIV/AIDS AND HOMELESSNESS

The Human Immunodeficiency Virus (HIV), which is found in bodily fluids such as blood, semen, vaginal secretions, and breast milk, destroys the immune system by inserting its own genetic material into white blood cells called T cells. Over time, T cells are killed and HIV replicates. As the concentration of T cells falls, the immune system weakens, leaving the body open to opportunistic infections. The disease progresses through four stages, the last of which is full-blown AIDS, when the body has little natural immunity left. The average time from HIV infection to AIDS is 10 years, and a person may live for several months to five years after the AIDS diagnosis (Straub, 2007).

PREVALENCE

At the end of 2006, 1,106,400 people were estimated to have HIV/AIDS in the United States (Centers for Disease Control and Prevention). By the end of 2007, 455,636 of these people had progressed to AIDS, including 889 children under the age of 13. In 2007, 14,110 people died of AIDS-related causes. In the homeless population, HIV/AIDS is even more prevalent. The National Alliance to End Homelessness estimates that 3.4% of homeless people were HIV-positive in 2006, compared to 0.4% of adults and adolescents in the general population (Centers for Disease Control and Prevention, 2008).

RELATIONSHIP TO HOMELESSNESS

HIV/AIDS and homelessness are intricately related. The costs of health care and medications for people living with HIV/AIDS (PLWHA) are often too high for people to keep up with. In addition, PLWHA are in danger of losing their jobs due to discrimination or as a result of frequent health-related absences. As a result, up to 50% of PLWHA in the United States are at risk of becoming homeless (National Alliance to End Homelessness, 2006).

http://www.nationalhomeless.org/factsheets/hiv.html

In addition, the conditions of homelessness may increase the risk of contracting HIV. A disproportionately large number of homeless people suffer from substance abuse disorders. Many homeless people inject drugs intravenously, and may share or reuse needles. This practice is responsible for 13% of HIV/AIDS diagnoses in the United States. An additional 50% of cases are a result of male-to-male sexual contact, and 33% are due to heterosexual sex (Centers for Disease Control and Prevention). Unfortunately, the conditions of homelessness may lead to sexual behaviors that increase the risk of contracting HIV. For example, many shelters are single sex, and most offer limited privacy, including communal sleeping and bathing. These circumstances make it difficult for shelter residents to form stable sexual relationships (University of California San Francisco Center for AIDS Prevention Studies, 2005).

Homeless people with HIV/AIDS encounter many challenges to their health. Due to factors such as poor hygiene, malnutrition, and exposure to cold and rainy weather, homeless people are already three to six times more likely than housed people to become ill (National Health Care for the Homeless Council, 2008). Since HIV targets the immune system, PLWHA do not have the ability to fight off disease, and their risk of illness is even higher. Additionally, crowded shelters with poor ventilation can endanger people with HIV/AIDS by exposing them to infections such as hepatitis A, pneumonia, tuberculosis, and skin infections. One study shows that people who sleep in a shelter are twice as likely to have tuberculosis if they are HIV-positive (National Alliance to End Homelessness, 2006).

Psychological factors play an additional role in the progression of HIV/AIDS. Psychological distress has been shown to increase the severity of the disease (Greeson et al., 2008). People who are homeless experience a great deal of stress on a daily basis, which exacerbates the progression of HIV/AIDS. Additionally, stress, depression, and other psychosocial factors that are common in homeless people affect behaviors, which in turn affect the progression of HIV/AIDS. For example, depression decreases a person's likelihood to adhere to medication, which is necessary to treat HIV/AIDS (Gore-Felton and Koopman, 2008).

It is very difficult for homeless PLWHA to adequately treat their disease. For example, homelessness makes it more difficult to obtain and use antiretroviral treatments (ARTs), the medication for HIV/AIDS medications. ARTs have complex regimens, and adherence is very difficult for people who don't have access to stable housing, clean water, bathrooms, refrigeration, and food (National Alliance to End Homelessness, 2006). Many homeless people also do not have health insurance and cannot pay for the medications and health services that are necessary to treat HIV/AIDS.

POLICY ISSUES

Homeless PLWHA need to be placed in supportive housing tailored to their needs. The experience of homelessness exacerbates the disease and hinders treatment. According to a New York study, formerly homeless people were four times more likely to get medical care once they had been placed in supportive housing than when they were in case management. Housing also increases the likelihood of receiving and adhering to ARTs (National Alliance to End Homelessness, 2006). The United States Department of Housing and Urban Development addresses this problem with the Housing Opportunities for Persons With AIDS (HOPWA) Program, but this program only serves 79 cities and 38 states (National Alliance to End Homelessness, 2006). More funding needs to be allocated to providing PLWHA with supportive housing.

Preventative and educational programs need to be provided at shelters, soup kitchens, and other locations that are easily accessible and comfortable for homeless people. Currently, many shelters only minimally address HIV/AIDS. Sex and drug use are strictly forbidden at most shelters, so many shelters do not allow outside HIV/AIDS education and prevention programs to openly discuss those topics or to distribute condoms. A few education programs, such as "Sex, Games, and Videotapes," have been effective in shelters. Programs such as these need to become federally funded and widespread (University of California San Francisco Center for AIDS Prevention Studies, 2005).

Comprehensive services such as health education, HIV testing, case management, mental health services, and basic health care also need to be provided to homeless PLWHA. Group interventions have been effective in some situations and should be replicated. Coordinated care networks need to be organized so that homeless PLWHA can receive the care that they need in a timely manner (University of California San Francisco Center for AIDS Prevention Studies, 2005).

APPENDIX

CITATIONS USING APA, 6TH EDITION, 2010

If your instructor has supplied you with a book or handout for APA citations, use that information rather than this handout. See the last page for a sample. If you need citations for items that are not listed in this guide sheet, contact the librarians. Page numbers refer to relevant pages in the APA *Publication Manual, 6th Edition.*

Important Information

If there is **no date listed**, use: (n.d.). If there is **no author listed**, start with the article title followed by the date.

Use the state abbreviation for all cities in the U.S. For cities in other countries, write out the country name. If the **state is given in the publisher's name**, do not include it in the location: East Lansing: University of Michigan Press

Shorten publisher names. For Harcourt Brace, use: Harcourt

Keep the word: Press. Keep the word: Books. Eliminate other words that do not identify the publisher, such as Inc. or Publishers.

If the author is Mary Sue Allen, use: **Allen, M. S.** Put a space between the initials.

List the authors or editors for **each** citation in the order given on the publication.

Capitalize proper nouns and the first word of a **book** title, **Internet** article title, a **magazine article** title and a **subtitle**.

Use **italics** for **book** *titles*, **magazine** *titles*, **newspaper** *names*, and **Internet** article *titles*.

Divide a URL after a slash or before a dot.

Books (Pages 202–206)

Single Author

Lampe, G. P. (1998). *Douglass spoke out: Freedom's voice.* Chicago, IL: American Press.

Two Authors

Curtis, M. T., & Andrews, K. A. (1998). *A changing Australia: The social, cultural and economic trends.* Annandale, VA: Federation Press.

Three to Seven Authors

Brown, C., Anderson, B. J., Ford, G. L., Bigelow, D. L., Card, A. B., Carey, D., & Smith, C. (2000). *Interesting topics for research papers.* Bethesda, MD: Roundtree Press.

More Than Seven Authors (p. 198)

Green, R. C., White, A. B., Brown, K. F., Red, C. F., Black, J. F., Gray, J. L., . . . Botos, G. (2000). *What color is your red wagon?* Philadelphia, PA: Liberty Books.

Second or Later Edition

Lerner, G. B. (1998). *The Grimke sisters from South Carolina* (2nd ed.). New York, NY: Oxford University Press.

Corporate Author and the Same Corporation as Publisher (p. 203)

American Association of Cereal Chemists. (1998). *Sweeteners*. St. Paul, MN: Author.

Reference Books and Book Chapters (Pages 202–203)

Signed Article (An author is listed, usually at the end of the article.) If there is a large editorial board, use the lead editor followed by et al.

Chaney, W. H., & Smith, G. (1996). Ventriloquism. In B. Smith, et al. (Eds.), *Collier's encyclopedia* (pp. 79–80). New York, NY: Collier's.

Unsigned Article (No author is listed.) If there are only a few editors, put (Eds.) after the editors' names.

Relativity. (1996). In D. Black & Q. Brown (Eds.), *The new encyclopaedia Britannica* (10th ed., Vol. 23, p. 766).
Chicago, IL: Encyclopaedia Britannica.

Edited Book

Smith, J. D., & Jolly, I. M. (Eds.). (1998). *Maternities and modernities: Colonial and postcolonial experiences in Asia and the Pacific*. Cambridge, MA: Cambridge University Press.

Chapter in Anthology or Compilation with the author of the chapter given

Explanation:

Author of Chapter (date of chapter or if none given, date of the book). Title of chapter. In Editor(s)' name(s) (Ed.), or (Eds.), of the book, *Title of the book in italics* (pages of the entire chapter). City, State: Publisher.

Example:

Deeb, R., & Brower, C. D. (1994). Law and justice. In R. Layman (Ed.), *American decades: 1950–1959* (pp. 225–256). Detroit, MI: Gale.

Separately Titled Volume in a Multivolume Work

Islamic state of Afghanistan. (1998). In G. P. Skabelund (Ed.), *Culturegrams: The nations around us: Vol. 2. Africa, Asia, and Oceania* (pp. 1–4). Provo, UT: Brigham Young University.

Literary Criticism

Magazine Article cited

Wilson, E. M. (1991). The ambiguity of Harry James. In T. Votteler (Ed.), *Short story criticism* (Vol. 8, pp. 274–276). Detroit, MI: Gale. (Reprinted from *The hound and horn*, Vol. 7, pp. 385–406, 1934).

Book cited

Smith, S. J. (1990). The nature walk. In T. Votteler (Ed.), *Contemporary literary criticism* (Vol. 20, pp. 23–26). Detroit, MI: Gale. (Reprinted from *Environmental protection*, pp. 34–36, 1990, New York, NY: Scribbs).

Brochure

American Red Cross. (2004). *Saving a life: Giving blood*. [Brochure]. Washington, DC: Author.

Government Publications

U.S. Census Bureau. (1999). *Statistical abstract of the United States: 1999*. Washington, DC: U.S. Government Printing Office.

Periodicals (Pages 198–202)

Periodicals include items published on a regular basis such as journals, magazines, newspapers, and newsletters.

Magazine

Brown, J. (1999, August 30). America's deadliest disaster. *Time*, 62(3), 58–59.

Journal Article with doi

Use the digital object identifier (doi) if it is available in the abstract in a database.

Herbst-Damm, K. L., & Kulik, J. A. (2005). Volunteer support, marital status, and the survival times of terminally ill patients. *Health Psychology, 24*, 225–229. doi: 10.1037/0278–6133.24.2.225

Journal Paginated by Issue with no doi

(The numbering of pages starts over with each issue.) Give the issue number.

In the following example, 181 is the volume and 3 is the issue. The volume is in italics, but the issue is not.

Kauffman, J. M., & Burbach, H. J., Jr. (1999). Creating classroom civility. *Journal of Education, 181*(3), 12–18.

Newspapers (Pages 200–201)

Signed Article (An author is listed, usually under the headline.)

Price, H. B. (1998, May 26). Tell me again: Why are S.A.T. scores so crucial? *The New York Times*, pp. A23, A25.

Unsigned Article

Kirkwood is great. (2011, January 14). *Gazette*, p. 14.

Editorial: Flood recovery slow. [Editorial]. (2011). *The Washington Post*, p. 16.

Internet Sources Divide a URL After a Slash or Before a Dot

With an author and date

Anderson, G. L. (2000, September 6). *Is Celebrex safe?* Retrieved from http://www.arthritisonline.com

Without an author or date

Home for the holidays. (n.d.). Retrieved from http://www.homeholidays.com

Electronic version of a book (p. 203)

Black, C. M. (2010). *Computers at work.* [DX Reader version]. Retrieved from http://www.ebook-storeco.uk

Online magazine article

Jones, B. (2011, January). Integrating technology. *Instruction, 40*(2). Retrieved from http://www.instr.org

Online Newspaper Article

Barrymore, C. F. (2010, December 30). Exercise is essential. *The New York Times.* Retrieved from http://www.nytimes.com

Personal Interviews, Letters or E-Mails

From the *Publication Manual of the American Psychological Association*, p. 179:

> Personal communications may be letters, memos, some electronic communications (e.g. e-mail or messages from nonarchived discussion groups or electronic bulletin boards), personal interviews, telephone conversations and the like. Because they do not provide recoverable data, **personal communications are not included in the reference list. Cite personal communications in text only.** Give the initials as well as the surname of the communicator, and provide as exact a date as possible:

> T. K. Lutes (personal communication, April 18, 2001)
> (V. G. Nguyen, personal communication, September 28, 1998)

Television Programs (Page 210)

Bradley, E. F. (Writer), & Brown, D. B. (Director). (2010). Desperate women [Television series episode]. In S. Smith (Executive Producer), *60 minutes.* New York, NY: Columbia Broadcasting.

Motion Pictures (Page 209)

Schimler, T. C. (Producer), & Mock, F. L. (Director). (1995). *Maya Lin: A strong clear vision* [Motion picture]. United States: Paramount Pictures.

In-Text Citations for APA (Pages 174–179)

- The quotation mark comes before the documentation.
- The punctuation at the end of the sentence comes after the documentation.

- If the documentation follows a BLOCK QUOTATION, place the punctuation before the documentation.
- All direct quotations need a specific part of the source documented.

Specific Parts of a Source (use page numbers)

"There were animals everywhere" (Stevens, 1998, p. 51).

Interview

"I was stationed at Pearl Harbor" (J. Rivera, personal communication, March 24, 2000).

On-line Reference

"The laughed" (Johnson, 1999, para. 23). OR (Heinz, 2002, chap. 3). OR (Jones, 2002, Conclusion section, para. 1)

If no author is given, use a shortened form of the title, including the first word listed in the list of references, in place of the author's name. Use n.d. if no date is given.

("Super," n.d., para. 5)

Secondary Source: Brown (as cited in Jones, 2010) wrote that…(Include Jones, not Brown, in the reference list.)

SEE THE SAMPLE ON THE BACK PAGE.

The reference list should be on a separate sheet of paper with one-inch margins.

The word, References, is centered.

Do not bold **any** information.

The **font and its size** should be the same throughout the list and the same as the text of the paper, usually size 12.

The entire list is **double-spaced** (one line in between each line of print).

Do not put extra spaces between the citations. The second and subsequent lines should be indented.

Alphabetize the citations in **one list**.

If there is an author or editor, use the last name for alphabetizing. If there is no author or editor, use the first word in the title, excluding A, An, and The when you alphabetize.

TABLE

IN-TEXT CITATION SAMPLES

Type of citation	First citation in text	Subsequent citations in text	Parenthetical format, first citation in text	Parenthetical format, subsequent citations in text
One work by one author	Walker (2007)	Walker {2007}	(Walker, 2007)	(Walker, 2007)
One work by two authors	Walker and Allen (2004)	Walker and Allen (2004)	(Walker & Allen, 2004)	(Walker & Allen, 2004)
One work by three authors	Bradley, Ramirez, and Soo (1999)	Bradley et al. (1999)	(Bradley, Ramirez, & Soo, 1999)	(Bradley et al., 1999)
One work by four authors	Bradley, Ramirez, Soo, and Walsh (2006)	Bradley etal. (2006)	(Bradley, Ramirez, Soo, & Walsh, 2006)	{Bradley et al., 2006)
One work by five authors	Walker, Allen, Bradley, Ramirez, and Soo (2008)	Walker etal. (2003)	(Walker, Allen, Bradley, Ramirez, & Soo, 2008)	(Walker etal., 2008)
One work by six or more authors	Wasserstein etal. (2005)	Wasserstein etal. (2005)	(Wasserstein et al.,2005)	(Wasserstein et a!., 2005)
Groups (readily identified through abbreviation) as authors	National Institute of Mental Health (NIMH, 2003)	NIMH (2003)	(National Institute of Mental Health [NIMH], 2003)	(NIMH, 2003)
Groups (no abbreviation) as authors	University of Pittsburgh (2005)	University of Pittsburgh (2005)	(University of Pittsburgh, 2005)	(University of Pitts¬burgh, 2005)

(American, 2010, p. 177)

REFERENCES

Bell, M. A. (2000). *Ringing forever.* Philadelphia, PA: Liberty Press.

Black, C. M. (2010). *Computers at work.* [DX Reader version]. Retrieved from http://www.ebookstoreco.uk

Free, R. U. (1999). *Sailing from England.* London, England: Cambridge Books.

The little known facts about America: From the beginning. (2001). *Journal of Education, 64*(2), 46-48. doi:10.2105/AJPH.2007.113571

Mayflower. (2000, September). Retrieved from http://www.plymouth.foundation.org

Updated February 2011, by Nancy Obermueller and Genny Yarne
American Psychological Association. (2010). *Publication manual of the American Psychological Association* (6th ed.). Washington, DC: Author.

INDEX

A

access, to records, 12
addiction, 76
administrative rules, 7
adolescents
    and alcohol abuse, 131–133
    and HIV, 96–98
    normal *vs.* drug-affected behavior, 135
    and substance abuse, 131–133, 135, 136
Adverse Childhood Experiences (ACE),
    284–289
    and adult medical disease, 285–286, 291–307
    factors that immunize damage from, 289
    and health care costs, 303
    health care implications, 305–307
    and health risks, 298–300
    and heart disease, 302
    and life expectancy, 304–305
    and medical disease, 300–303
    and mental health disorders, 284–285
    outline of study, 292–294
    and poor adult outcomes, 288
    and psychiatric disorders, 294–297
    and sexual behavior, 300
    and toxic stress, 287, 288–289
alcohol, 168
    education guide, 178
    effects on the brain, 136–137
    overview, 126–127
    pre-test, 126

alcohol abuse, 20, 88, 127, 168. *see also*
    substance abuse
    and adolescents, 131–133
    and family influence, 134
    health risks of, 129
    physiological effects of, 136–138
    and pregnancy, 130
    and women, 128–131
alcohol abuse continuum, 129
alcohol screening, 22
Alzheimer's Association, 325
Alzheimer's Disease, 320–326
    Alzheimer's Disease Genetics Fact Sheet,
    323
    causes of, 322–323
    diagnosis, 323–324
    early signs and symptoms of, 321
    medications for, 324
    mild, 321
    moderate, 321–322
    severe, 322
    support for caregivers, 325
    treatment of, 324–325
Alzheimer's Disease Centers, 325
American Medical Association (AMA), 127
American Psychiatric Association (APA), 43
anabolic steroids, 170
anorexia nervosa, 77–78, 78–79, 79
anxiety disorder, 81–82
    and demographics, 3

general anxiety disorder (GAD), 73
obsessive compulsive disorder (OCD), 73–74
panic disorder, 74
post-traumatic stress disorder (PTSD), 74
social anxiety disorder, 74–75
types of, 73
Asperger's syndrome, 47, 49
assertive outreach, 89, 166
at-risk populations
African Americans, 314
Hispanic Americans, 314
LGBT, 314
Native Americans, 314
race/ethnicity in population *vs.* foster care, 316
women and children, 312–313
youths, 313
Attention Deficit Disorder (ADD), 75
Attention Deficit Hyperactivity Disorder (ADHD), 43, 55, 75
autism, 47–48, 52, 57–58
autism spectrum disorder, 43

B
Bachelor degree, social work, 6
behavior or emotional disability, 55
benzodiazepines, 156–157
billing and fees, 12
binge-eating disorder, 78, 79, 80
bipolar disorder, 70–72, 82–83
defined, 70
diagnosis, 83
symptoms of, 70–72, 83
blindness, 56–57
bloodborne pathogens, 30–37
blood pressure, 34–35
bloodstream, and alcohol, 137–138
Board, 6, 19, 22
boarding homes, 263
Braille, 57
brain, effects of alcohol on, 136–137, 138
breast cancer, and alcohol, 129
Bridges to the Future program, 29
bulimia nervosa, 78, 79
business practices, 18

C
cancer, 28
cannabinoids, 168
Cannabis sativa, 147
cardiovascular disease (CVD), 27
case management, 87
causation and correlation, 162–165
Census Bureau, 29
Centers for Disease Control (CDC), 35
Centers of Excellence program, 28
cerebral palsy, 53
child abuse
behavior indicators of, 197–198
child prostitution, 204
children as caretakers, 200
defined by Iowa law, 198–200
denial of critical care, 202–204
and DHS assessment, 206–218
legal provisions, 283
and mandatory reporting, 182, 182–193
mental injury, 201
overview, 185–189
physical abuse, 200–201
physical indicators of, 196–197
presence of illegal drugs, 204–205
removal of child, 220–226
report form, 246
reporting procedures, 193–195
sexual abuse, 202
Child and Family Services Reviews (CFSRs), 317
cirrhosis, 129
client, 7
clinical services, 7
Clinical Trial Networks, 29
club drugs, 169
cocaine, 148–149, 169
education guide, 178
co-curring disorders, 76, 160–161
cognitive performance, 105
communication disorder, 43
Community-Based Participatory Research, 28
competence, 5, 8
Competitive Research (SCORE) programs, 29
computerized tomography (CT), 324
confidentiality, 9–11

conflict of interest, 13–14
controlled study, 163
counseling, 7, 90, 167

D
deaf, 57
Department of Human Services (DHS), 183, 184
dependent adult abuse, 184, 247–249
   denial of critical care, 257–258
   and DHS assessment, 261–264
   financial exploitation, 256
   legal provisions, 281, 283
   physical abuse, 256
   sexual abuse, 257
dependent adult abuse report form, 277
depressants, education guide, 178
depression, 64, 83–84
   among Veterans, 327–334
   causes of, 65
   and demographics, 3
   diagnosis, 83–84
   help for, 66, 67–68
   and illnesses, 69–70
   prevention, 68
   signs of, 65–66, 69
   symptoms of, 71, 83
   treatment, 84
   treatment of, 67
developmental disability, 43–44, 58, 58–59
dignity, 5
directly observed therapy of highly active ART (DOT-HAART), 105–108
disability
   by age, 41
   characteristics of people with, 43
   defined, 40
   developmental, 43–44
   intellectual, 53
   physical and neurological, 53–54
   understanding, 53
discipline
   definitions, 19
   grounds for, 19–22
   methods of, 22
disclosure, 10, 16–17

discretion of Board, 22
discrimination, 18
disparities, in health, 26
dissociate drugs, 169
drinking pattern, women, 128
drug abuse, 20, 88. *see also* substance abuse
drug screening, 22
DSM-5, 43, 121–123
dual diagnosis, 76, 86–88
   defined, 76
   demographics, 86–87
   treatment of, 87–90
dual relationship, 13
dual relationship, and conflicts of interest, 13

E
eating disorder, 77–81
   anorexia nervosa, 77, 78–79
   binge-eating disorder, 78, 79, 80
   bulimia nervosa, 78, 79
   defined, 77
elder abuse, 185
electronic thermometer, 34
epilepsy, 54
esophagus, and alcohol, 137
ethanol, 126
ethical practice, 2–23
ethical principles, 4–5
ethyl alcohol, 126
executive functioning, 46

F
fatigue, 104
financial exploitation, 184–185
fraud, in procuring license, 19

G
general anxiety disorder (GAD), 73, 81–82
glove removal, 37
gloves, protective, 36
gown/apron, for protection, 36
guardianship, 269–270

H
hallucinogens, 169
   education guide, 178

hand care, 35–36
hard of hearing, 57
harm-reduction model of prevention, 167
health. *see* physical health and safety, social
        detriments of, 28
health disparities, 26–29
    in 1980s, 26
    NIH efforts to eliminate, 27–30
    research, 27–28
    social detriments of, 28
    today, 26–27
health education, 28
health equity, 26
health-related quality of life (HRQOL),
    108–109
heart disease, and alcohol, 129, 138
hepatitis, 129
heroin, 150–152, 169
    short-and long-term effects of use, 151
HIV/AIDS, 27, 31
    adherence to treatment, 105–108
    and adolescents, 96–98
    and cocaine, 148
    and homelessness, 342–344
    medical care, 103
    neuropsychological assessment, 101–102
    prevention, 96–98
    psychiatric assessment, 99–100, 99–101
    spiritual care, 103–105
    treatment, 103
homelessness
    among families, 335—336
    among Veterans, 334
    among youth, 334–335
    definitions and statistics, 338–339
    and HIV/AIDS, 342–344
    methods for measuring, 339–340
    national estimates of, 340–341
    policy issues, 344
human relationships, 5
hydrocodone, 154–155

I
imminent danger, 194
impairments, 17
incompetency, 19

informed consent, 7–8
inhalants, 170
    education guide, 178
integrated treatment, 88–90, 165–167
    key factors in, 166–167
integrity, 5
intellectual disability, 43, 53
Intelligence Quotient (I.Q), 44–45
Internet research exercises, mental health, 95
Internet research questions, for at-risk and
        developmental disabilities, 60
Internet research questions, substance abuse,
        159
Internet sites, for at-risk and developmental
        disabilities, 59
intoxication, 126
Iowa Adult Methamphetamine Treatment
        Project, 152
Iowa Code, 5, 7
    administrative rules, 7
    and child abuse, 187–188, 195–196, 198–206
    definitions, 6–7, 7
    and dependent adult abuse, 248–261
    discipline, 19–22
    order for competency or drug screening, 22
    rules of conduct, 7–19

K
kidneys, and alcohol, 138

L
laws, 5–23. *see also* Iowa Code
learning disability, 54–55
learning disorder, 43
license, 19
    fraud in procuring, 19
licensee, 6
liver damage, and alcohol, 129, 138
Loan Repayment program, 29
long-term community-based approach, to
        treatment, 90, 167
low vision, 56–57

M
magnetic resonance imaging (MRI), 324
major depressive episode, 327–330

mandatory reporter, 182–184, 185
  and child abuse, 182–193
  child care provider, 192
  defined by Iowa law, 255
  and dependent adult abuse, 249–255
  educator, 191–192
  law enforcement officer, 192–193
  mental health professional, 192
  reporting procedures, 193–195
  reports and forms, 216–218
  training, 233–234
manic episode, 71
marijuana, 147, 168
  education guide, 178
marijuana use and mental illness, 161
mask/eye protection, 36
Master's degree, social work, 6
mental health. *see also* neurodevelopmental
    disorders
  anxiety disorder, 73, 81–82
  Attention Deficit Hyperactivity Disorder
    (ADHD), 75
  bipolar disorder, 70–72
  depression, 64–69, 64–70
  dual diagnosis, 76, 86–88
  generalized anxiety disorder (GAD), 81–82
  mood disorder, 81–82
  obsessive compulsive disorder (OCD),
    73–74
  panic disorder, 74
  post-traumatic stress disorder (PTSD), 74
  schizophrenia, 75–76
  social anxiety disorder, 74–75
  U.S. statistics for, 3
mental retardation levels, 44–45
methamphetamine, 149–150, 152–154, 169
  vs. cocaine, 150
methylphenidate, 157
Minority Biomedical Research Support, 29
Minority Health and Health Disparities
    International Research Training
    program, 29
misrepresentation, 16–17
modafinil, 103, 105
mood disorder, 71, 82–84

motivational intervention, 90, 166
mouth, and alcohol, 137

N
narcotics, education guide, 178
National Association of Social Workers
    (NASW)
  ethical principles, 4–5
  and rules of conduct, 18–23
National Association of Social Workers
    (NASW) Code of Ethics, 18
National Association of State Alcohol and
    Drug Abuse Directors (NASADAD),
    160
National Association of State Mental Health
    Program Directors (NASMHPD), 160
National Center on Minority Health and
    Health Disparities (NCMHD), 26
National Coalition for the Homeless, 341
National Forensic Laboratory Information
    System (NFLIS), 154
National Institute on Minority Health and
    Health Disparities (NIMHD), 26, 28, 29
National Institutes of Health (NIH), 26, 27
National Law Center on Homelessness and
    Poverty, 340
National Survey on Drug Use and Health
    (NSDUH), 120, 328
neurodevelopmental disorders
  Asperger's syndrome, 47, 49
  autism, 47–48, 52
  and learning issues, 45
  pervasive developmental disorders (PDD),
    47
  traumatic brain injury (TBI), 45–46, 50–51
neurodevelopmental motor disorders, 43
Newborn Safe Haven Act, 244–245

O
obsessive compulsive disorder (OCD), 73–74
opioids, 123, 168
organization relationships, 18
OSHA, 30–31, 37
oxycodone, 155–156

P

pancreas, and alcohol, 138

panic disorder, 74

period prevalence, in homelessness, 339

personal protective equipment (PPE), 30–31
   decontaminating and disposing of, 31
   exceptions to use of, 31
   selecting, 30–31

pervasive developmental disorders (PDD), 47

physical and neurological disability, 53–54
   cerebral palsy, 53
   epilepsy, 54
   muscular dystrophy, 54
   spina bifida, 54

physical contact, 14

physical health and safety, health disparities, 26–29

point-in-time counts, in homelessness, 339

post-traumatic stress disorder (PTSD), 74, 161–162
   and substance abuse, 161–162

practice of social work, 6, 7

pregnancy, and alcohol, 130

privacy, 9–11

private practice, 6–7

pro bono service, 5

psychopharmacology, 103–105

psychosocial rehabilitation
   defined, 2
   principles of, 2

psychosocial therapy, 7

pulse, taking, 32–33

Q

Quadrants of Care, 160

R

racial disproportionality in child welfare, 315–317

record keeping, 11–12

records, access to, 12

relationships, 5
   sexual, 14

release of child abuse information form, 282

release of dependent adult abuse information form, 280

request for dependent adult abuse registry information form, 279

research, 17

respiration, 32

rules of conduct, 7–19
   and National Association of Social Workers (NASW), 18–23

S

schizophrenia, 75–76, 84–85
   diagnosis, 85
   symptoms of, 84–85

service, 4–5

Severe Opioid Use Disorder, 123

sex glands, and alcohol, 138

sexual harassment, 18

sexual relationships, 14

sexual risk behaviors, 96, 97

sharps, 36

Sheehan Disability Scale (SDS), 329

small ear thermometer, 32

social anxiety disorder, 74–75

social detriments of health, 28

social justice, 5

Social Readjustment Rating Scale (SRRS), 318

social support, 90, 167

speech and language disorders, 56

spina bifida, 54

spiritual care, 103

stimulants, 169
   education guide, 178

stomach, and alcohol, 137

stroke, 27

substance abuse, 88, 120–123
   and adolescents, 131–133, 135, 136
   alcohol, 126–147
   benzodiazepines, 156–157
   causation and correlation, 162–165
   cocaine, 148–149
   and co-curring disorders, 161
   diagnostic criteria for, 121–123
   drug education guide, 178
   drugs commonly abused, 168–170
   and enabling behavior, 133
   harm-reduction model of prevention, 167
   heroin, 150–152

hydrocodone, 154–155
legal drugs of, 154–157
marijuana, 147
methamphetamine, 149–150, 152
methylphenidate, 157
oxycodone, 155–156
and post-traumatic stress disorder (PTSD), 161—162
principles of treatment, 171–173
scale of severity, 122
services for, 157–158
symptoms of, 179
synthetic drugs, 174–177
treatment, 165–167, 171–173
Substance Abuse and Mental Health Services Administration (SAMHSA), 120, 332, 333
suicide, 113–115
age group differences in, 113
attempts in U.S., 113
deaths in U.S., 113
gender disparities in, 113
racial and ethnic disparities in, 114
risk factors, 114
terminology, 114–115
supervision, 9
support group, 88
Surgeon General's Report on Mental Health, 3
synthetic drugs, 174–177

T
Task Force on Black and Minority Health, 26
temperature, taking, 33–34
termination of services, 15
tobacco, 120, 168

toxic stress, 287, 288–289
trauma, childhood experience of, 284–307
traumatic brain injury (TBI), 45–46, 50–51, 58
treatment, 87–88
treatment, stages of, 89–90

U
unethical conduct, 21
U.S. Advisory Board on Child Abuse, 187
U.S. Food and Drug Administration, 324

V
veterans
and depression, 327–334
and homelessness, 334
visual impairment, 56–57
vital signs, 32
blood pressure, 34–35
precautions in taking, 35–37
pulse, 32–33
respiration, 32
temperature, 33, 34

W
washing hands, 36
waste/linen, 36
women, and alcohol abuse, 128–131
worth, 5

Y
young adults
and alcohol abuse, 136–147
and HIV prevention, 96
Youth Empowerment Program (YEP), Ohio, 336